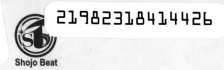
Yona of the Dawn

9

Story & Art by

Mizuho Kusanagi

yona of the Dawn

Volume 9

CONTENTS

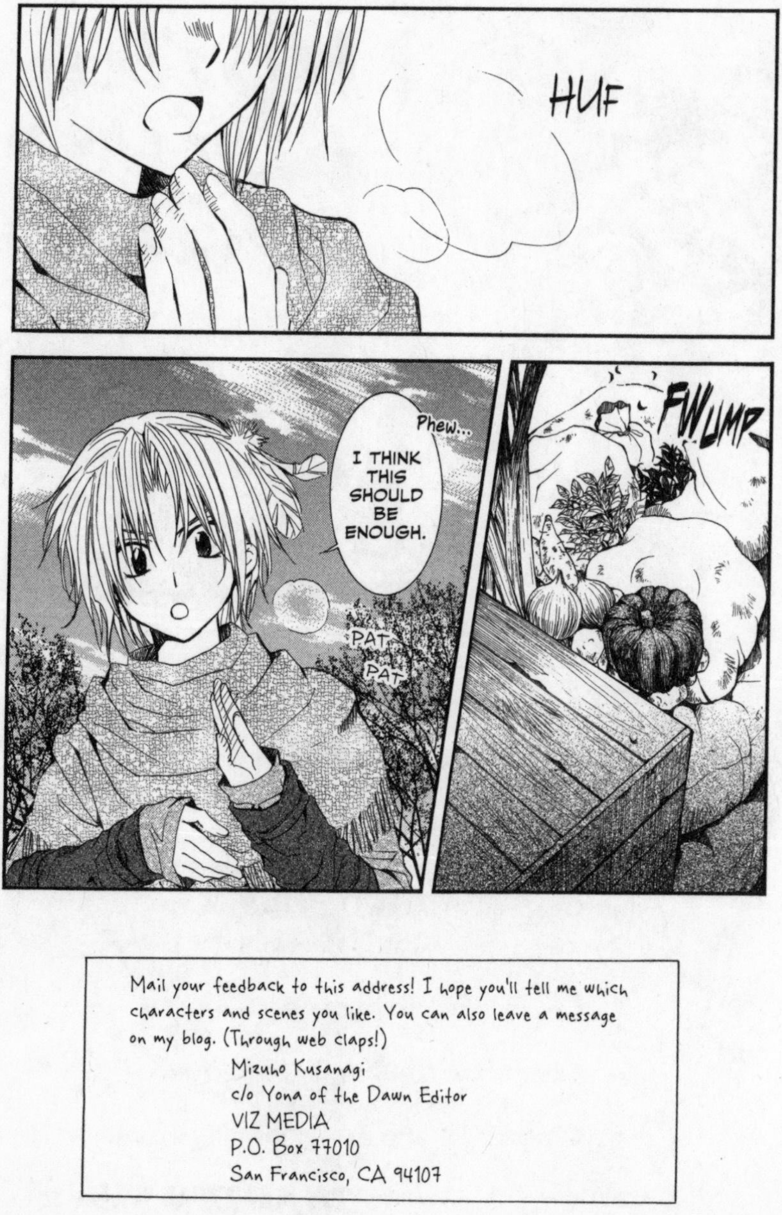
HUF
FWUMP
Phew...
I THINK THIS SHOULD BE ENOUGH.
PAT PAT

Mail your feedback to this address! I hope you'll tell me which characters and scenes you like. You can also leave a message on my blog. (Through web claps!)

Mizuho Kusanagi
c/o Yona of the Dawn Editor
VIZ MEDIA
P.O. Box 77010
San Francisco, CA 94107

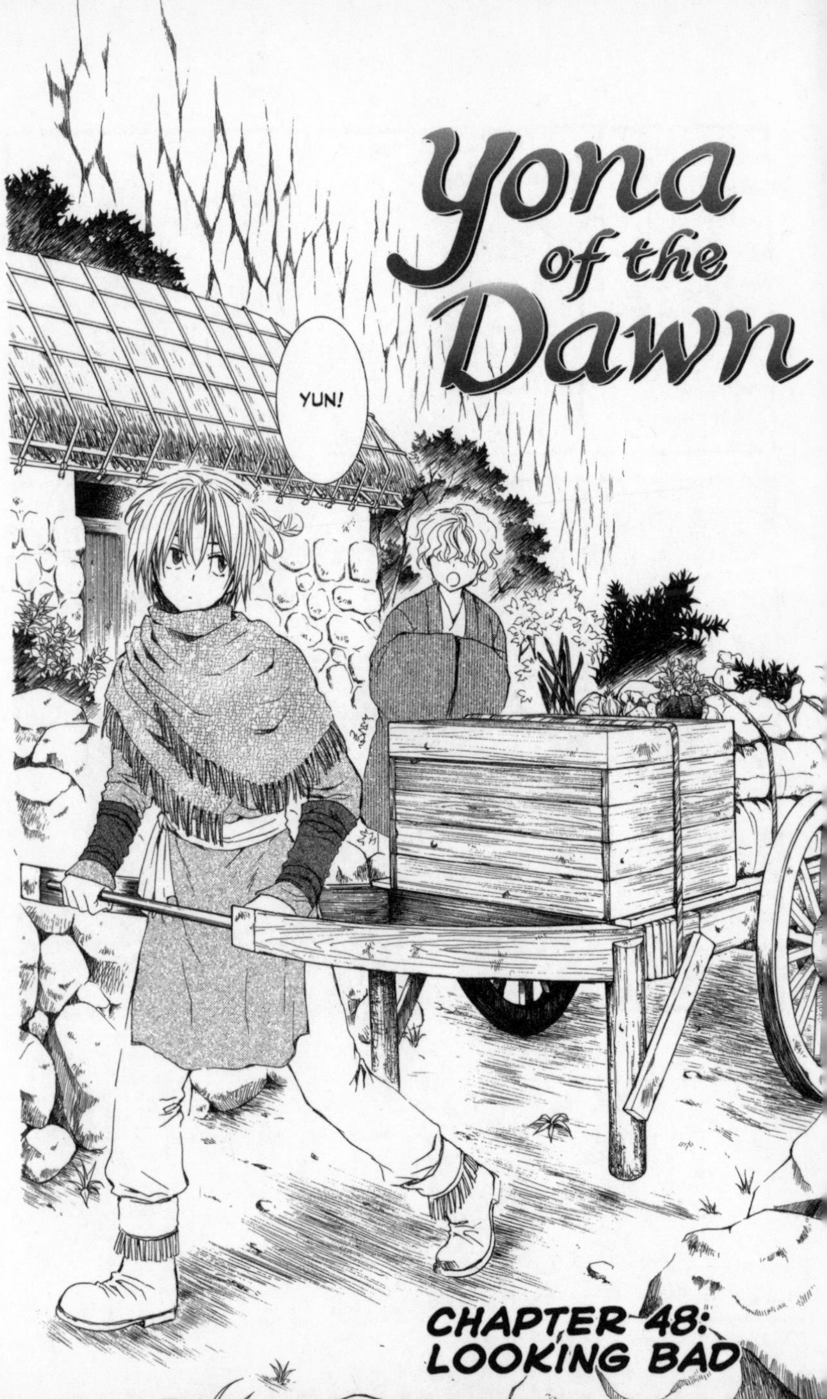
Yona of the Dawn
YUN!
CHAPTER 48:
LOOKING BAD

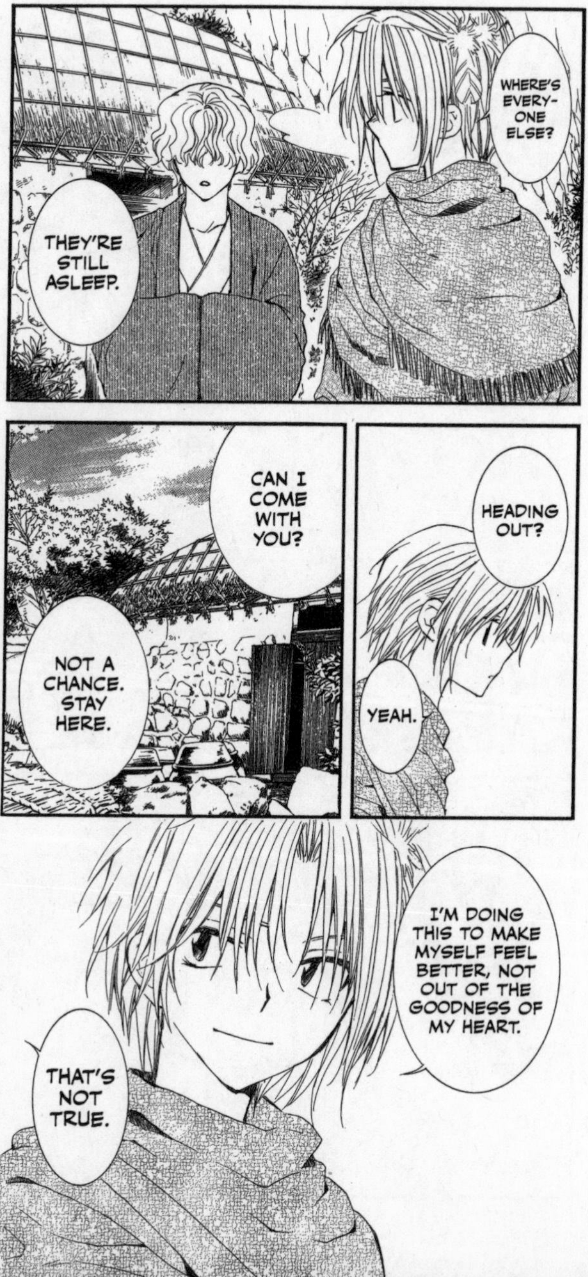
WHERE'S EVERY-ONE ELSE?
THEY'RE STILL ASLEEP.
HEADING OUT?
YEAH.
CAN I COME WITH YOU?
NOT A CHANCE. STAY HERE.
I'M DOING THIS TO MAKE MYSELF FEEL BETTER, NOT OUT OF THE GOODNESS OF MY HEART.
THAT'S NOT TRUE.

Hello! This is Mizuho Kusanagi. Thank you very much for picking up volume 9 of Yona of the Dawn!

Volume 9! It's the same number of volumes I reached with my previous series, *NG Life*. I'm glad I made it this far. This volume is extra special for me. I'm putting out a deluxe version that comes with a CD!!* It's the first time there's been an audio version of any of my work. I'm very appreciative, but also nervous. I couldn't have done it without your support!

My staff has been such a big help. They've worked so hard! ♡

I'm so grateful!

To be continued in the next column...

*Only available in Japan

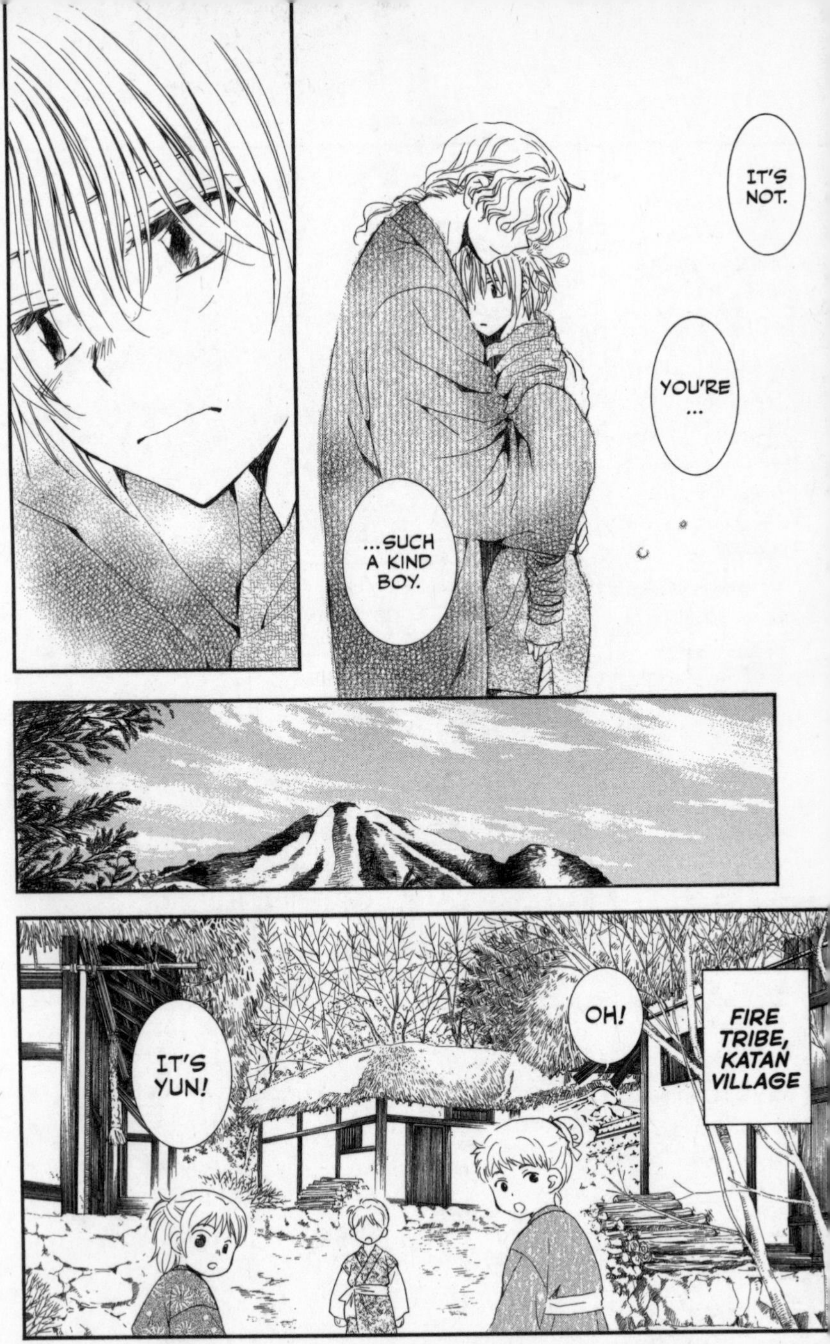
IT'S NOT.
YOU'RE ...
...SUCH A KIND BOY.
FIRE TRIBE, KATAN VILLAGE
OH!
IT'S YUN!

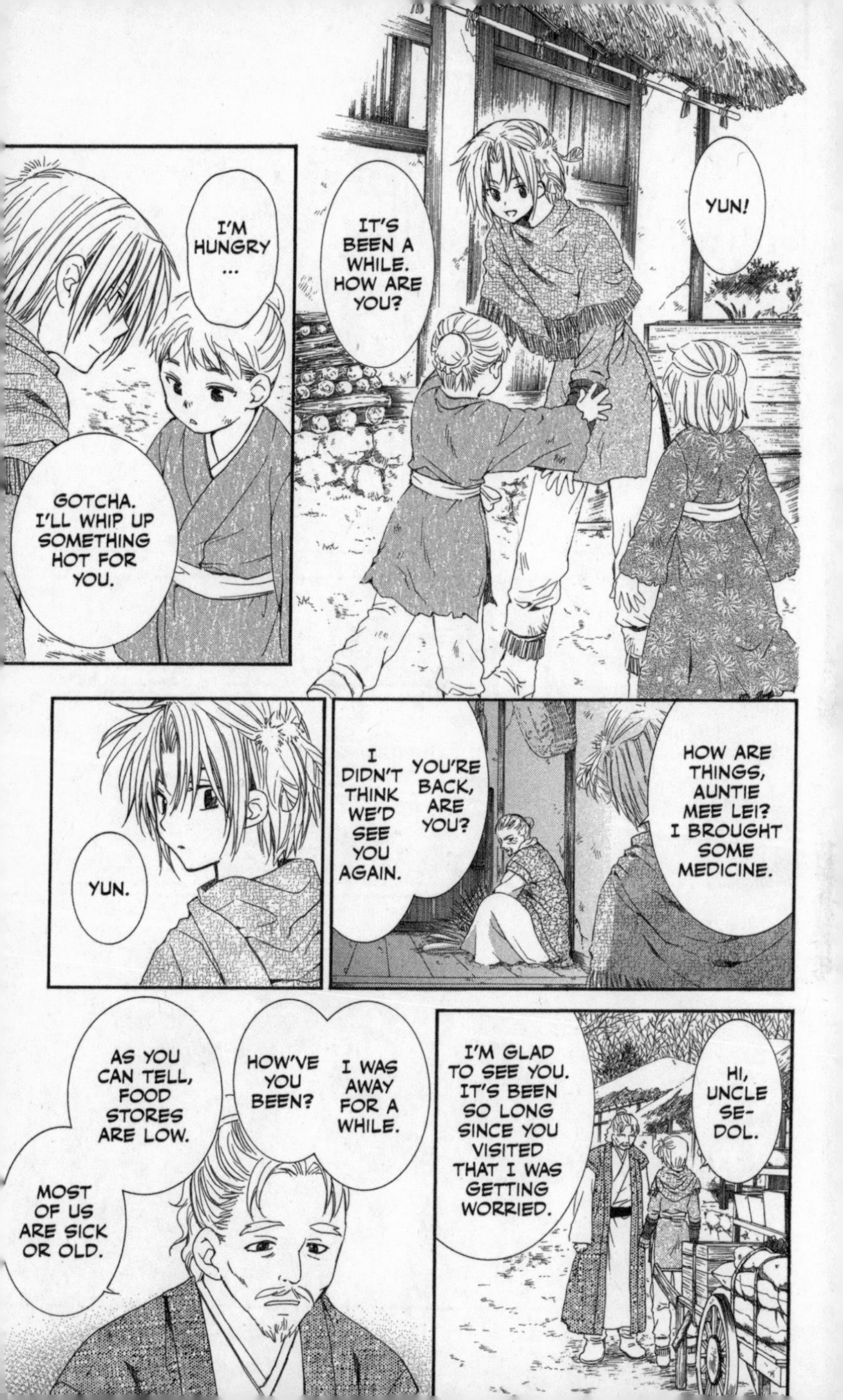
YUN!
IT'S BEEN A WHILE. HOW ARE YOU?
I'M HUNGRY ...
GOTCHA. I'LL WHIP UP SOMETHING HOT FOR YOU.
HOW ARE THINGS, AUNTIE MEE LEI? I BROUGHT SOME MEDICINE.
YOU'RE BACK, ARE YOU?
I DIDN'T THINK WE'D SEE YOU AGAIN.
YUN.
HI, UNCLE SE-DOL.
I'M GLAD TO SEE YOU. IT'S BEEN SO LONG SINCE YOU VISITED THAT I WAS GETTING WORRIED.
I WAS AWAY FOR A WHILE.
HOW'VE YOU BEEN?
AS YOU CAN TELL, FOOD STORES ARE LOW.
MOST OF US ARE SICK OR OLD.

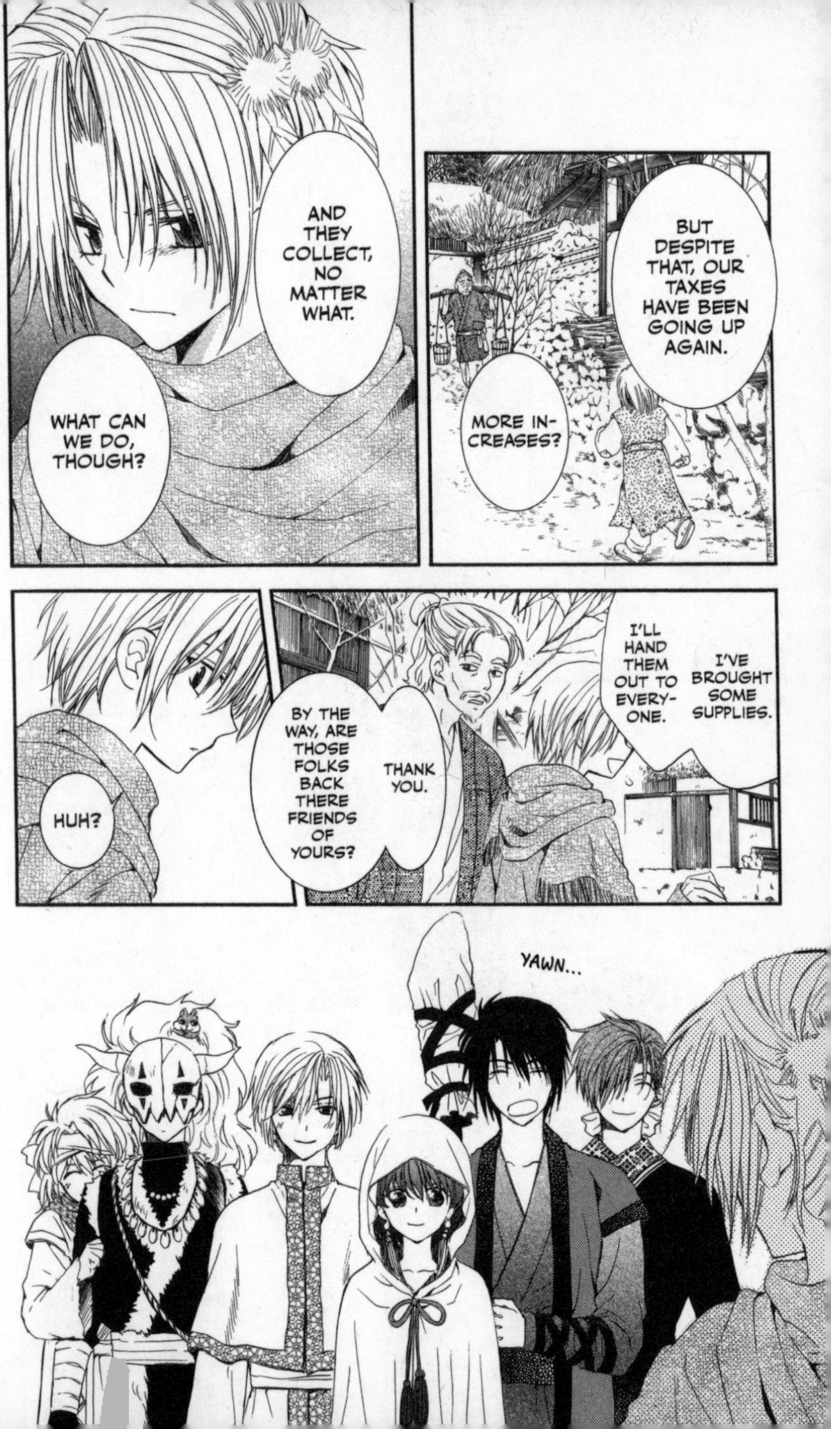
BUT DESPITE THAT, OUR TAXES HAVE BEEN GOING UP AGAIN.
MORE IN-CREASES?
AND THEY COLLECT, NO MATTER WHAT.
WHAT CAN WE DO, THOUGH?
I'VE BROUGHT SOME SUPPLIES.
I'LL HAND THEM OUT TO EVERY-ONE.
THANK YOU.
BY THE WAY, ARE THOSE FOLKS BACK THERE FRIENDS OF YOURS?
HUH?
YAWN...

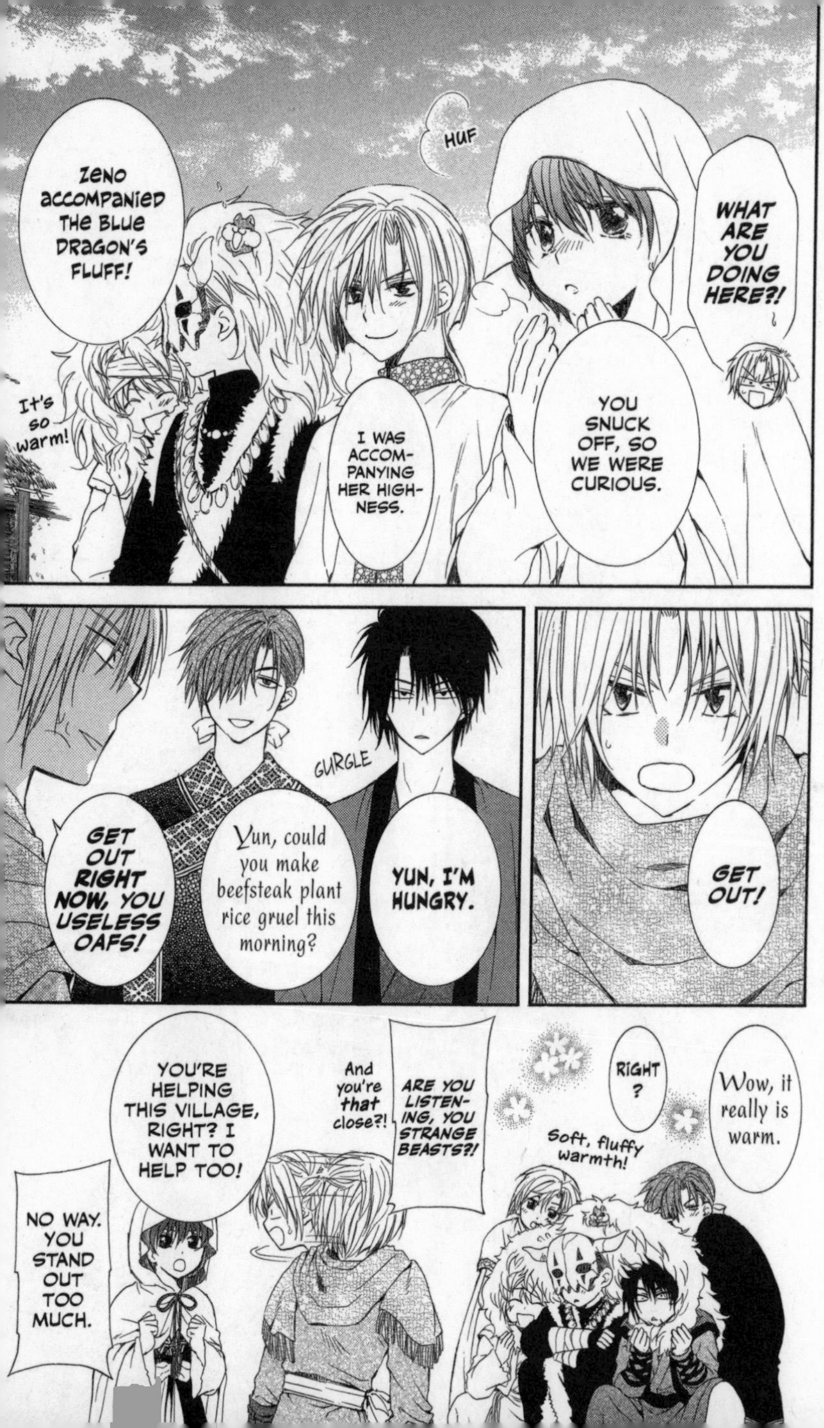
WHAT ARE YOU DOING HERE?!
HUF
YOU SNUCK OFF, SO WE WERE CURIOUS.
I WAS ACCOMPANYING HER HIGHNESS.
Zeno accompanied the blue dragon's fluff!
It's so warm!
GET OUT!
YUN, I'M HUNGRY.
GURGLE
Yun, could you make beefsteak plant rice gruel this morning?
GET OUT RIGHT NOW, YOU USELESS OAFS!
Wow, it really is warm.
RIGHT?
Soft, fluffy warmth!
ARE YOU LISTENING, YOU STRANGE BEASTS?!
And you're that close?!
YOU'RE HELPING THIS VILLAGE, RIGHT? I WANT TO HELP TOO!
NO WAY. YOU STAND OUT TOO MUCH.

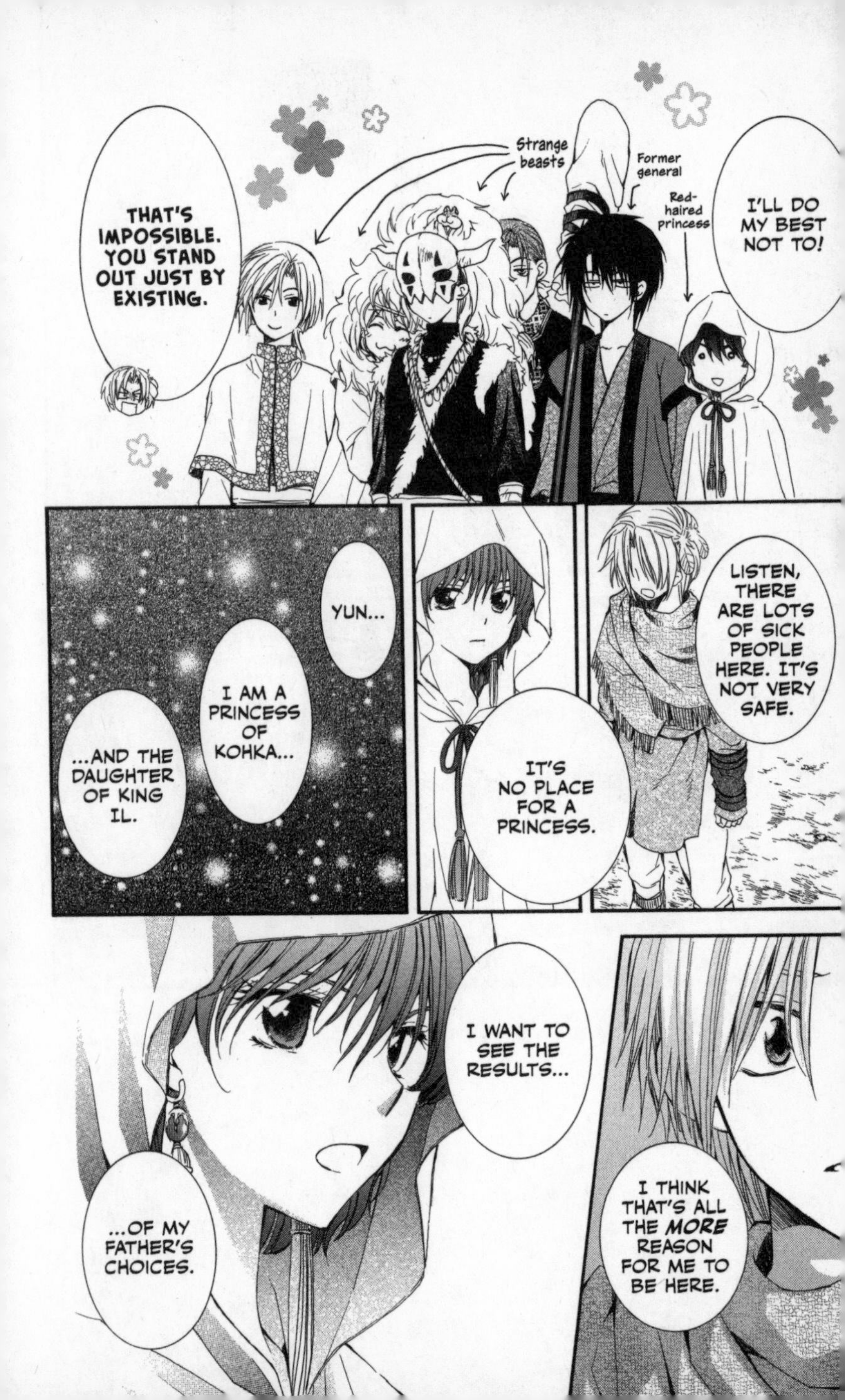
I'LL DO MY BEST NOT TO!
Red-haired princess
Former general
Strange beasts
THAT'S IMPOSSIBLE. YOU STAND OUT JUST BY EXISTING.
LISTEN, THERE ARE LOTS OF SICK PEOPLE HERE. IT'S NOT VERY SAFE.
IT'S NO PLACE FOR A PRINCESS.
YUN...
I AM A PRINCESS OF KOHKA...
...AND THE DAUGHTER OF KING IL.
I THINK THAT'S ALL THE *MORE* REASON FOR ME TO BE HERE.
I WANT TO SEE THE RESULTS...
...OF MY FATHER'S CHOICES.

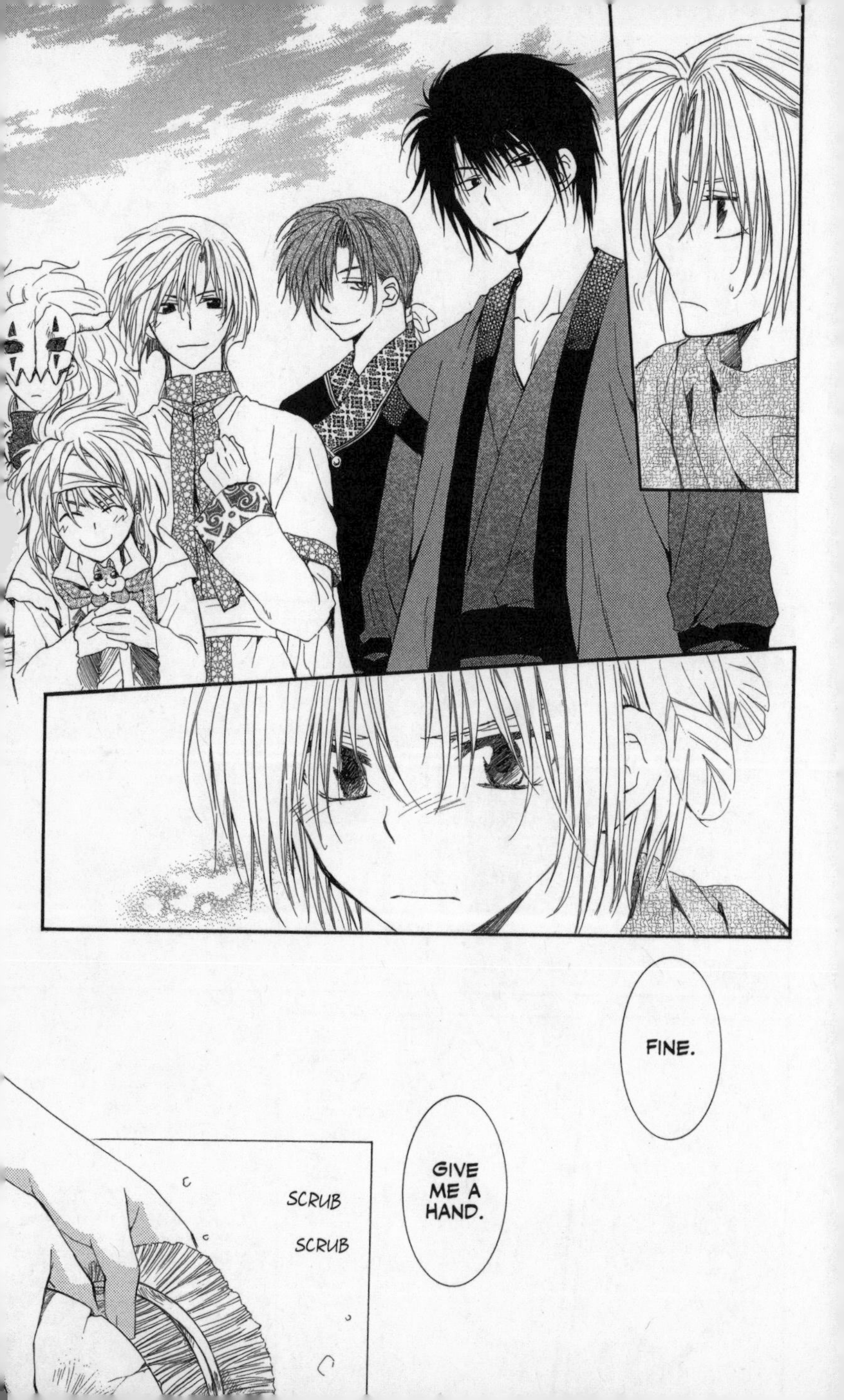
FINE.
GIVE ME A HAND.
SCRUB
SCRUB

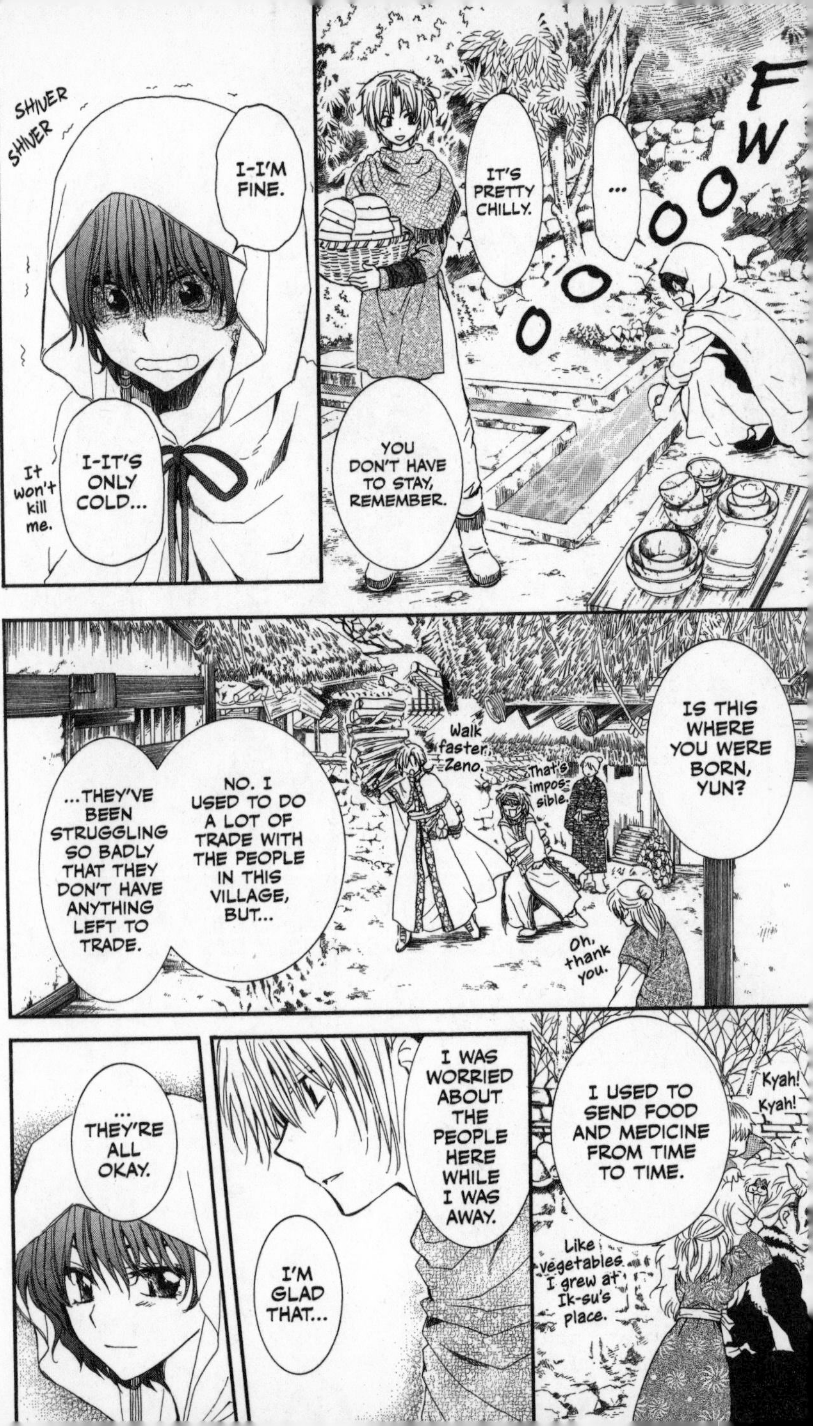
FWOOOOOO
...
IT'S PRETTY CHILLY.
YOU DON'T HAVE TO STAY, REMEMBER.
SHIVER SHIVER
I-I'M FINE.
I-IT'S ONLY COLD...
It won't kill me.
IS THIS WHERE YOU WERE BORN, YUN?
Walk faster, Zeno.
That's impossible.
Oh, thank you.
NO. I USED TO DO A LOT OF TRADE WITH THE PEOPLE IN THIS VILLAGE, BUT...
...THEY'VE BEEN STRUGGLING SO BADLY THAT THEY DON'T HAVE ANYTHING LEFT TO TRADE.
Kyah! Kyah!
I USED TO SEND FOOD AND MEDICINE FROM TIME TO TIME.
Like vegetables I grew at Ik-su's place.
I WAS WORRIED ABOUT THE PEOPLE HERE WHILE I WAS AWAY.
I'M GLAD THAT...
... THEY'RE ALL OKAY.

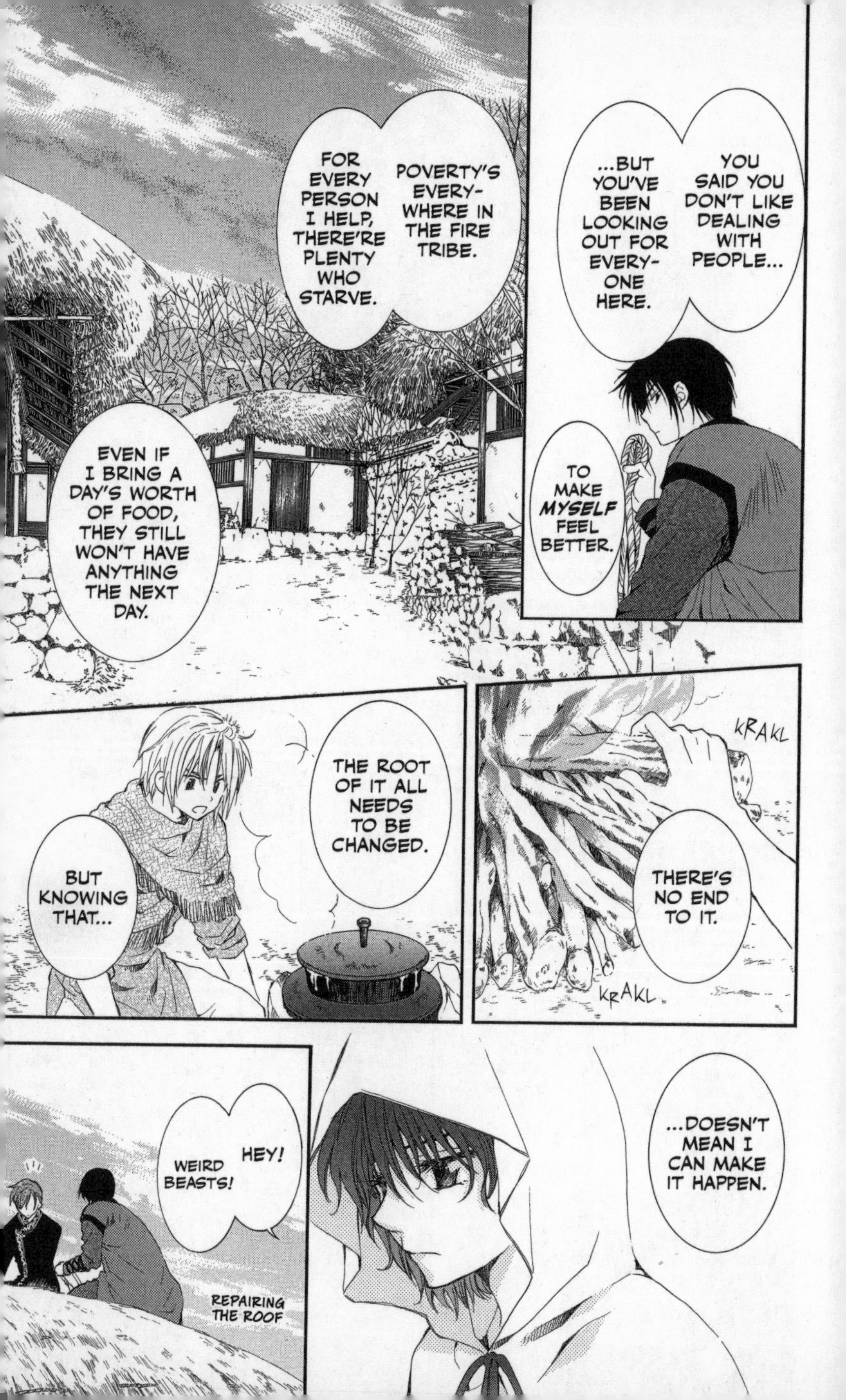
YOU SAID YOU DON'T LIKE DEALING WITH PEOPLE...
...BUT YOU'VE BEEN LOOKING OUT FOR EVERY-ONE HERE.
TO MAKE *MYSELF* FEEL BETTER.
POVERTY'S EVERY-WHERE IN THE FIRE TRIBE.
FOR EVERY PERSON I HELP, THERE'RE PLENTY WHO STARVE.
EVEN IF I BRING A DAY'S WORTH OF FOOD, THEY STILL WON'T HAVE ANYTHING THE NEXT DAY.
KRAKL
THERE'S NO END TO IT.
KRAKL
THE ROOT OF IT ALL NEEDS TO BE CHANGED.
BUT KNOWING THAT...
...DOESN'T MEAN I CAN MAKE IT HAPPEN.
HEY!
WEIRD BEASTS!
REPAIRING THE ROOF

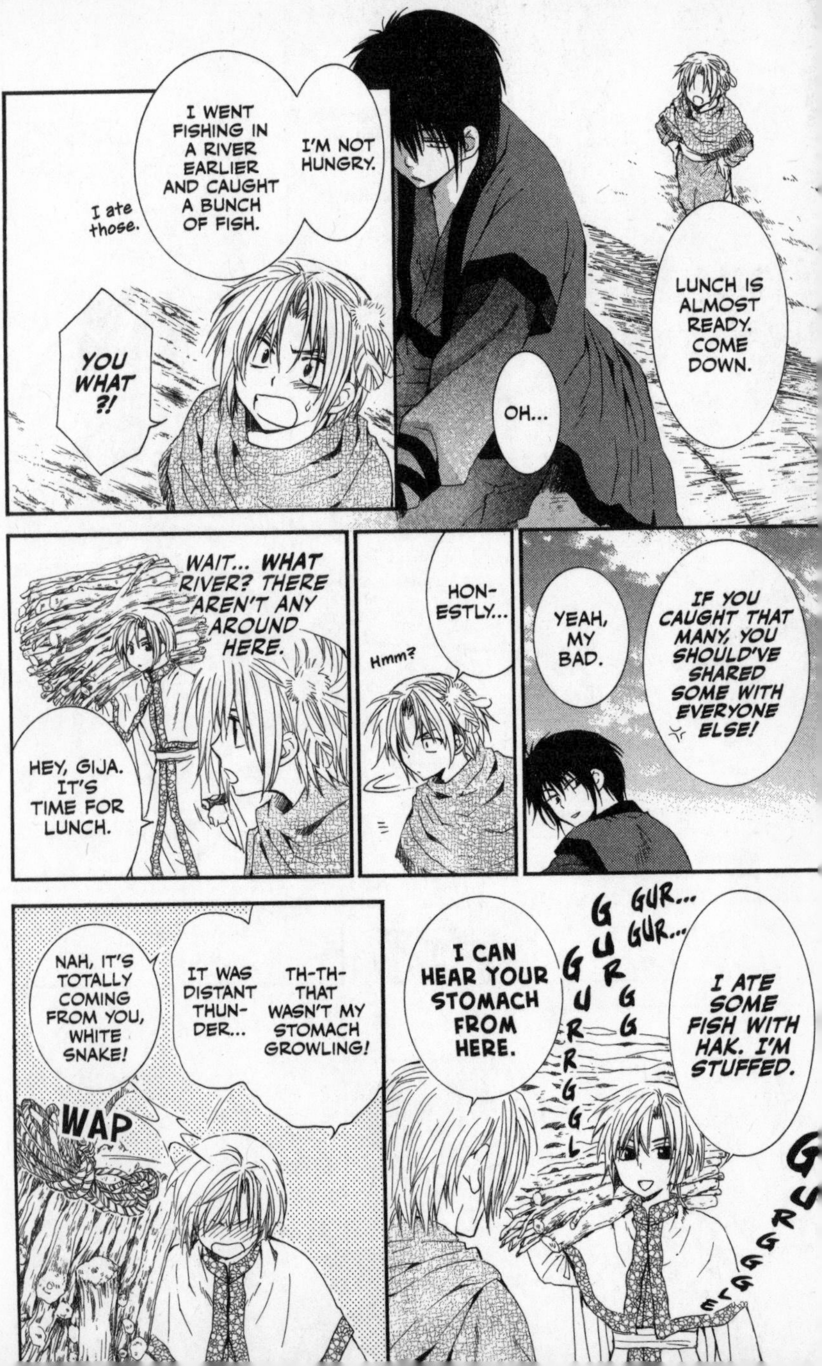
LUNCH IS ALMOST READY. COME DOWN.
OH...
I'M NOT HUNGRY.
I WENT FISHING IN A RIVER EARLIER AND CAUGHT A BUNCH OF FISH.
I ate those.
YOU WHAT ?!
IF YOU CAUGHT THAT MANY, YOU SHOULD'VE SHARED SOME WITH EVERYONE ELSE!
YEAH, MY BAD.
HON-ESTLY...
Hmm?
WAIT... WHAT RIVER? THERE AREN'T ANY AROUND HERE.
HEY, GIJA. IT'S TIME FOR LUNCH.
GUR... GUR...
I ATE SOME FISH WITH HAK. I'M STUFFED.
GURGG
GURRGGL
I CAN HEAR YOUR STOMACH FROM HERE.
TH-TH-THAT WASN'T MY STOMACH GROWLING!
IT WAS DISTANT THUNDER...
NAH, IT'S TOTALLY COMING FROM YOU, WHITE SNAKE!
WAP

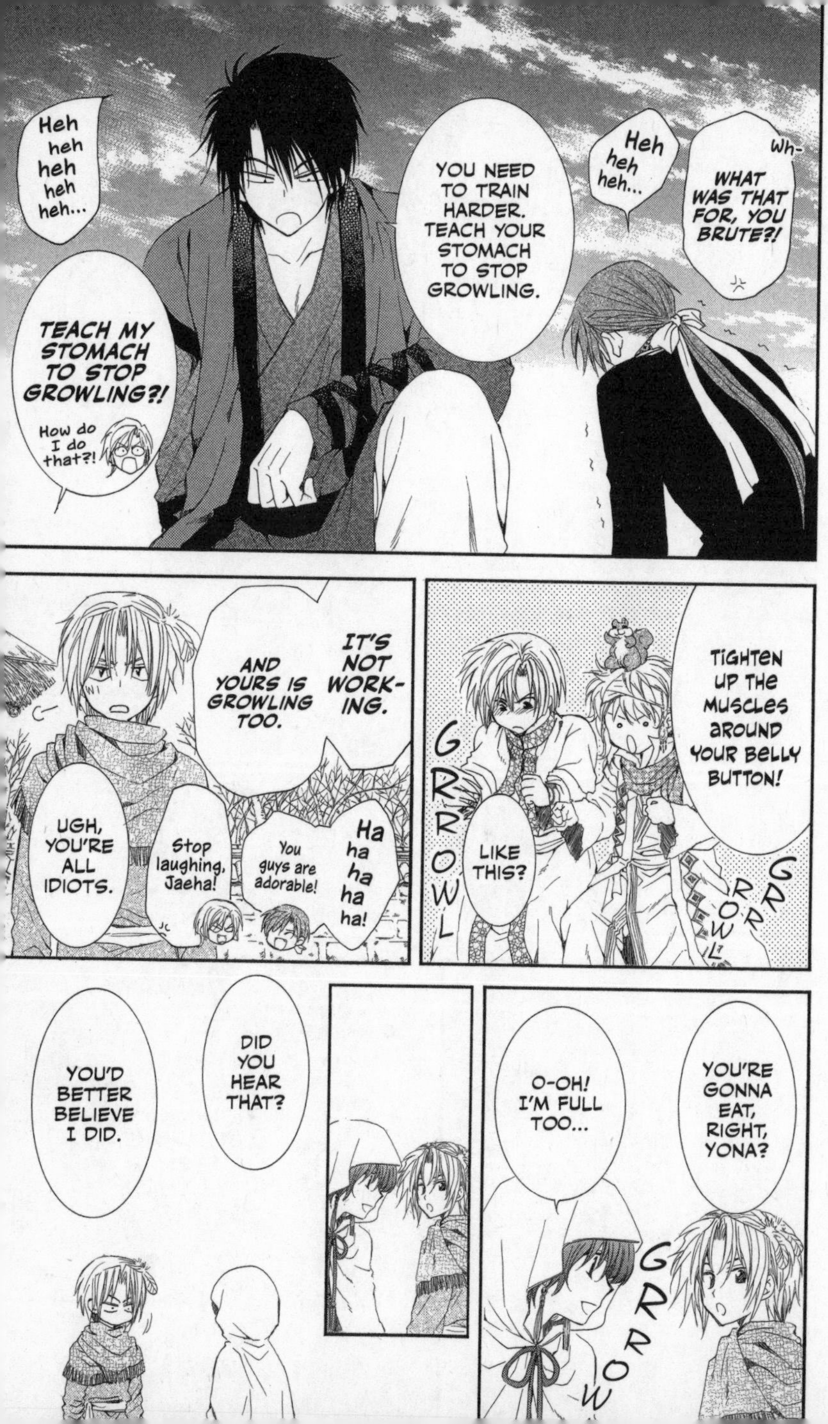
Wh- WHAT WAS THAT FOR, YOU BRUTE?!
Heh heh heh...
YOU NEED TO TRAIN HARDER. TEACH YOUR STOMACH TO STOP GROWLING.
Heh heh heh heh heh...
TEACH MY STOMACH TO STOP GROWLING?!
How do I do that?!
TIGHTEN UP THE MUSCLES AROUND YOUR BELLY BUTTON!
GRROWL
LIKE THIS?
GRROWL
IT'S NOT WORKING.
AND YOURS IS GROWLING TOO.
Ha ha ha ha ha!
You guys are adorable!
Stop laughing, Jaeha!
UGH, YOU'RE ALL IDIOTS.
YOU'RE GONNA EAT, RIGHT, YONA?
O-OH! I'M FULL TOO...
GRROWW
DID YOU HEAR THAT?
YOU'D BETTER BELIEVE I DID.

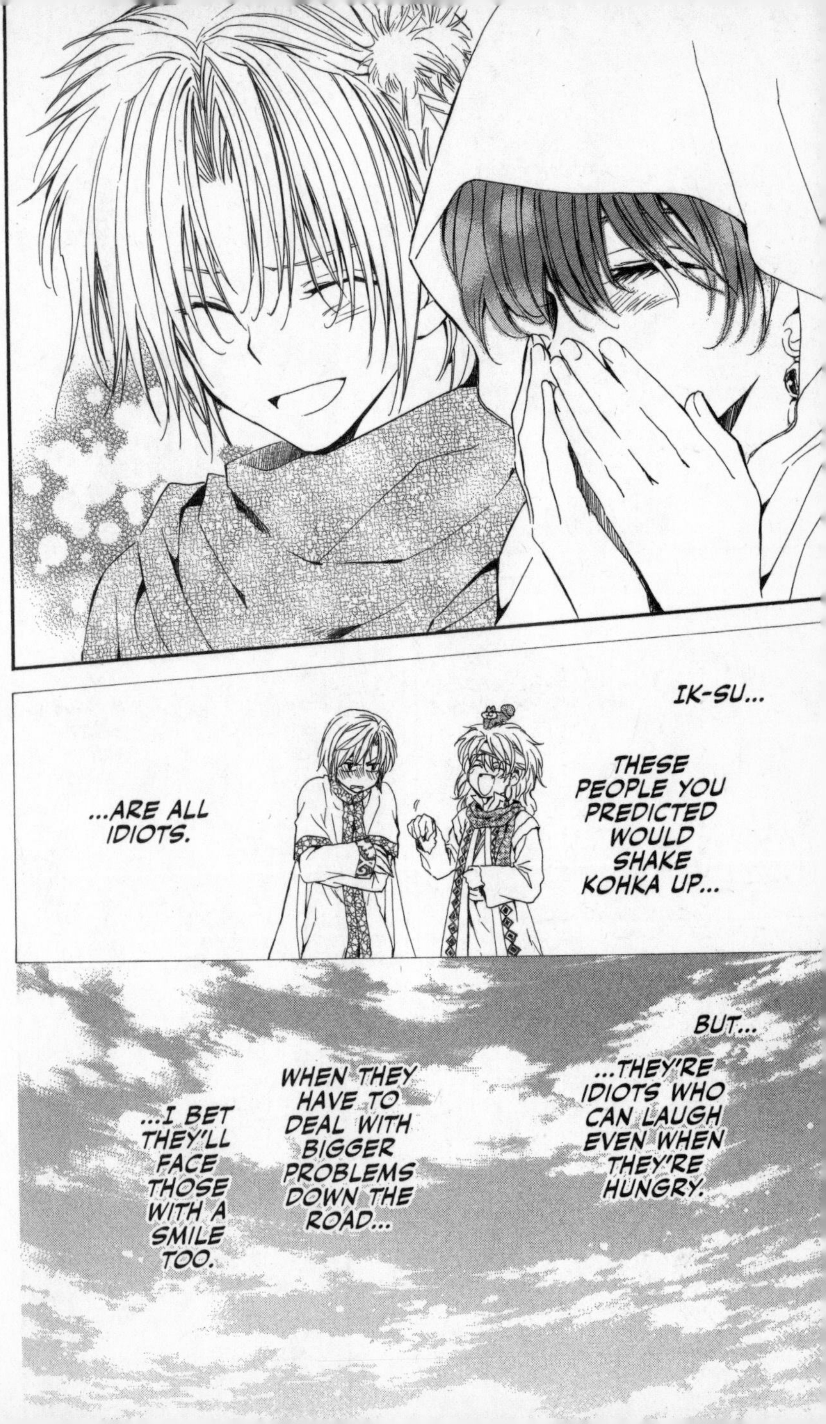
IK-SU...
THESE PEOPLE YOU PREDICTED WOULD SHAKE KOHKA UP...
...ARE ALL IDIOTS.
BUT...
...THEY'RE IDIOTS WHO CAN LAUGH EVEN WHEN THEY'RE HUNGRY.
WHEN THEY HAVE TO DEAL WITH BIGGER PROBLEMS DOWN THE ROAD...
...I BET THEY'LL FACE THOSE WITH A SMILE TOO.

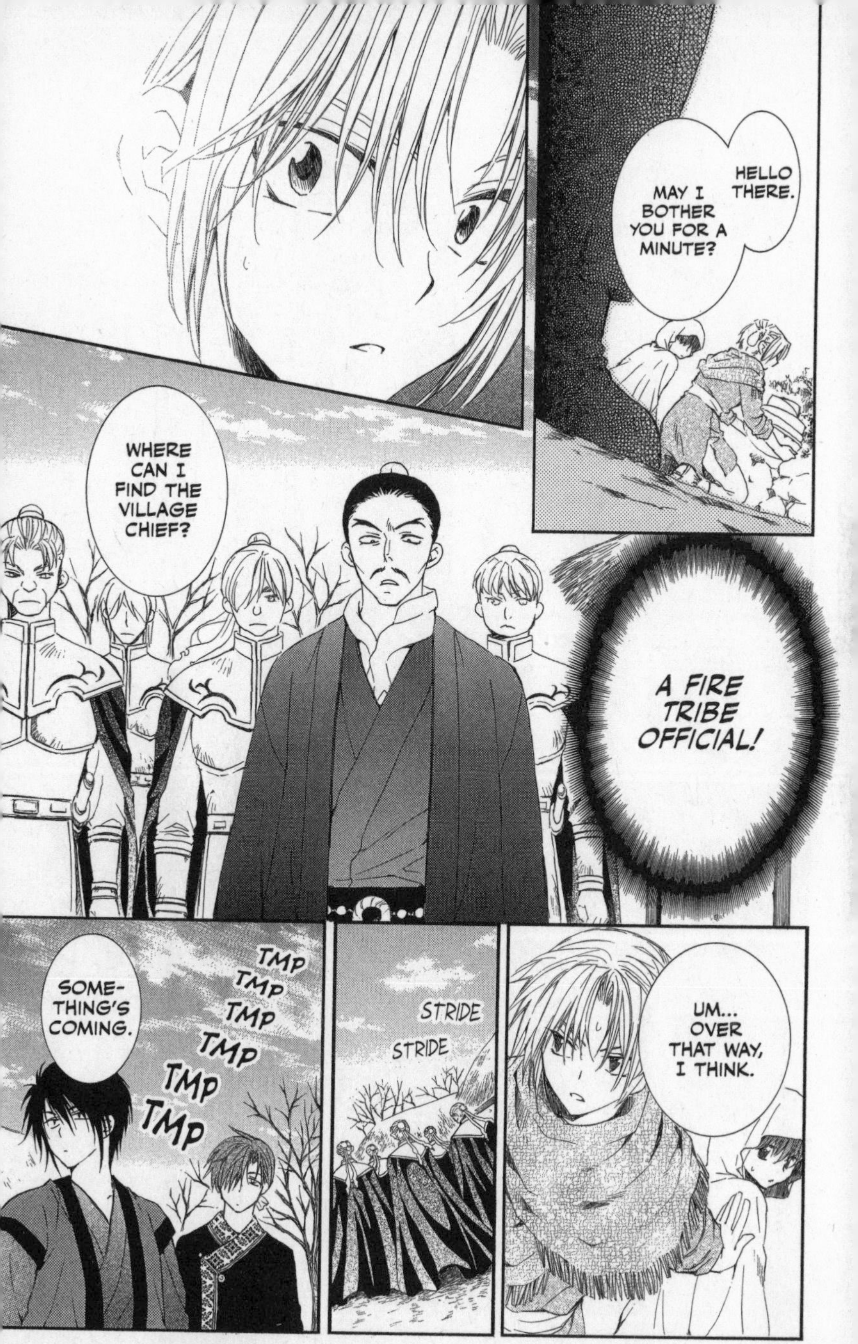
HELLO THERE.
MAY I BOTHER YOU FOR A MINUTE?
WHERE CAN I FIND THE VILLAGE CHIEF?
A FIRE TRIBE OFFICIAL!
UM... OVER THAT WAY, I THINK.
STRIDE
STRIDE
TMp TMp TMp TMp TMp TMp
SOME-THING'S COMING.

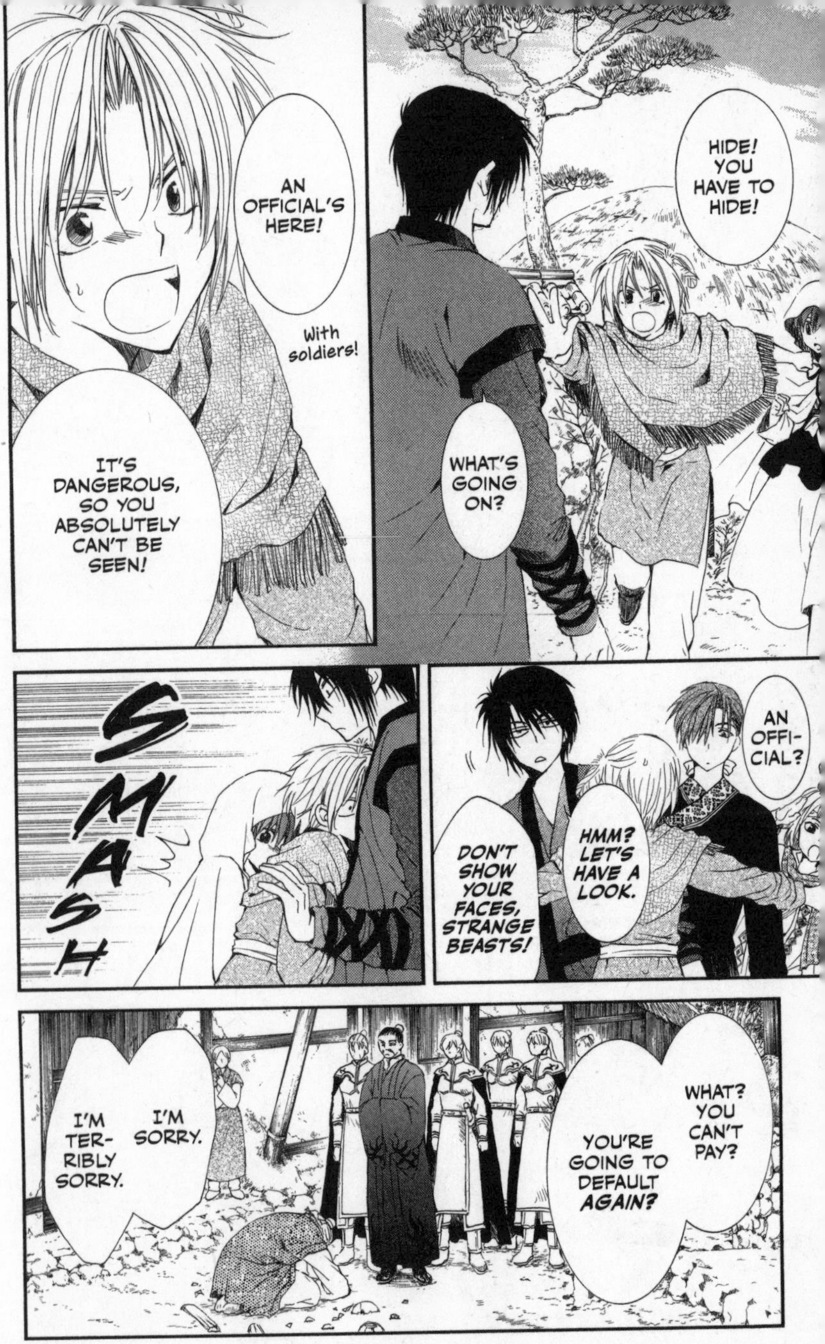
HIDE! YOU HAVE TO HIDE!
WHAT'S GOING ON?
AN OFFICIAL'S HERE!
With soldiers!
IT'S DANGEROUS, SO YOU ABSOLUTELY CAN'T BE SEEN!
AN OFFI-CIAL?
HMM? LET'S HAVE A LOOK.
DON'T SHOW YOUR FACES, STRANGE BEASTS!
SMASH
WHAT? YOU CAN'T PAY?
YOU'RE GOING TO DEFAULT AGAIN?
I'M SORRY.
I'M TER-RIBLY SORRY.

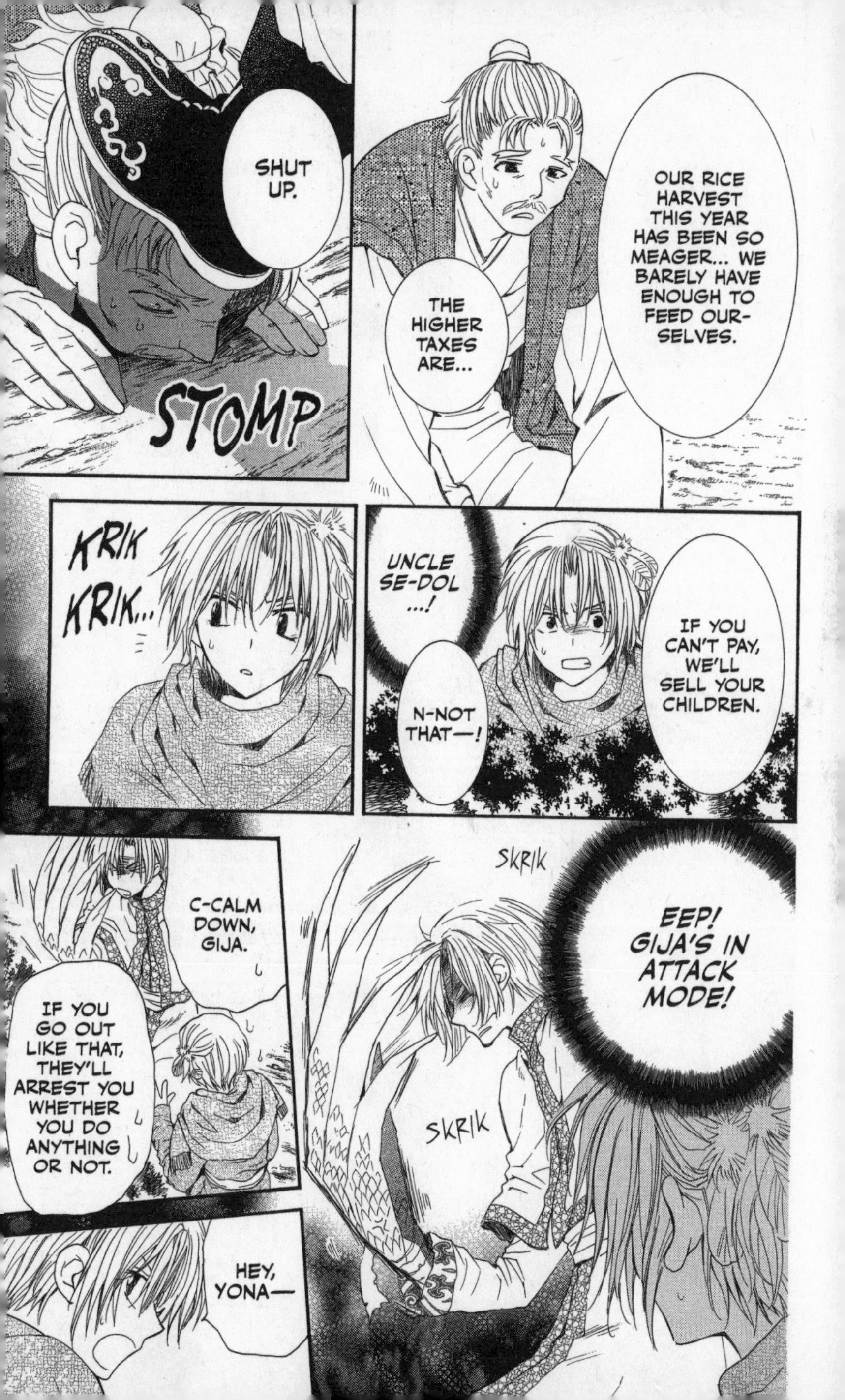
OUR RICE HARVEST THIS YEAR HAS BEEN SO MEAGER... WE BARELY HAVE ENOUGH TO FEED OUR-SELVES.
THE HIGHER TAXES ARE...
SHUT UP.
STOMP
IF YOU CAN'T PAY, WE'LL SELL YOUR CHILDREN.
N-NOT THAT—!
UNCLE SE-DOL ...!
KRIK KRIK...
SKRIK
EEP! GIJA'S IN ATTACK MODE!
SKRIK
C-CALM DOWN, GIJA.
IF YOU GO OUT LIKE THAT, THEY'LL ARREST YOU WHETHER YOU DO ANYTHING OR NOT.
HEY, YONA—

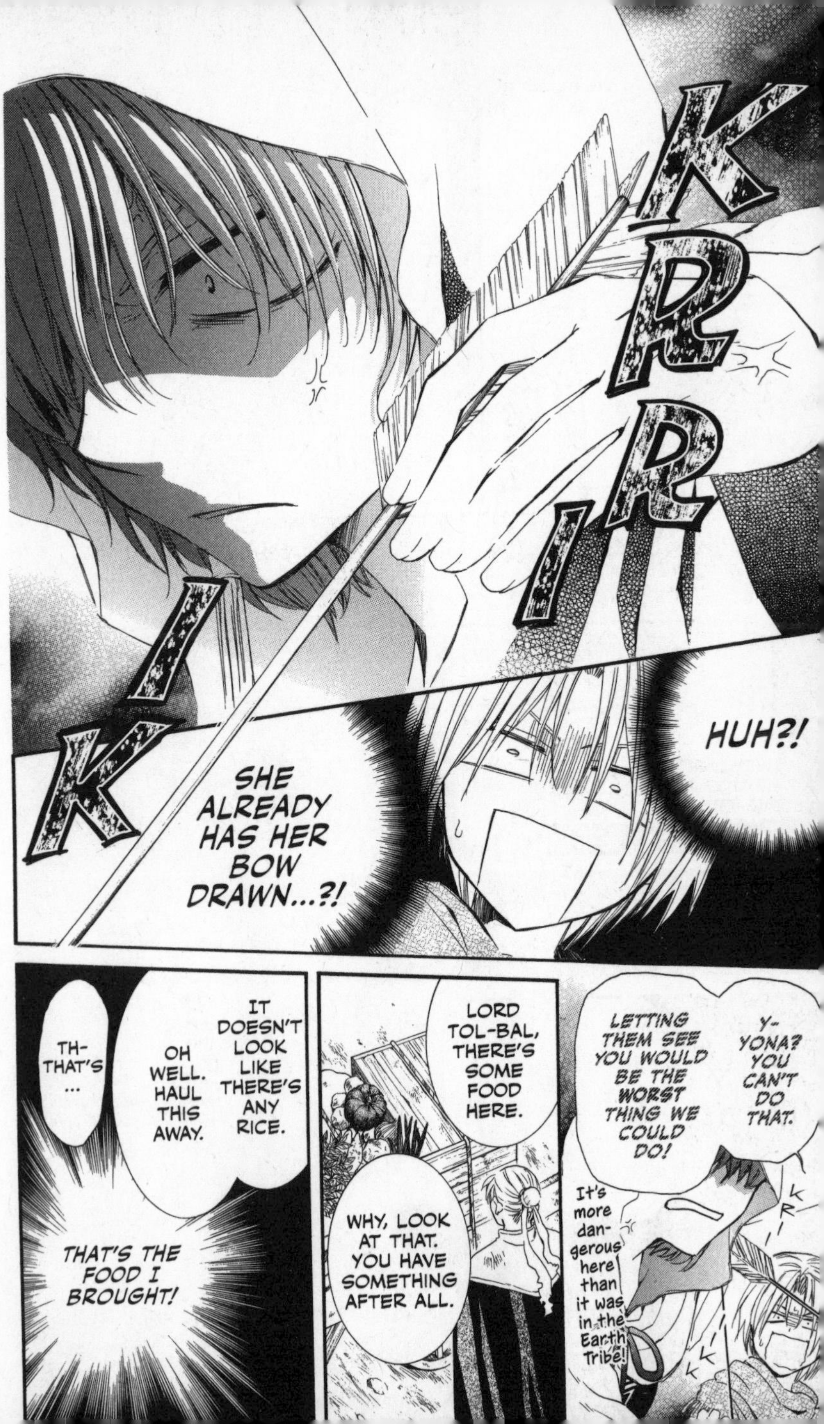
KRRIIK
HUH?!
SHE ALREADY HAS HER BOW DRAWN...?!
Y-YONA? YOU CAN'T DO THAT.
LETTING THEM SEE YOU WOULD BE THE WORST THING WE COULD DO!
It's more dangerous here than it was in the Earth Tribe!
LORD TOL-BAL, THERE'S SOME FOOD HERE.
WHY, LOOK AT THAT. YOU HAVE SOMETHING AFTER ALL.
IT DOESN'T LOOK LIKE THERE'S ANY RICE.
OH WELL. HAUL THIS AWAY.
TH-THAT'S...
THAT'S THE FOOD I BROUGHT!

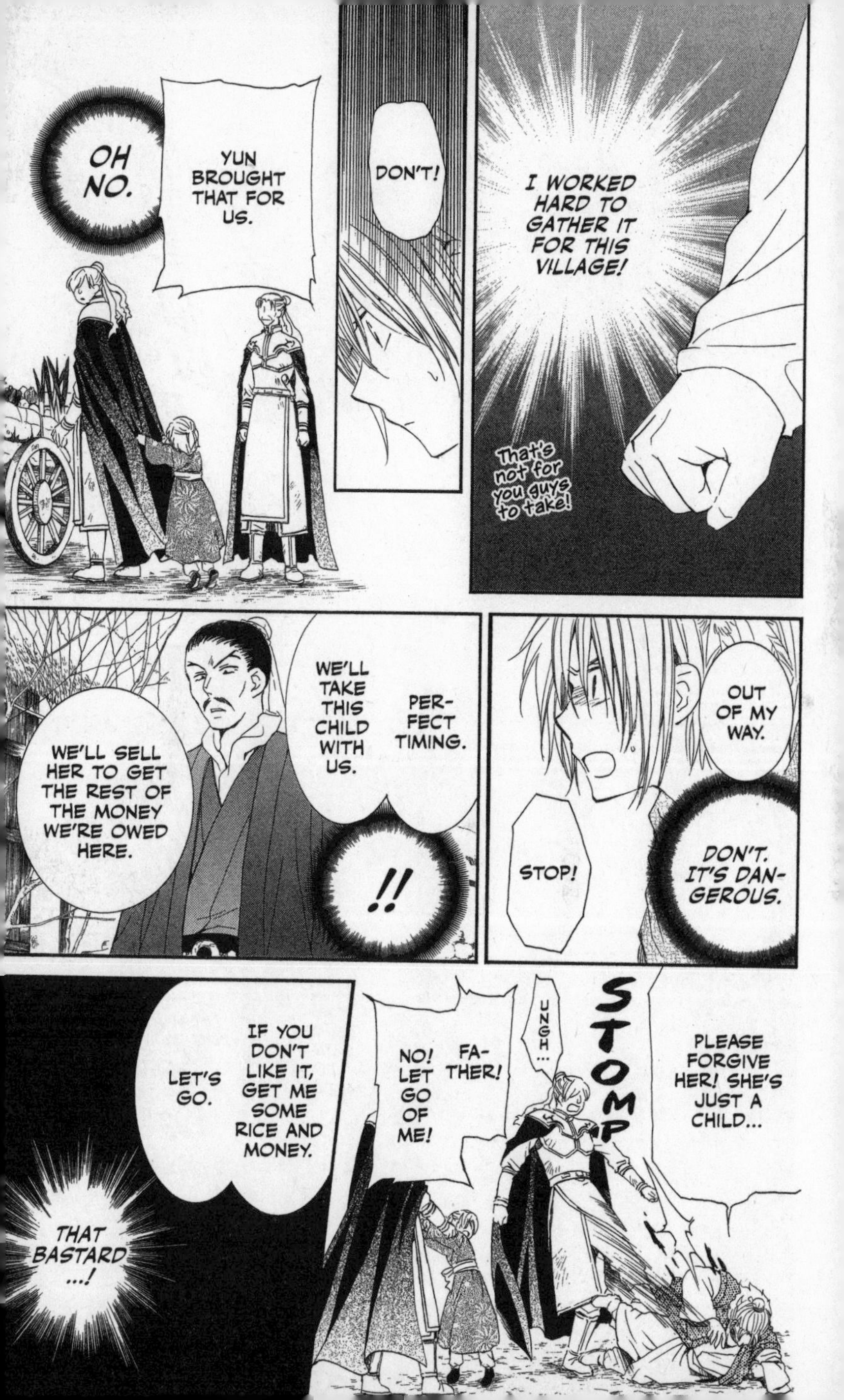
I WORKED HARD TO GATHER IT FOR THIS VILLAGE!
That's not for you guys to take!
DON'T!
YUN BROUGHT THAT FOR US.
OH NO.
OUT OF MY WAY.
DON'T. IT'S DAN-GEROUS.
STOP!
PER-FECT TIMING.
WE'LL TAKE THIS CHILD WITH US.
!!
WE'LL SELL HER TO GET THE REST OF THE MONEY WE'RE OWED HERE.
PLEASE FORGIVE HER! SHE'S JUST A CHILD...
STOMP
UNGH...
FA-THER!
NO! LET GO OF ME!
IF YOU DON'T LIKE IT, GET ME SOME RICE AND MONEY.
LET'S GO.
THAT BASTARD ...!

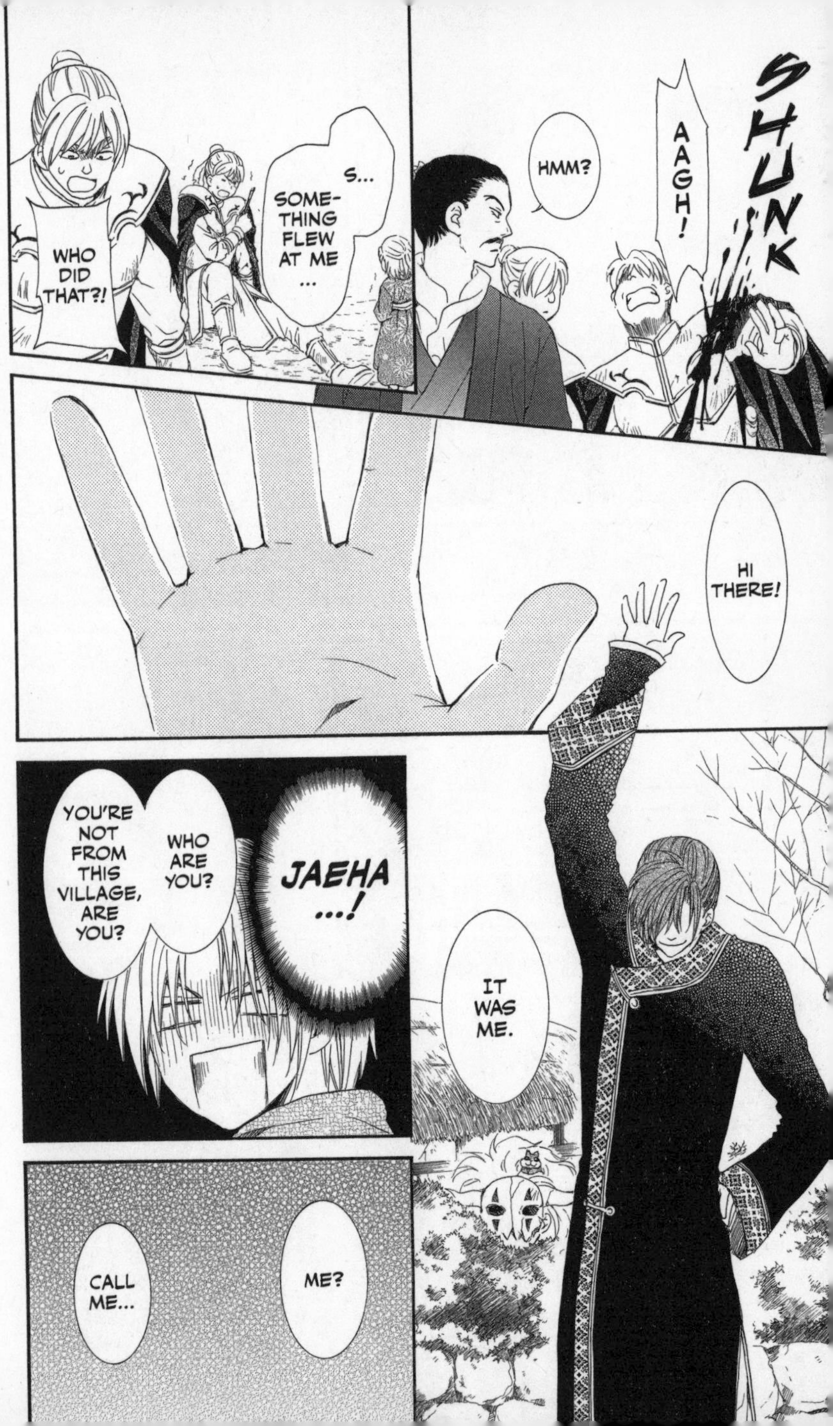
SHUNK
AAGH!
HMM?
S... SOMETHING FLEW AT ME...
WHO DID THAT?!
HI THERE!
IT WAS ME.
JAEHA...!
WHO ARE YOU?
YOU'RE NOT FROM THIS VILLAGE, ARE YOU?
ME?
CALL ME...

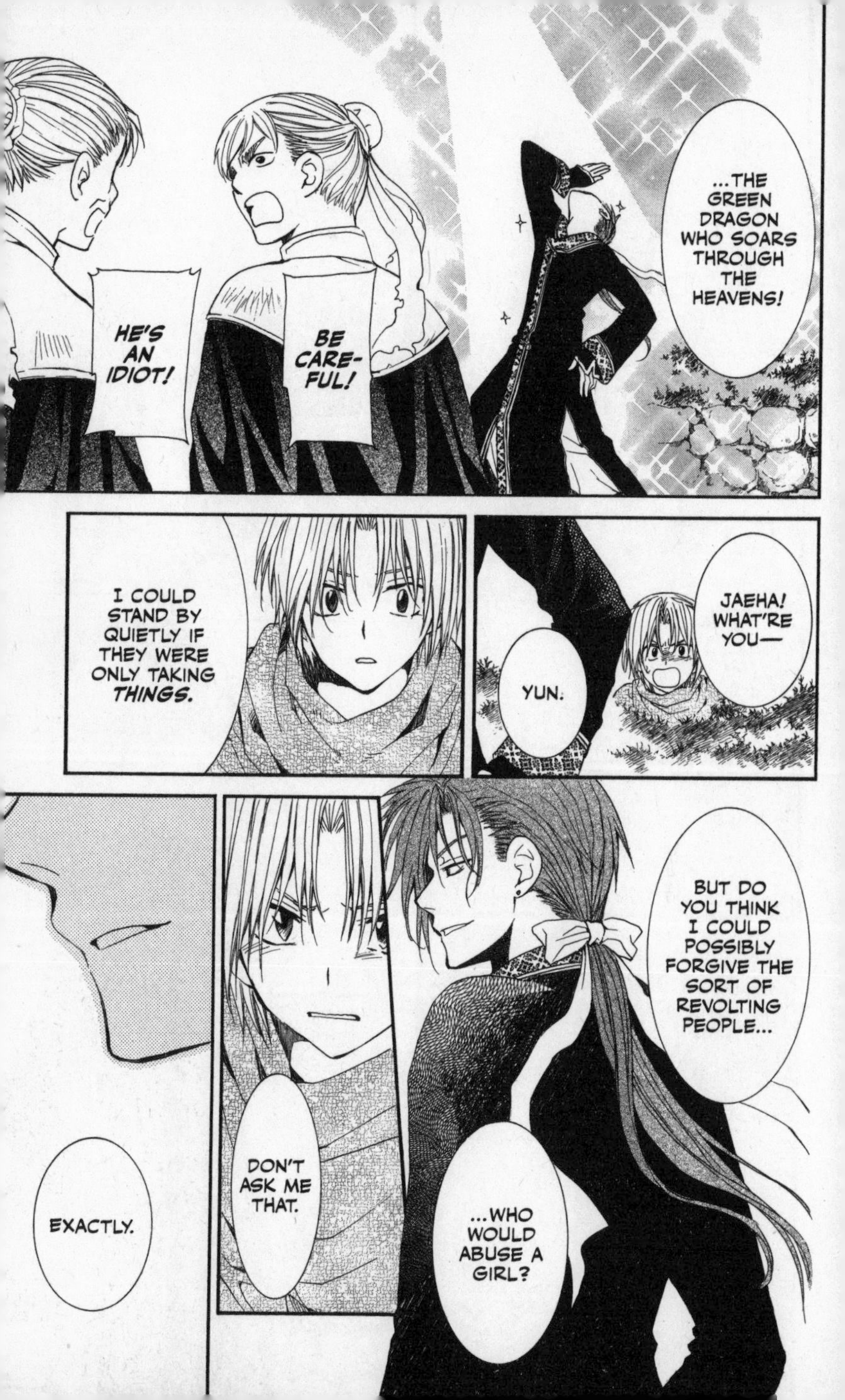
...THE GREEN DRAGON WHO SOARS THROUGH THE HEAVENS!
BE CARE-FUL!
HE'S AN IDIOT!
JAEHA! WHAT'RE YOU—
YUN.
I COULD STAND BY QUIETLY IF THEY WERE ONLY TAKING *THINGS.*
BUT DO YOU THINK I COULD POSSIBLY FORGIVE THE SORT OF REVOLTING PEOPLE...
...WHO WOULD ABUSE A GIRL?
DON'T ASK ME THAT.
EXACTLY.

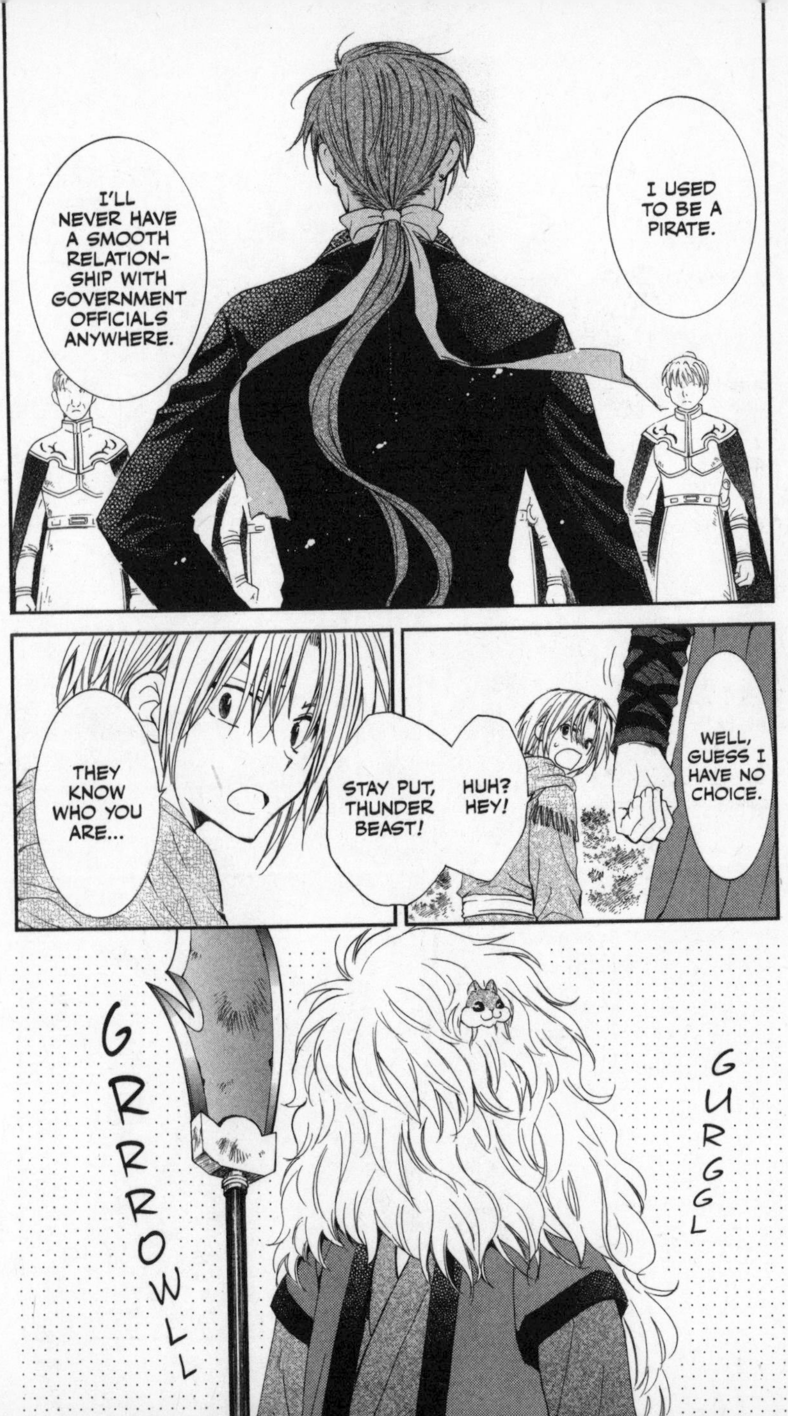
I USED TO BE A PIRATE.
I'LL NEVER HAVE A SMOOTH RELATION-SHIP WITH GOVERNMENT OFFICIALS ANYWHERE.
WELL, GUESS I HAVE NO CHOICE.
HUH? HEY!
STAY PUT, THUNDER BEAST!
THEY KNOW WHO YOU ARE...
GURGGL
GRRROWLL

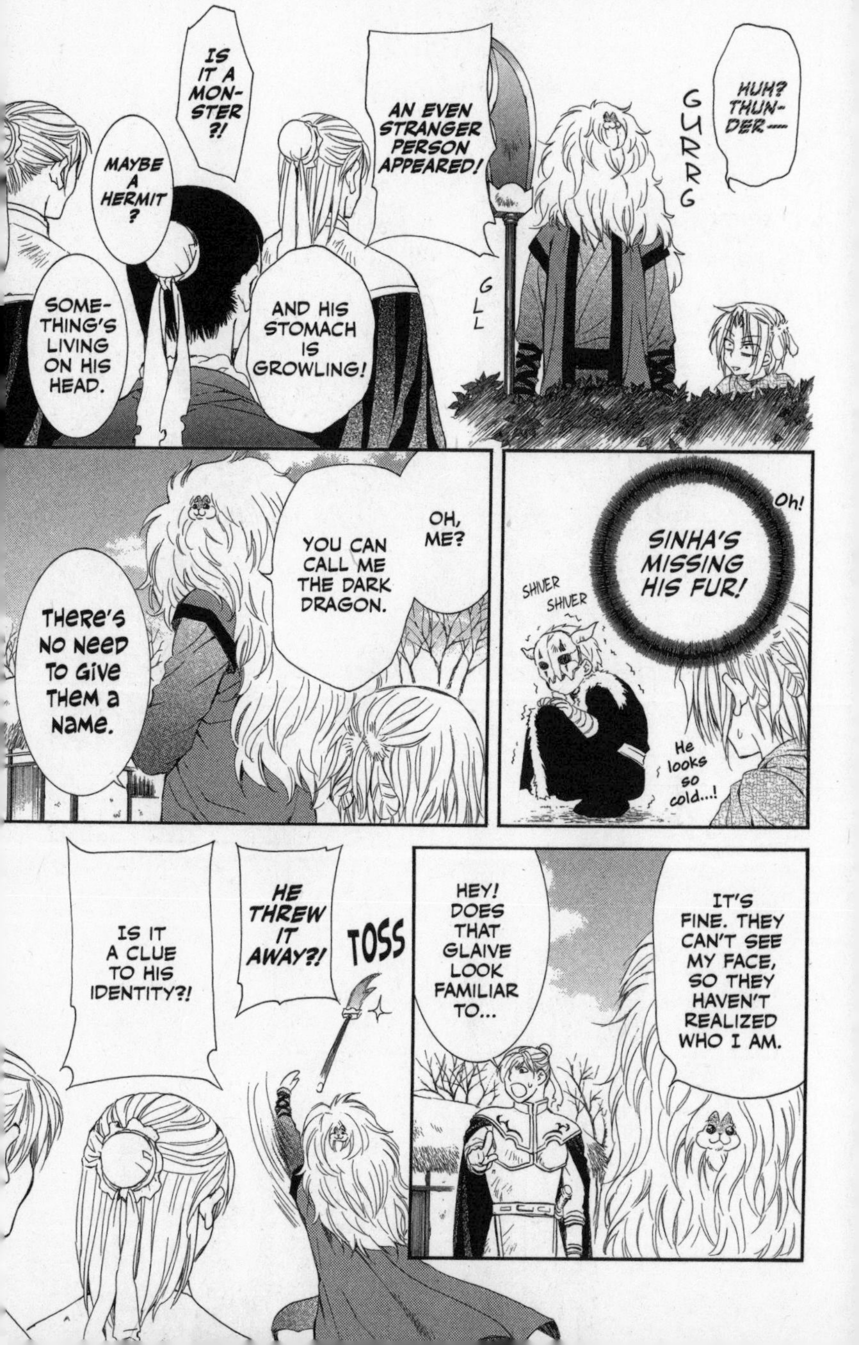
HUH? THUNDER---
GURRG
AN EVEN STRANGER PERSON APPEARED!
IS IT A MONSTER?!
GLL
AND HIS STOMACH IS GROWLING!
MAYBE A HERMIT?
SOMETHING'S LIVING ON HIS HEAD.
Oh!
SINHA'S MISSING HIS FUR!
SHIVER SHIVER
He looks so cold...!
OH, ME?
YOU CAN CALL ME THE DARK DRAGON.
There's no need to give them a name.
IT'S FINE. THEY CAN'T SEE MY FACE, SO THEY HAVEN'T REALIZED WHO I AM.
HEY! DOES THAT GLAIVE LOOK FAMILIAR TO...
TOSS
HE THREW IT AWAY?!
IS IT A CLUE TO HIS IDENTITY?!

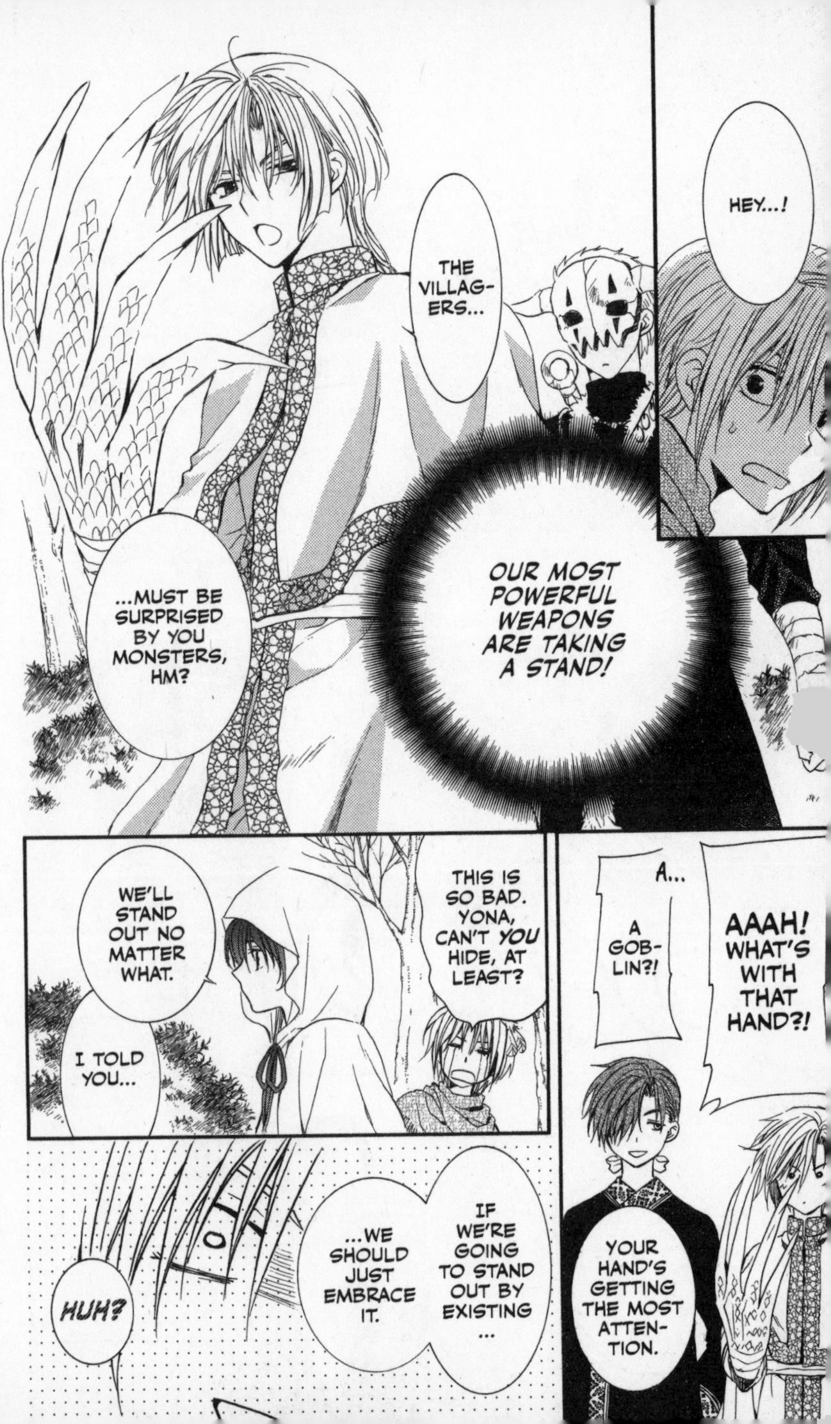

HEY...!
THE VILLAGERS...
...MUST BE SURPRISED BY YOU MONSTERS, HM?
OUR MOST POWERFUL WEAPONS ARE TAKING A STAND!
A...
A GOBLIN?!
AAAH! WHAT'S WITH THAT HAND?!
YOUR HAND'S GETTING THE MOST ATTENTION.
THIS IS SO BAD. YONA, CAN'T *YOU* HIDE, AT LEAST?
WE'LL STAND OUT NO MATTER WHAT.
I TOLD YOU...
IF WE'RE GOING TO STAND OUT BY EXISTING...
...WE SHOULD JUST EMBRACE IT.
HUH?

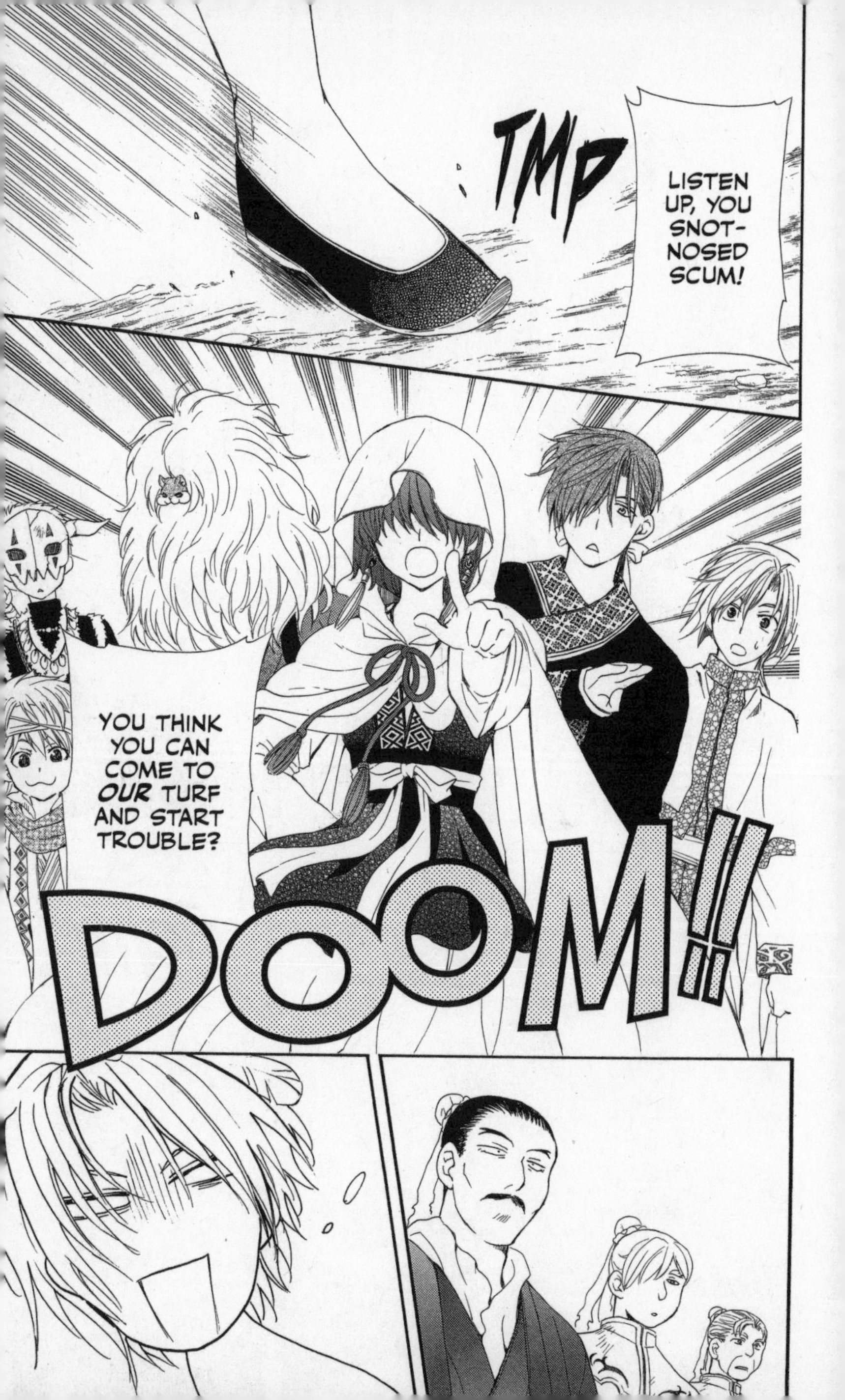
LISTEN UP, YOU SNOT-NOSED SCUM!
TMP
YOU THINK YOU CAN COME TO *OUR* TURF AND START TROUBLE?
DOOM!!

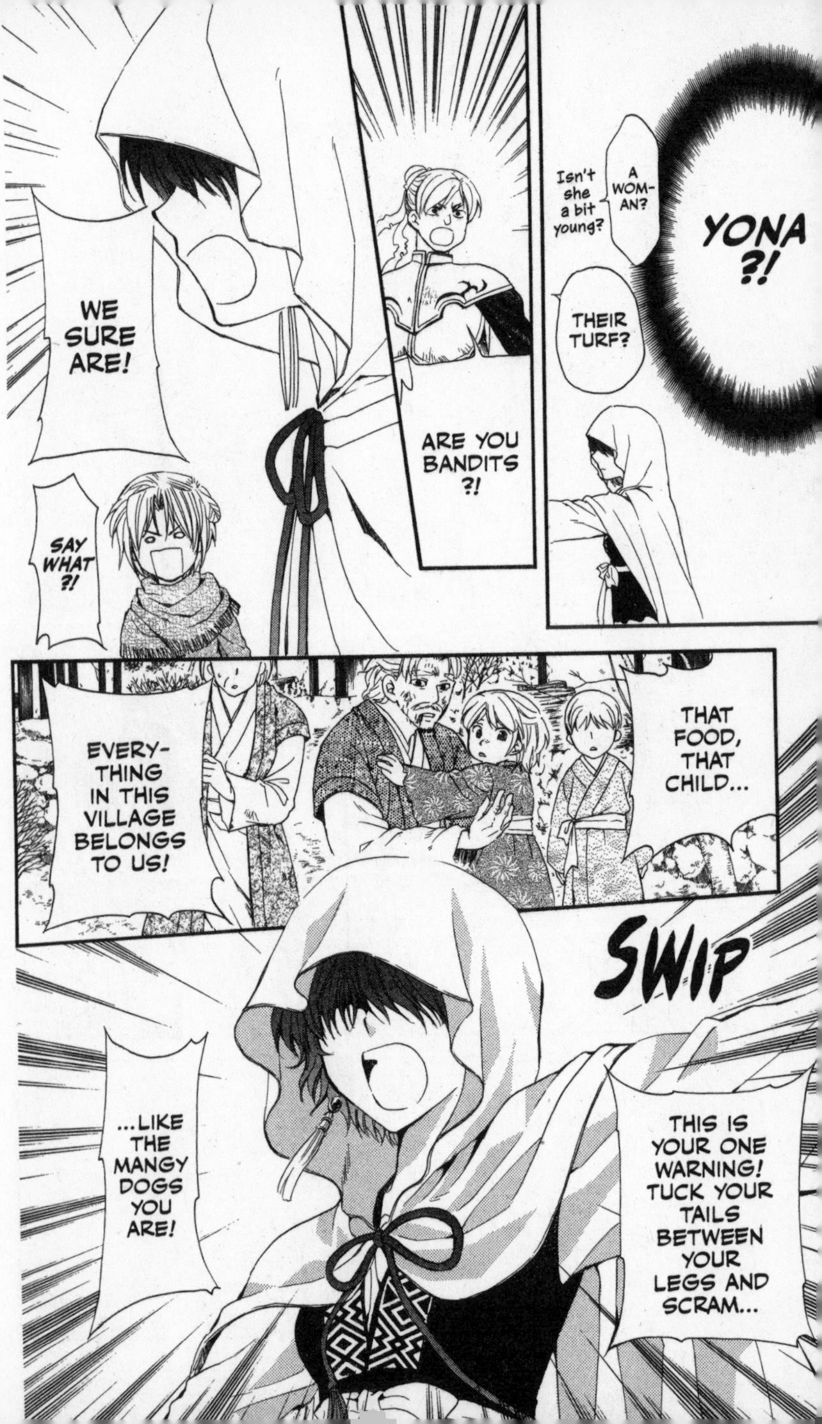
YONA ?!
A WOM- AN?
Isn't she a bit young?
THEIR TURF?
ARE YOU BANDITS ?!
WE SURE ARE!
SAY WHAT ?!
THAT FOOD, THAT CHILD...
EVERY- THING IN THIS VILLAGE BELONGS TO US!
SWIP
THIS IS YOUR ONE WARNING! TUCK YOUR TAILS BETWEEN YOUR LEGS AND SCRAM...
...LIKE THE MANGY DOGS YOU ARE!

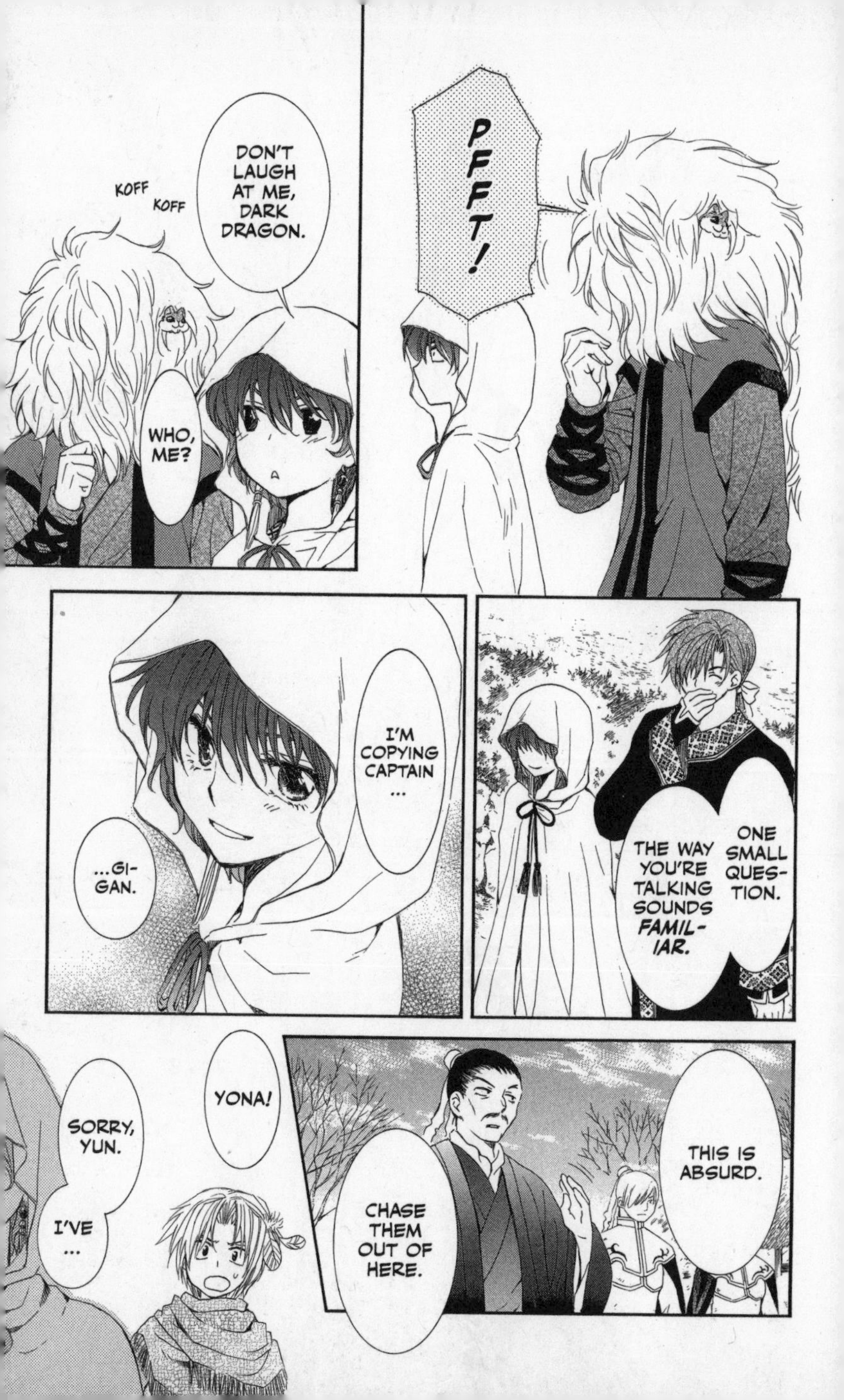
PFFT!
DON'T LAUGH AT ME, DARK DRAGON.
KOFF KOFF
WHO, ME?
ONE SMALL QUES- TION.
THE WAY YOU'RE TALKING SOUNDS FAMIL- IAR.
I'M COPYING CAPTAIN ...
...GI- GAN.
THIS IS ABSURD.
CHASE THEM OUT OF HERE.
YONA!
SORRY, YUN.
I'VE ...

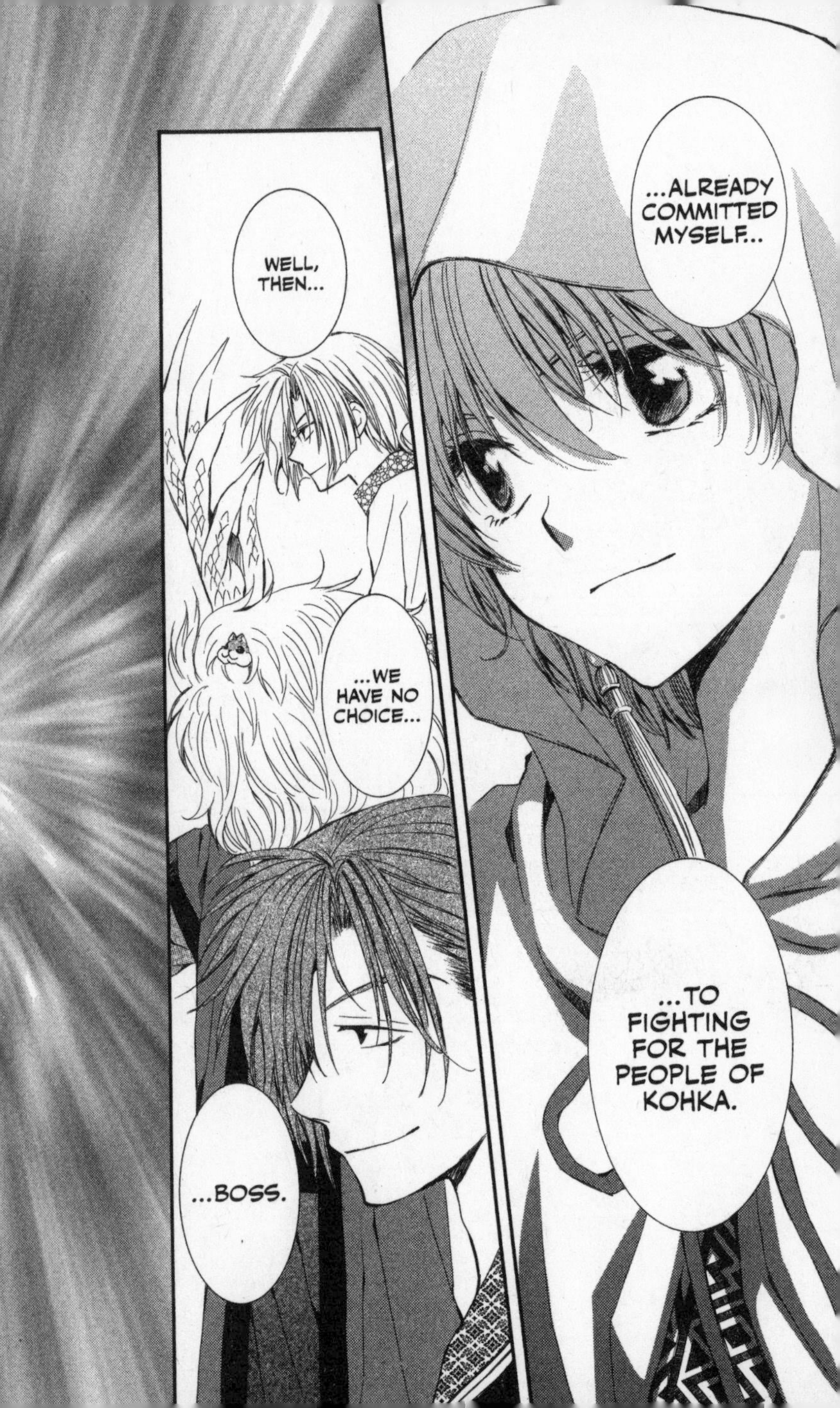
...ALREADY COMMITTED MYSELF...
...TO FIGHTING FOR THE PEOPLE OF KOHKA.
WELL, THEN...
...WE HAVE NO CHOICE...
...BOSS.

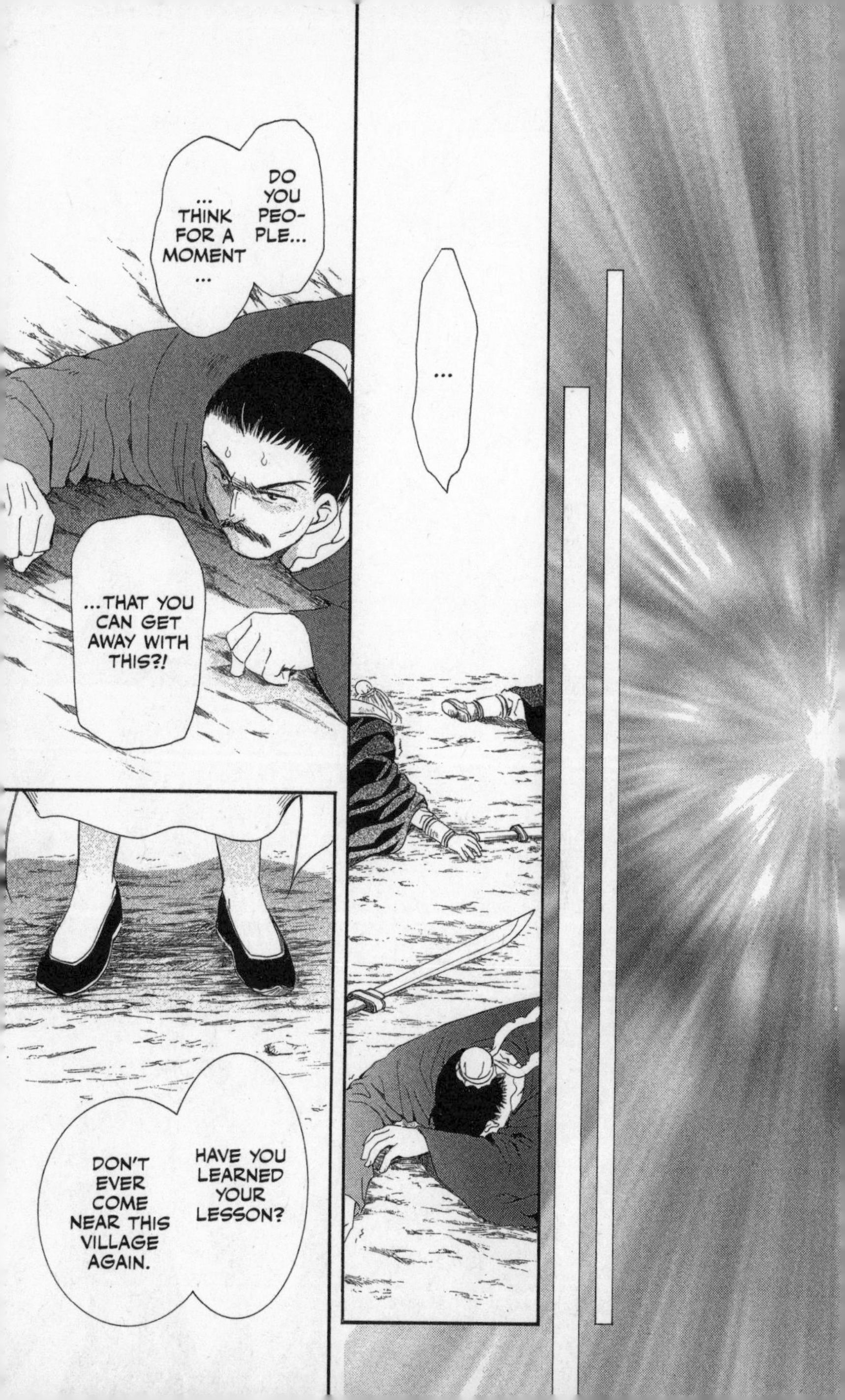
...
DO YOU PEOPLE...
...THINK FOR A MOMENT...
...THAT YOU CAN GET AWAY WITH THIS?!
HAVE YOU LEARNED YOUR LESSON?
DON'T EVER COME NEAR THIS VILLAGE AGAIN.

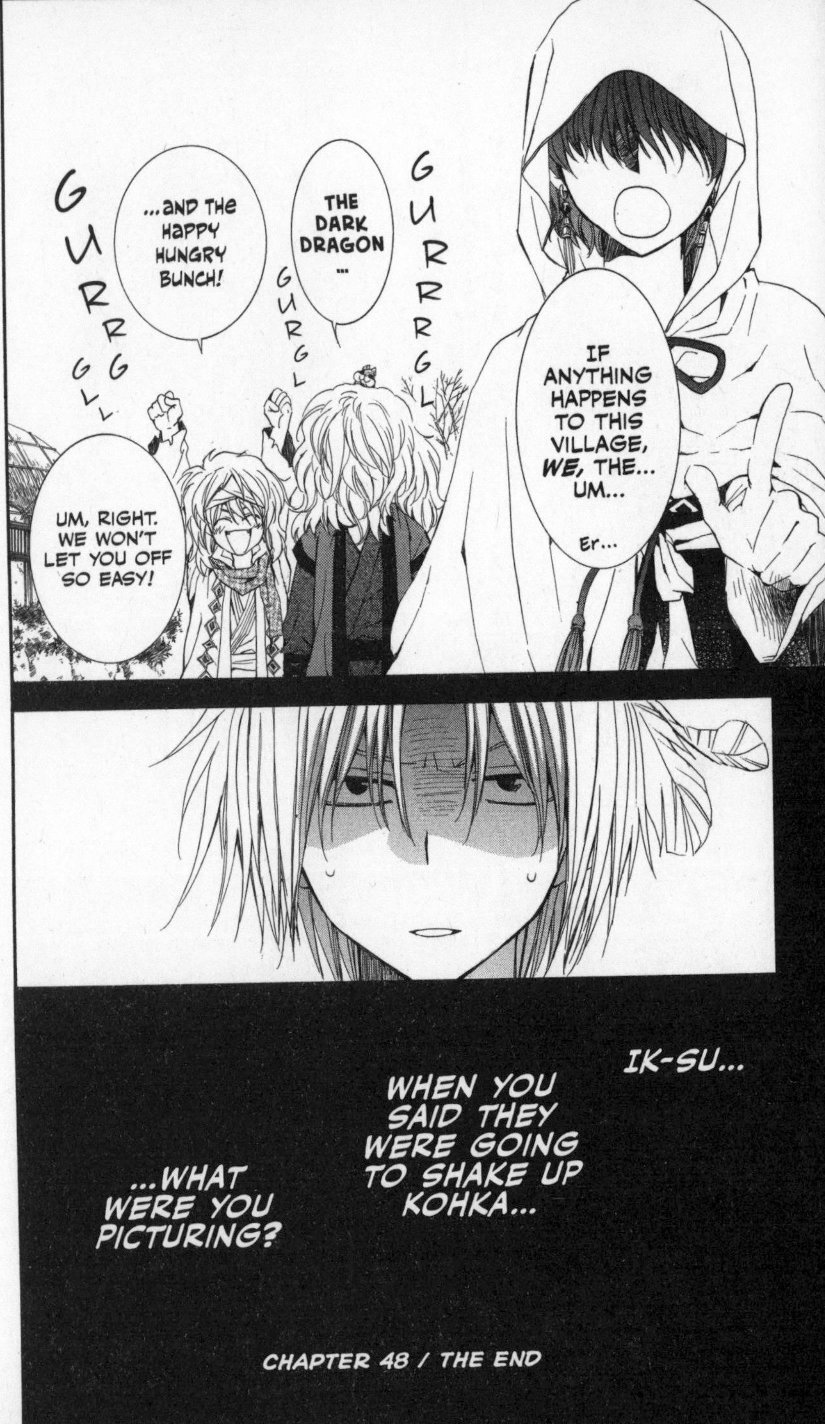
IF ANYTHING HAPPENS TO THIS VILLAGE, WE, THE... UM...
Er...
GURRRGL
THE DARK DRAGON...
GURGL
...and the Happy Hungry Bunch!
GURRGGLL
UM, RIGHT. WE WON'T LET YOU OFF SO EASY!
IK-SU...
WHEN YOU SAID THEY WERE GOING TO SHAKE UP KOHKA...
...WHAT WERE YOU PICTURING?
CHAPTER 48 / THE END

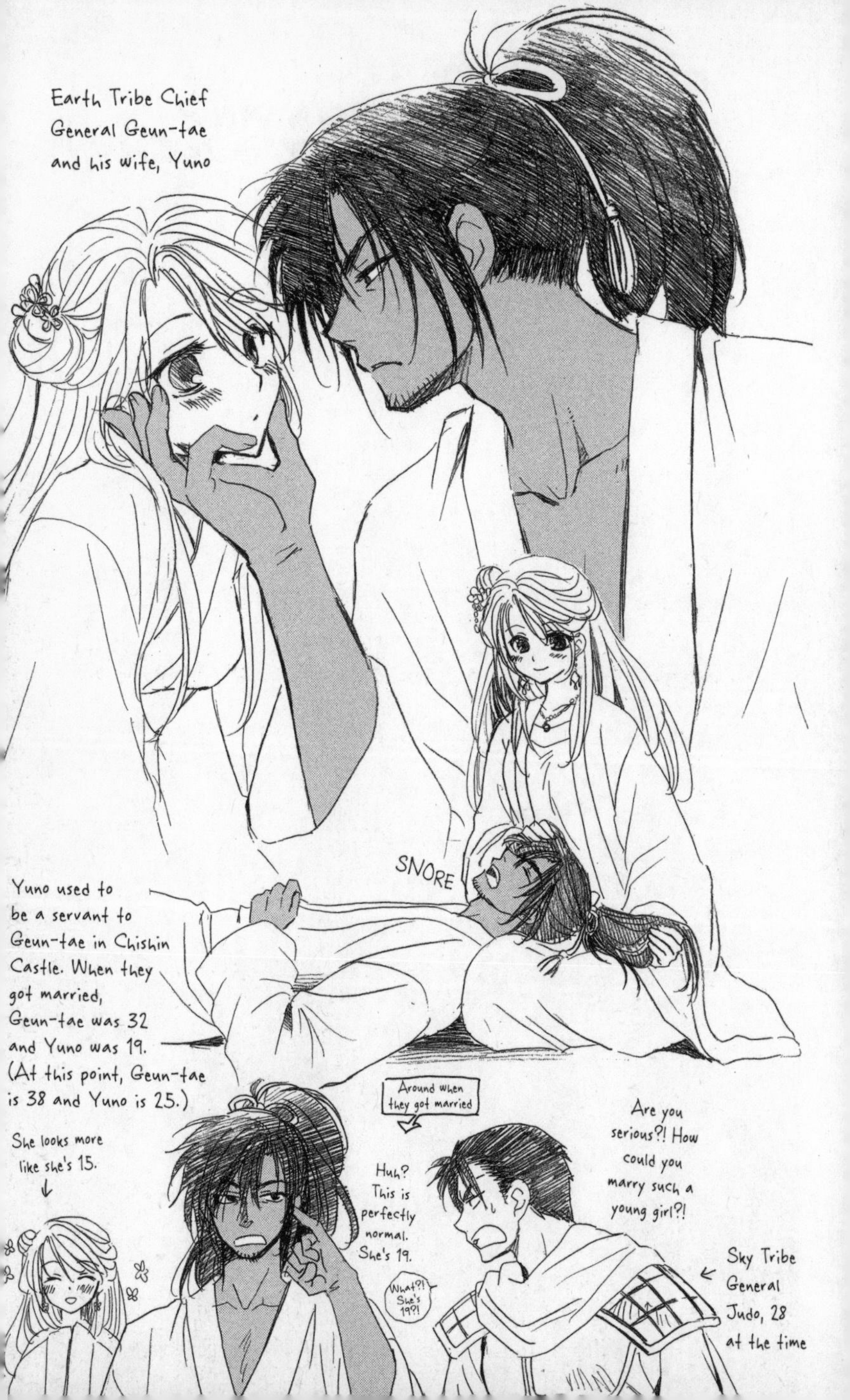
Earth Tribe Chief General Geun-tae and his wife, Yuno
SNORE
Yuno used to be a servant to Geun-tae in Chishin Castle. When they got married, Geun-tae was 32 and Yuno was 19. (At this point, Geun-tae is 38 and Yuno is 25.)
Around when they got married
Sky Tribe General Judo, 28 at the time
Are you serious?! How could you marry such a young girl?!
Huh? This is perfectly normal. She's 19.
What?! She's 19?!
She looks more like she's 15.

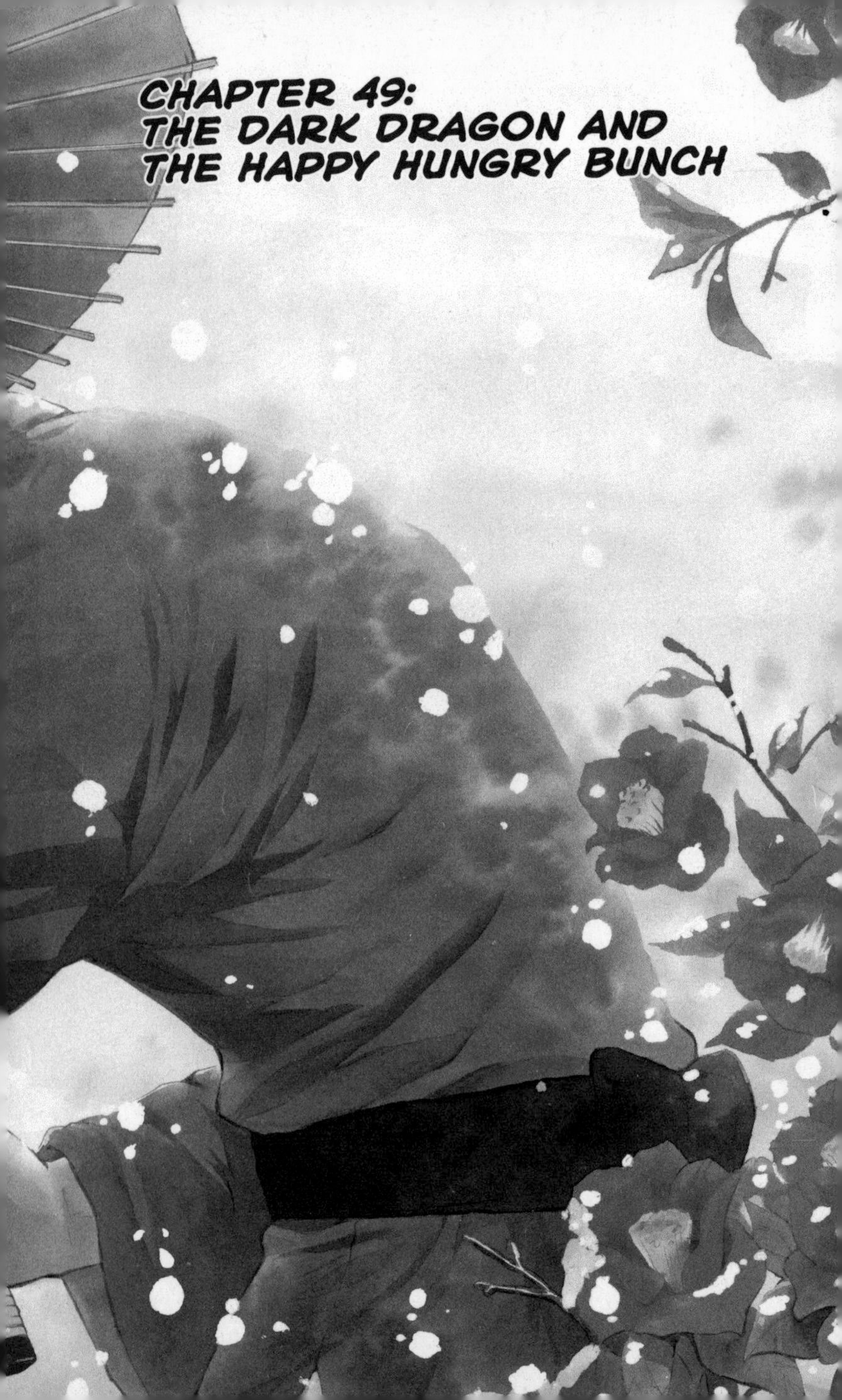
CHAPTER 49:
THE DARK DRAGON AND
THE HAPPY HUNGRY BUNCH

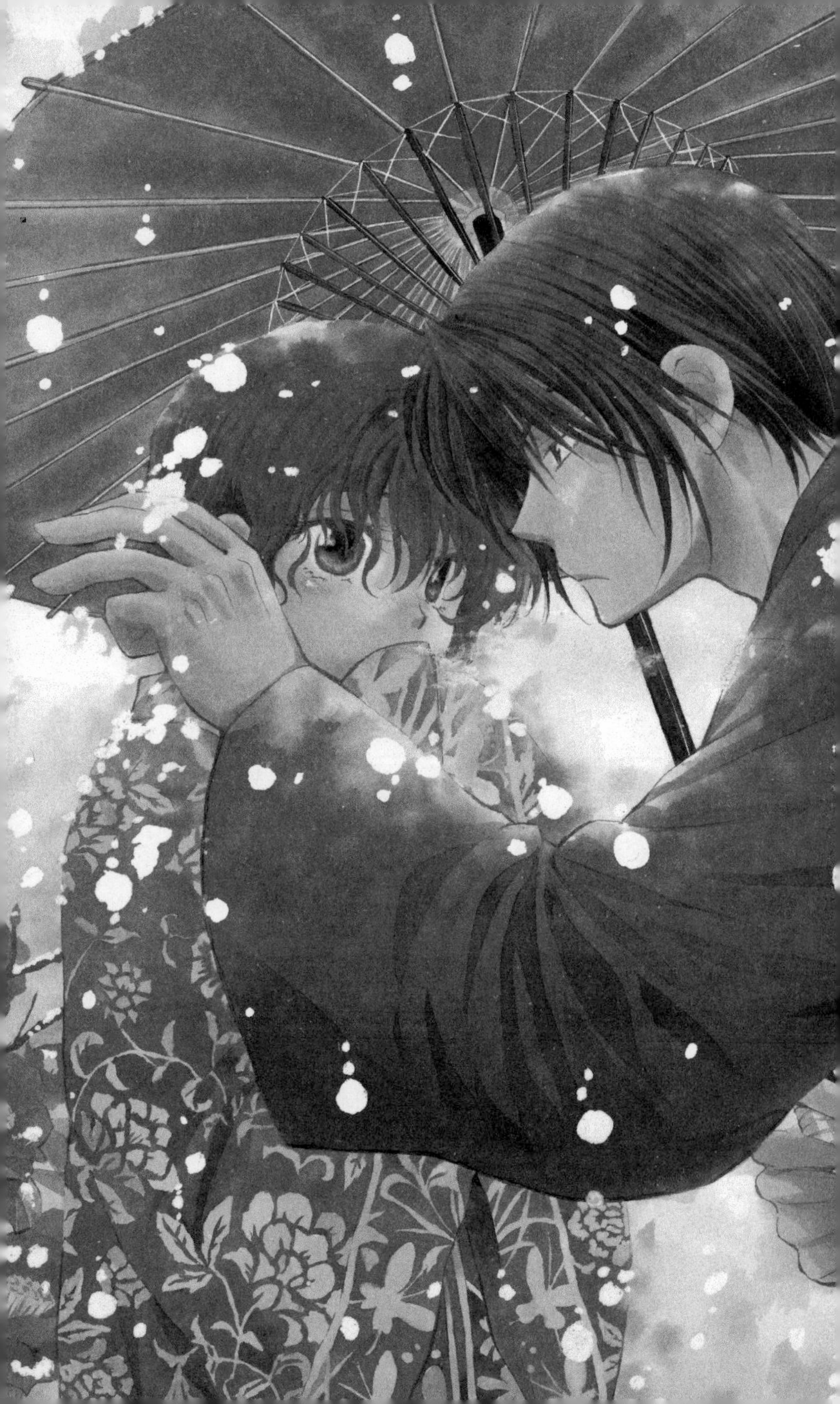

Doodle of Hak and Yona

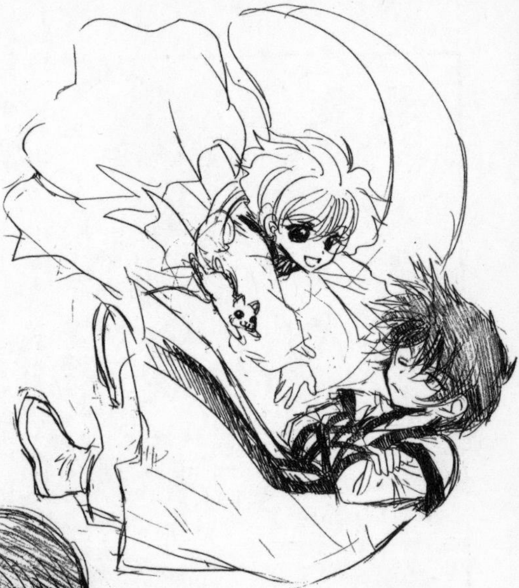

A rejected rough sketch for a bookstore handout →

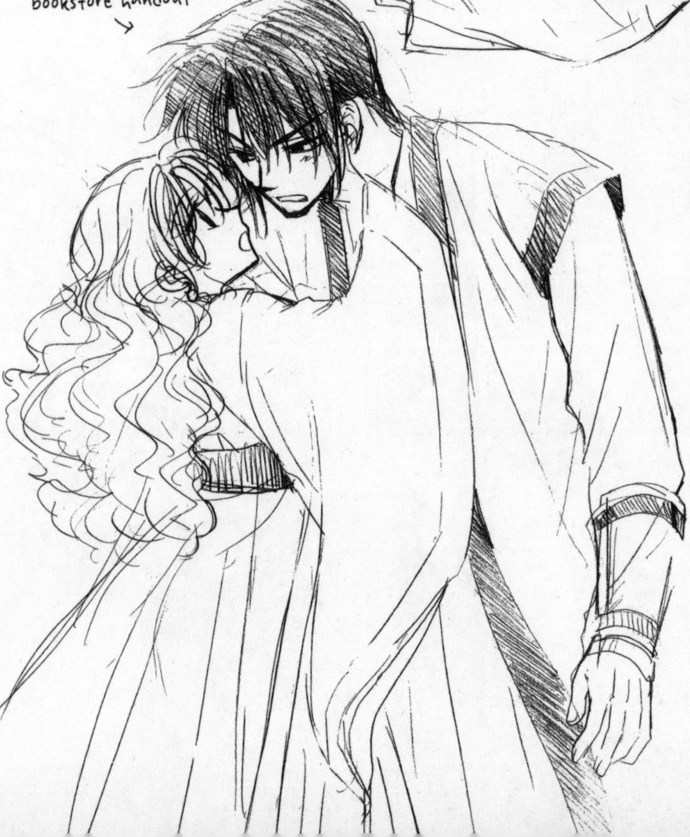

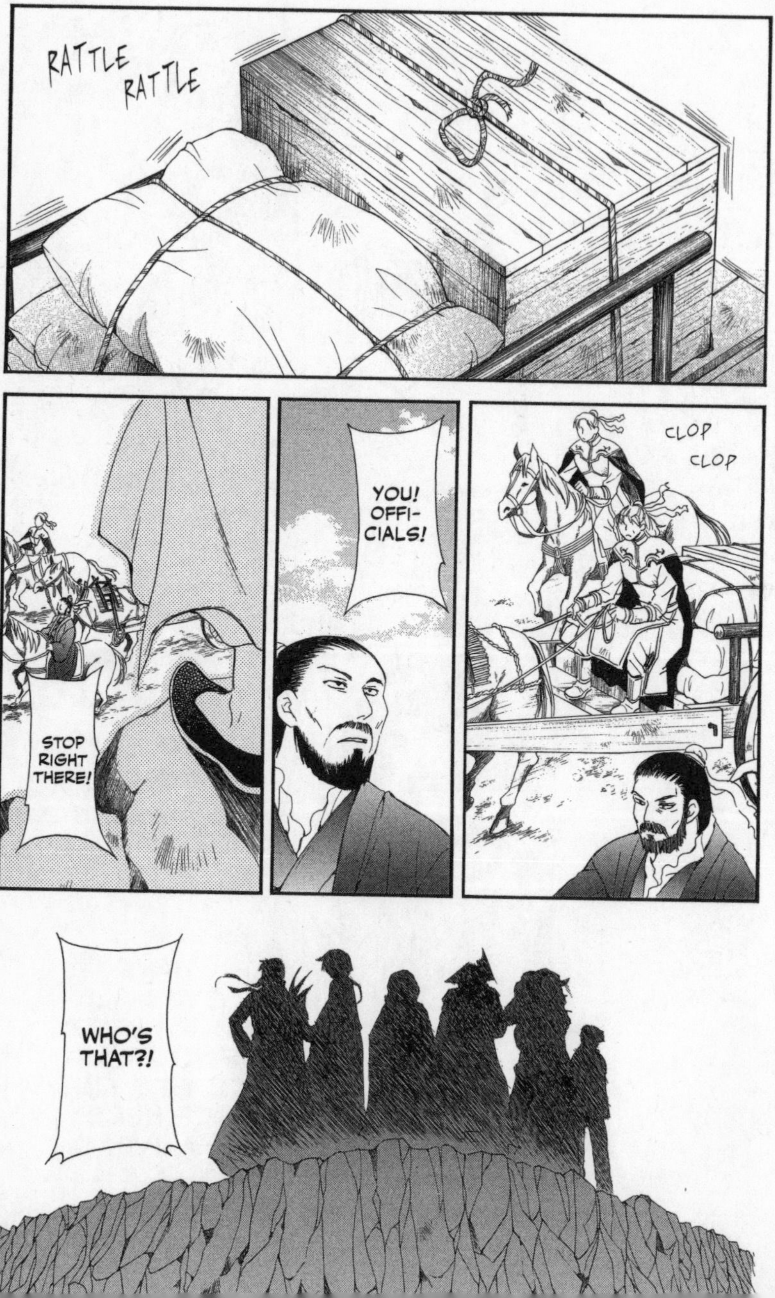
RATTLE RATTLE
CLOP CLOP
YOU! OFFI-CIALS!
STOP RIGHT THERE!
WHO'S THAT?!

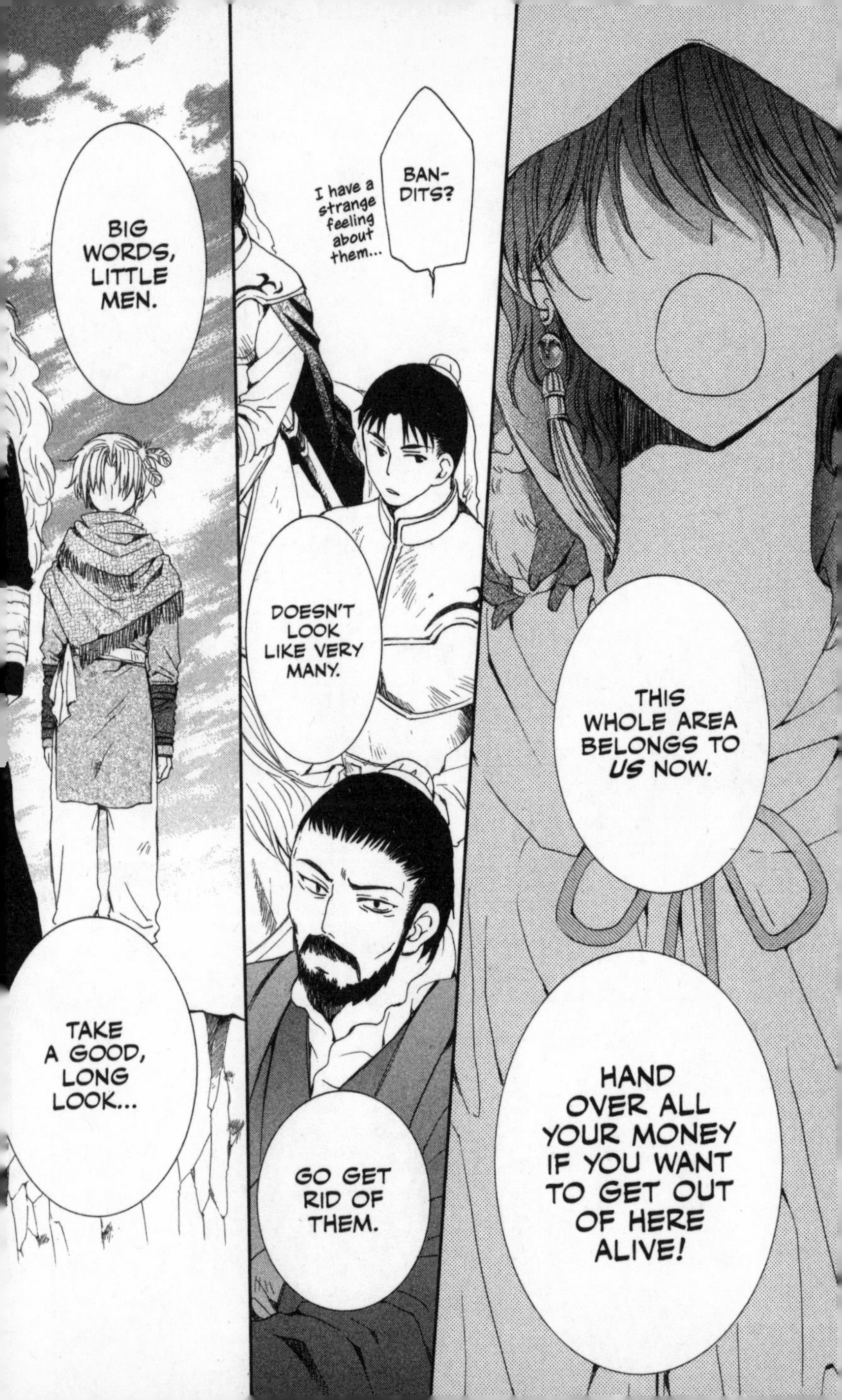
THIS WHOLE AREA BELONGS TO *US* NOW.
HAND OVER ALL YOUR MONEY IF YOU WANT TO GET OUT OF HERE ALIVE!
BAN-DITS?
I have a strange feeling about them...
DOESN'T LOOK LIKE VERY MANY.
GO GET RID OF THEM.
BIG WORDS, LITTLE MEN.
TAKE A GOOD, LONG LOOK...

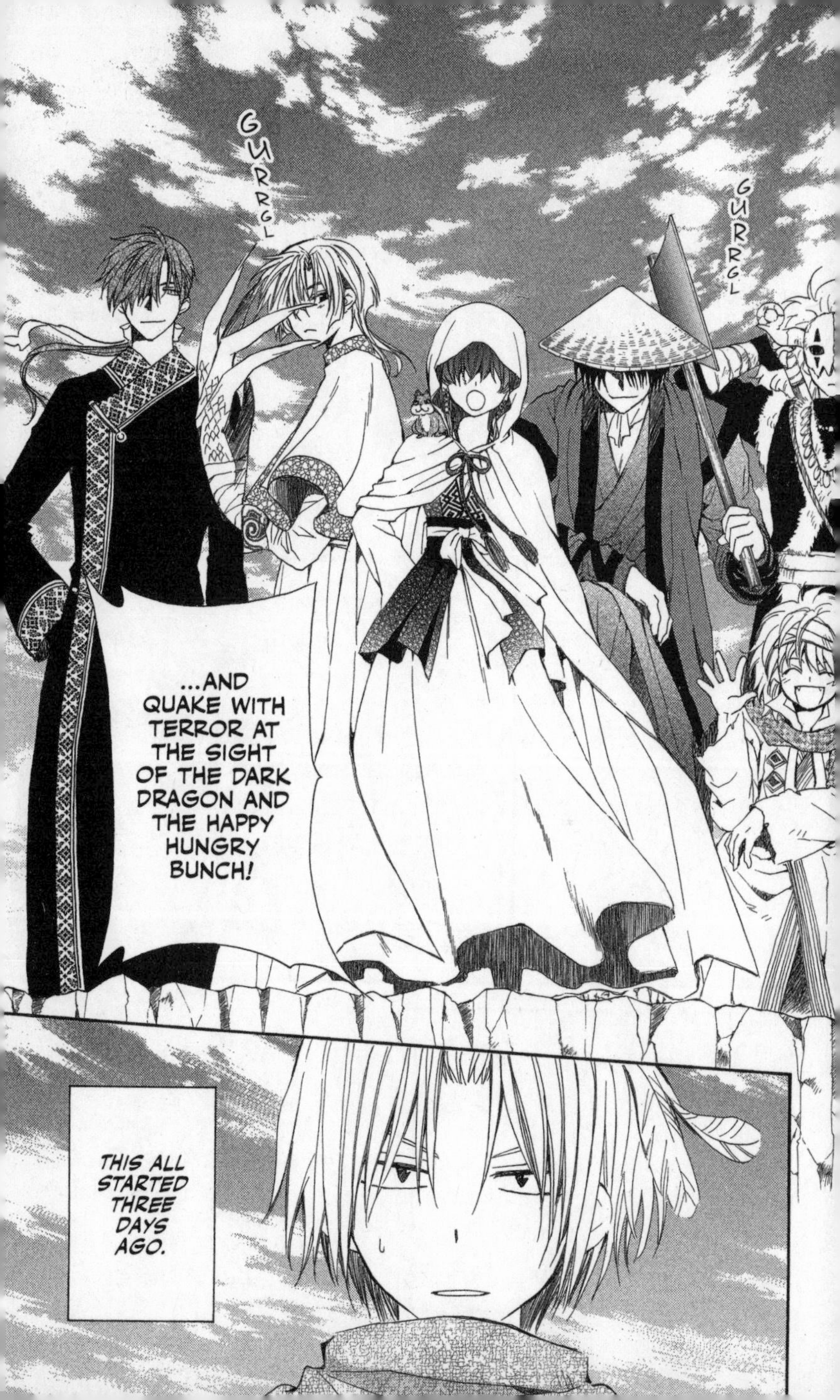
GURRGL
GURRGL
...AND QUAKE WITH TERROR AT THE SIGHT OF THE DARK DRAGON AND THE HAPPY HUNGRY BUNCH!
THIS ALL STARTED THREE DAYS AGO.

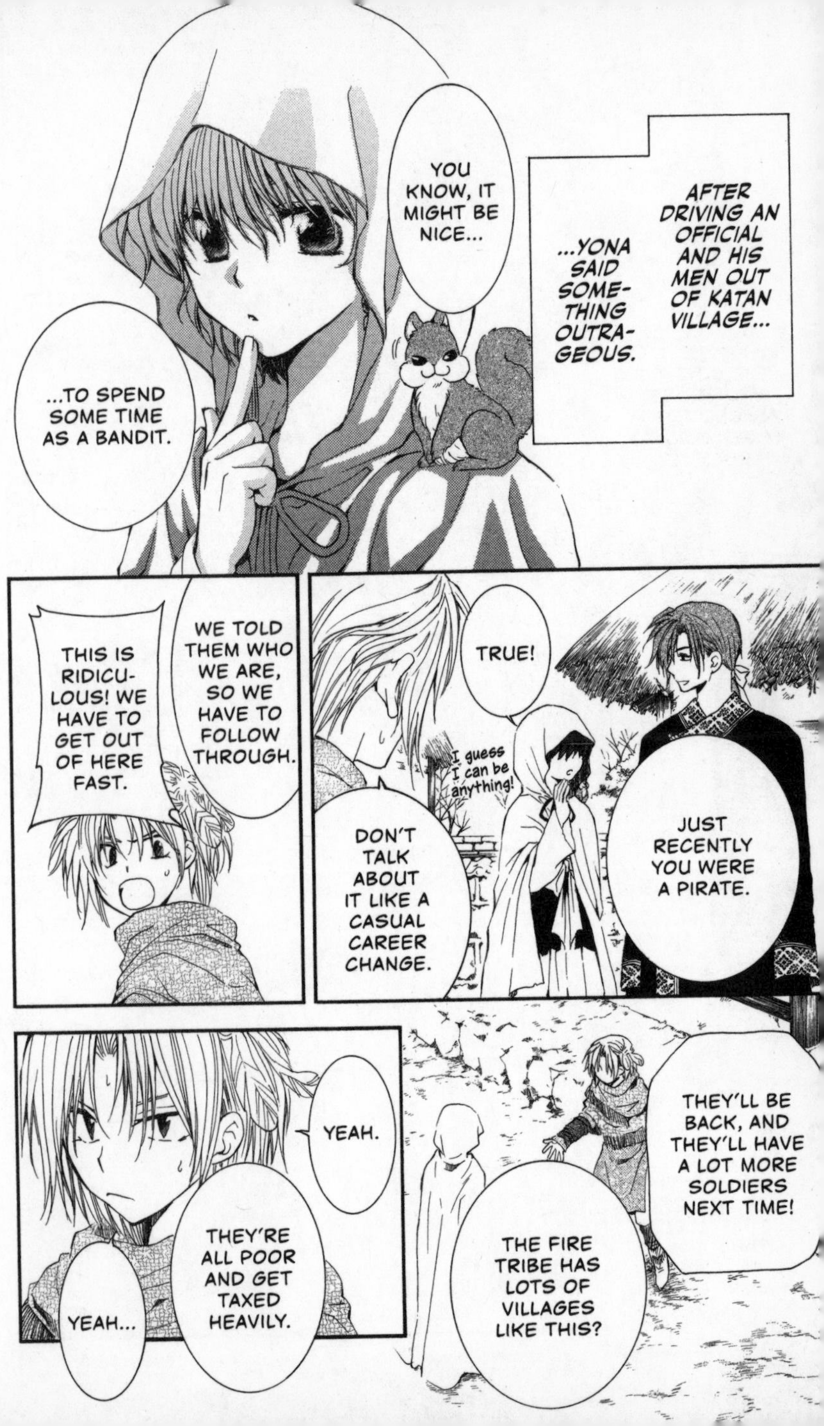
AFTER DRIVING AN OFFICIAL AND HIS MEN OUT OF KATAN VILLAGE...
...YONA SAID SOMETHING OUTRAGEOUS.
YOU KNOW, IT MIGHT BE NICE...
...TO SPEND SOME TIME AS A BANDIT.
JUST RECENTLY YOU WERE A PIRATE.
TRUE!
I guess I can be anything!
DON'T TALK ABOUT IT LIKE A CASUAL CAREER CHANGE.
WE TOLD THEM WHO WE ARE, SO WE HAVE TO FOLLOW THROUGH.
THIS IS RIDICULOUS! WE HAVE TO GET OUT OF HERE FAST.
THEY'LL BE BACK, AND THEY'LL HAVE A LOT MORE SOLDIERS NEXT TIME!
THE FIRE TRIBE HAS LOTS OF VILLAGES LIKE THIS?
YEAH.
THEY'RE ALL POOR AND GET TAXED HEAVILY.
YEAH...

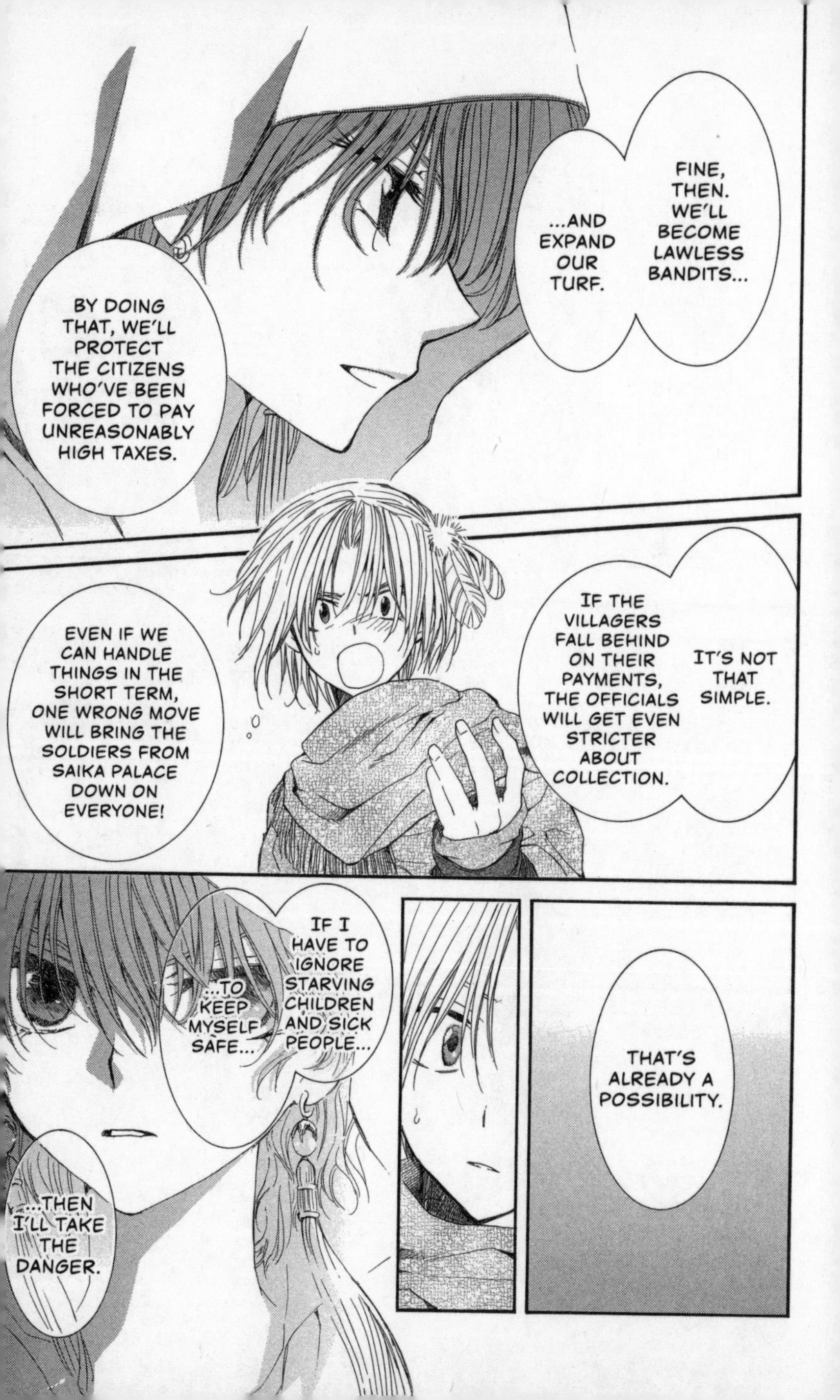
FINE, THEN. WE'LL BECOME LAWLESS BANDITS...
...AND EXPAND OUR TURF.
BY DOING THAT, WE'LL PROTECT THE CITIZENS WHO'VE BEEN FORCED TO PAY UNREASONABLY HIGH TAXES.
IT'S NOT THAT SIMPLE.
IF THE VILLAGERS FALL BEHIND ON THEIR PAYMENTS, THE OFFICIALS WILL GET EVEN STRICTER ABOUT COLLECTION.
EVEN IF WE CAN HANDLE THINGS IN THE SHORT TERM, ONE WRONG MOVE WILL BRING THE SOLDIERS FROM SAIKA PALACE DOWN ON EVERYONE!
THAT'S ALREADY A POSSIBILITY.
IF I HAVE TO IGNORE STARVING CHILDREN AND SICK PEOPLE...
...TO KEEP MYSELF SAFE...
...THEN I'LL TAKE THE DANGER.

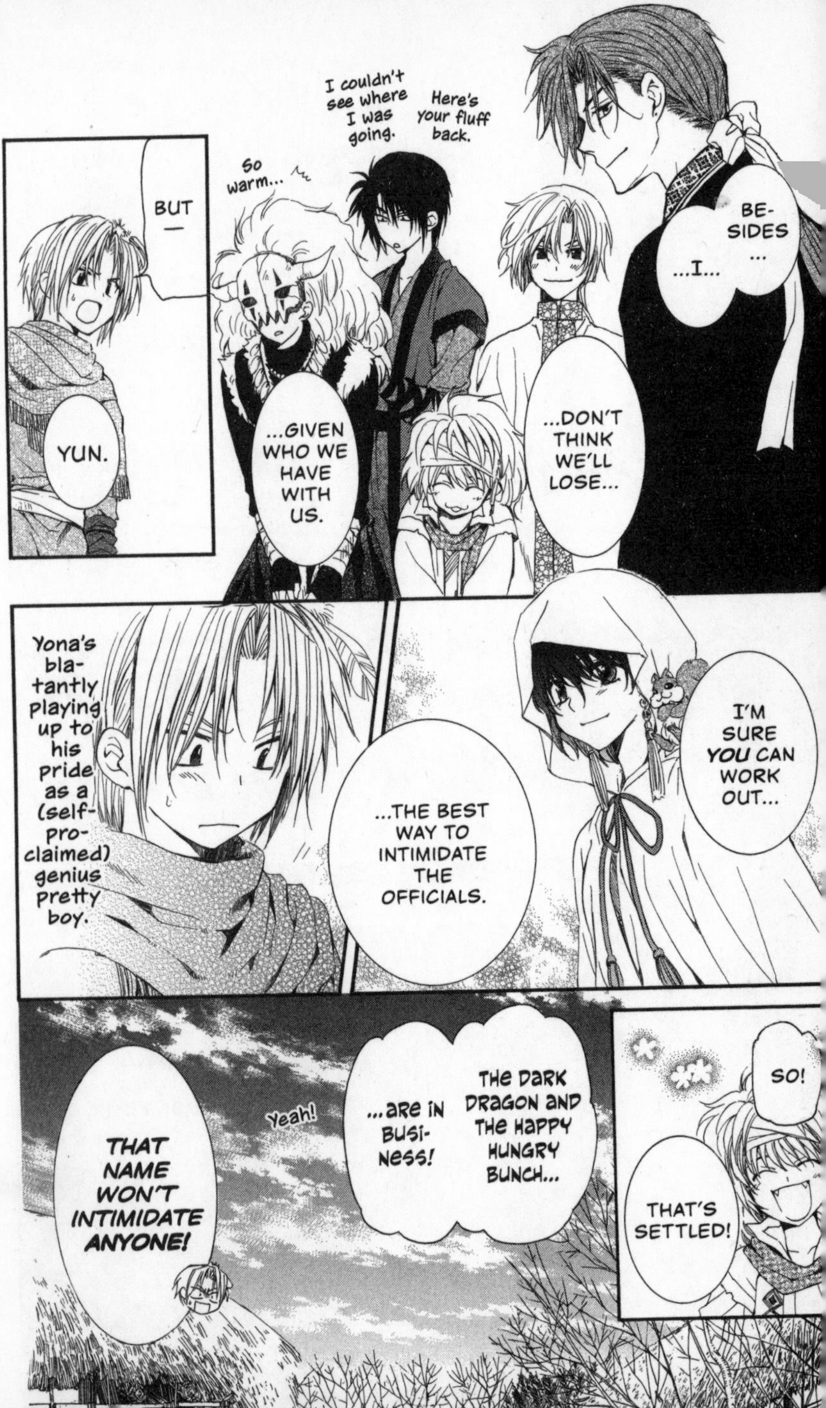
BE-SIDES...
...I...
Here's your fluff back.
I couldn't see where I was going.
So warm...
...DON'T THINK WE'LL LOSE...
...GIVEN WHO WE HAVE WITH US.
BUT —
YUN.
I'M SURE *YOU* CAN WORK OUT...
...THE BEST WAY TO INTIMIDATE THE OFFICIALS.
Yona's blatantly playing up to his pride as a (self-proclaimed) genius pretty boy.
SO!
THAT'S SETTLED!
The Dark Dragon and the Happy Hungry Bunch...
...are in Business!
Yeah!
THAT NAME WON'T INTIMIDATE ANYONE!

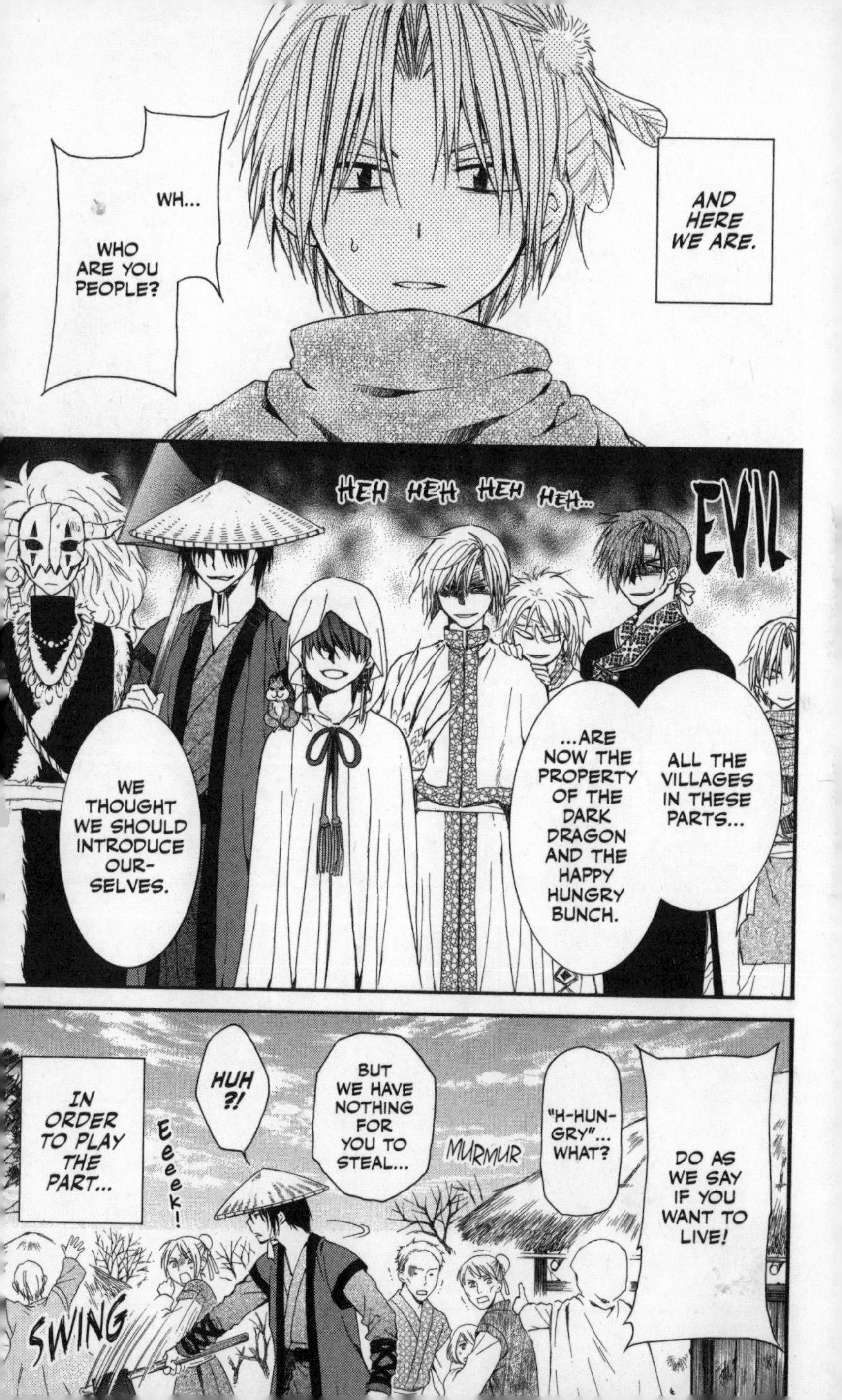
AND HERE WE ARE.
WH... WHO ARE YOU PEOPLE?
EVIL
HEH HEH HEH HEH...
ALL THE VILLAGES IN THESE PARTS...
...ARE NOW THE PROPERTY OF THE DARK DRAGON AND THE HAPPY HUNGRY BUNCH.
WE THOUGHT WE SHOULD INTRODUCE OUR-SELVES.
DO AS WE SAY IF YOU WANT TO LIVE!
"H-HUN-GRY"... WHAT?
MURMUR
BUT WE HAVE NOTHING FOR YOU TO STEAL...
HUH?!
Eeeek!
IN ORDER TO PLAY THE PART...
SWING

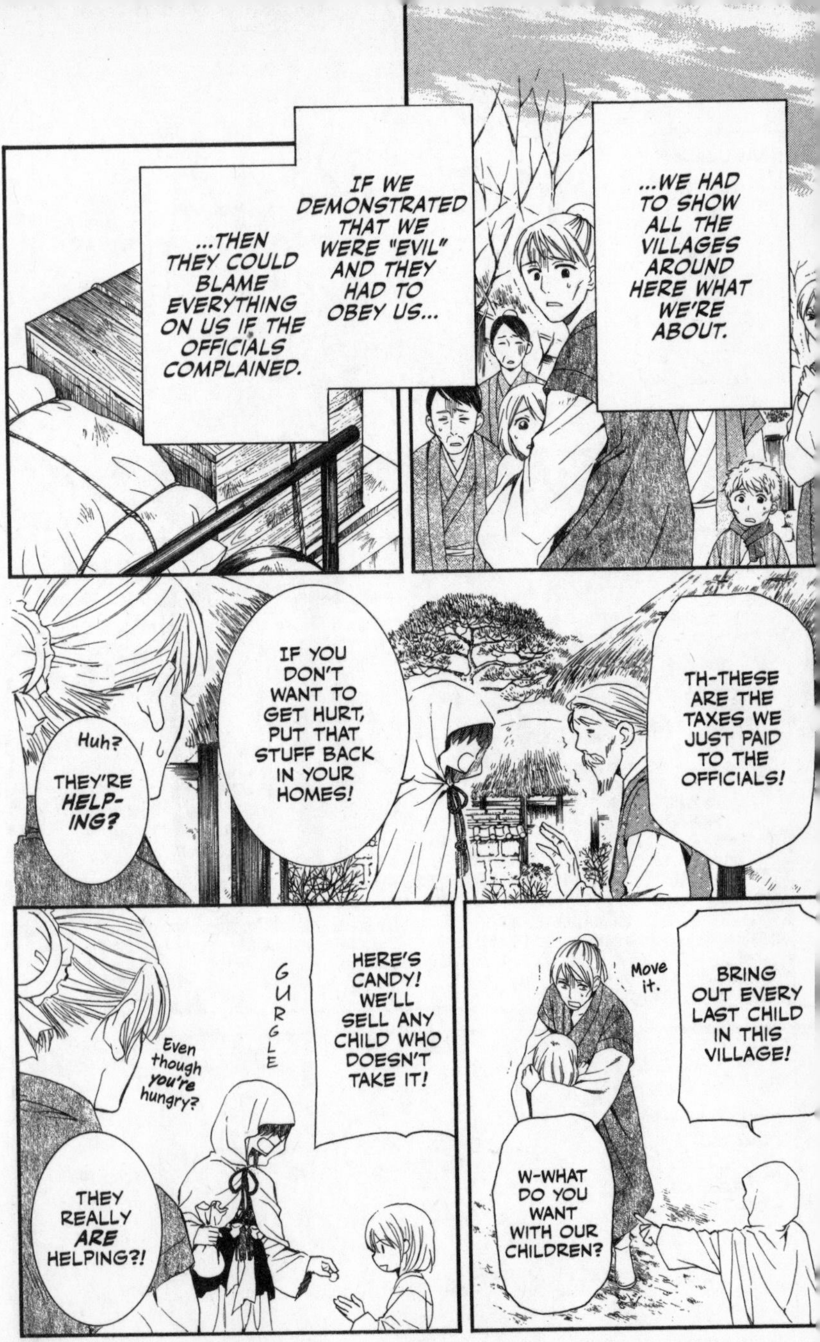
...WE HAD TO SHOW ALL THE VILLAGES AROUND HERE WHAT WE'RE ABOUT.
IF WE DEMONSTRATED THAT WE WERE "EVIL" AND THEY HAD TO OBEY US...
...THEN THEY COULD BLAME EVERYTHING ON US IF THE OFFICIALS COMPLAINED.
TH-THESE ARE THE TAXES WE JUST PAID TO THE OFFICIALS!
IF YOU DON'T WANT TO GET HURT, PUT THAT STUFF BACK IN YOUR HOMES!
Huh?
THEY'RE HELPING?
BRING OUT EVERY LAST CHILD IN THIS VILLAGE!
Move it.
W-WHAT DO YOU WANT WITH OUR CHILDREN?
HERE'S CANDY! WE'LL SELL ANY CHILD WHO DOESN'T TAKE IT!
GURGLE
Even though you're hungry?
THEY REALLY ARE HELPING?!

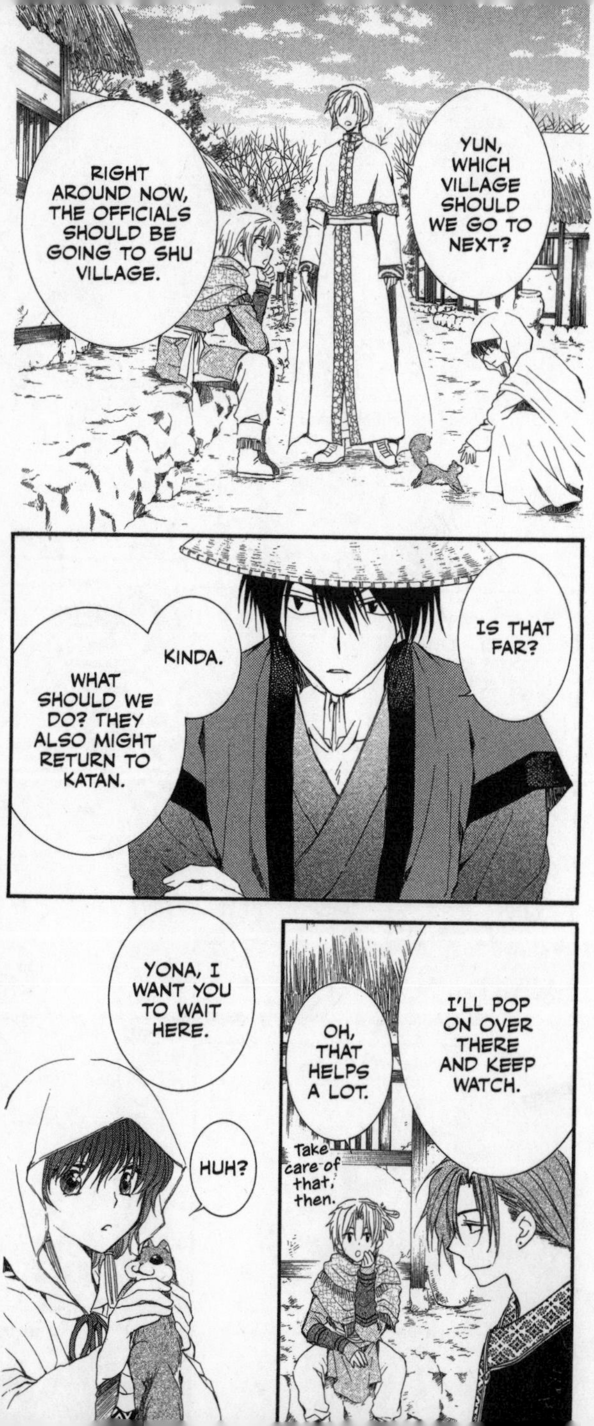
YUN, WHICH VILLAGE SHOULD WE GO TO NEXT?
RIGHT AROUND NOW, THE OFFICIALS SHOULD BE GOING TO SHU VILLAGE.
IS THAT FAR?
KINDA.
WHAT SHOULD WE DO? THEY ALSO MIGHT RETURN TO KATAN.
I'LL POP ON OVER THERE AND KEEP WATCH.
OH, THAT HELPS A LOT.
Take care of that, then.
YONA, I WANT YOU TO WAIT HERE.
HUH?

Now, about the cast for the Yona CD!

Yona→Chiwa Saito
Hak→Tomoaki Maeno
Yun→
Junko Minagawa
Gija→
Masakazu Morita
Sinha→
Nobuhiko Okamoto
Ao (Pu-kyu)→
Nozomi Yamamoto
Il→Susumu Akagi

I made suggestions about who to cast in each role, and after consulting with the personnel in charge of producing the CD, we made our final decisions. I'm so glad I asked these people to do this! *Yona of the Dawn* is very lucky!

Thank you very much to the entire cast! Sorry for barging in during recording, but I was very impressed. For those of you who bought the deluxe CD version, I drew an account of what happened.

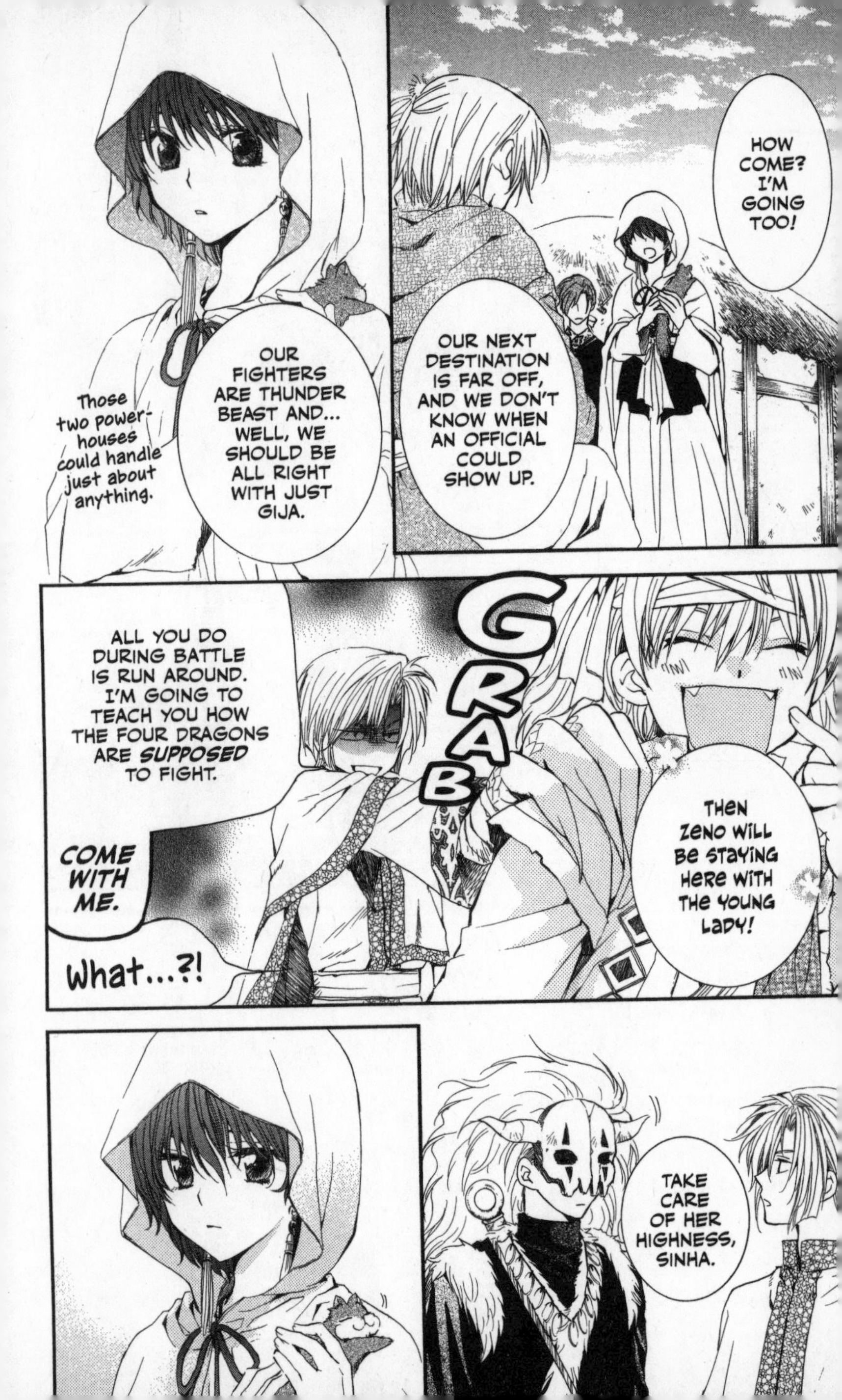
HOW COME? I'M GOING TOO!
OUR NEXT DESTINATION IS FAR OFF, AND WE DON'T KNOW WHEN AN OFFICIAL COULD SHOW UP.
OUR FIGHTERS ARE THUNDER BEAST AND... WELL, WE SHOULD BE ALL RIGHT WITH JUST GIJA.
Those two power-houses could handle just about anything.
THEN ZENO WILL BE STAYING HERE WITH THE YOUNG LADY!
GRAB
ALL YOU DO DURING BATTLE IS RUN AROUND. I'M GOING TO TEACH YOU HOW THE FOUR DRAGONS ARE *SUPPOSED* TO FIGHT.
COME WITH ME.
What...?!
TAKE CARE OF HER HIGHNESS, SINHA.

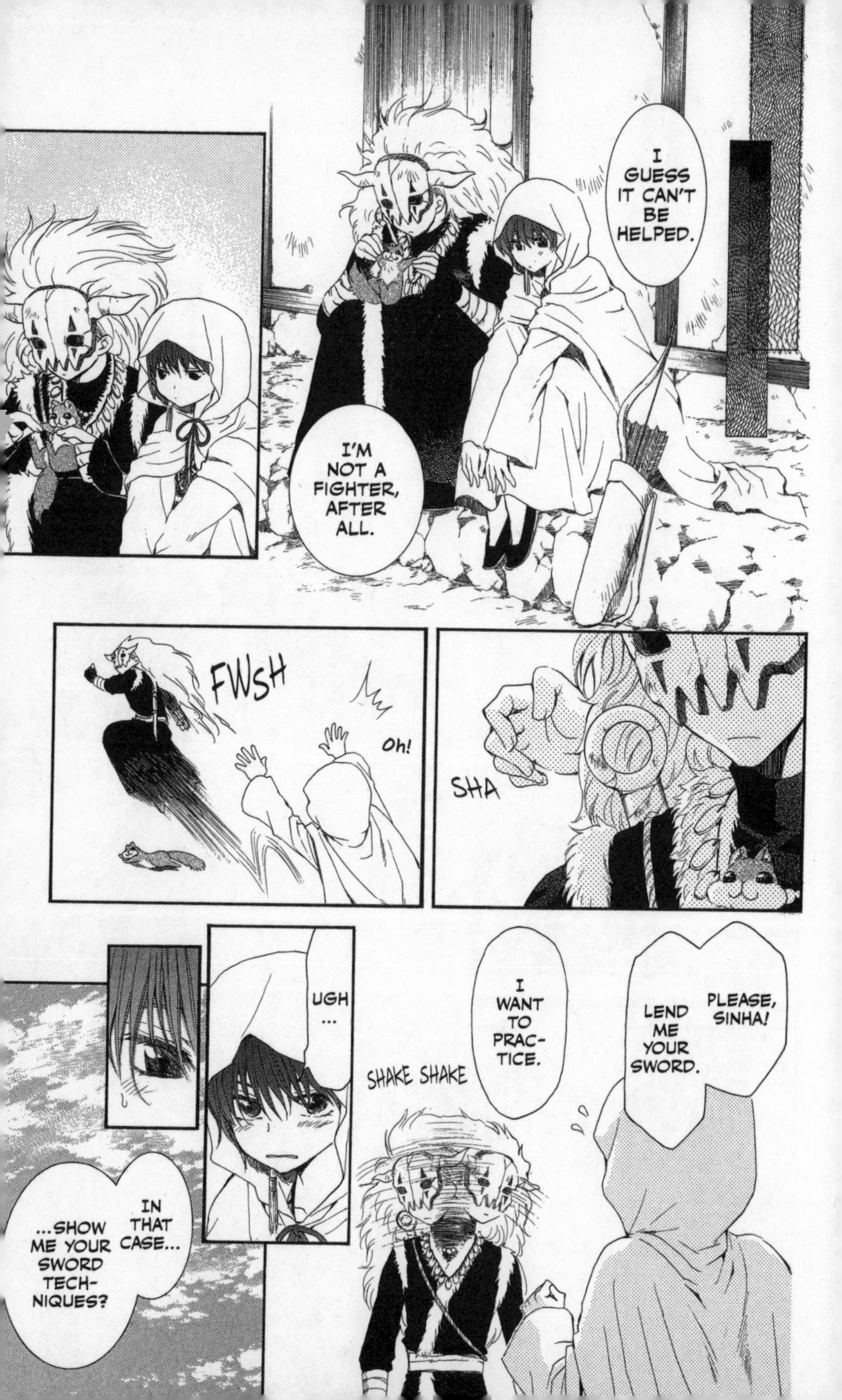
I GUESS IT CAN'T BE HELPED.
I'M NOT A FIGHTER, AFTER ALL.
SHA
FWSH
Oh!
PLEASE, SINHA!
LEND ME YOUR SWORD.
I WANT TO PRAC-TICE.
SHAKE SHAKE
UGH ...
IN THAT CASE...
...SHOW ME YOUR SWORD TECH-NIQUES?

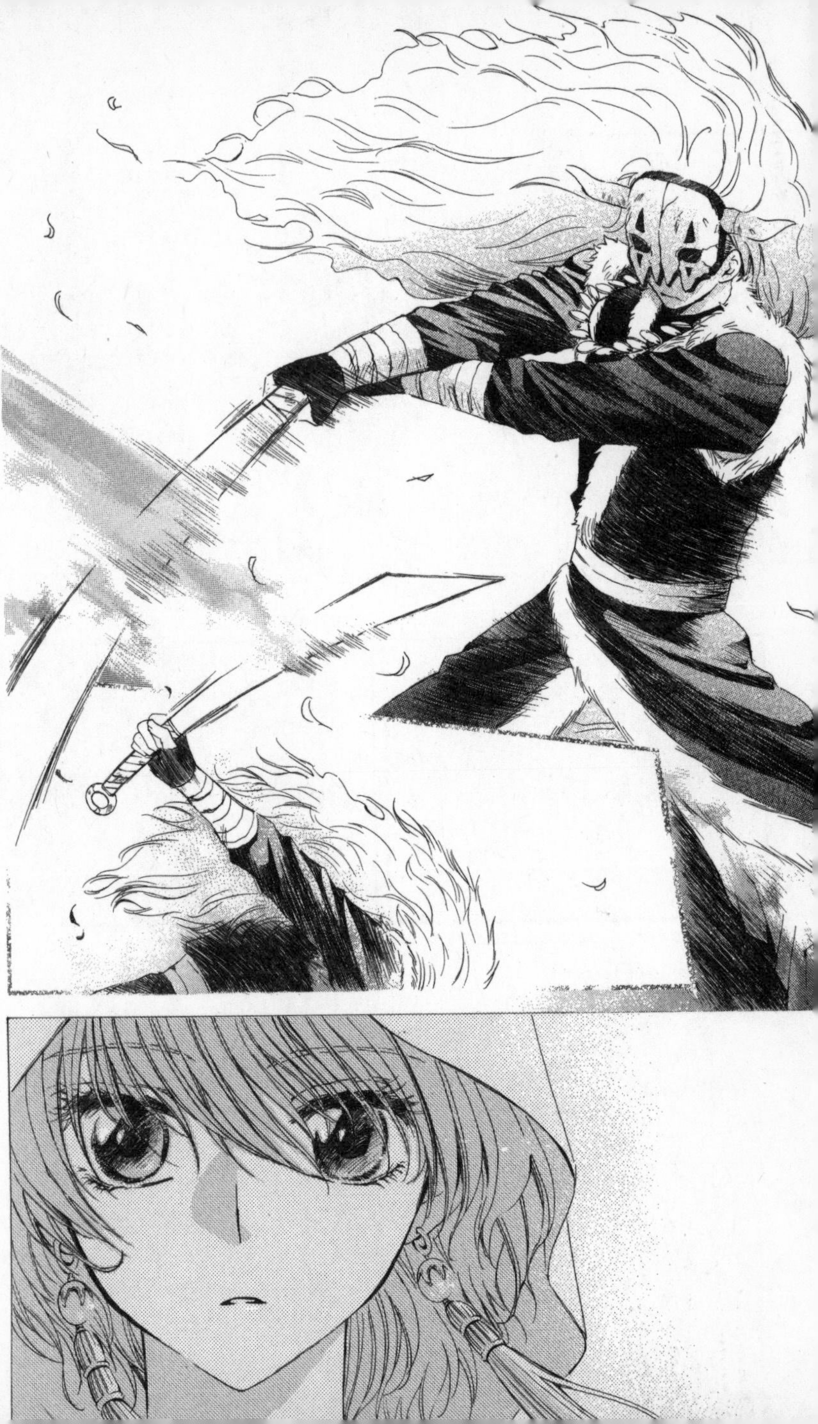

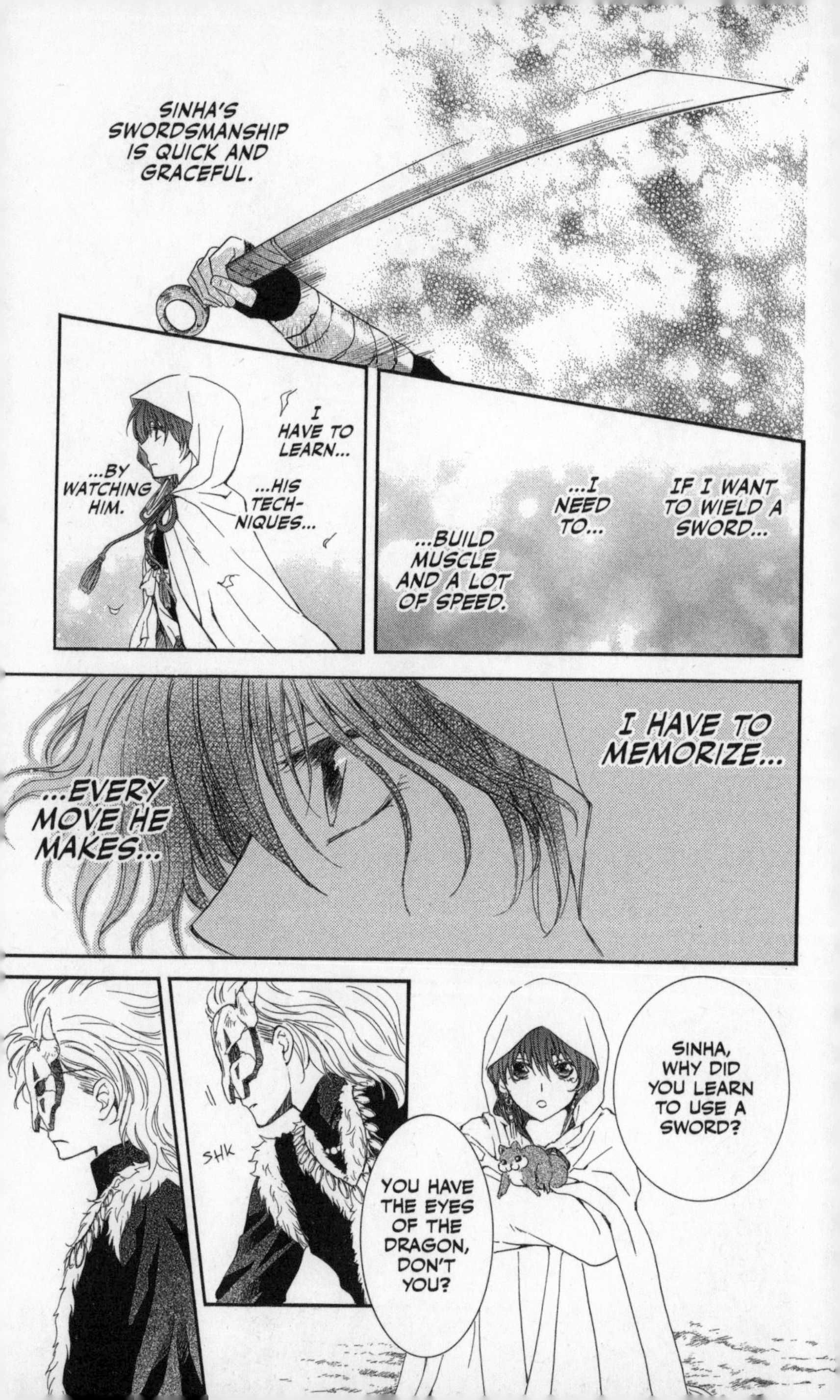
SINHA'S SWORDSMANSHIP IS QUICK AND GRACEFUL.
IF I WANT TO WIELD A SWORD...
...I NEED TO...
...BUILD MUSCLE AND A LOT OF SPEED.
I HAVE TO LEARN...
...HIS TECH-NIQUES...
...BY WATCHING HIM.
I HAVE TO MEMORIZE...
...EVERY MOVE HE MAKES...
SINHA, WHY DID YOU LEARN TO USE A SWORD?
YOU HAVE THE EYES OF THE DRAGON, DON'T YOU?
SHK

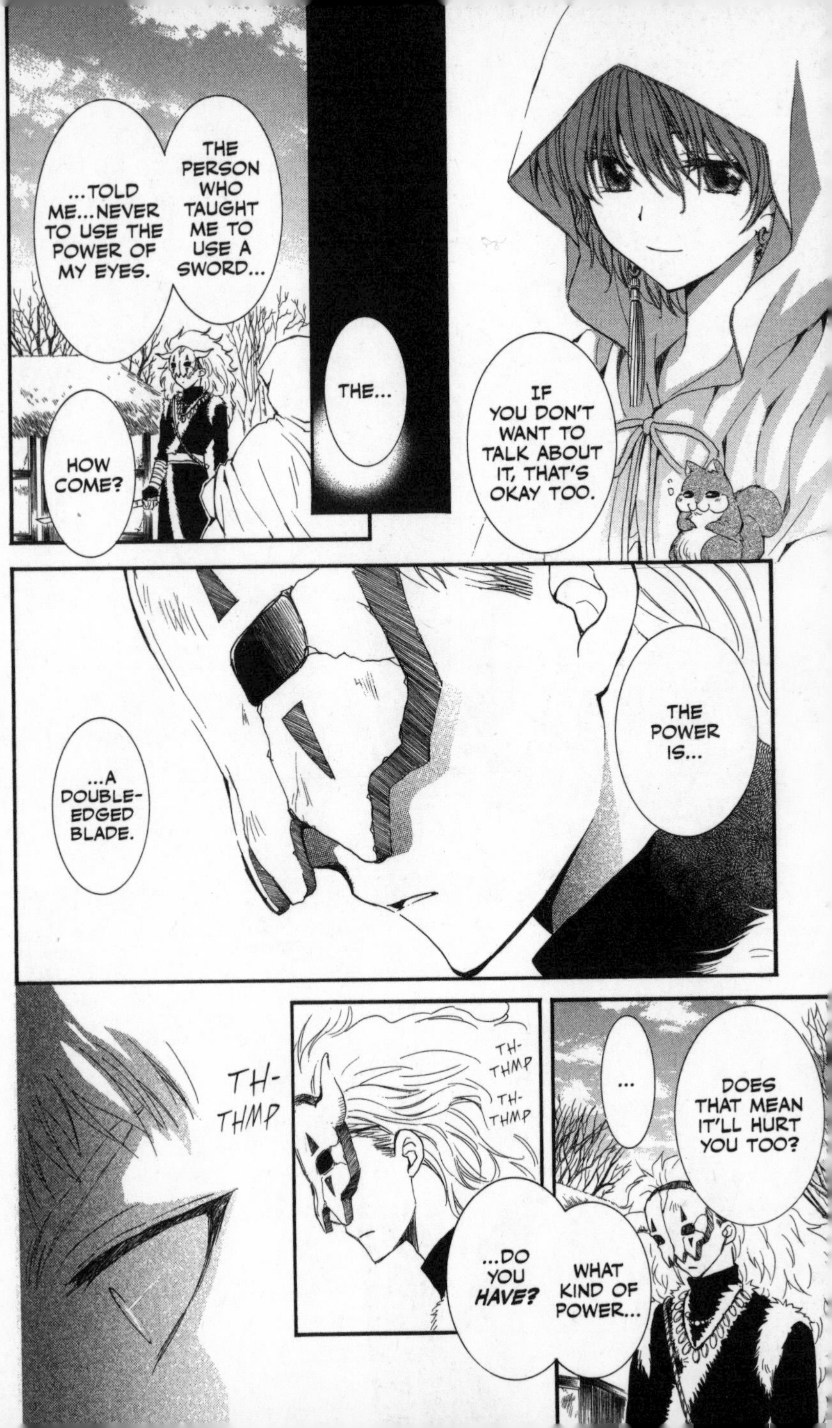
IF YOU DON'T WANT TO TALK ABOUT IT, THAT'S OKAY TOO.
THE...
THE PERSON WHO TAUGHT ME TO USE A SWORD...
...TOLD ME...NEVER TO USE THE POWER OF MY EYES.
HOW COME?
THE POWER IS...
...A DOUBLE-EDGED BLADE.
...
DOES THAT MEAN IT'LL HURT YOU TOO?
WHAT KIND OF POWER...
...DO YOU *HAVE?*
TH-THMP
TH-THMP
TH-THMP

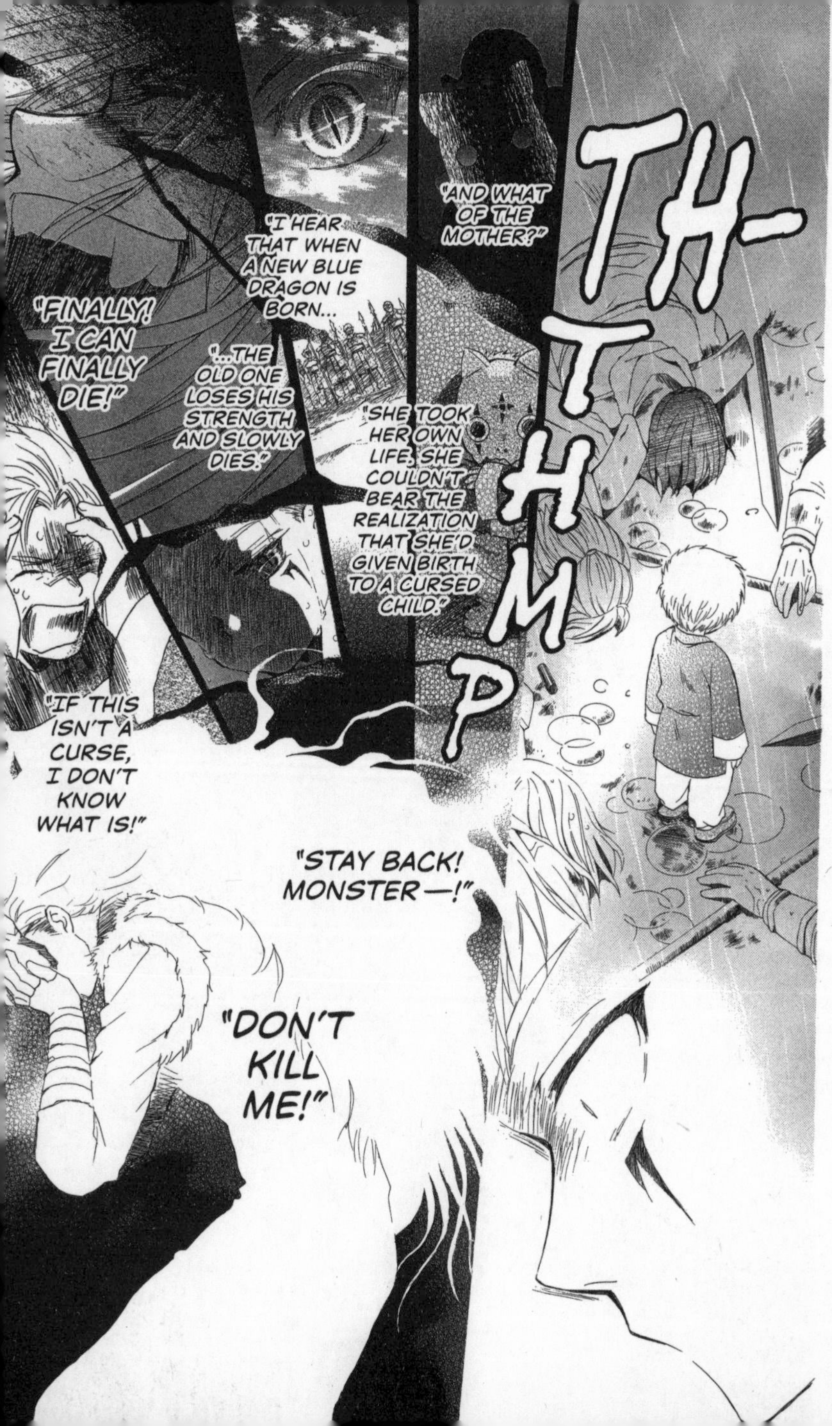
TH-THMP
"AND WHAT OF THE MOTHER?"
"SHE TOOK HER OWN LIFE. SHE COULDN'T BEAR THE REALIZATION THAT SHE'D GIVEN BIRTH TO A CURSED CHILD."
"I HEAR THAT WHEN A NEW BLUE DRAGON IS BORN...
"...THE OLD ONE LOSES HIS STRENGTH AND SLOWLY DIES."
"FINALLY! I CAN FINALLY DIE!"
"IF THIS ISN'T A CURSE, I DON'T KNOW WHAT IS!"
"STAY BACK! MONSTER—!"
"DON'T KILL ME!"

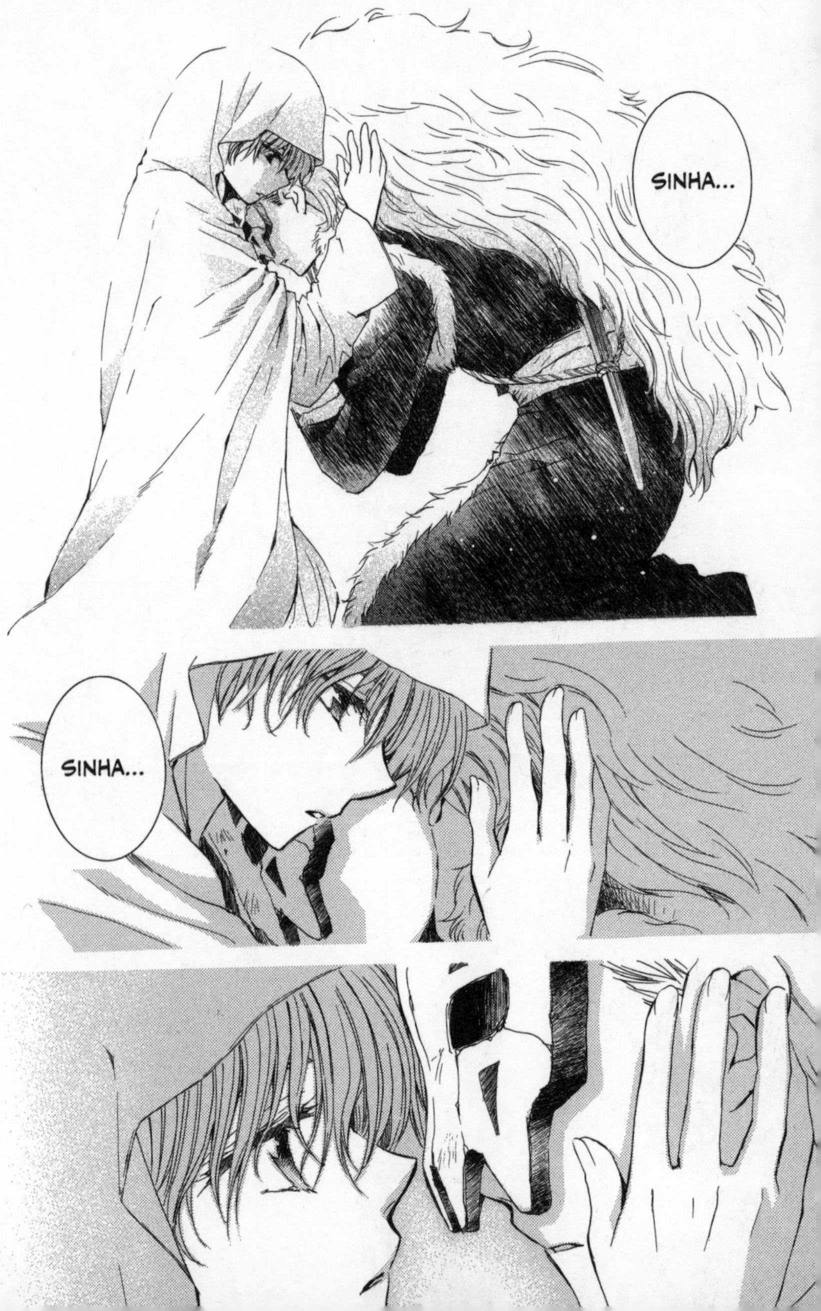
SINHA...
SINHA...

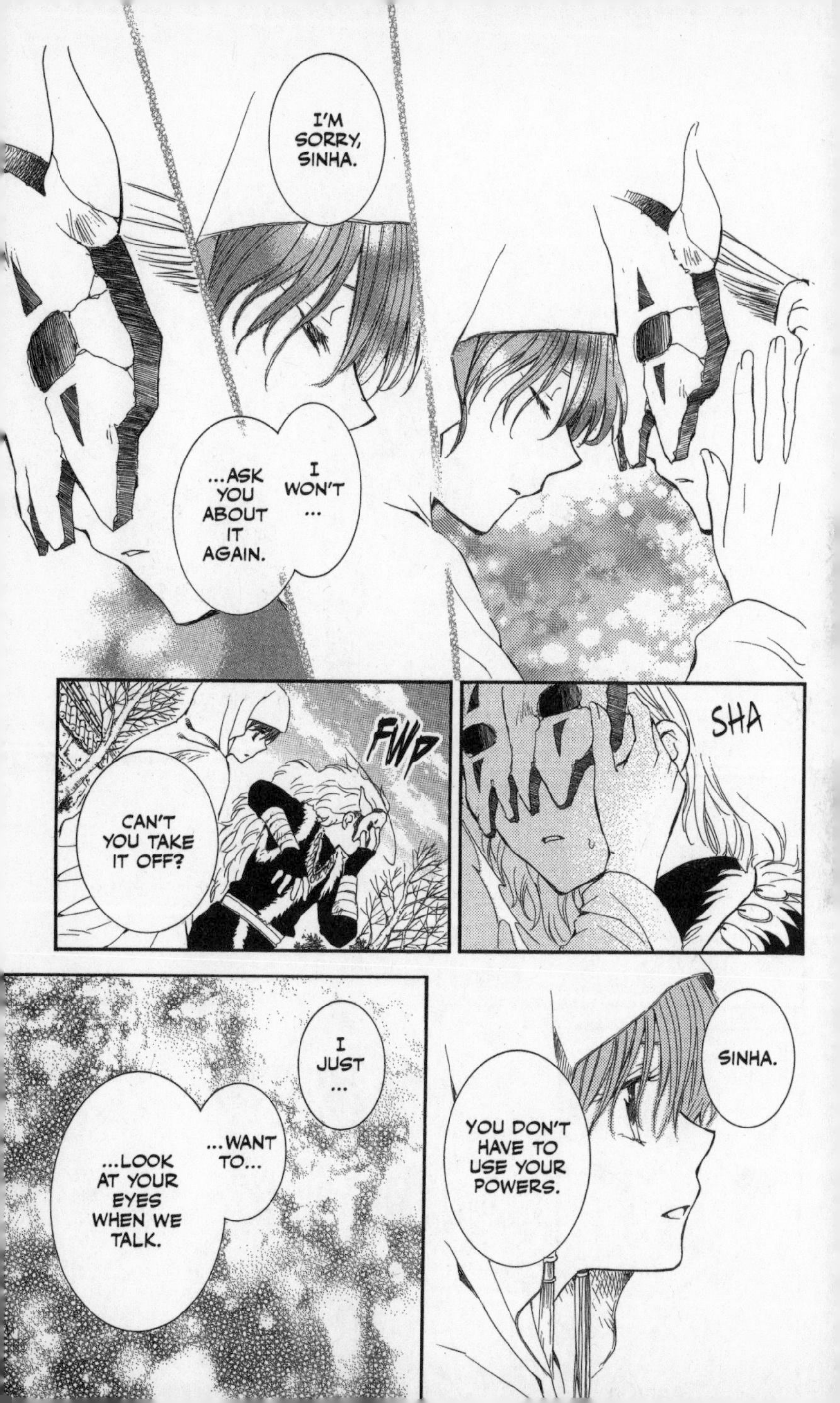
I'M SORRY, SINHA.
I WON'T ...
...ASK YOU ABOUT IT AGAIN.
SHA
FWP
CAN'T YOU TAKE IT OFF?
SINHA.
YOU DON'T HAVE TO USE YOUR POWERS.
I JUST ...
...WANT TO...
...LOOK AT YOUR EYES WHEN WE TALK.

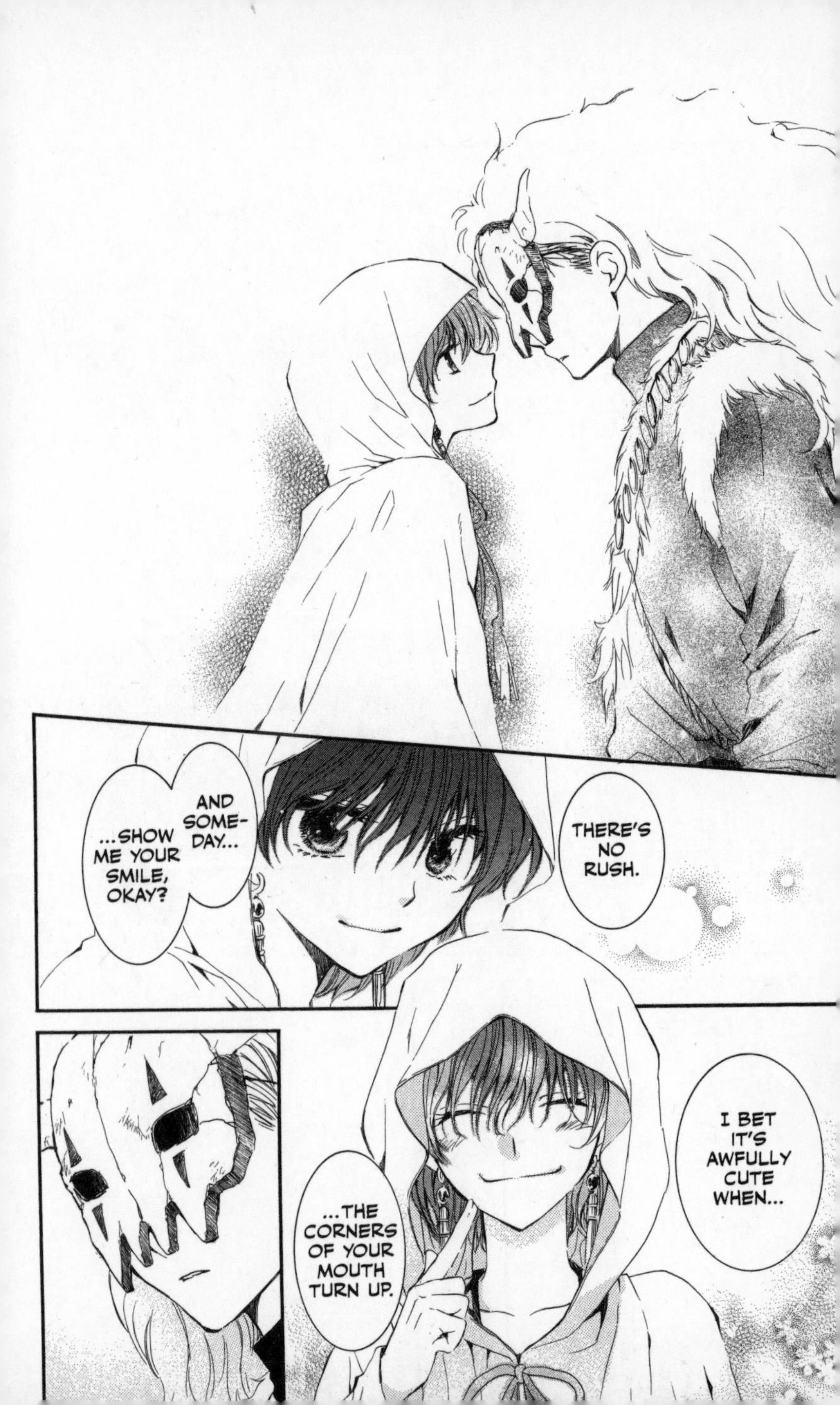
THERE'S NO RUSH.
AND SOME-DAY...
...SHOW ME YOUR SMILE, OKAY?
I BET IT'S AWFULLY CUTE WHEN...
...THE CORNERS OF YOUR MOUTH TURN UP.

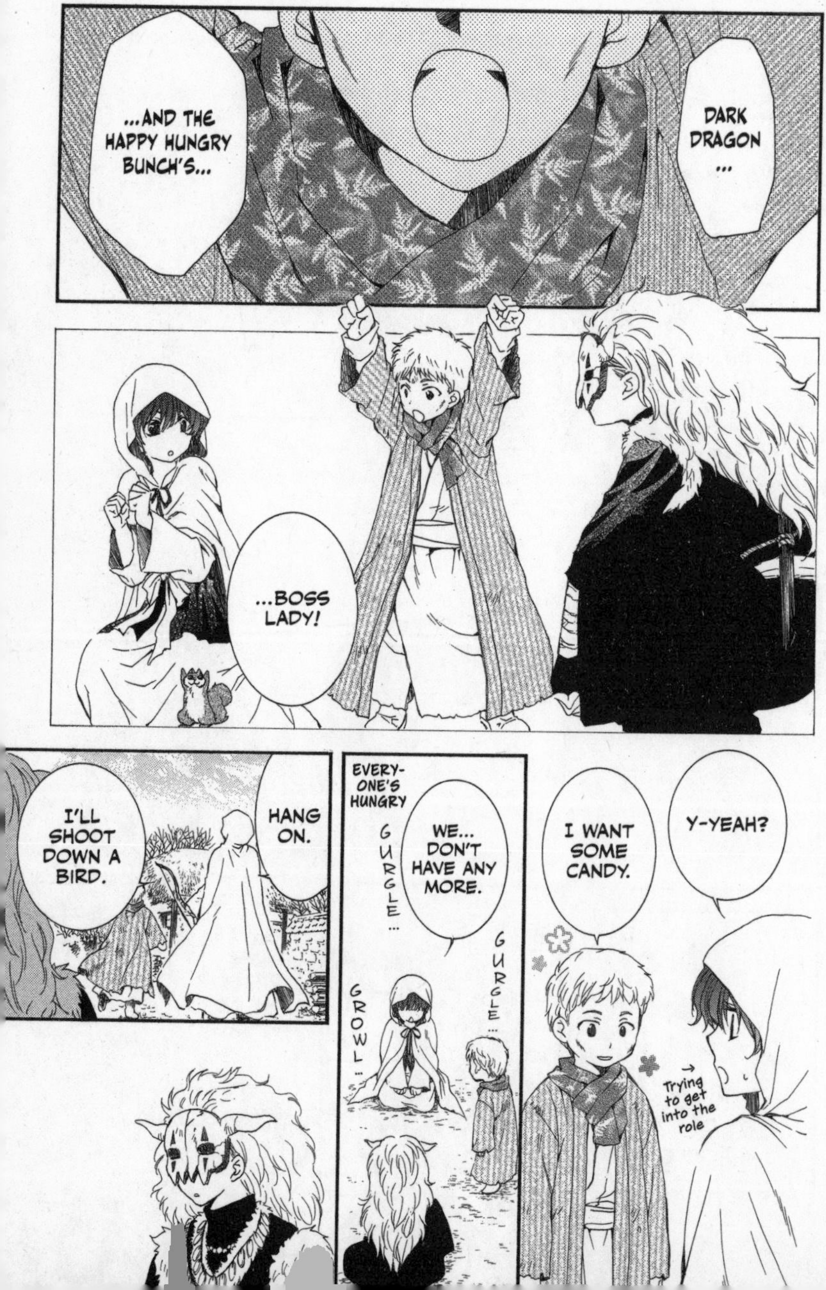
DARK DRAGON ...
...AND THE HAPPY HUNGRY BUNCH'S...
...BOSS LADY!
Y-YEAH?
I WANT SOME CANDY.
Trying to get into the role
EVERY-ONE'S HUNGRY
WE... DON'T HAVE ANY MORE.
GURGLE...
GURGLE...
GROWL...
HANG ON.
I'LL SHOOT DOWN A BIRD.

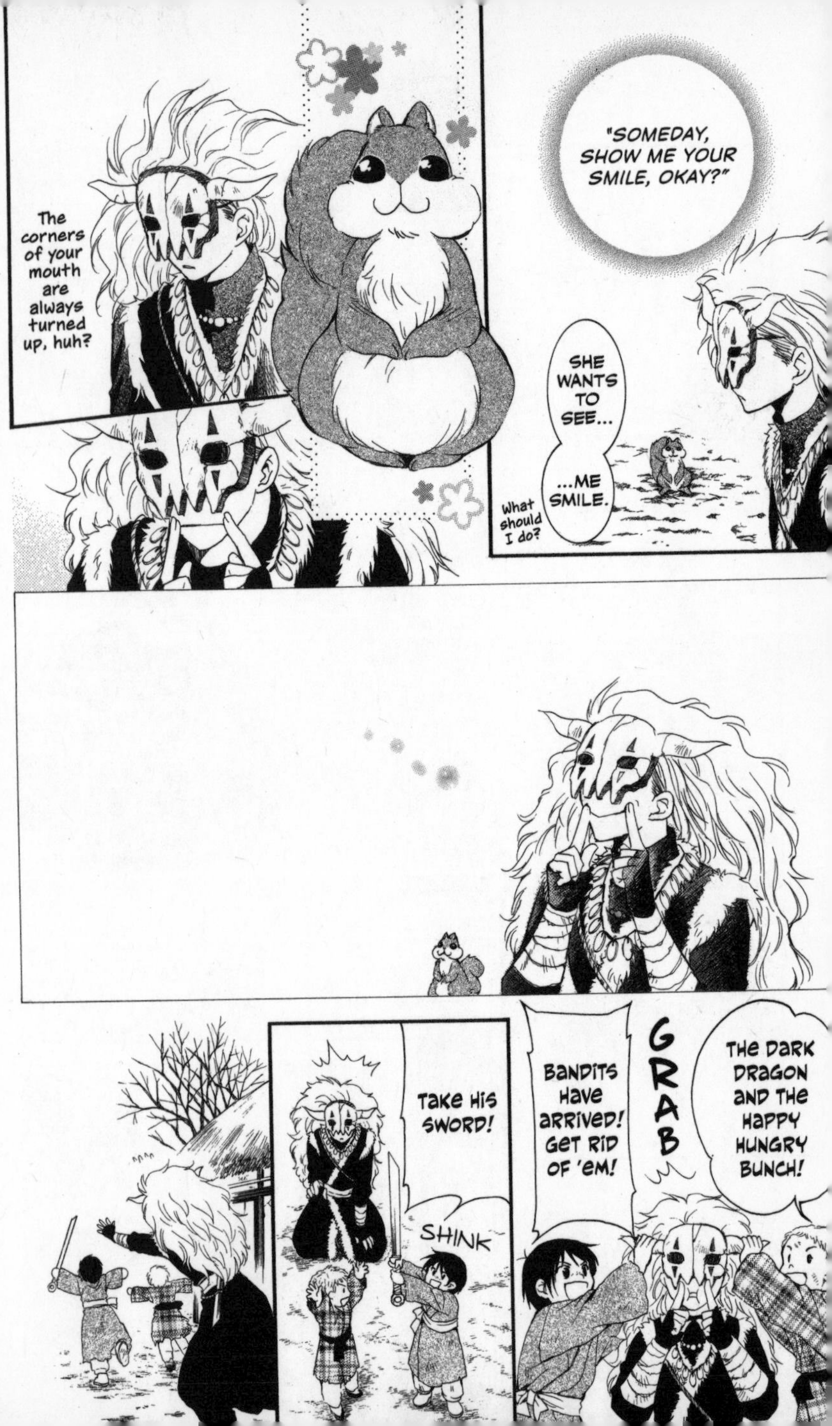
"SOMEDAY, SHOW ME YOUR SMILE, OKAY?"
SHE WANTS TO SEE...
...ME SMILE.
What should I do?
The corners of your mouth are always turned up, huh?
THE DARK DRAGON AND THE HAPPY HUNGRY BUNCH!
GRAB
BANDITS HAVE ARRIVED! GET RID OF 'EM!
TAKE HIS SWORD!
SHINK

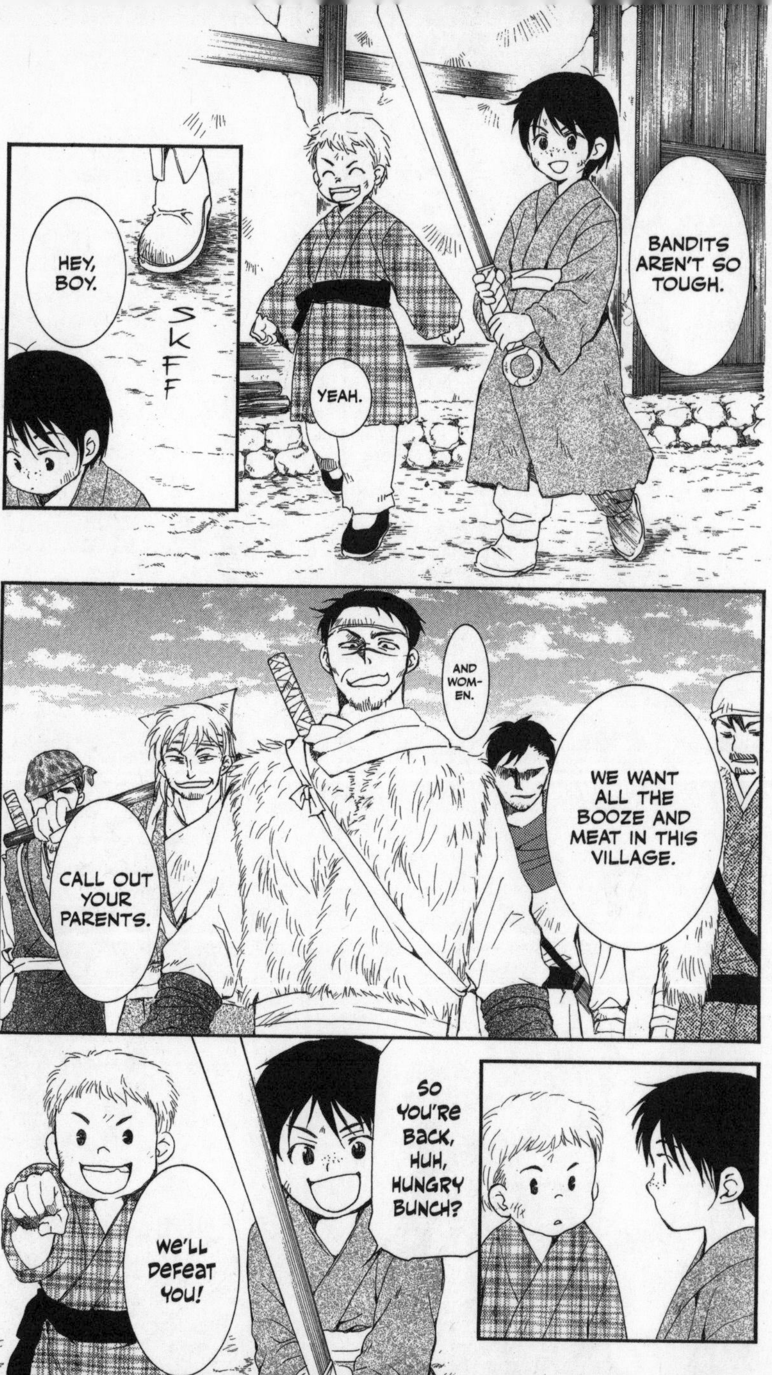
BANDITS AREN'T SO TOUGH.
YEAH.
HEY, BOY.
SKFF
WE WANT ALL THE BOOZE AND MEAT IN THIS VILLAGE.
AND WOM-EN.
CALL OUT YOUR PARENTS.
SO YOU'RE BACK, HUH, HUNGRY BUNCH?
WE'LL DEFEAT YOU!

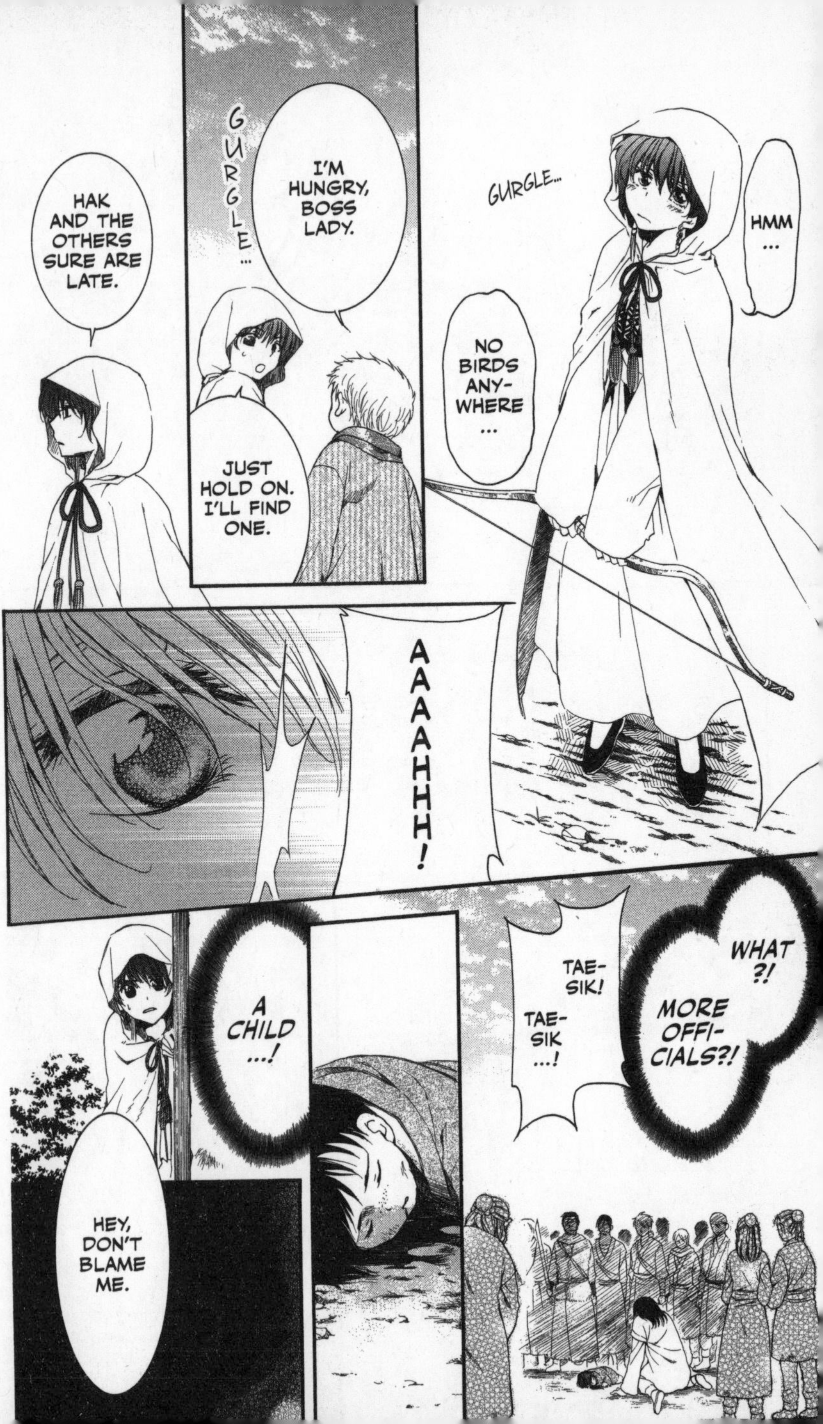
HMM ...
GURGLE...
NO BIRDS ANY-WHERE ...
GURGLE...
I'M HUNGRY, BOSS LADY.
JUST HOLD ON. I'LL FIND ONE.
HAK AND THE OTHERS SURE ARE LATE.
AAAAHHH!
WHAT?! MORE OFFI-CIALS?!
TAE-SIK! TAE-SIK ...!
A CHILD ...!
HEY, DON'T BLAME ME.

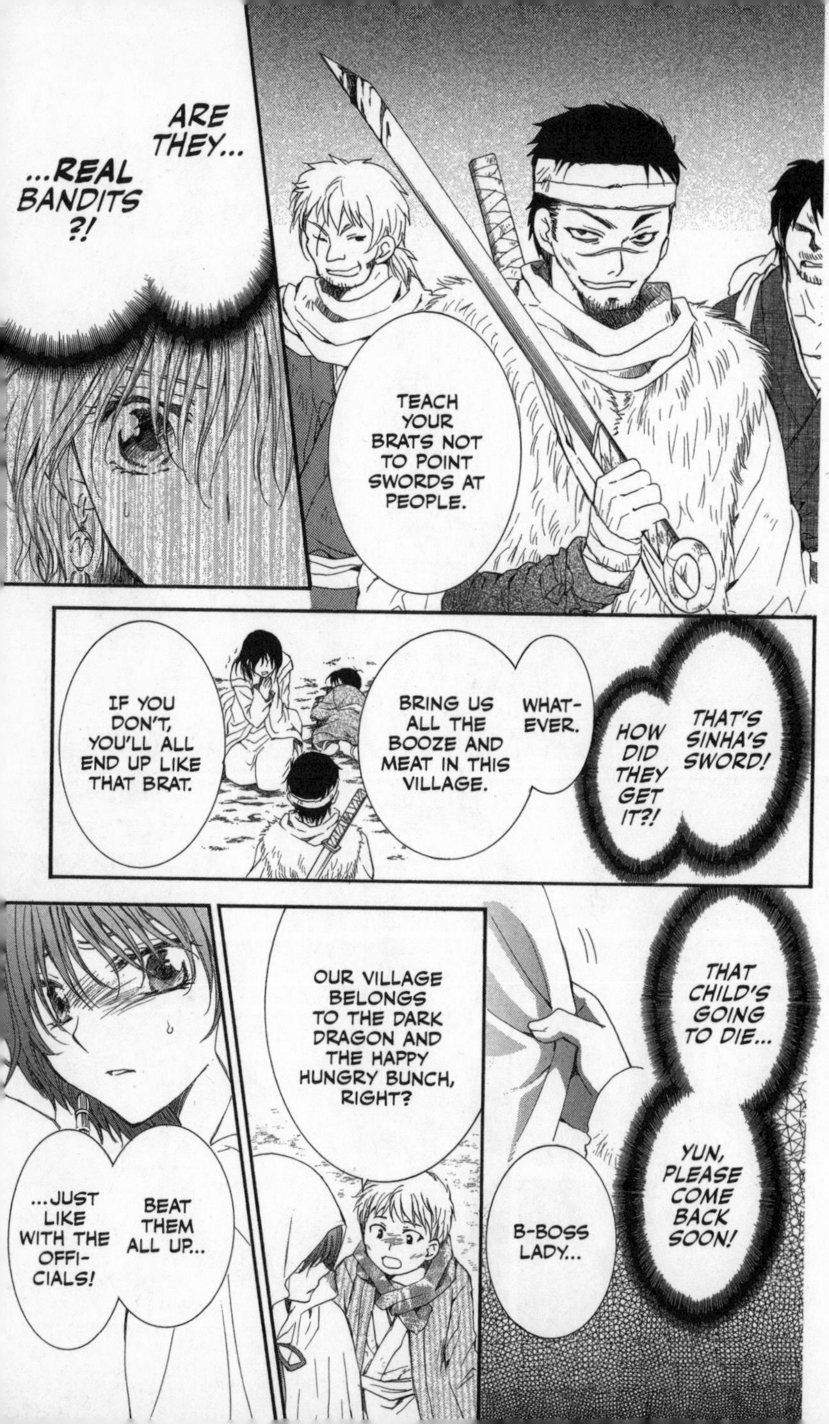
TEACH YOUR BRATS NOT TO POINT SWORDS AT PEOPLE.
ARE THEY...
...REAL BANDITS?!
THAT'S SINHA'S SWORD!
HOW DID THEY GET IT?!
WHATEVER.
BRING US ALL THE BOOZE AND MEAT IN THIS VILLAGE.
IF YOU DON'T, YOU'LL ALL END UP LIKE THAT BRAT.
THAT CHILD'S GOING TO DIE...
YUN, PLEASE COME BACK SOON!
B-BOSS LADY...
OUR VILLAGE BELONGS TO THE DARK DRAGON AND THE HAPPY HUNGRY BUNCH, RIGHT?
BEAT THEM ALL UP...
...JUST LIKE WITH THE OFFICIALS!

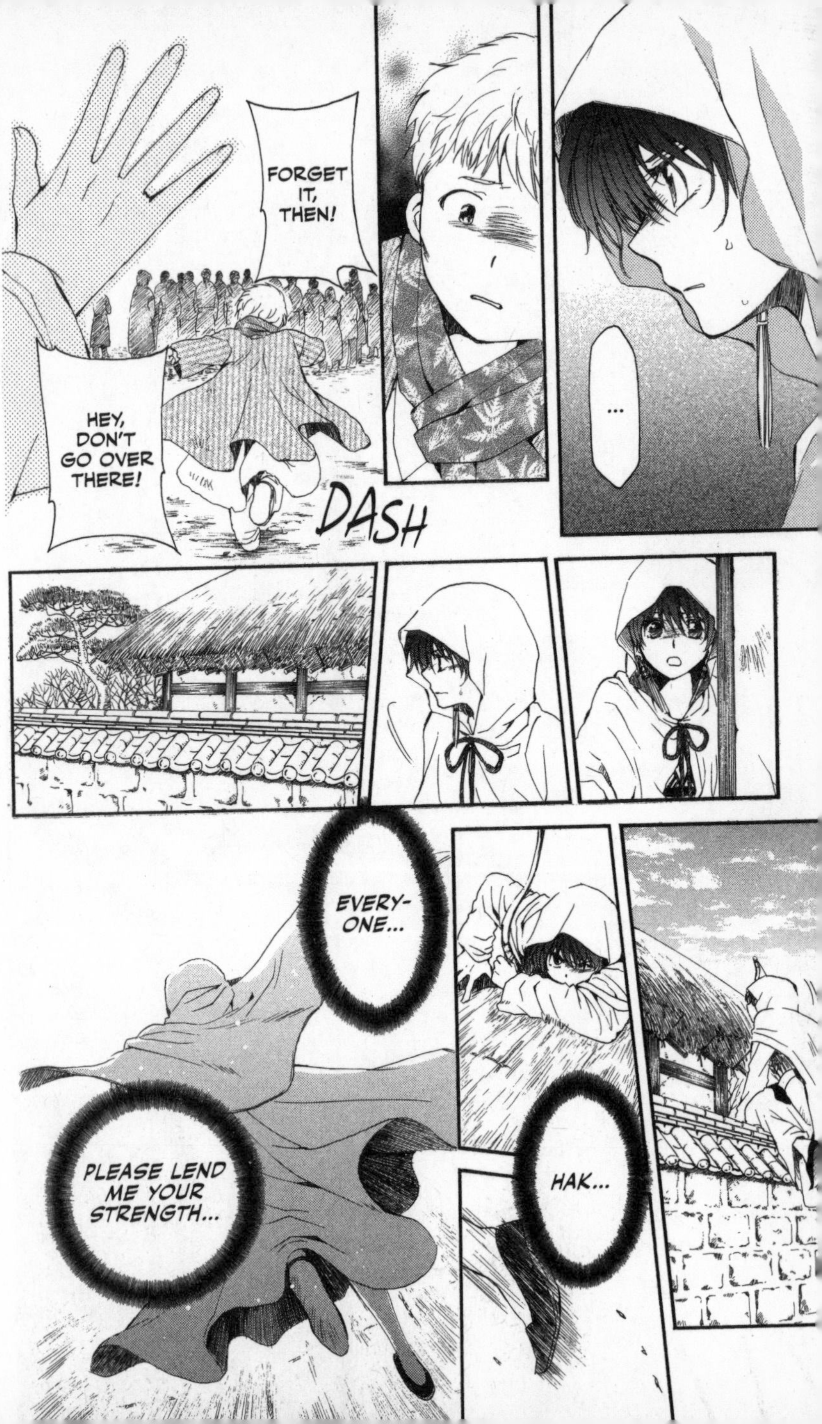
...
FORGET IT, THEN!
HEY, DON'T GO OVER THERE!
DASH
HAK...
EVERY-ONE...
PLEASE LEND ME YOUR STRENGTH...

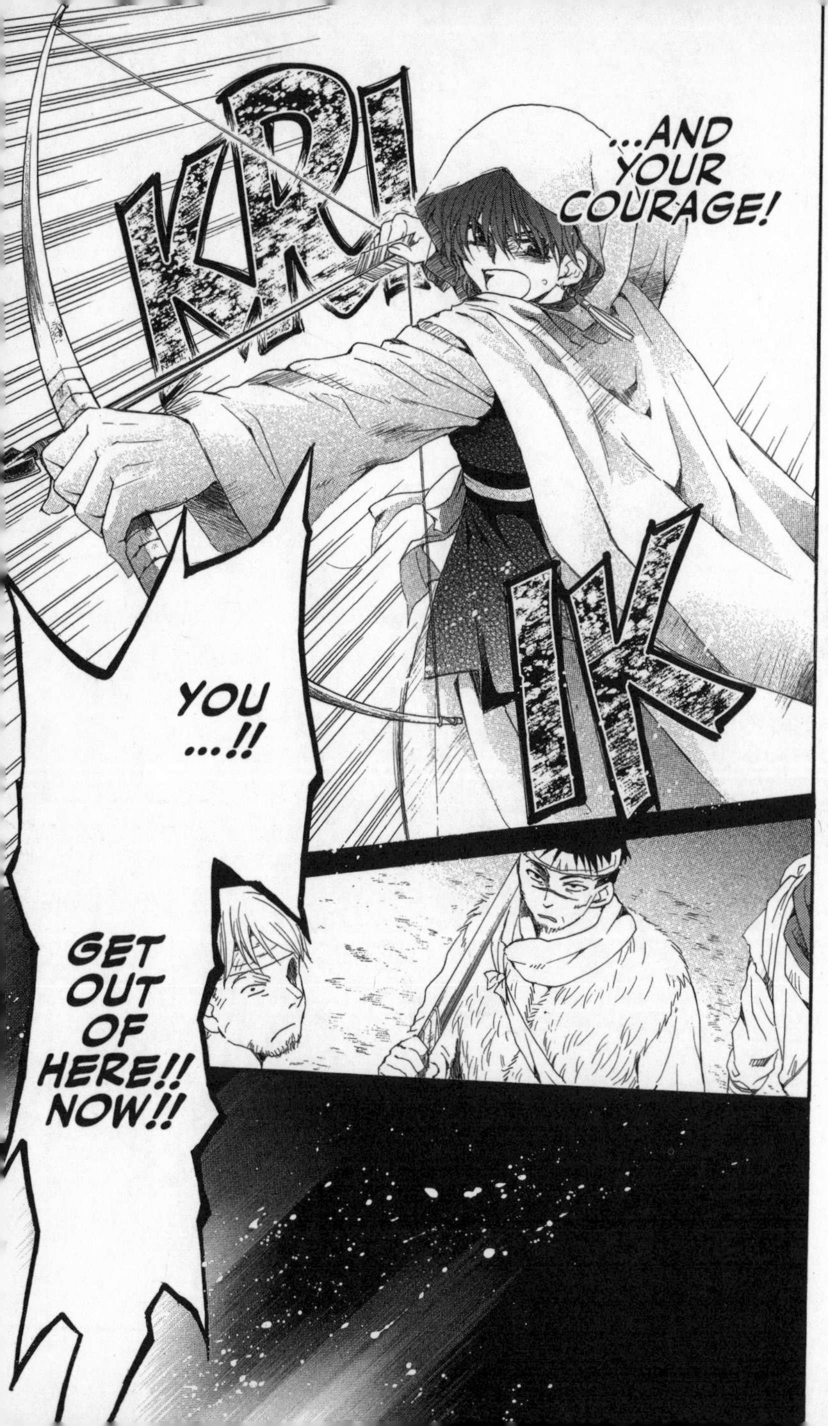
...AND YOUR COURAGE!
KRI
IK
YOU ...!!
GET OUT OF HERE!! NOW!!

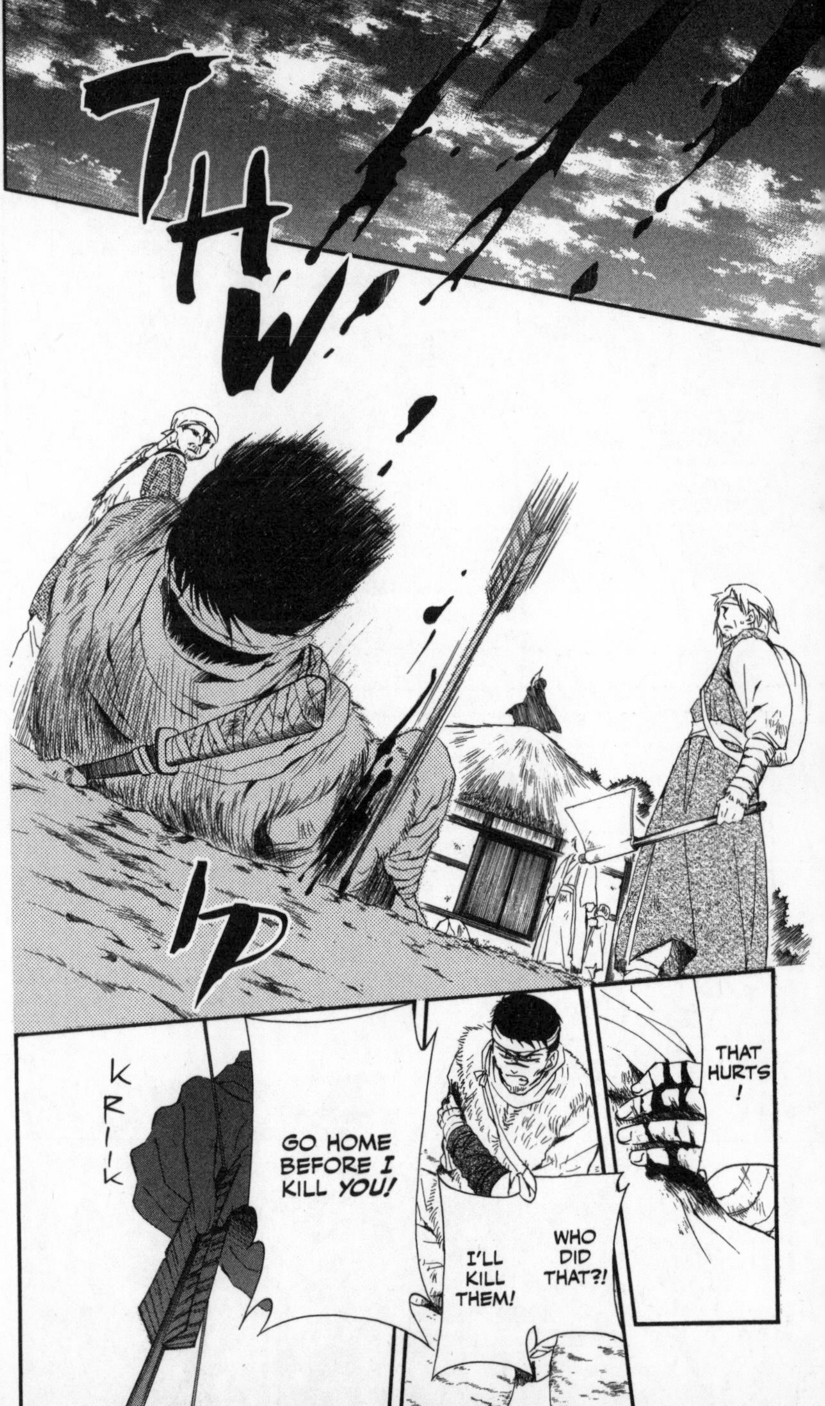
THWK
THAT HURTS!
WHO DID THAT?!
I'LL KILL THEM!
GO HOME BEFORE I KILL YOU!
KRIK

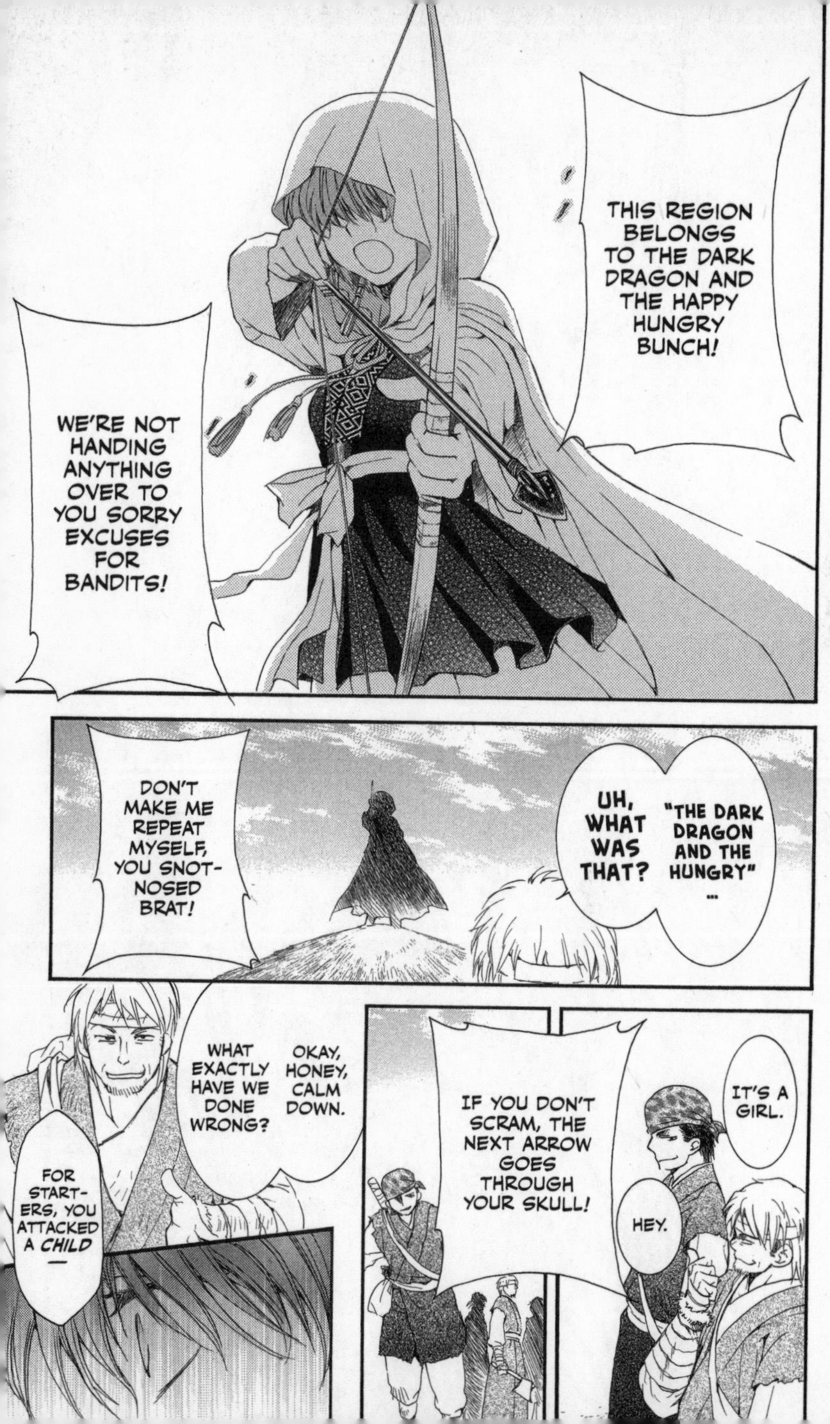
THIS REGION BELONGS TO THE DARK DRAGON AND THE HAPPY HUNGRY BUNCH!
WE'RE NOT HANDING ANYTHING OVER TO YOU SORRY EXCUSES FOR BANDITS!
UH, WHAT WAS THAT? "THE DARK DRAGON AND THE HUNGRY"...
DON'T MAKE ME REPEAT MYSELF, YOU SNOT-NOSED BRAT!
IT'S A GIRL.
HEY.
IF YOU DON'T SCRAM, THE NEXT ARROW GOES THROUGH YOUR SKULL!
OKAY, HONEY, CALM DOWN.
WHAT EXACTLY HAVE WE DONE WRONG?
FOR STARTERS, YOU ATTACKED A *CHILD*—

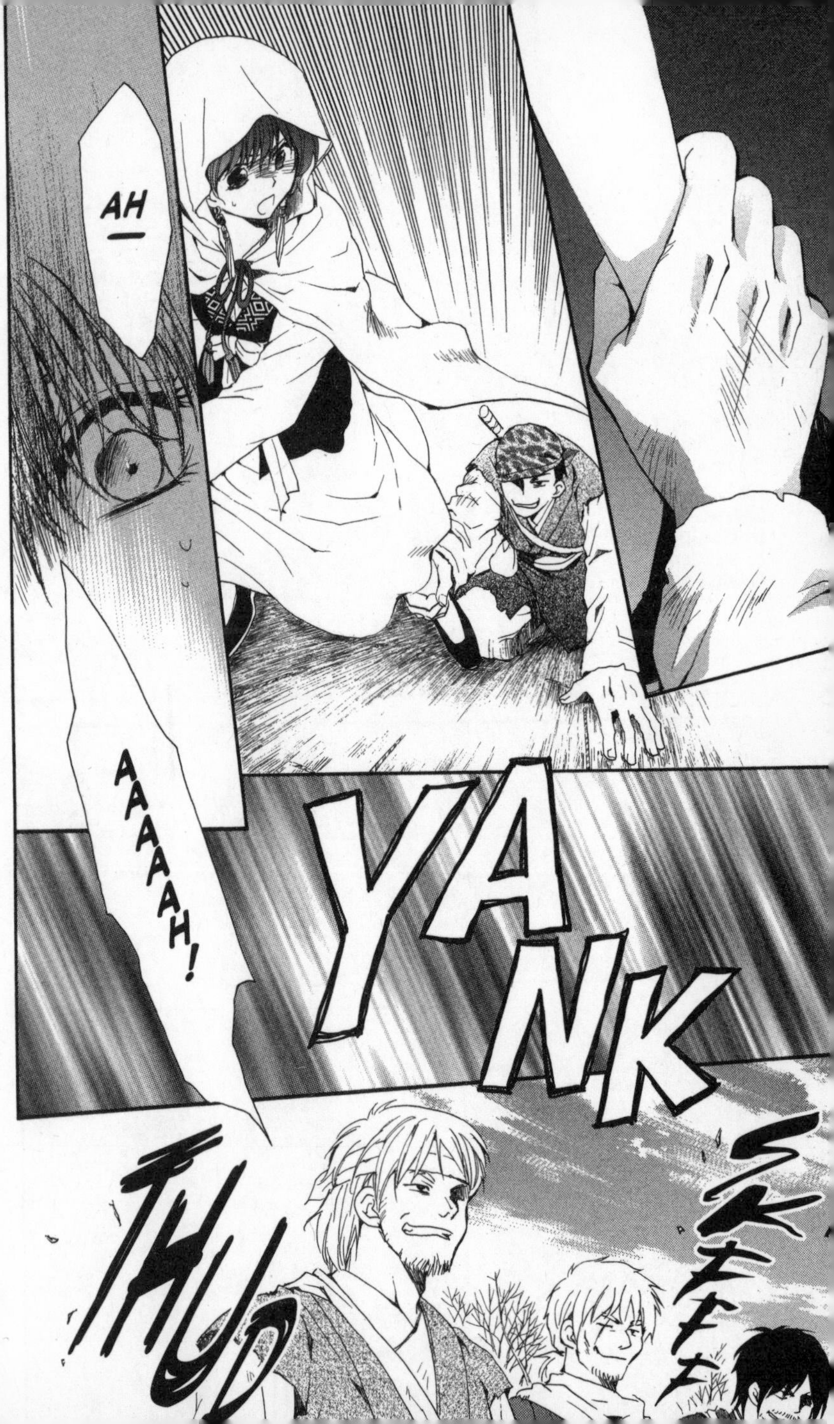

AH—
AAAAAAH!
YANK
SKEEEE
THUD

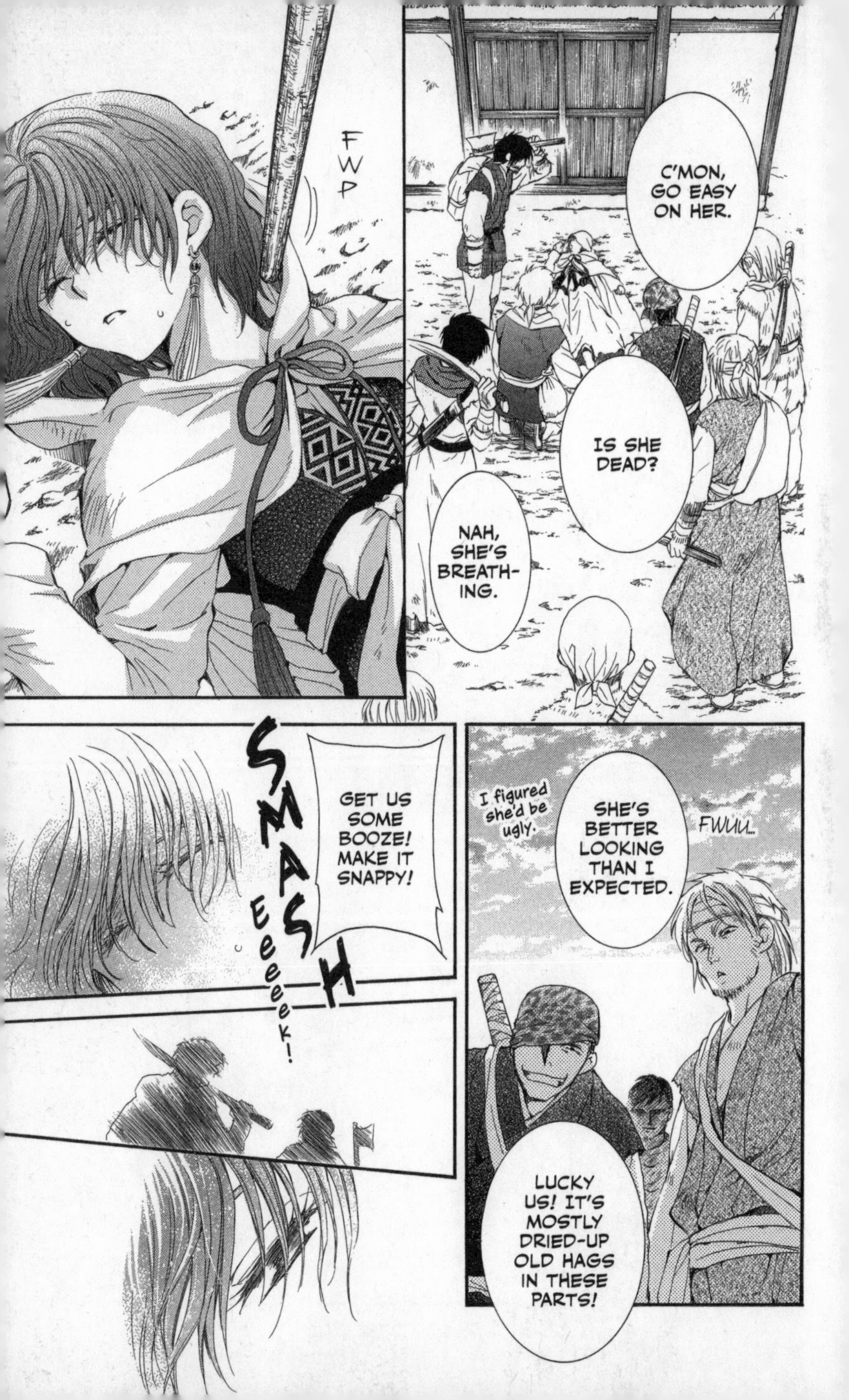
C'MON, GO EASY ON HER.
IS SHE DEAD?
NAH, SHE'S BREATHING.
FWP
FWUU...
SHE'S BETTER LOOKING THAN I EXPECTED.
I figured she'd be ugly.
LUCKY US! IT'S MOSTLY DRIED-UP OLD HAGS IN THESE PARTS!
GET US SOME BOOZE! MAKE IT SNAPPY!
SMASH
Eeeeeek!

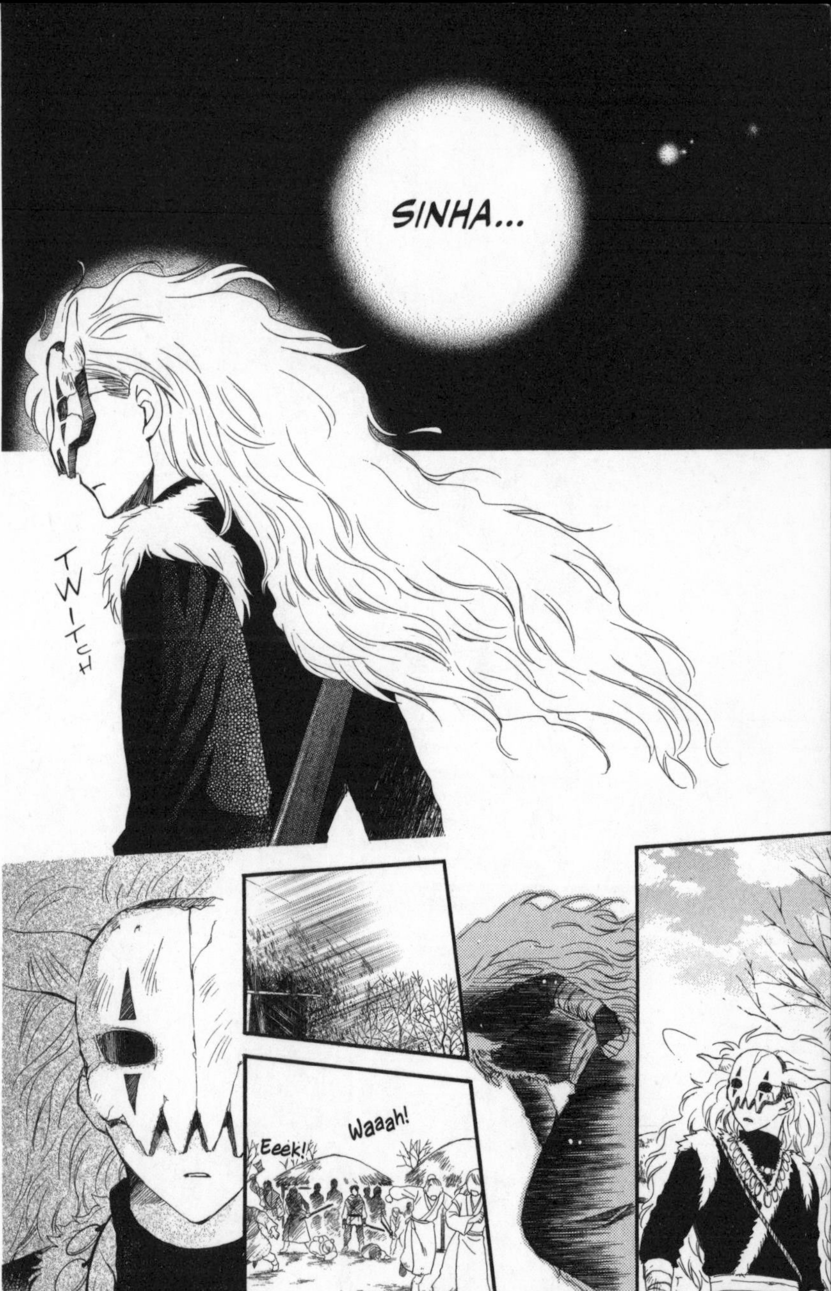
SINHA...
TWITCH
Waaah!
Eeek!
DASH

CHAPTER 49 / THE END

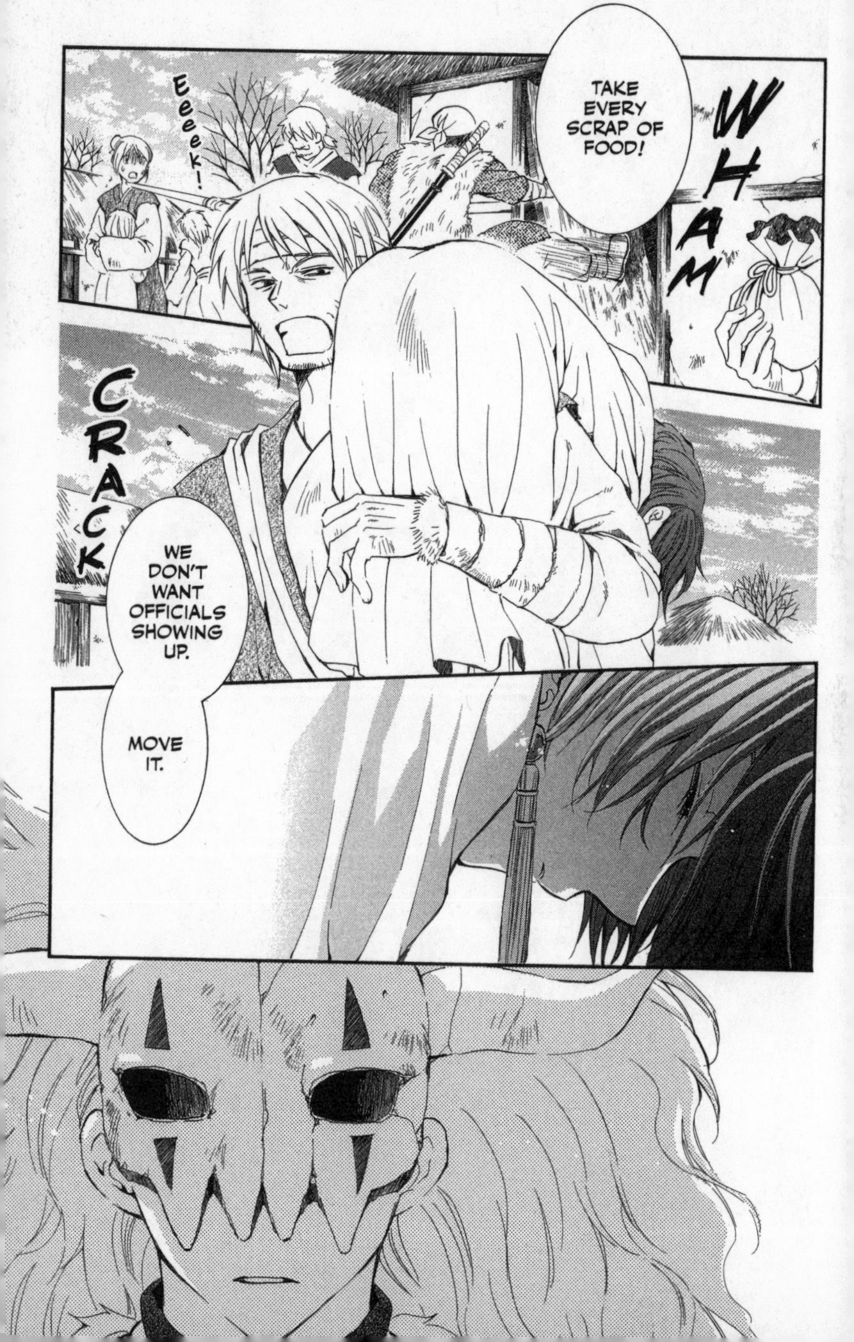
TAKE EVERY SCRAP OF FOOD!
WHAM
Eeeek!
CRACK
WE DON'T WANT OFFICIALS SHOWING UP.
MOVE IT.

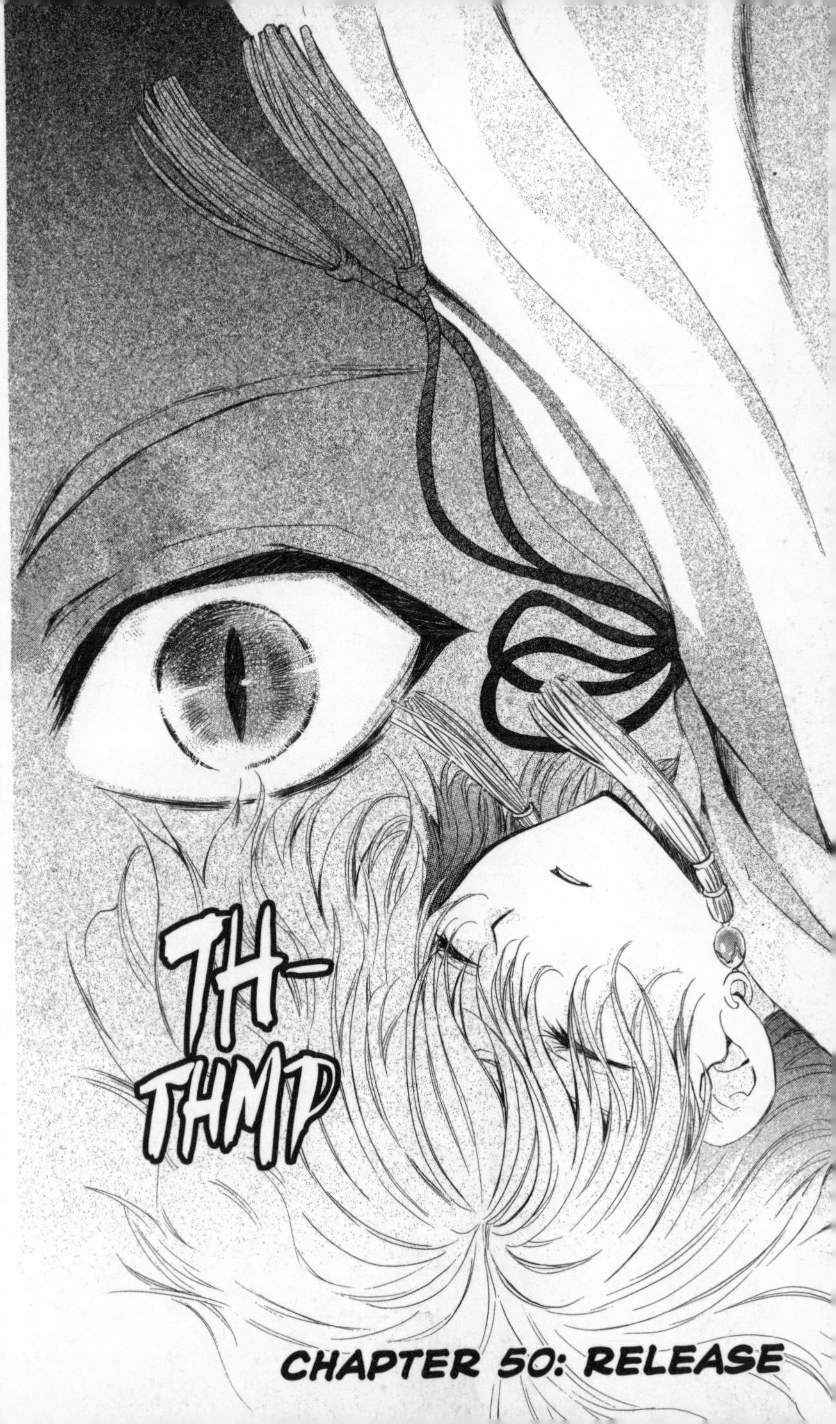
TH-THMP
CHAPTER 50: RELEASE

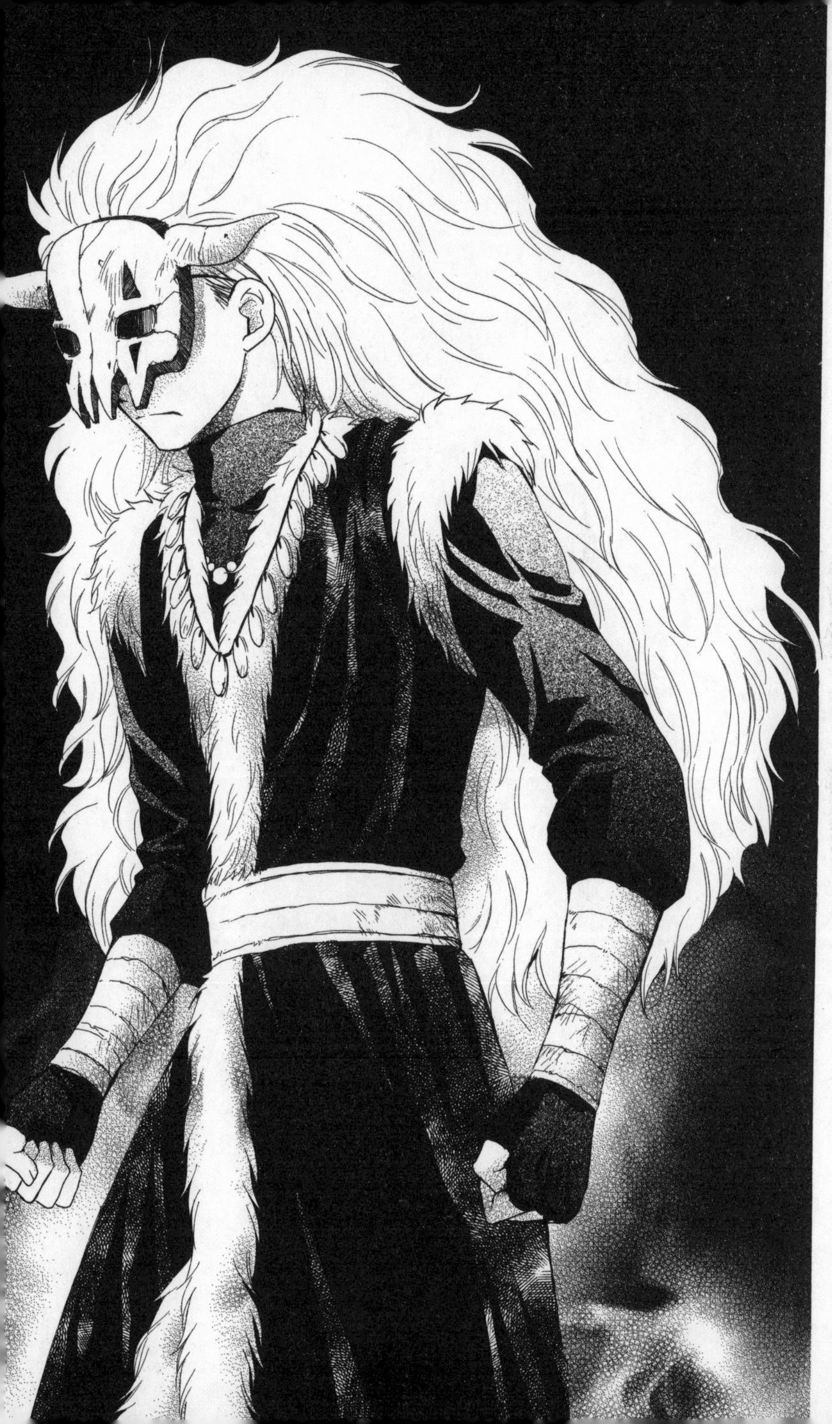

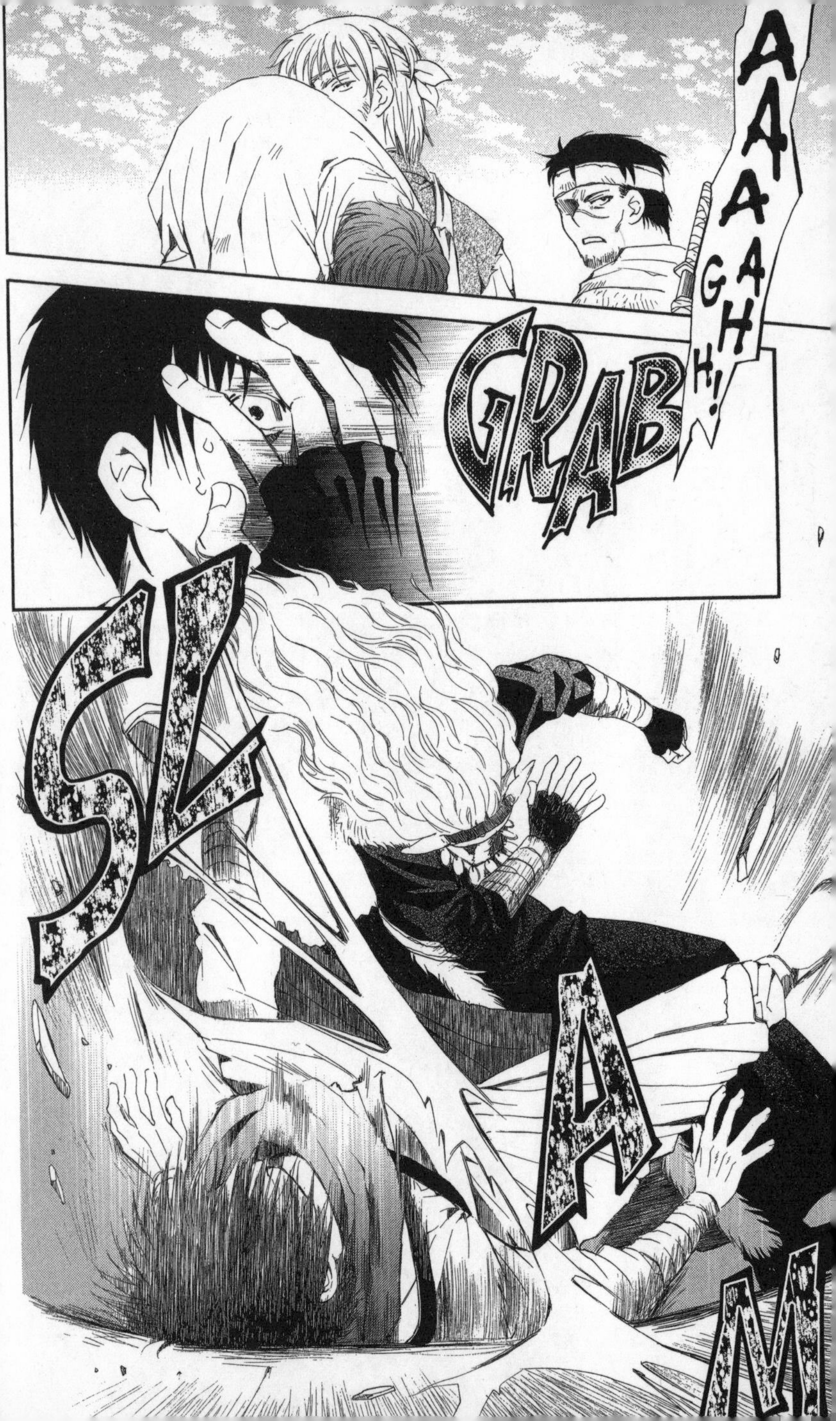

AAAAAGHH!
GRAB
SLAM

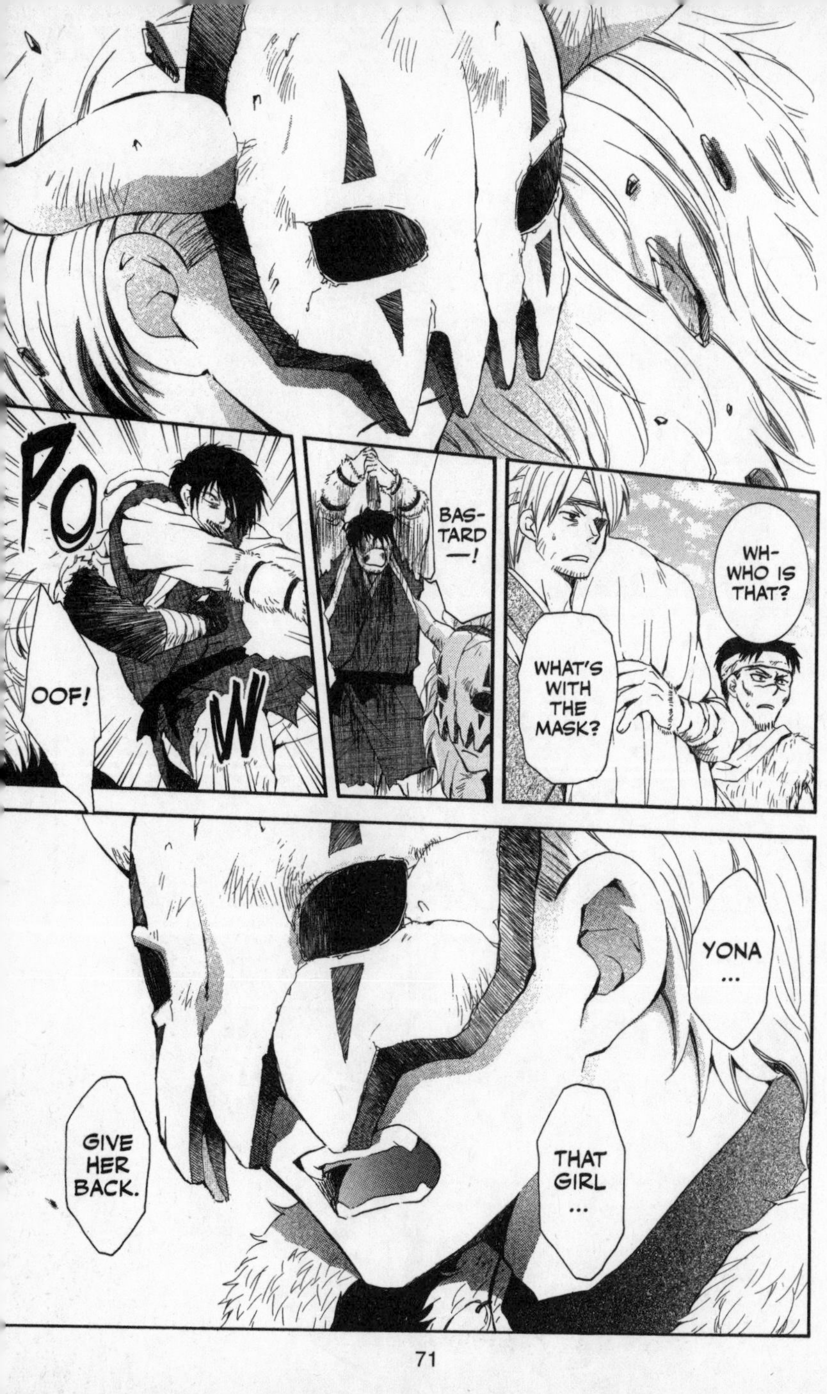
WH- WHO IS THAT?
WHAT'S WITH THE MASK?
BAS-TARD—!
POW
OOF!
YONA ...
THAT GIRL ...
GIVE HER BACK.

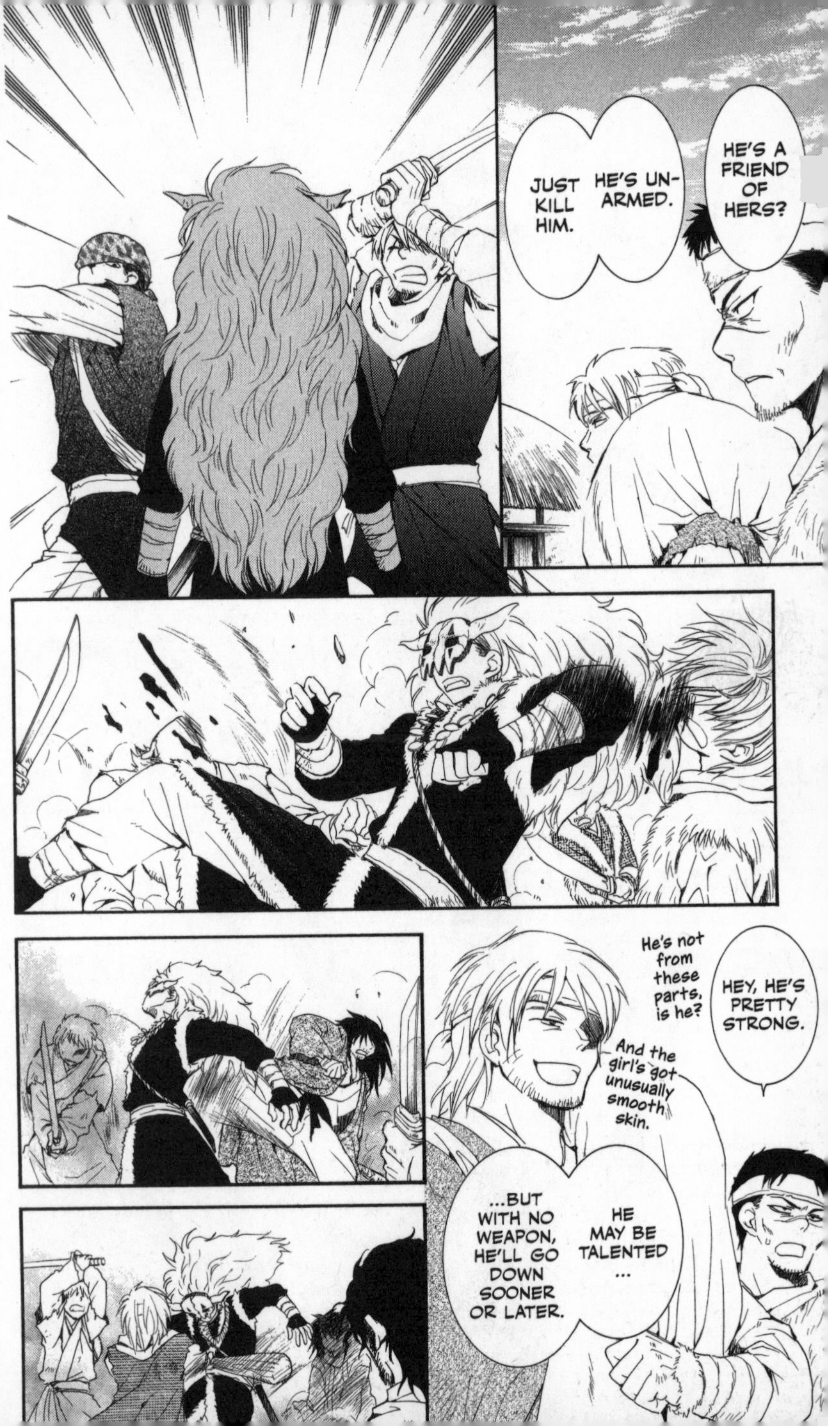
HE'S A FRIEND OF HERS?
HE'S UN-ARMED.
JUST KILL HIM.
HEY, HE'S PRETTY STRONG.
He's not from these parts, is he?
And the girl's got unusually smooth skin.
HE MAY BE TALENTED ...
...BUT WITH NO WEAPON, HE'LL GO DOWN SOONER OR LATER.

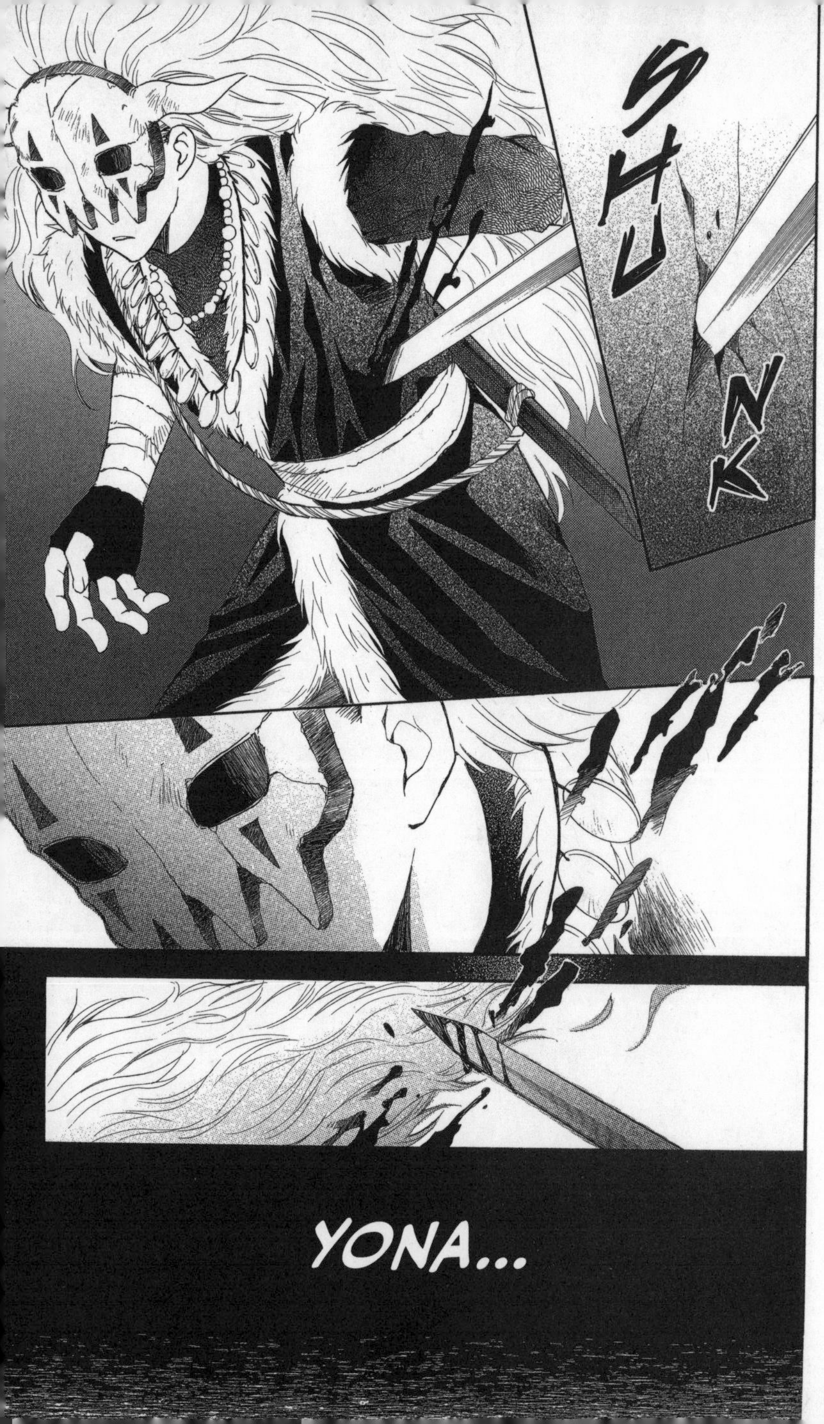
SHUNK
YONA...

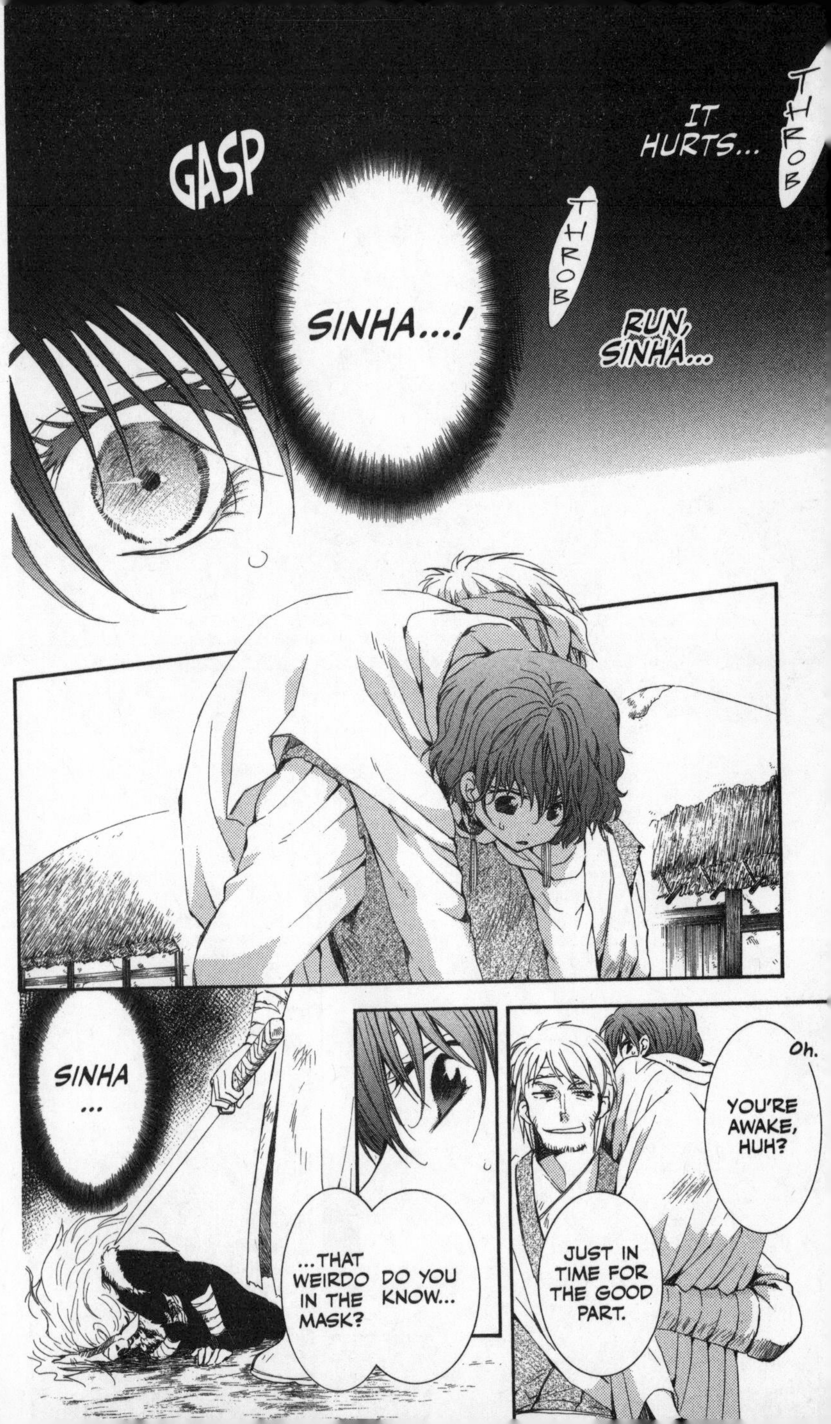

THROB
IT HURTS...
THROB
GASP
RUN, SINHA...
SINHA...!
Oh.
YOU'RE AWAKE, HUH?
JUST IN TIME FOR THE GOOD PART.
DO YOU KNOW...
...THAT WEIRDO IN THE MASK?
SINHA ...

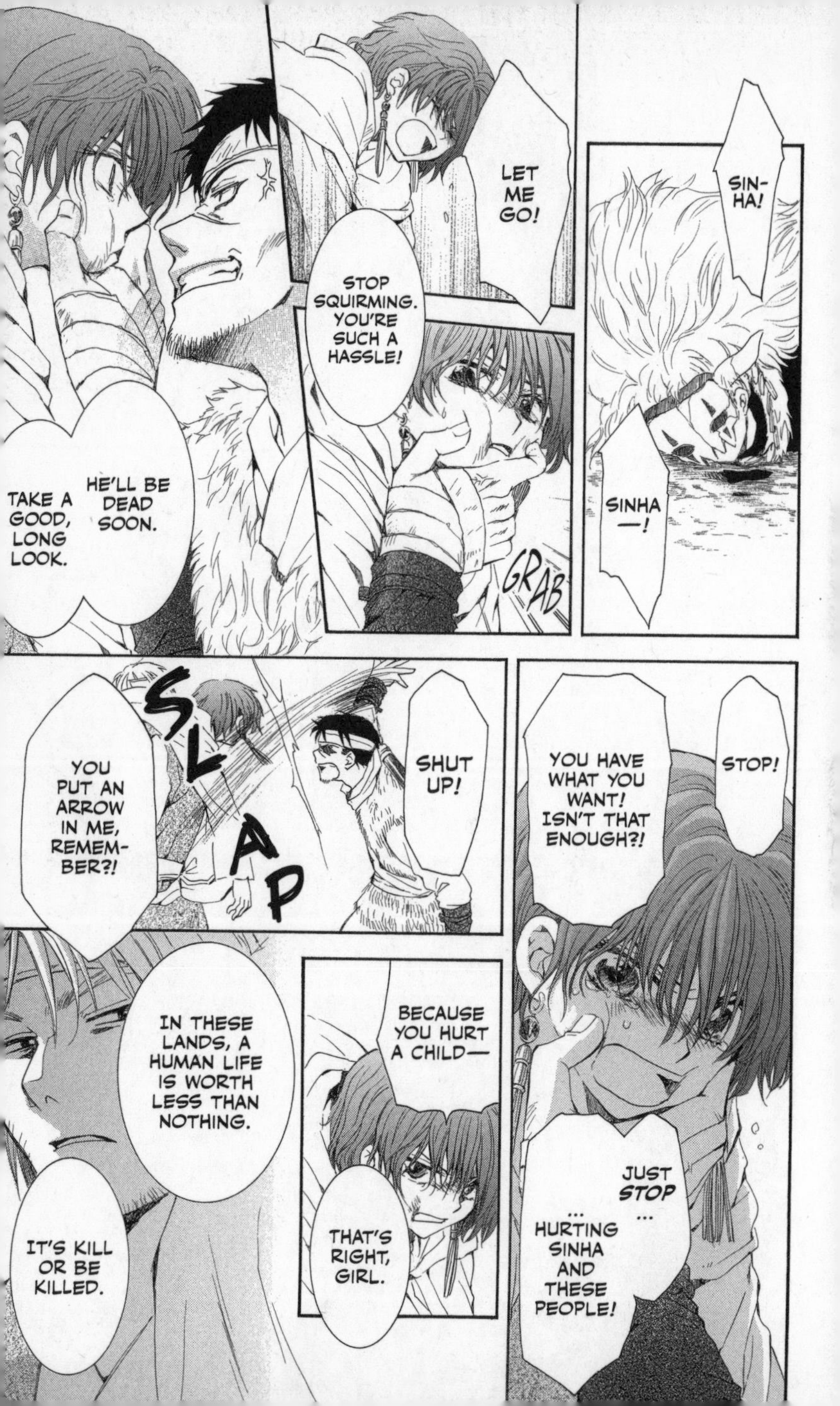
SIN-HA!
SINHA—!
LET ME GO!
STOP SQUIRMING. YOU'RE SUCH A HASSLE!
GRAB
HE'LL BE DEAD SOON.
TAKE A GOOD, LONG LOOK.
STOP!
YOU HAVE WHAT YOU WANT! ISN'T THAT ENOUGH?!
JUST *STOP* ... ... HURTING SINHA AND THESE PEOPLE!
SHUT UP!
SLAP
YOU PUT AN ARROW IN ME, REMEMBER?!
BECAUSE YOU HURT A CHILD—
THAT'S RIGHT, GIRL.
IN THESE LANDS, A HUMAN LIFE IS WORTH LESS THAN NOTHING.
IT'S KILL OR BE KILLED.

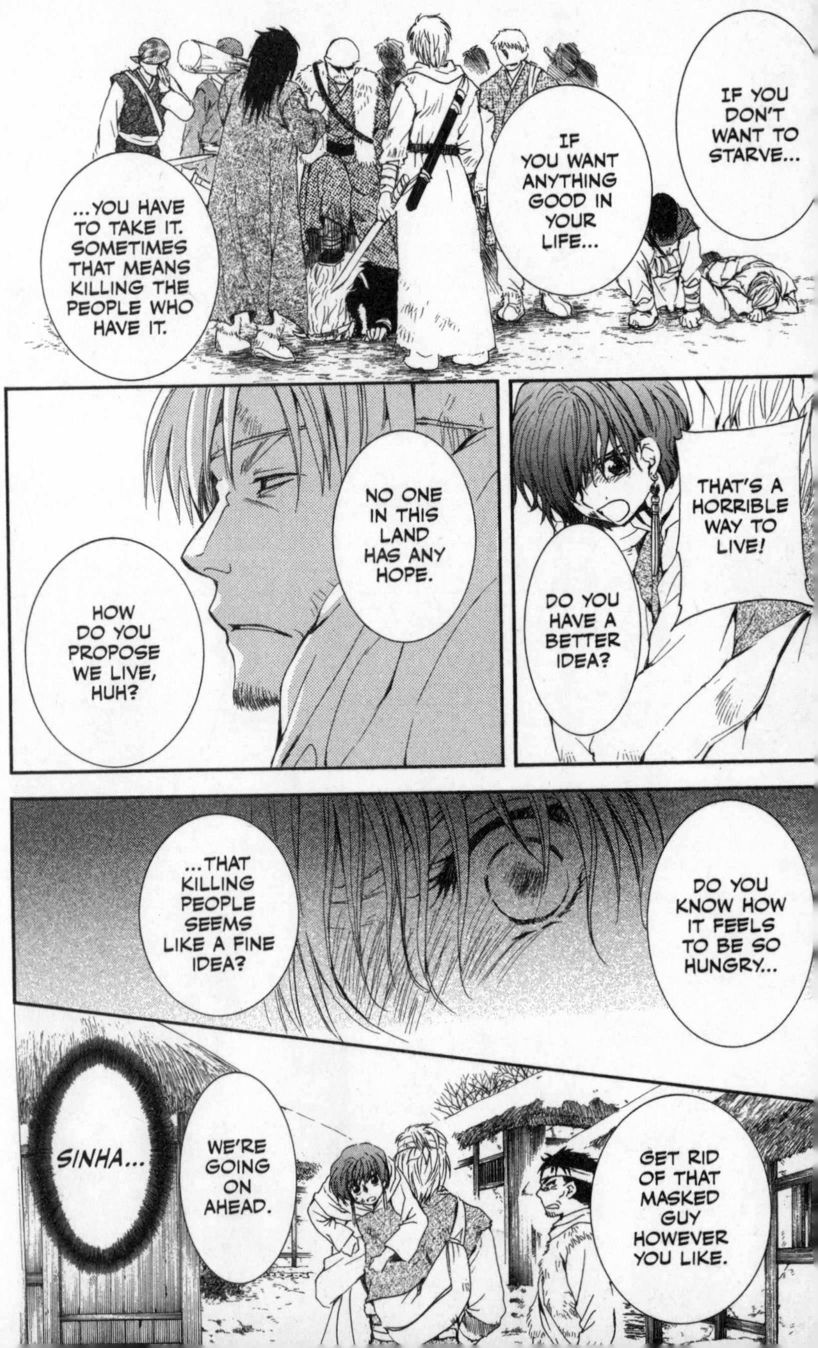
IF YOU DON'T WANT TO STARVE...
IF YOU WANT ANYTHING GOOD IN YOUR LIFE...
...YOU HAVE TO TAKE IT. SOMETIMES THAT MEANS KILLING THE PEOPLE WHO HAVE IT.
THAT'S A HORRIBLE WAY TO LIVE!
DO YOU HAVE A BETTER IDEA?
NO ONE IN THIS LAND HAS ANY HOPE.
HOW DO YOU PROPOSE WE LIVE, HUH?
DO YOU KNOW HOW IT FEELS TO BE SO HUNGRY...
...THAT KILLING PEOPLE SEEMS LIKE A FINE IDEA?
GET RID OF THAT MASKED GUY HOWEVER YOU LIKE.
WE'RE GOING ON AHEAD.
SINHA...

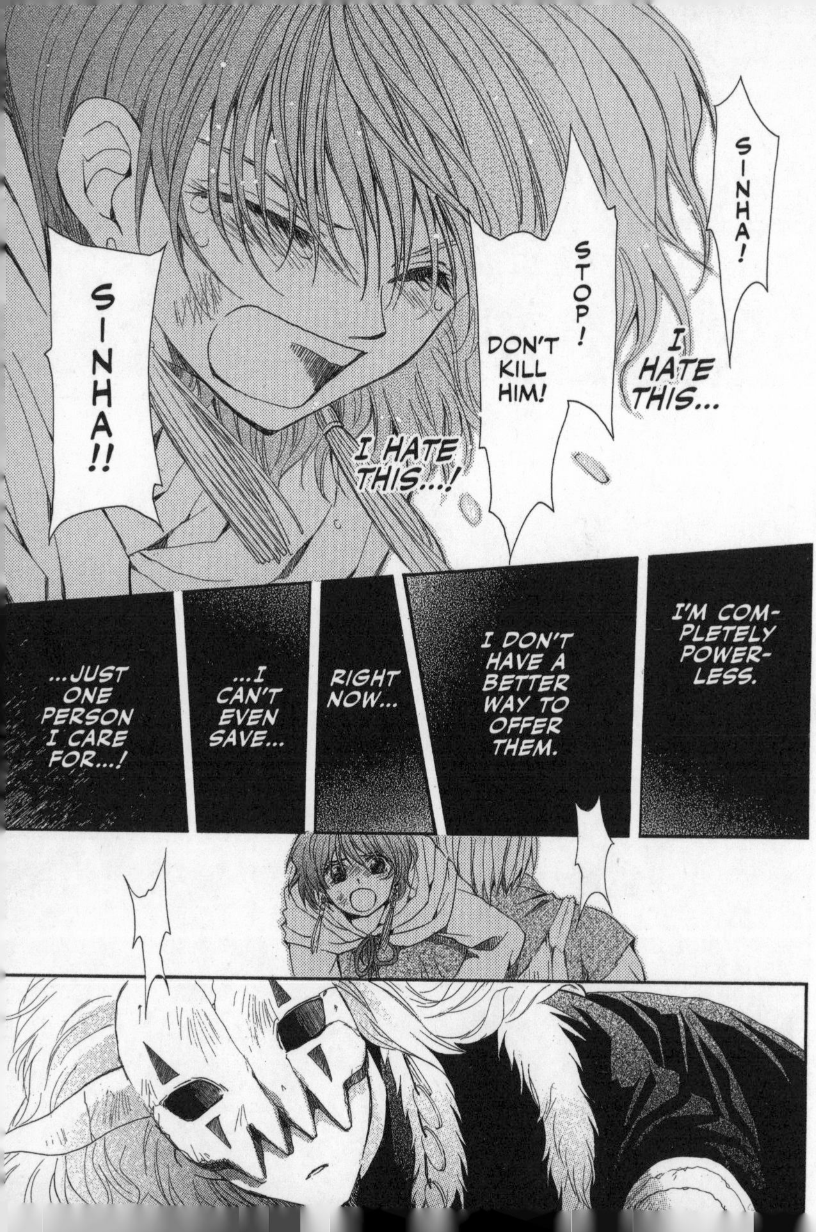
SINHA!
I HATE THIS...
STOP!
DON'T KILL HIM!
I HATE THIS...!
SINHA!!
I'M COM-PLETELY POWER-LESS.
I DON'T HAVE A BETTER WAY TO OFFER THEM.
RIGHT NOW...
...I CAN'T EVEN SAVE...
...JUST ONE PERSON I CARE FOR...!

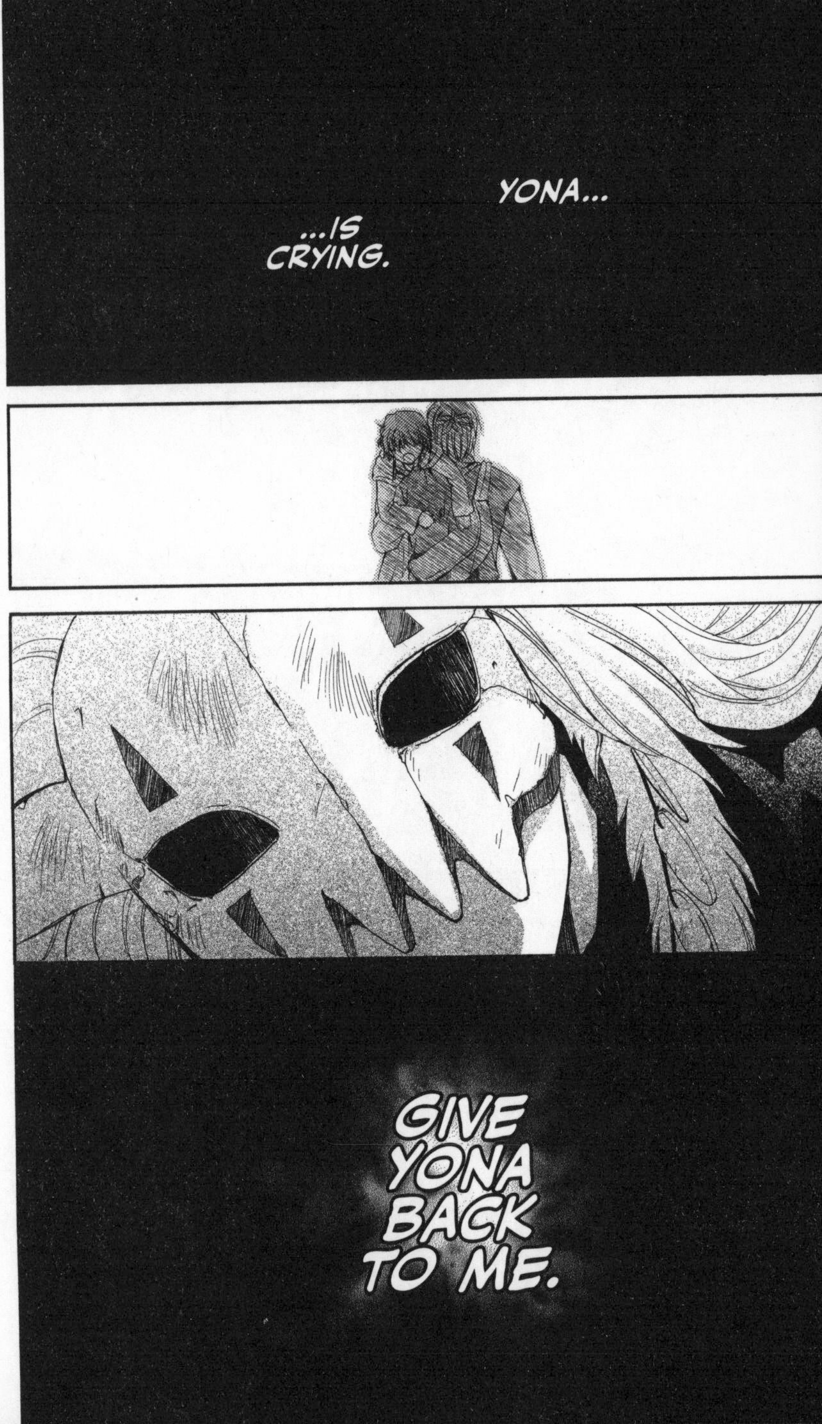
YONA...
...IS CRYING.
GIVE YONA BACK TO ME.

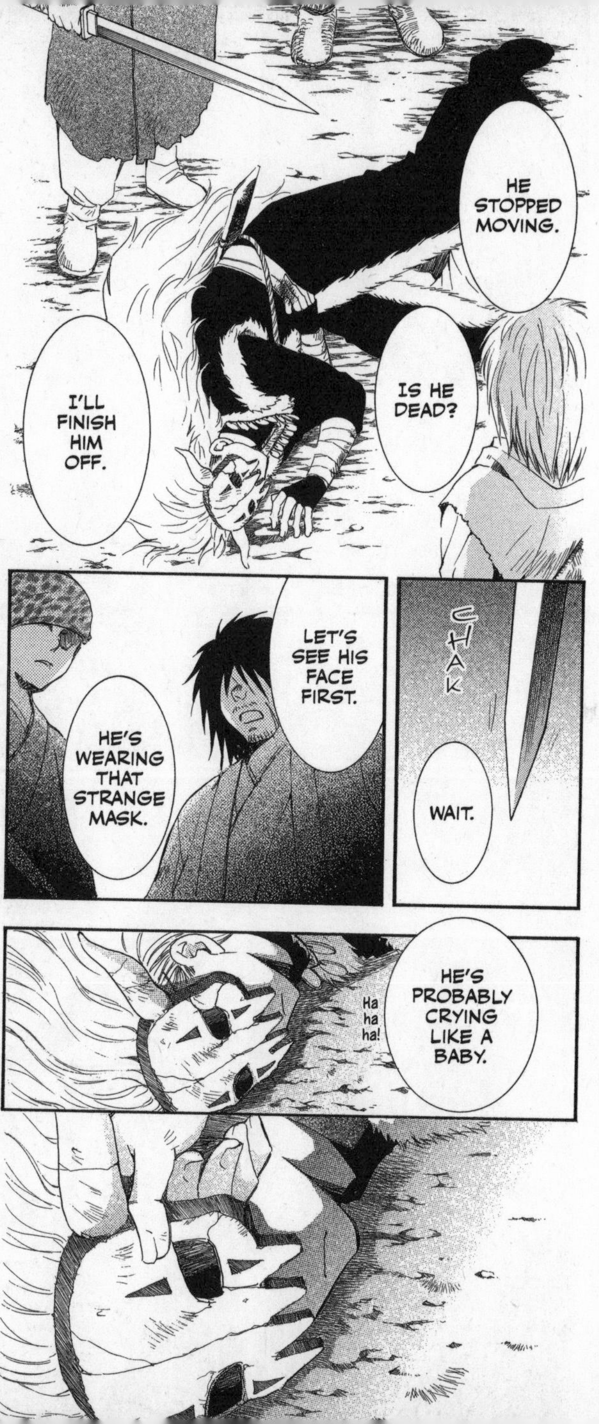
HE STOPPED MOVING.
IS HE DEAD?
I'LL FINISH HIM OFF.
CHAK
WAIT.
LET'S SEE HIS FACE FIRST.
HE'S WEARING THAT STRANGE MASK.
HE'S PROBABLY CRYING LIKE A BABY.
Ha ha ha!

I love actors—or I should say I love people who do theater. I can't resist a wonderful voice. They make my heart skip a beat.

I really admire voice actors. It feels so generous of them to deliver lines that I wrote with those amazing voices that I admire so much. It makes me feel bashful...and nervous.

Thoughts like that left me flustered, but I was so blown away by the voice cast that I had no time to be shy. They'd all read the source material. Sometimes they acted cute, and other times they were sad. They took their work so seriously! I was keenly aware of why I love them so much!

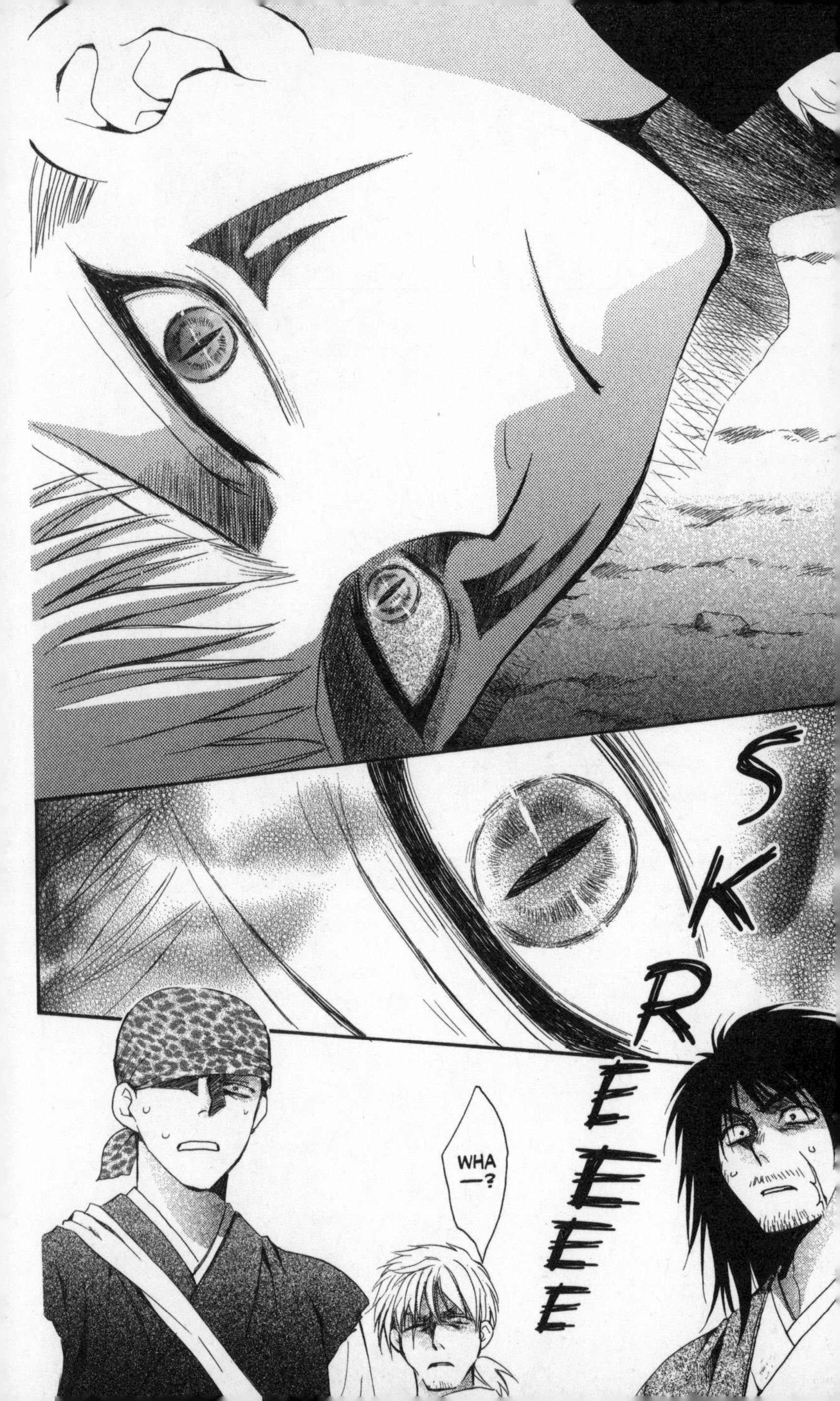
SKREEEEEEE
WHA—?

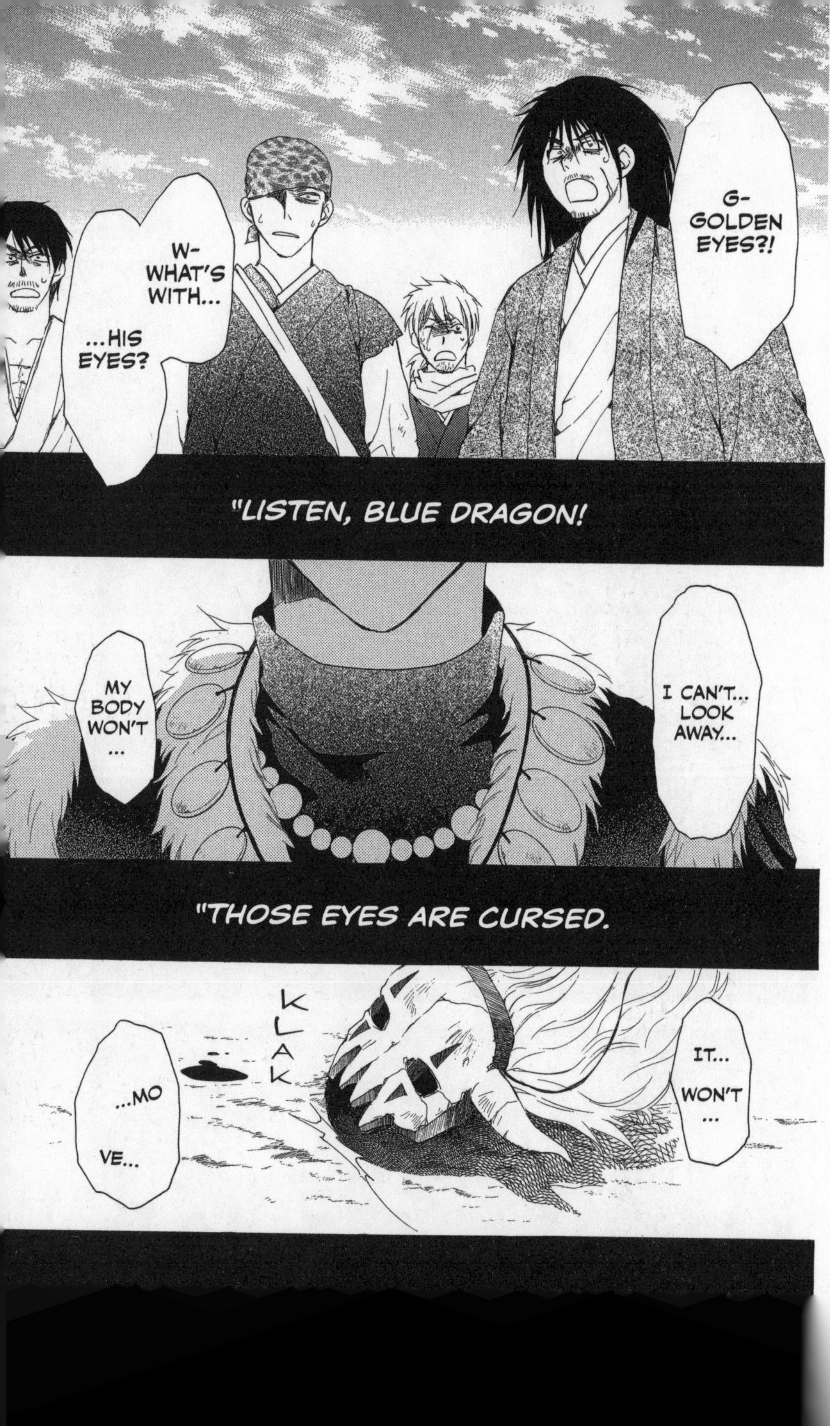
G- GOLDEN EYES?!
W- WHAT'S WITH...
...HIS EYES?
"LISTEN, BLUE DRAGON!
I CAN'T... LOOK AWAY...
MY BODY WON'T ...
"THOSE EYES ARE CURSED.
IT... WON'T ...
KLAK
...MO VE...

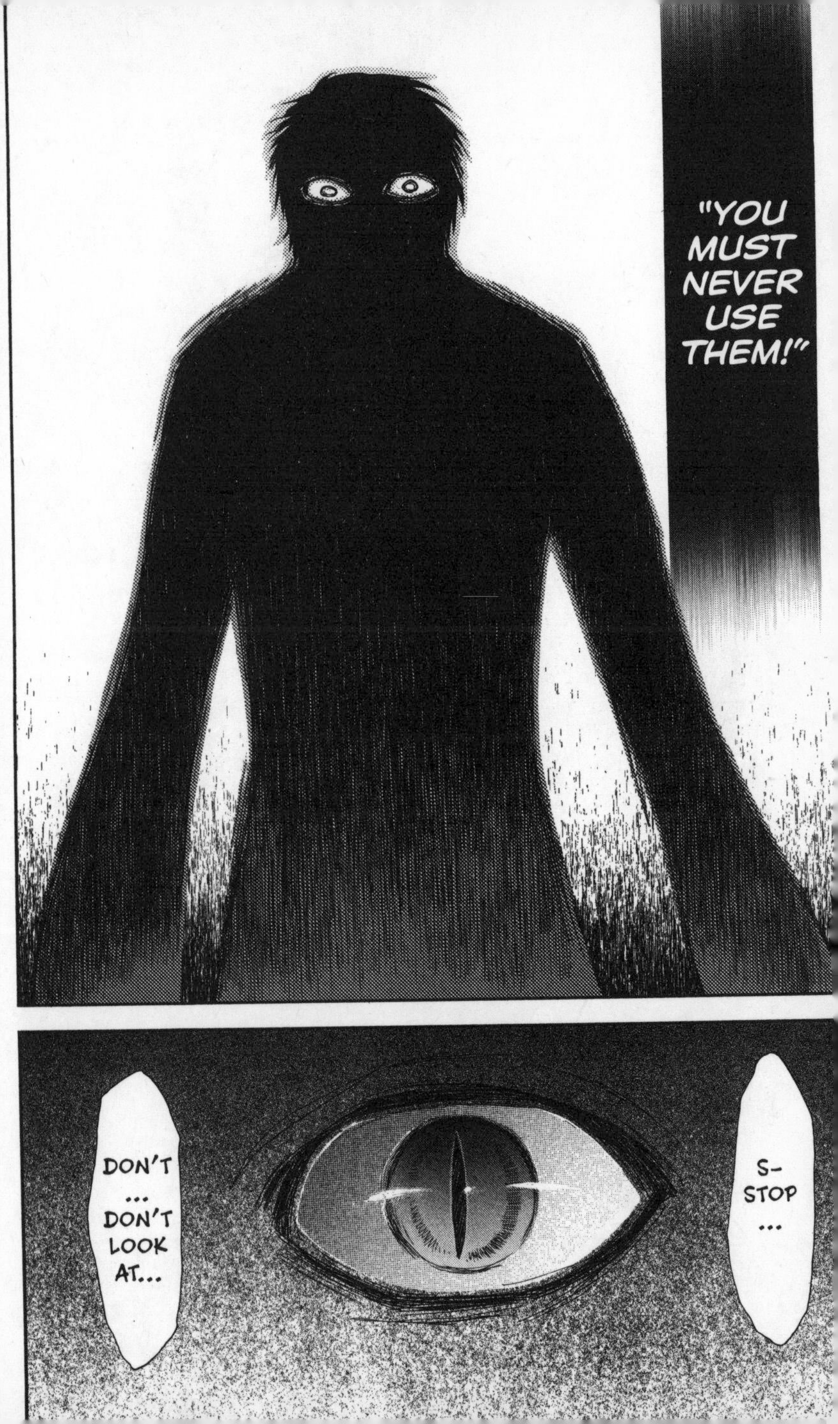
"YOU MUST NEVER USE THEM!"
S-STOP ...
DON'T ... DON'T LOOK AT...

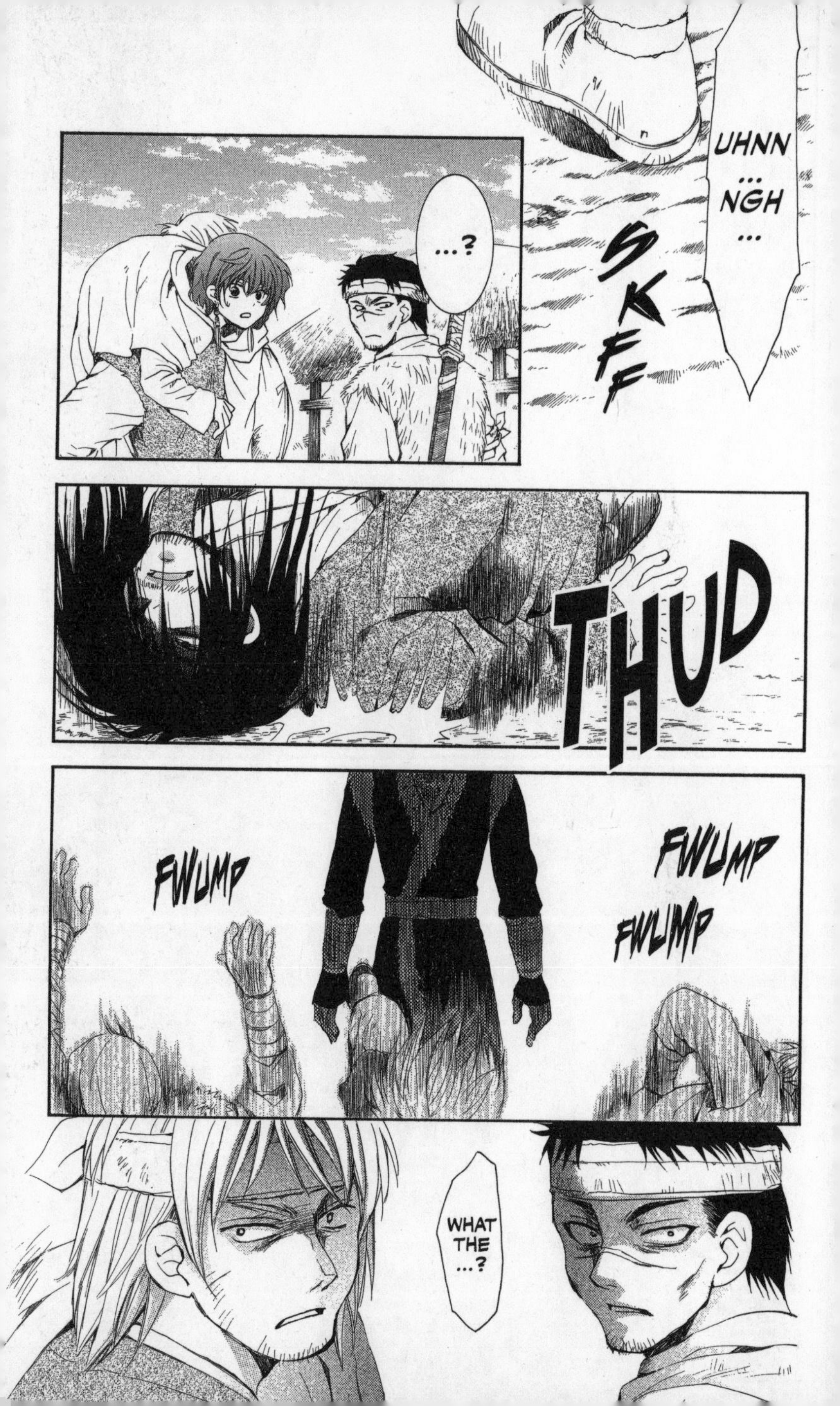
UHNN ... NGH ...
SKFF
...?
THUD
FWUMP
FWUMP
FWUMP
WHAT THE ...?

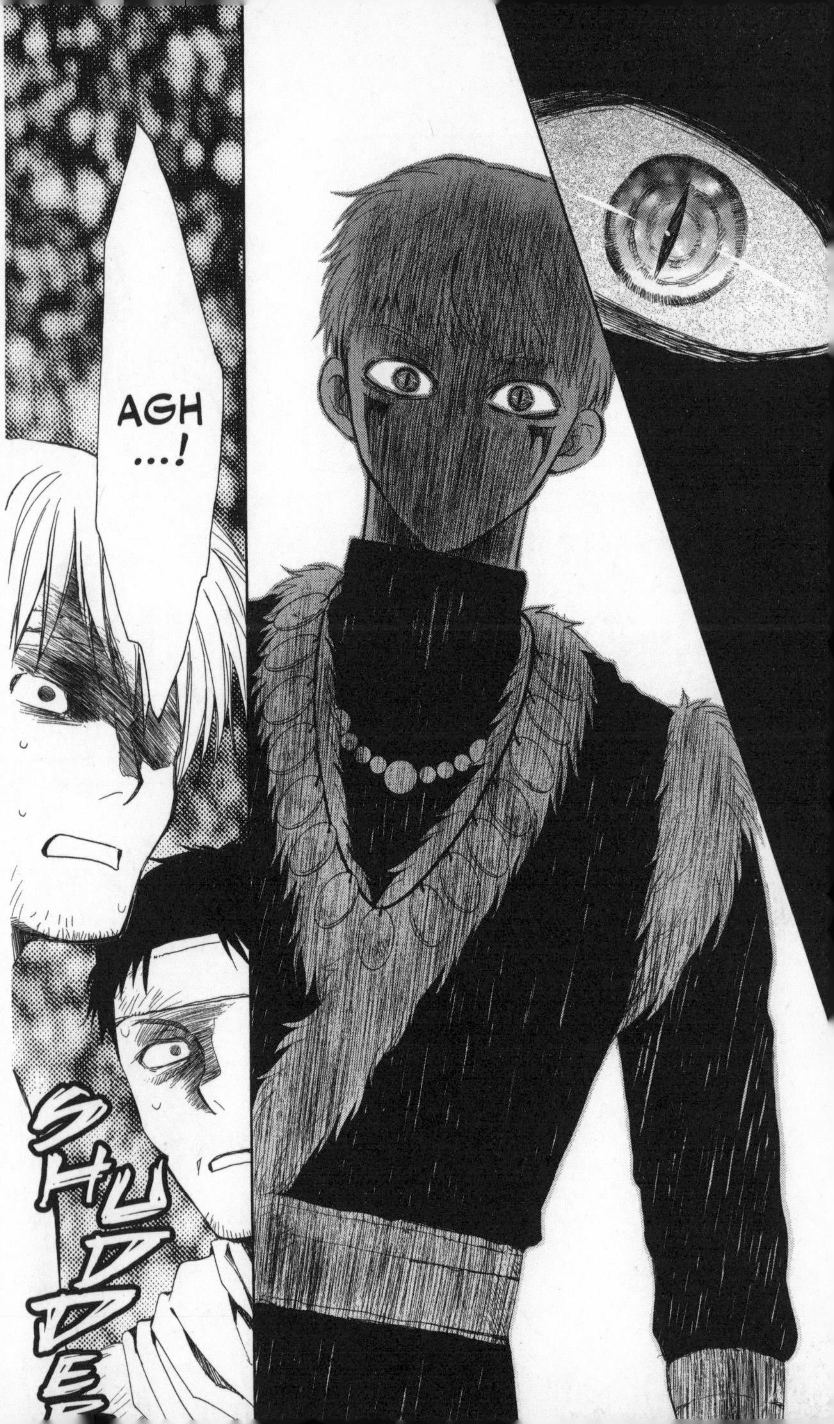
AGH ...!
SHUDDE

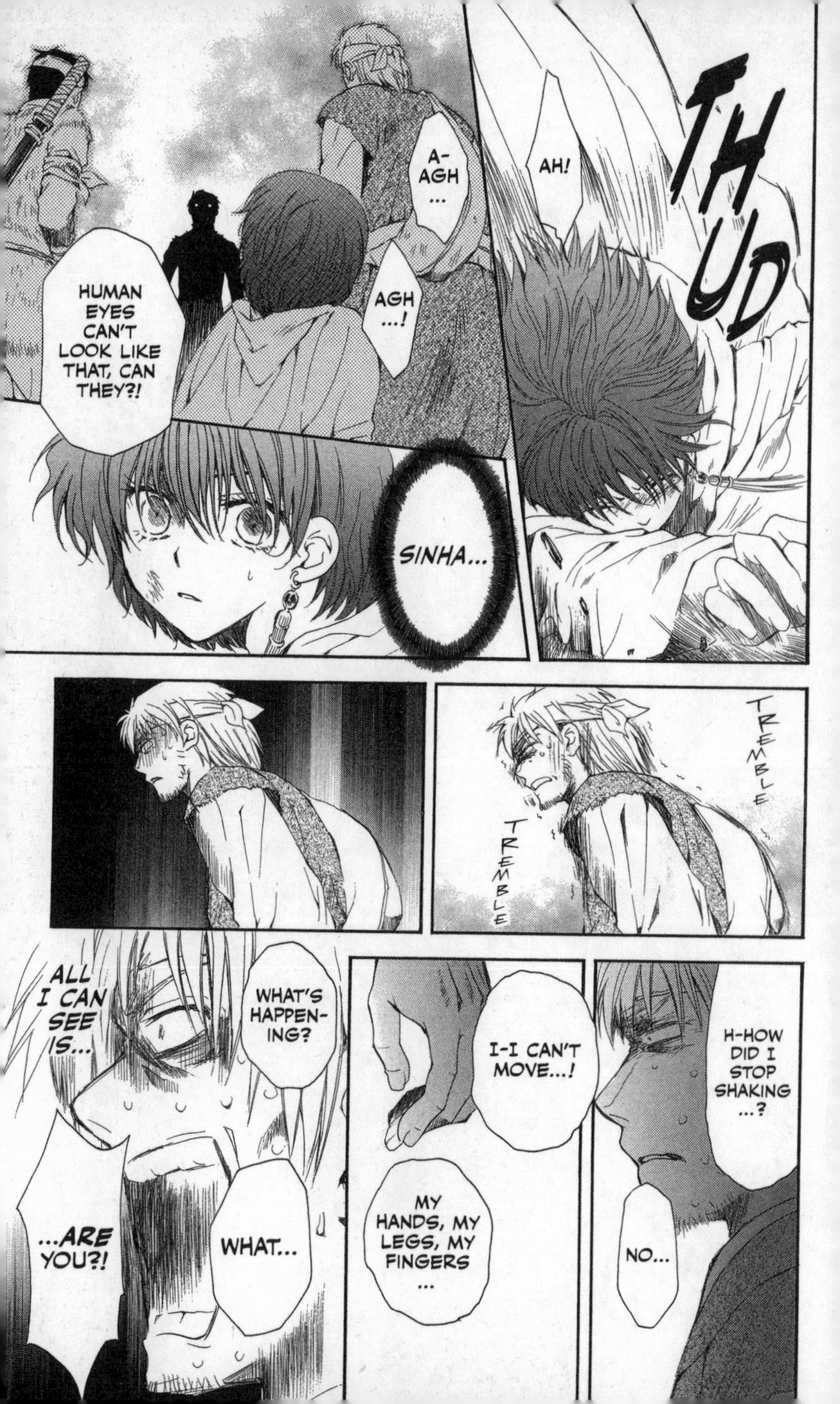

AH!
THUD
A-AGH...
AGH...!
HUMAN EYES CAN'T LOOK LIKE THAT, CAN THEY?!
SINHA...
TREMBLE
TREMBLE
H-HOW DID I STOP SHAKING...?
NO...
I-I CAN'T MOVE...!
MY HANDS, MY LEGS, MY FINGERS...
WHAT'S HAPPENING-ING?
ALL I CAN SEE IS...
WHAT...
...ARE YOU?!

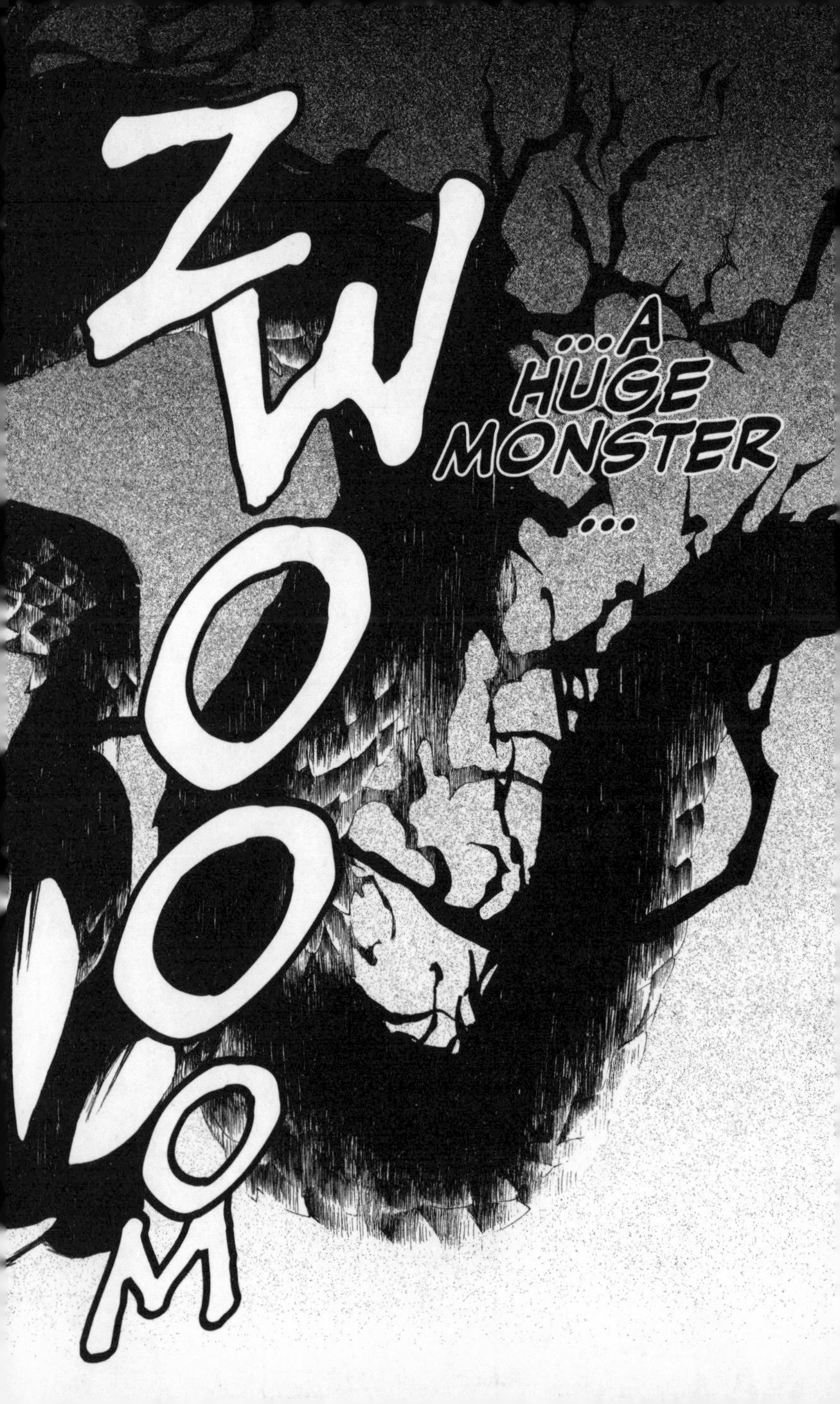
ZWOOOM
...A HUGE MONSTER...

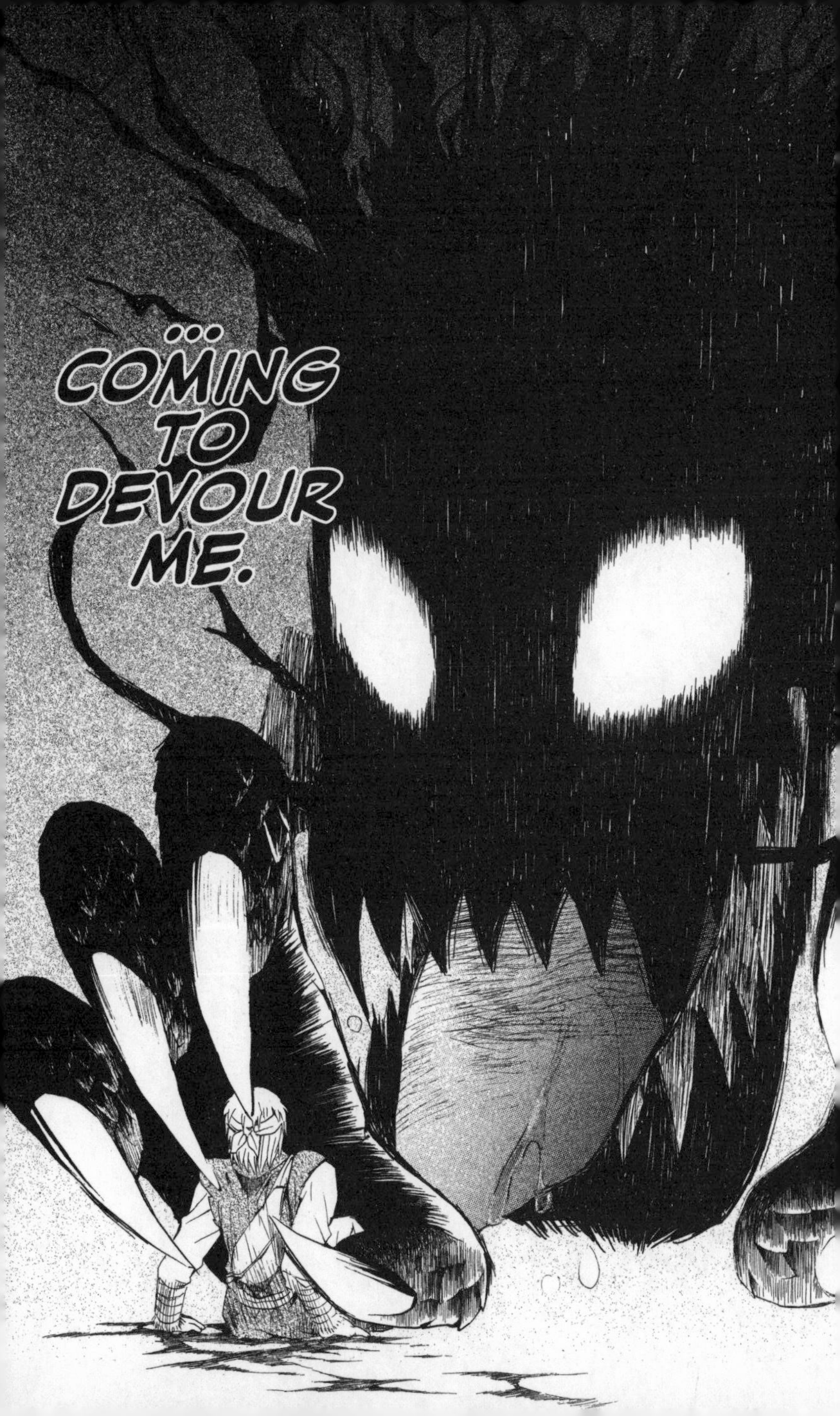
...COMING TO DEVOUR ME.

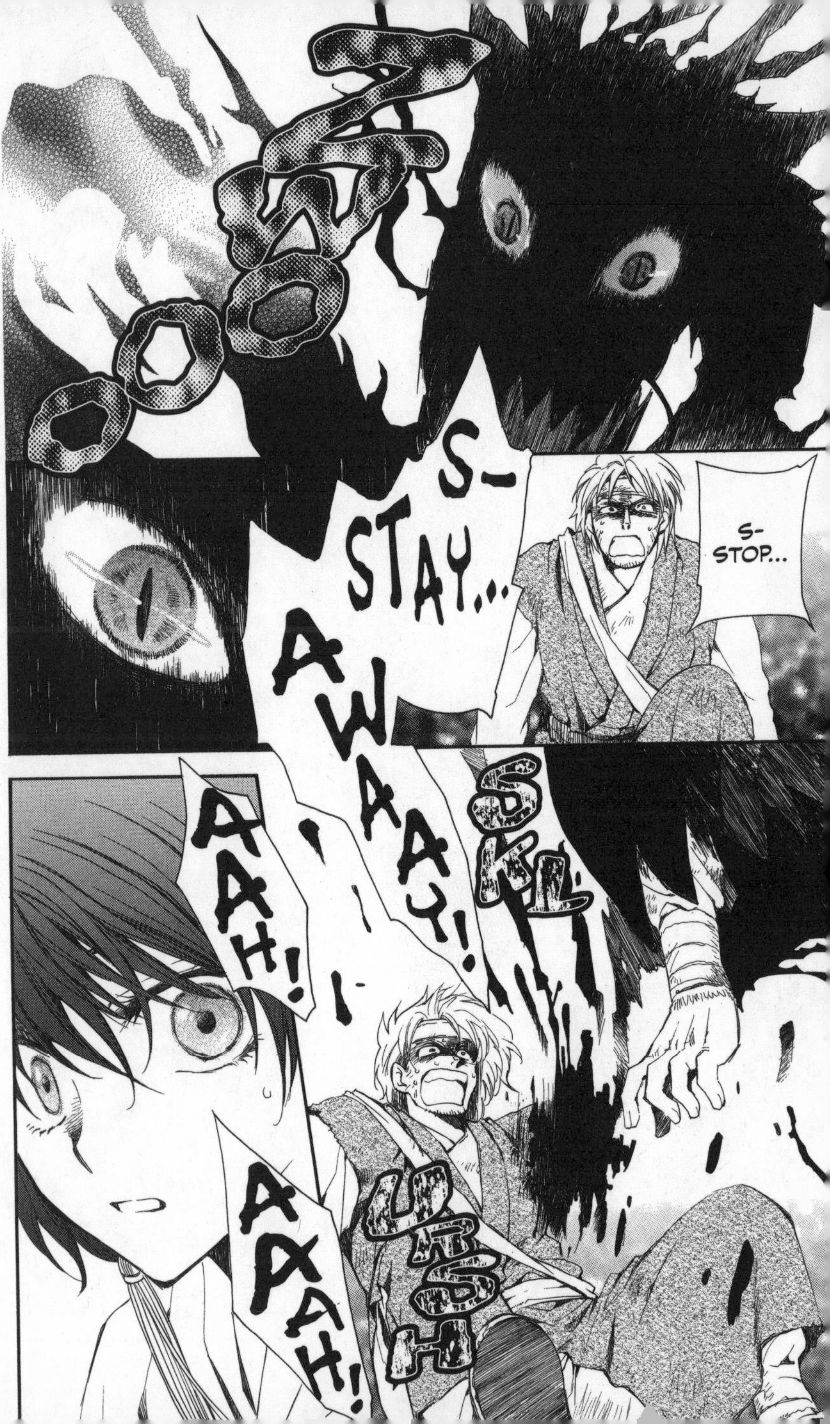
S-
STOP...
S-
STAY...
AWAAAY!
AAH!!
AAAAH!

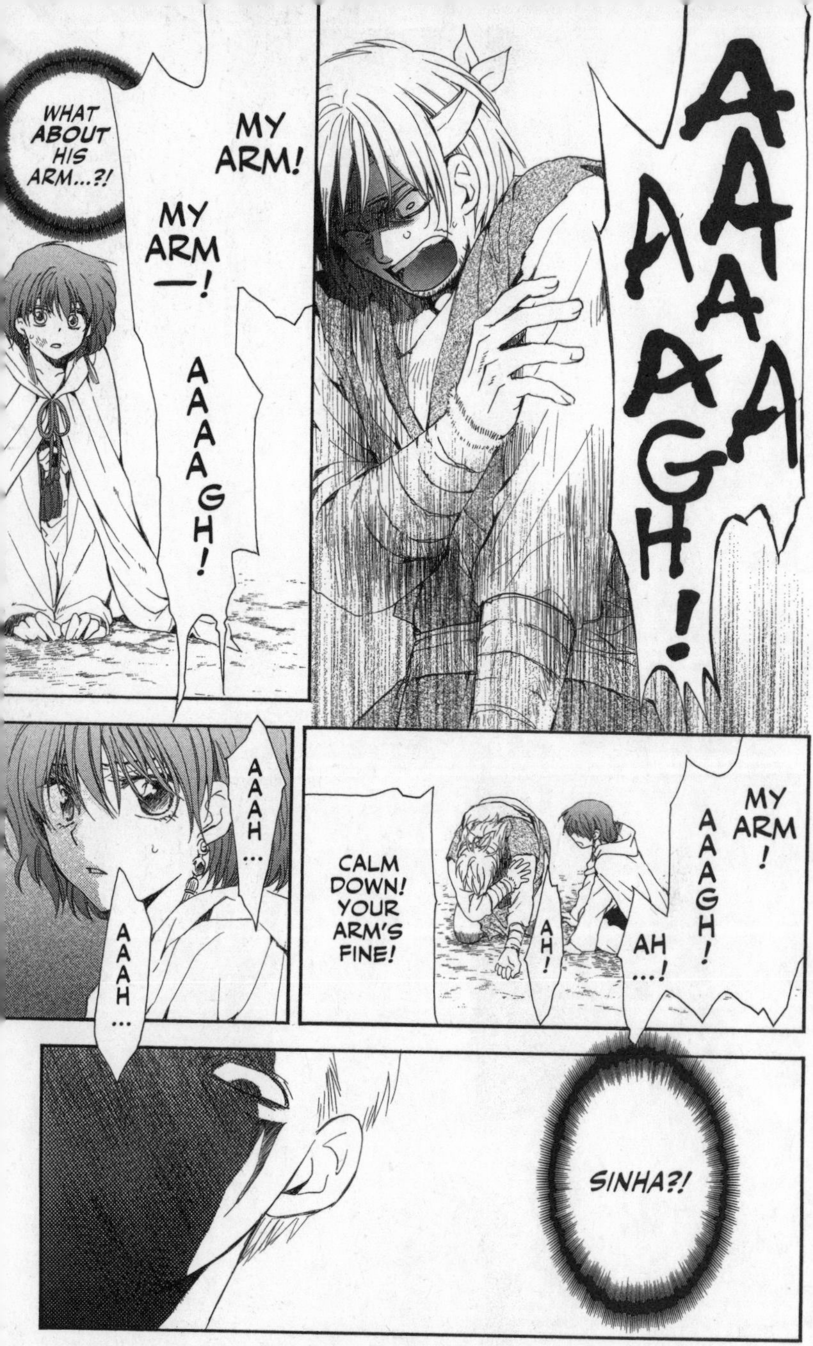
AAAAAAGH!
MY ARM!
MY ARM—!
AAAAGH!
WHAT ABOUT HIS ARM...?!
MY ARM! AAAAGH!
AH ...!
AH!
CALM DOWN! YOUR ARM'S FINE!
AAAH ...
AAAH ...
SINHA?!

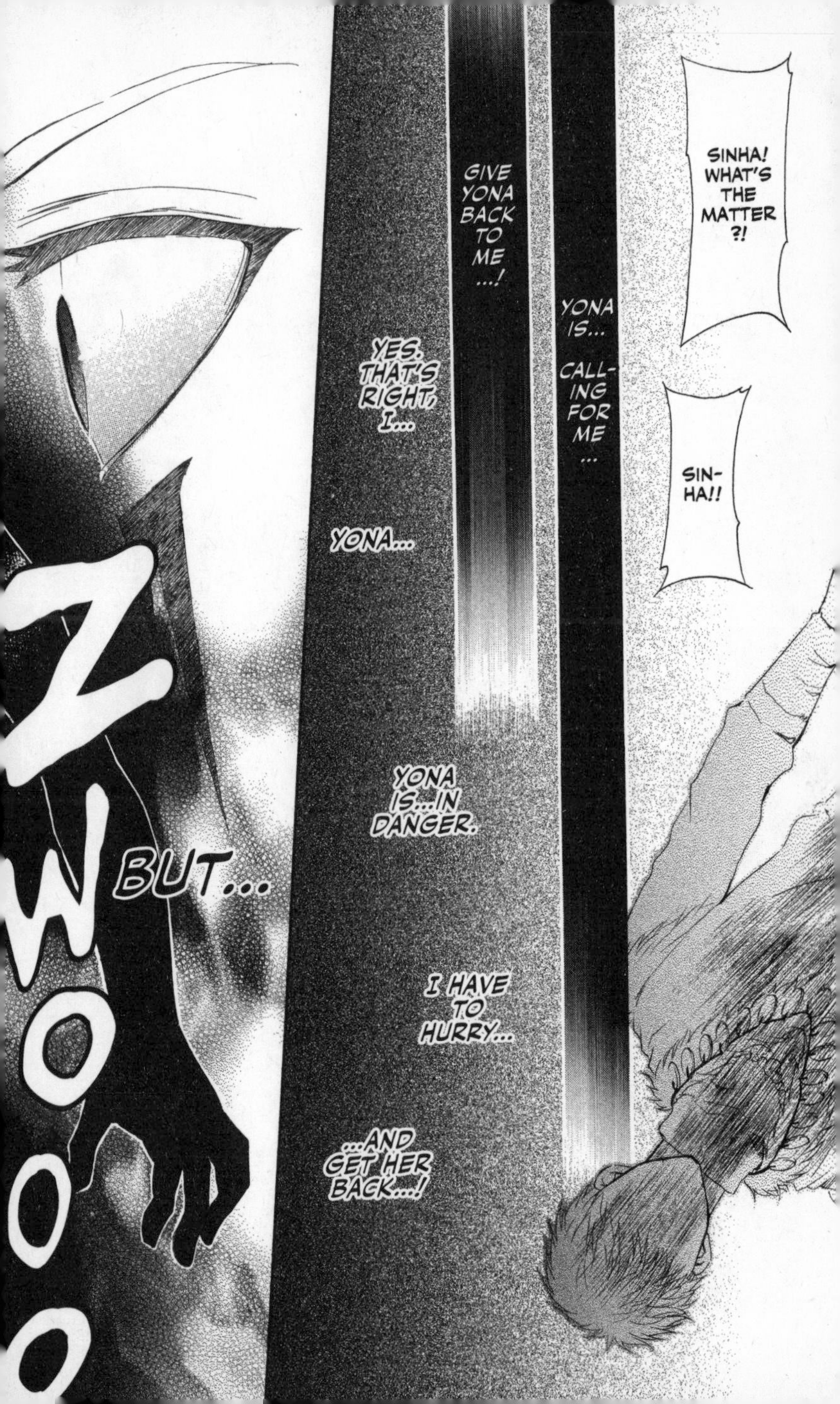
SINHA! WHAT'S THE MATTER?!
SIN-HA!!
YONA IS... CALLING FOR ME...
GIVE YONA BACK TO ME...!
YES. THAT'S RIGHT, I...
YONA...
YONA IS...IN DANGER.
I HAVE TO HURRY...
...AND GET HER BACK...!
BUT...
ZWOOO

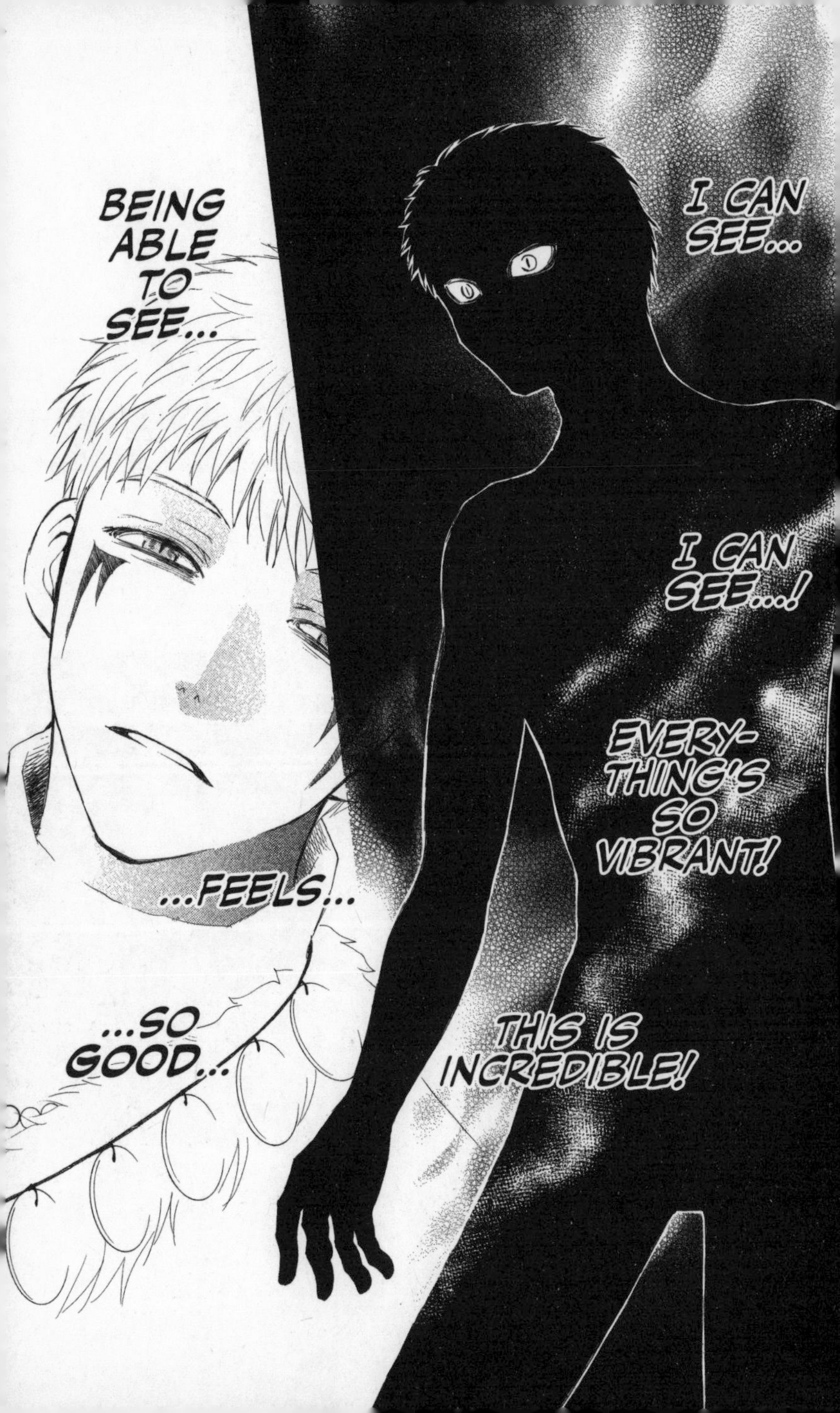
I CAN SEE...
I CAN SEE...!
EVERY-THING'S SO VIBRANT!
THIS IS INCREDIBLE!
BEING ABLE TO SEE...
...FEELS...
...SO GOOD...

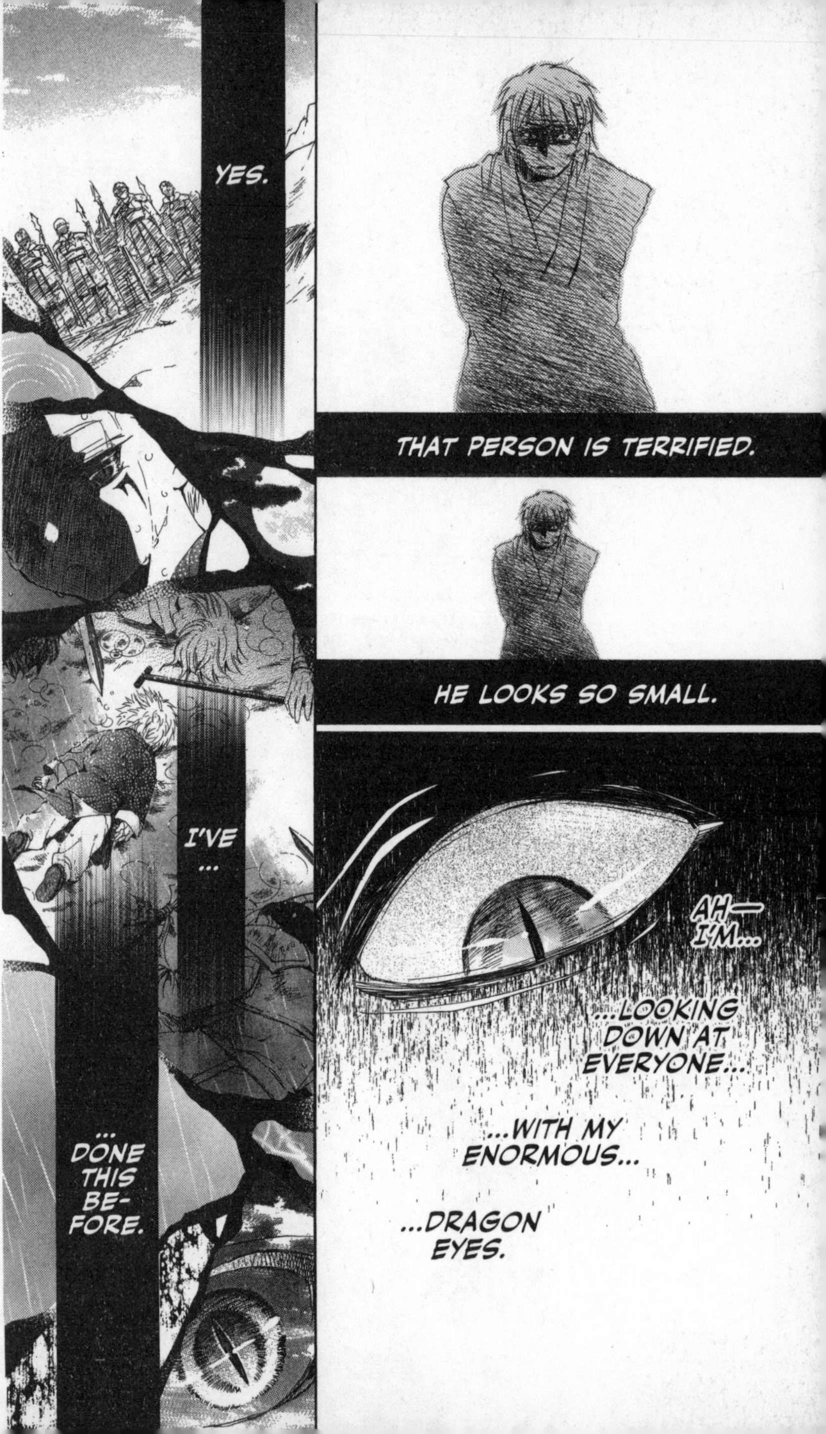

THAT PERSON IS TERRIFIED.
HE LOOKS SO SMALL.
AH— I'M...
...LOOKING DOWN AT EVERYONE...
...WITH MY ENORMOUS...
...DRAGON EYES.
YES.
I'VE ...
... DONE THIS BE- FORE.

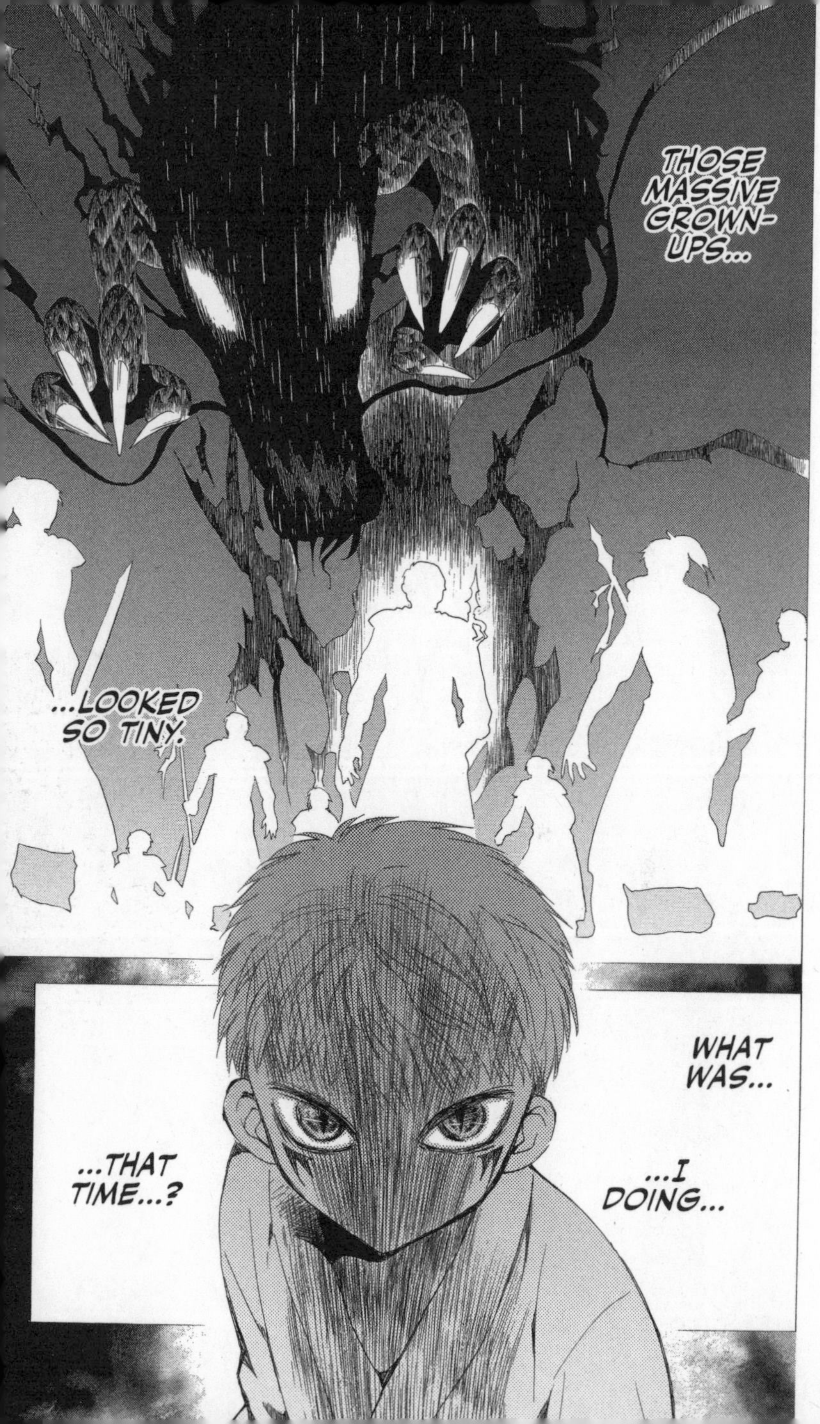
THOSE MASSIVE GROWN-UPS...
...LOOKED SO TINY.
WHAT WAS...
...I DOING...
...THAT TIME...?

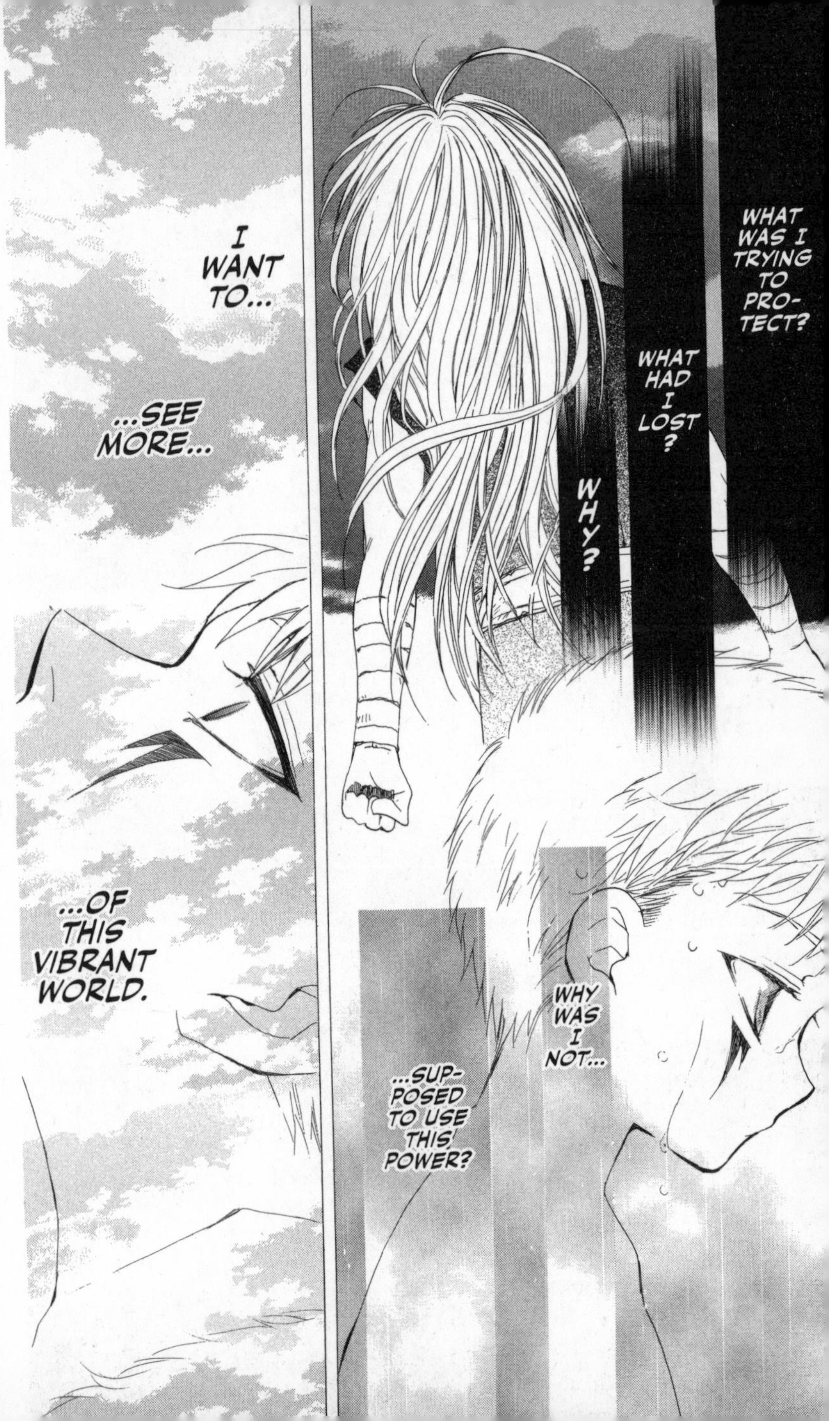
WHAT WAS I TRYING TO PRO-TECT?
WHAT HAD I LOST?
WHY?
WHY WAS I NOT...
...SUP-POSED TO USE THIS POWER?
I WANT TO...
...SEE MORE...
...OF THIS VIBRANT WORLD.

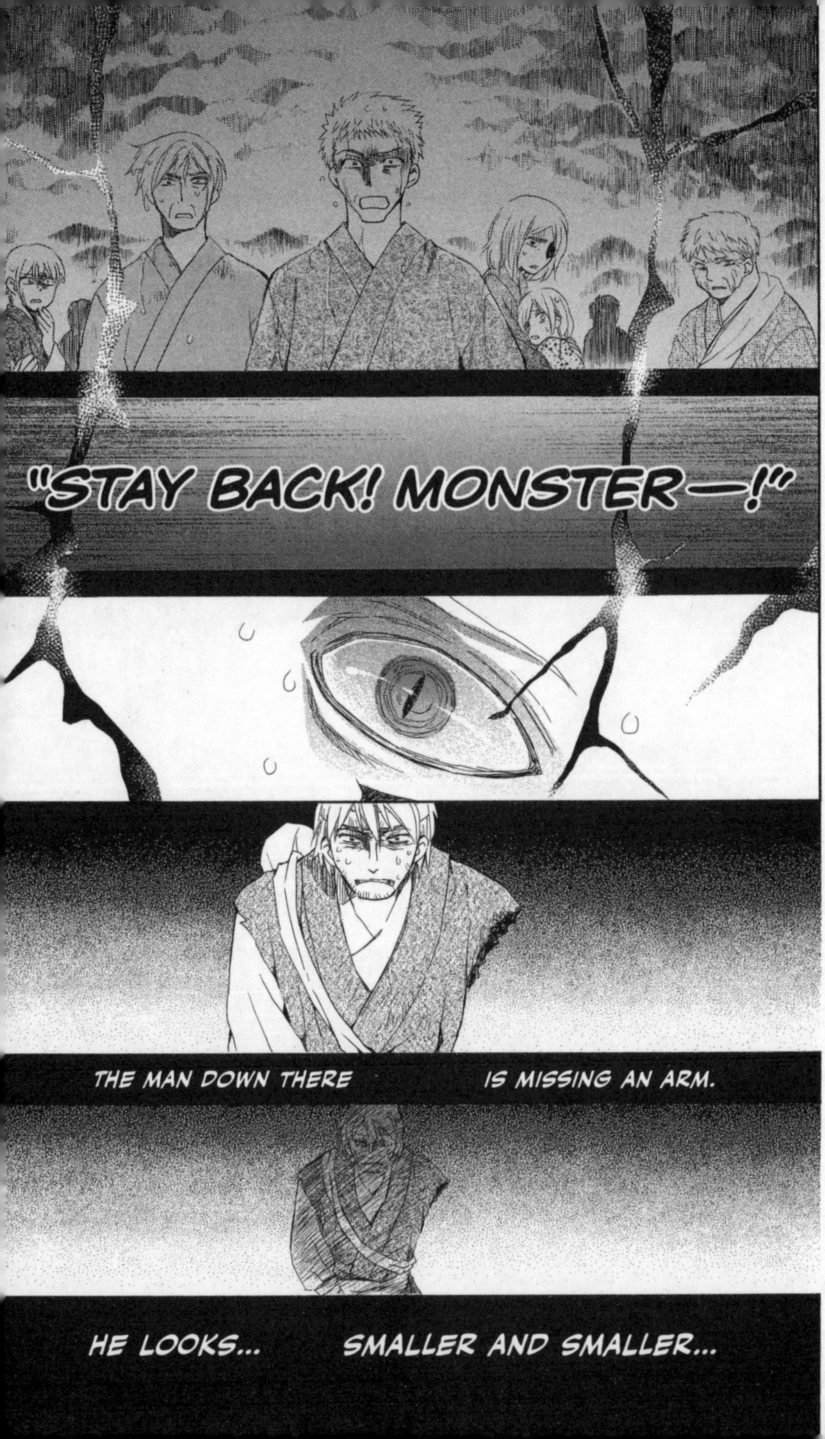
"STAY BACK! MONSTER—!"
IS MISSING AN ARM.
THE MAN DOWN THERE
SMALLER AND SMALLER...
HE LOOKS...

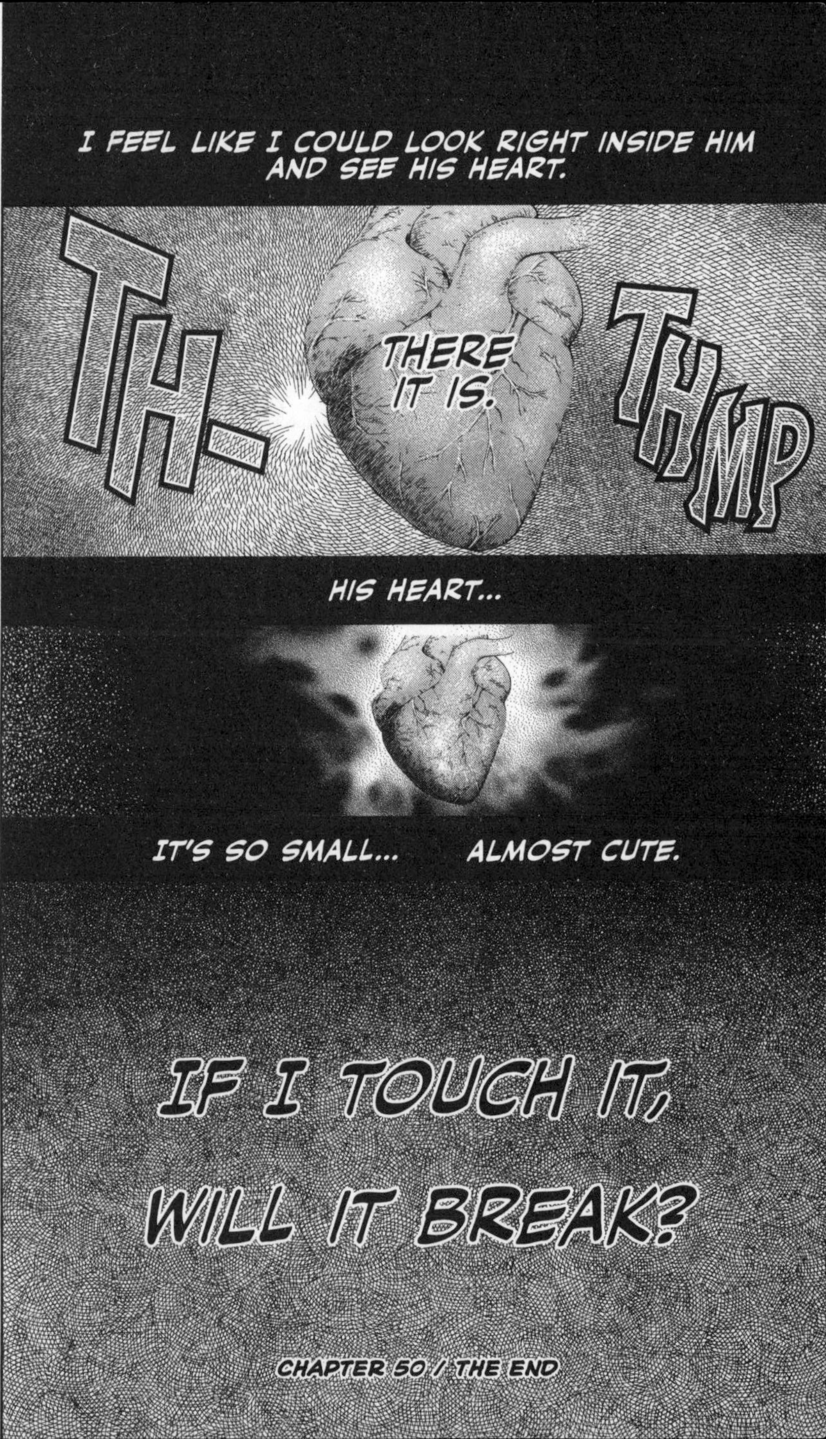

I FEEL LIKE I COULD LOOK RIGHT INSIDE HIM AND SEE HIS HEART.

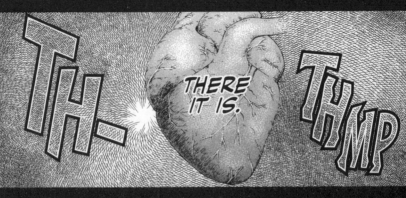

TH-

THERE IT IS.

THMP

HIS HEART...

IT'S SO SMALL... ALMOST CUTE.

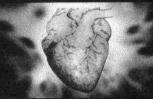

IF I TOUCH IT, WILL IT BREAK?

CHAPTER 50 / THE END

CHAPTER 51: LOSING YOURSELF

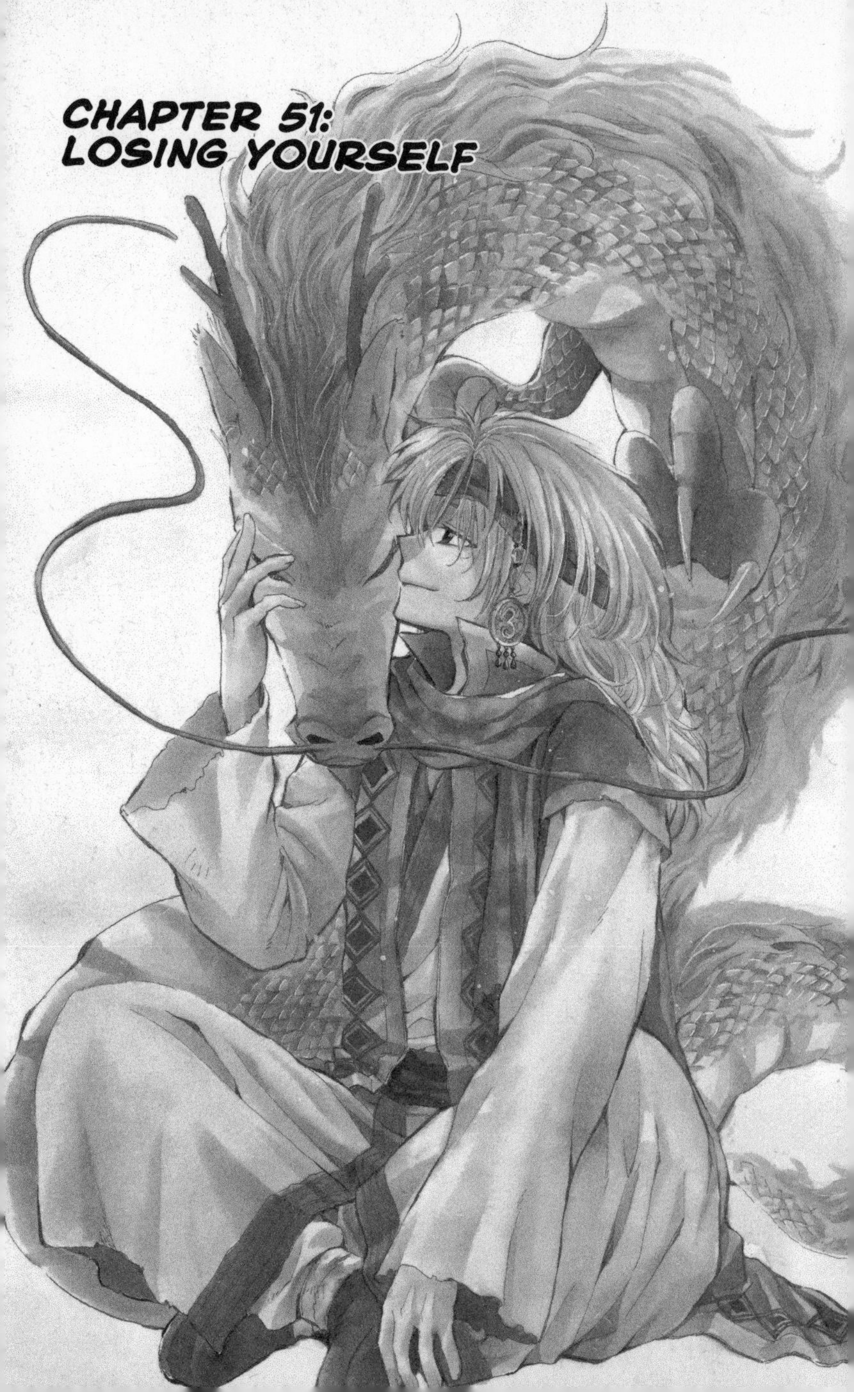

While I was
drawing this,
I didn't realize
Pu-kyu was
floating. →

THERE IT IS.

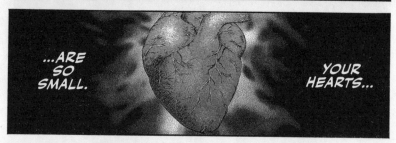

...ARE
SO
SMALL.

YOUR
HEARTS...

...SHOULD
I
CHOOSE?

WHICH
ONE...

Special thanks to all the people who've helped me.

My assistants → Mikorun, Kyoko, Oka, C.F., Ryo and my little sister...

My editor Yamashita, the Hana to Yume editorial office...

Everyone who has helped me create and sell this manga...

Family, friends and readers who've supported me...!

I'm truly grateful that you've all supported Yona!

I'll keep dedicating myself to working on this manga every day.

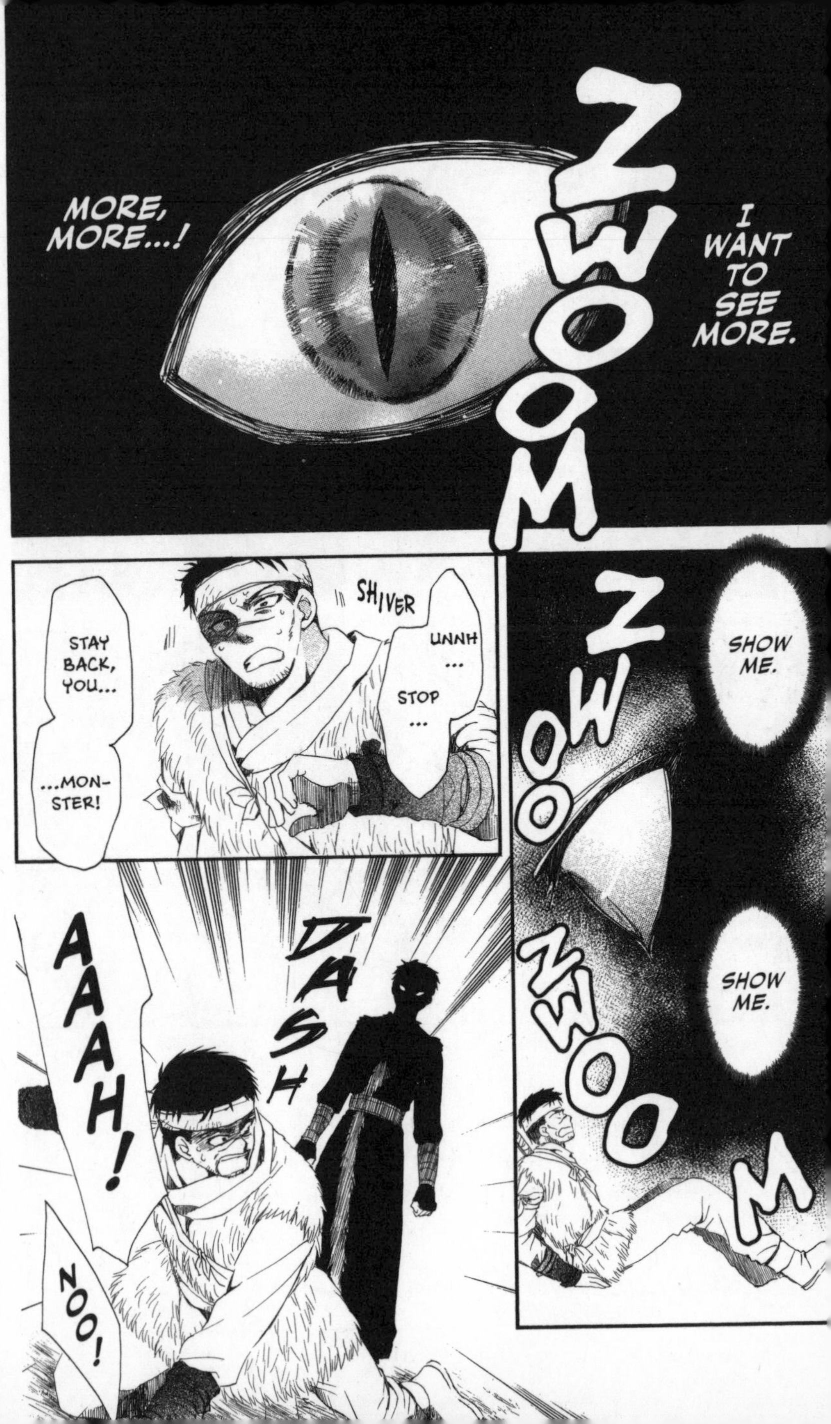
I WANT TO SEE MORE.
ZWOOOM
MORE, MORE...!
SHOW ME.
ZWOOOOM
SHOW ME.
SHIVER
UNNH ... STOP ...
STAY BACK, YOU...
...MON-STER!
DASH
AAAH!
NOO!

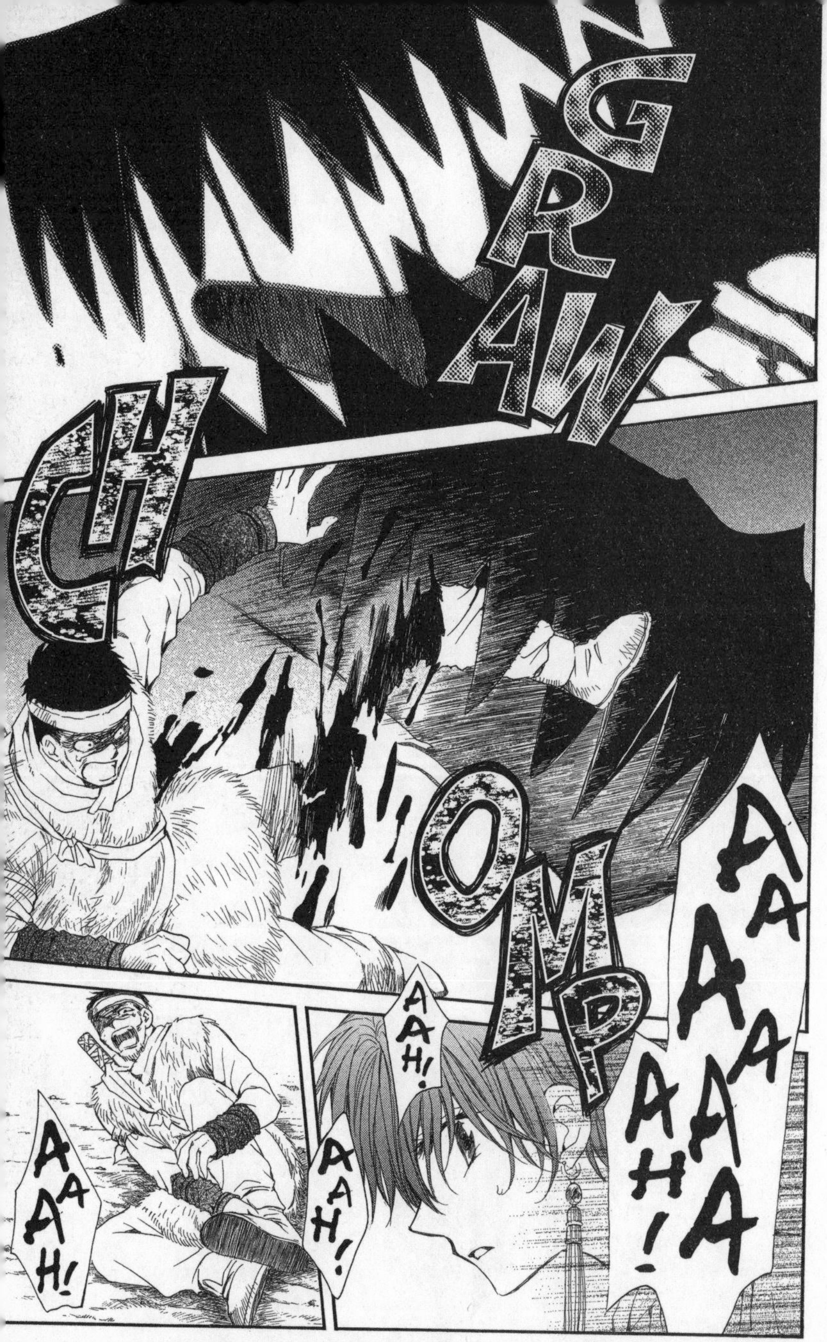
GRAW
CHOMP
AAAAAAAAAH!
AAH!
AAH!
AAAH!

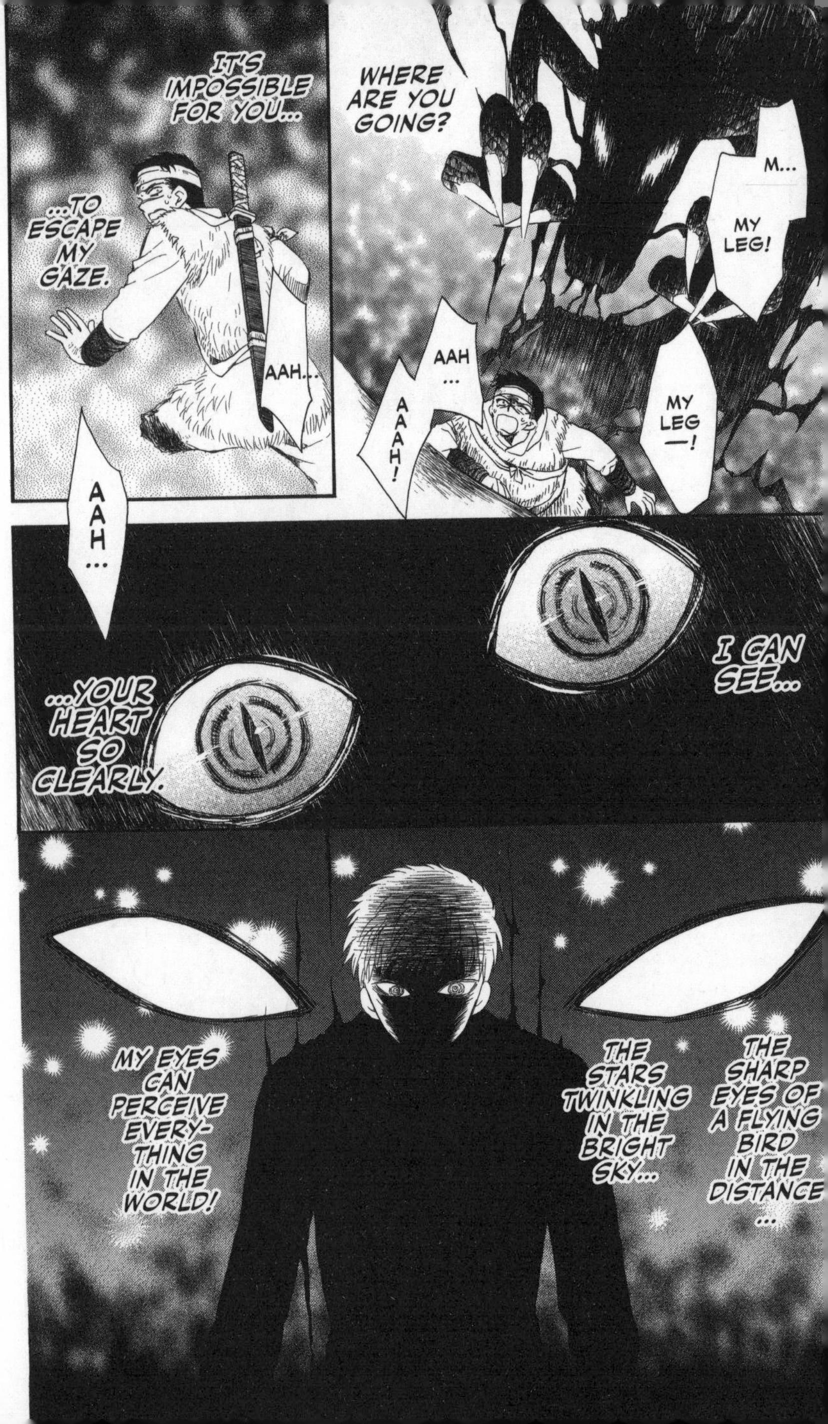
M...
MY LEG!
WHERE ARE YOU GOING?
MY LEG—!
AAH...
AAAAH!
IT'S IMPOSSIBLE FOR YOU...
...TO ESCAPE MY GAZE.
AAH...
AAH...
I CAN SEE...
...YOUR HEART SO CLEARLY.
THE SHARP EYES OF A FLYING BIRD IN THE DISTANCE...
THE STARS TWINKLING IN THE BRIGHT SKY...
MY EYES CAN PERCEIVE EVERY-THING IN THE WORLD!

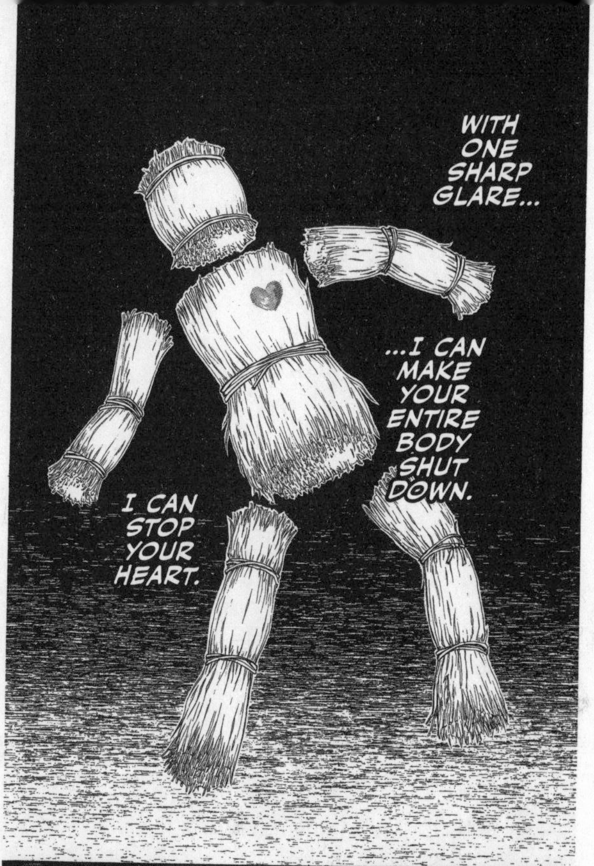

WITH ONE SHARP GLARE...
...I CAN MAKE YOUR ENTIRE BODY SHUT DOWN.
I CAN STOP YOUR HEART.

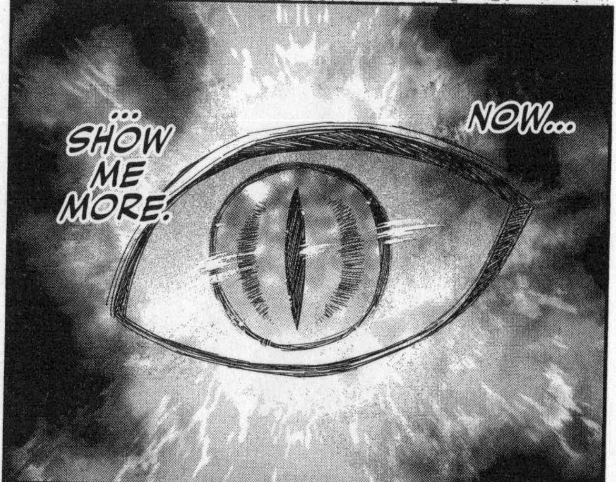

NOW...
...SHOW ME MORE.

I'm sure that those of you who bought the manga edition that included the CD already know that the CD is based on "A Name Is Given," chapter 25 of volume 5. The CD really is a limited item, so any of you who bought the regular version but want to know what's on the CD, please make sure to pick it up soon! I even illustrated the jacket cover!

Also, the packet that comes with the August 8, 2012, issue of *Hana to Yume* will include the second Yona CD! You can get a drama CD that has approximately 60 minutes of wonderful voices for a reasonable price! Please get it! I strongly suggest that you do.

For details, check out my blog or the *Hana to Yume* blog.

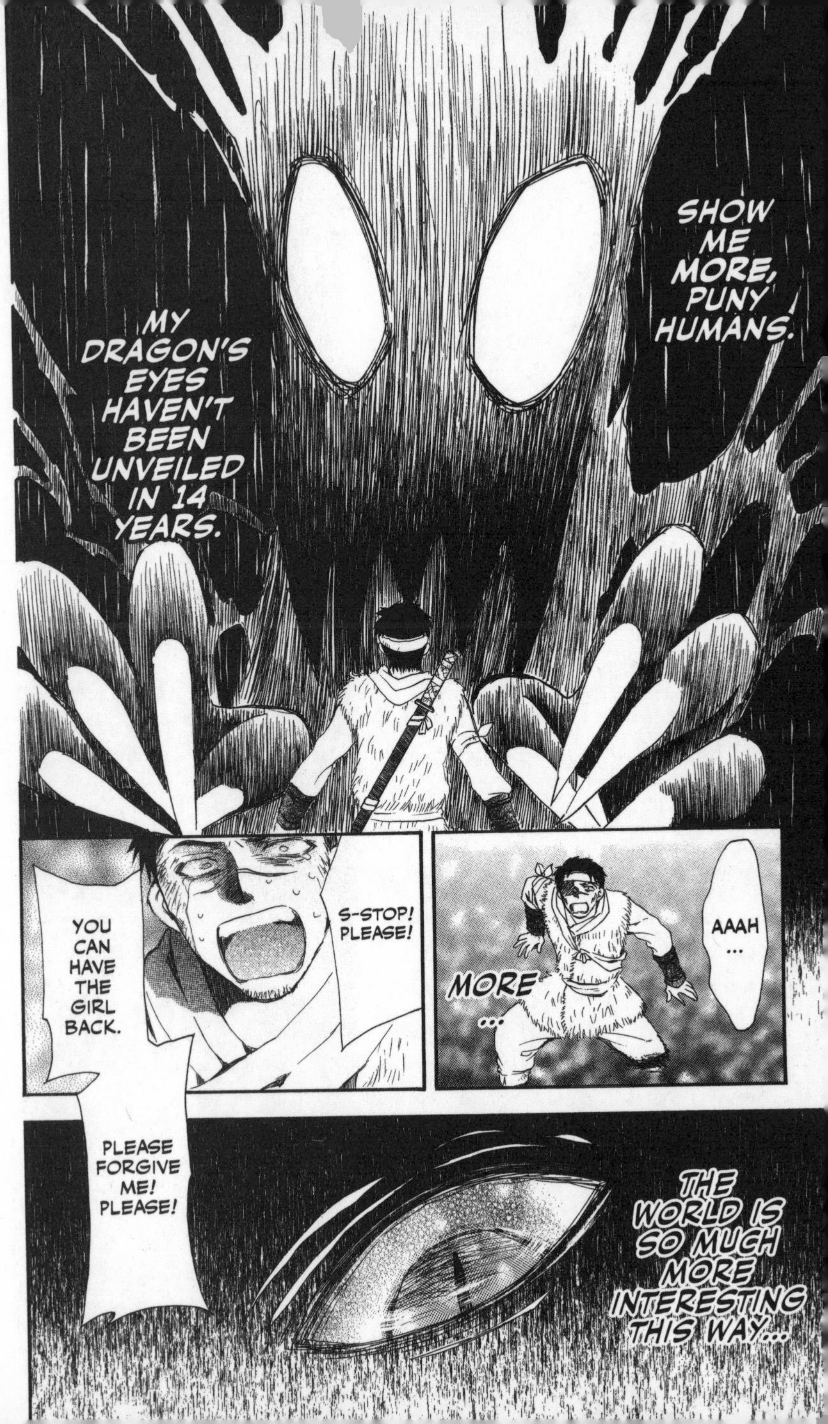
SHOW ME MORE, PUNY HUMANS.
MY DRAGON'S EYES HAVEN'T BEEN UNVEILED IN 14 YEARS.
AAAH ...
MORE ...
S-STOP! PLEASE!
YOU CAN HAVE THE GIRL BACK.
THE WORLD IS SO MUCH MORE INTERESTING THIS WAY...
PLEASE FORGIVE ME! PLEASE!

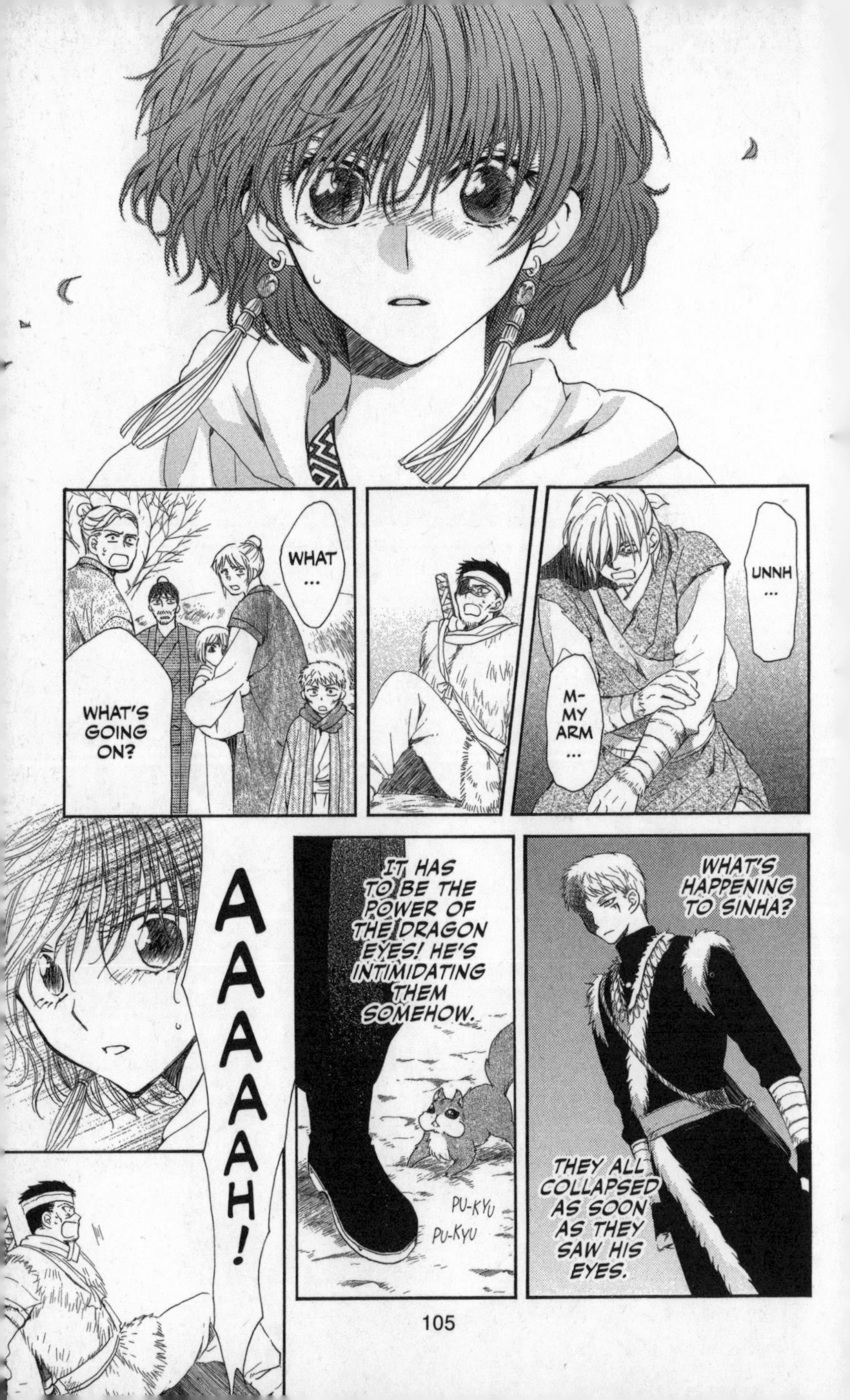
UNNH ...
M- MY ARM ...
WHAT ...
WHAT'S GOING ON?
WHAT'S HAPPENING TO SINHA?
THEY ALL COLLAPSED AS SOON AS THEY SAW HIS EYES.
IT HAS TO BE THE POWER OF THE DRAGON EYES! HE'S INTIMIDATING THEM SOMEHOW.
PU-KYU
PU-KYU
AAAAAH!

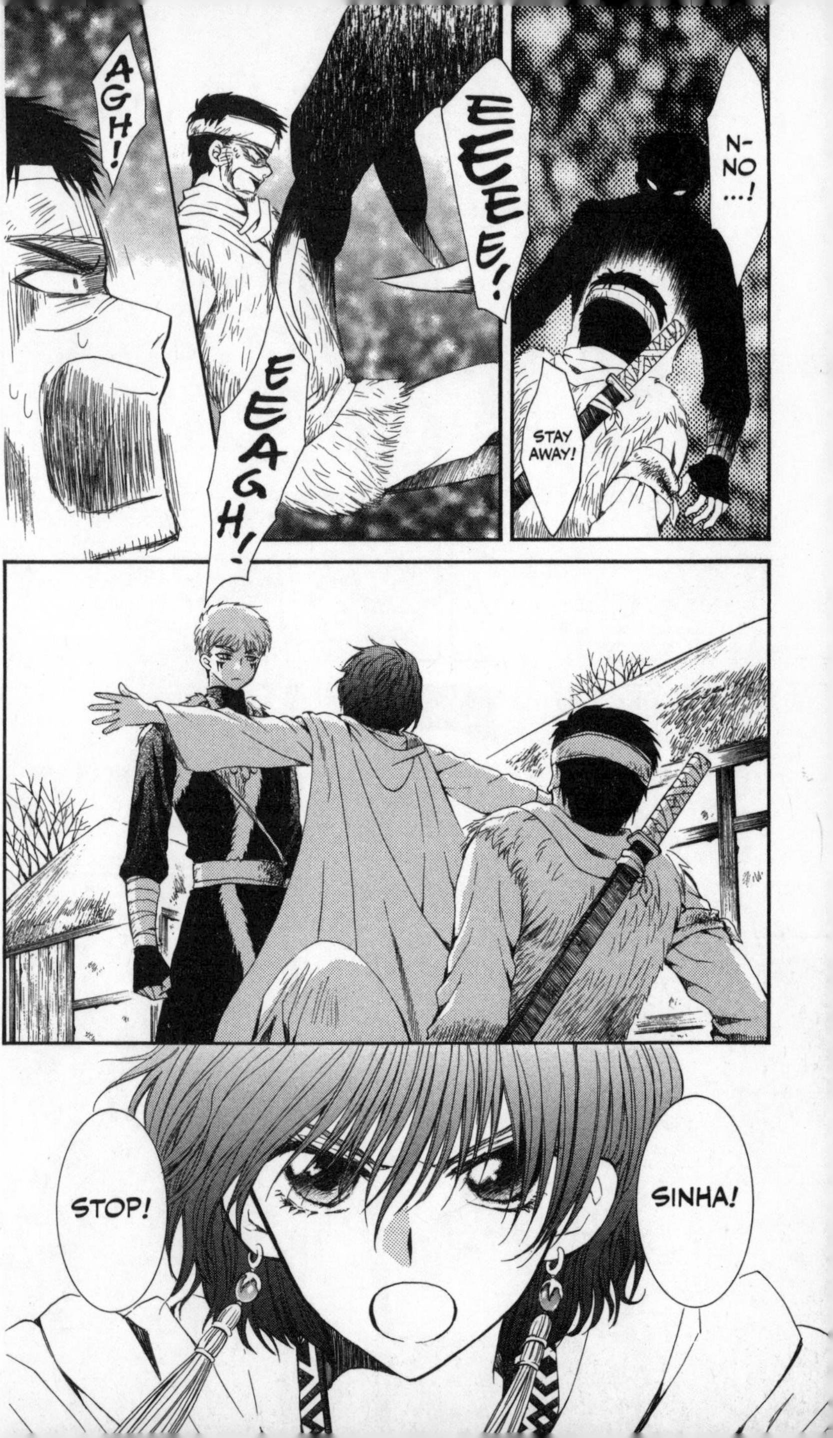

N-NO...!
STAY AWAY!
EEEEE!
AGH!
EEAGH!
SINHA!
STOP!

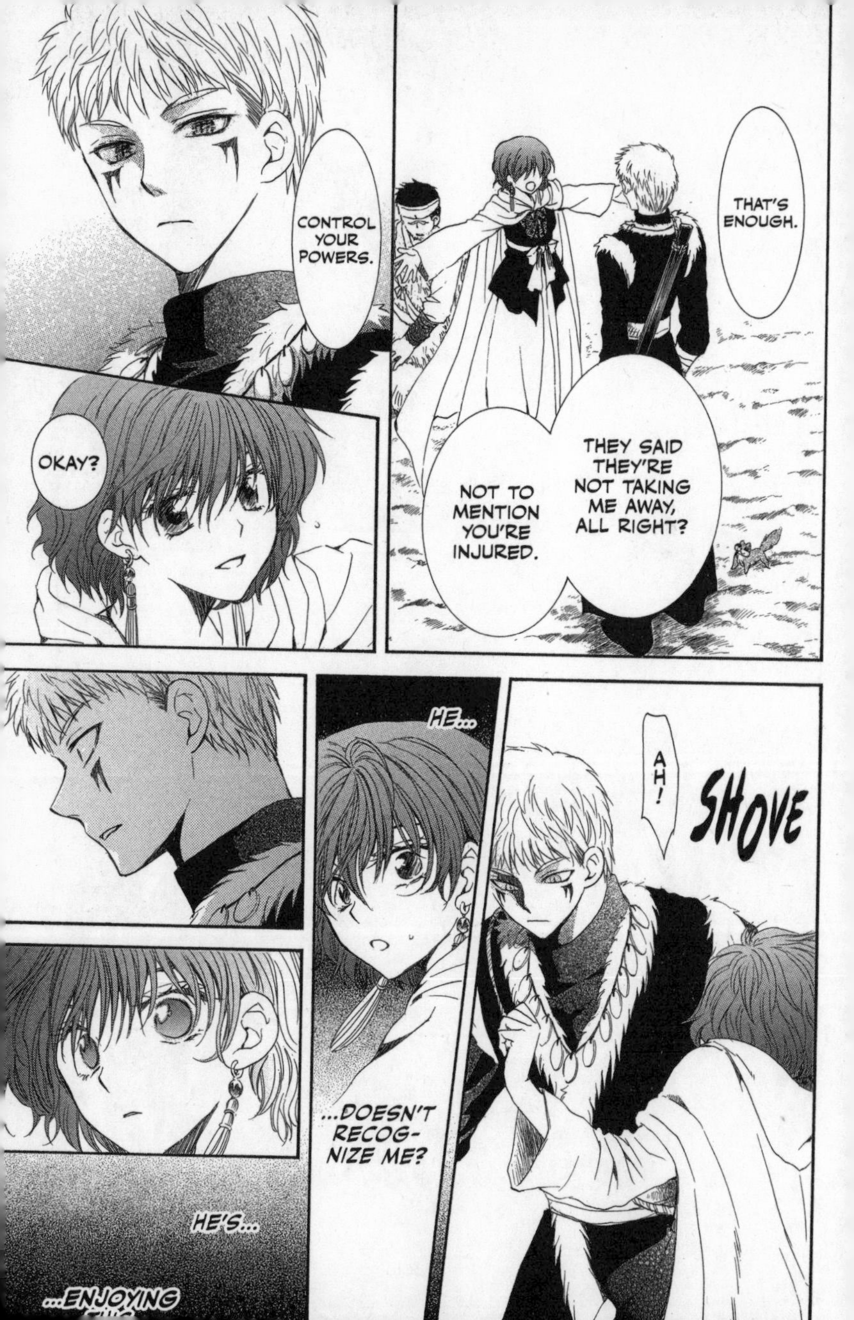
THAT'S ENOUGH.
THEY SAID THEY'RE NOT TAKING ME AWAY, ALL RIGHT?
NOT TO MENTION YOU'RE INJURED.
CONTROL YOUR POWERS.
OKAY?
AH!
SHOVE
HE...
...DOESN'T RECOG-NIZE ME?
HE'S...
...ENJOYING

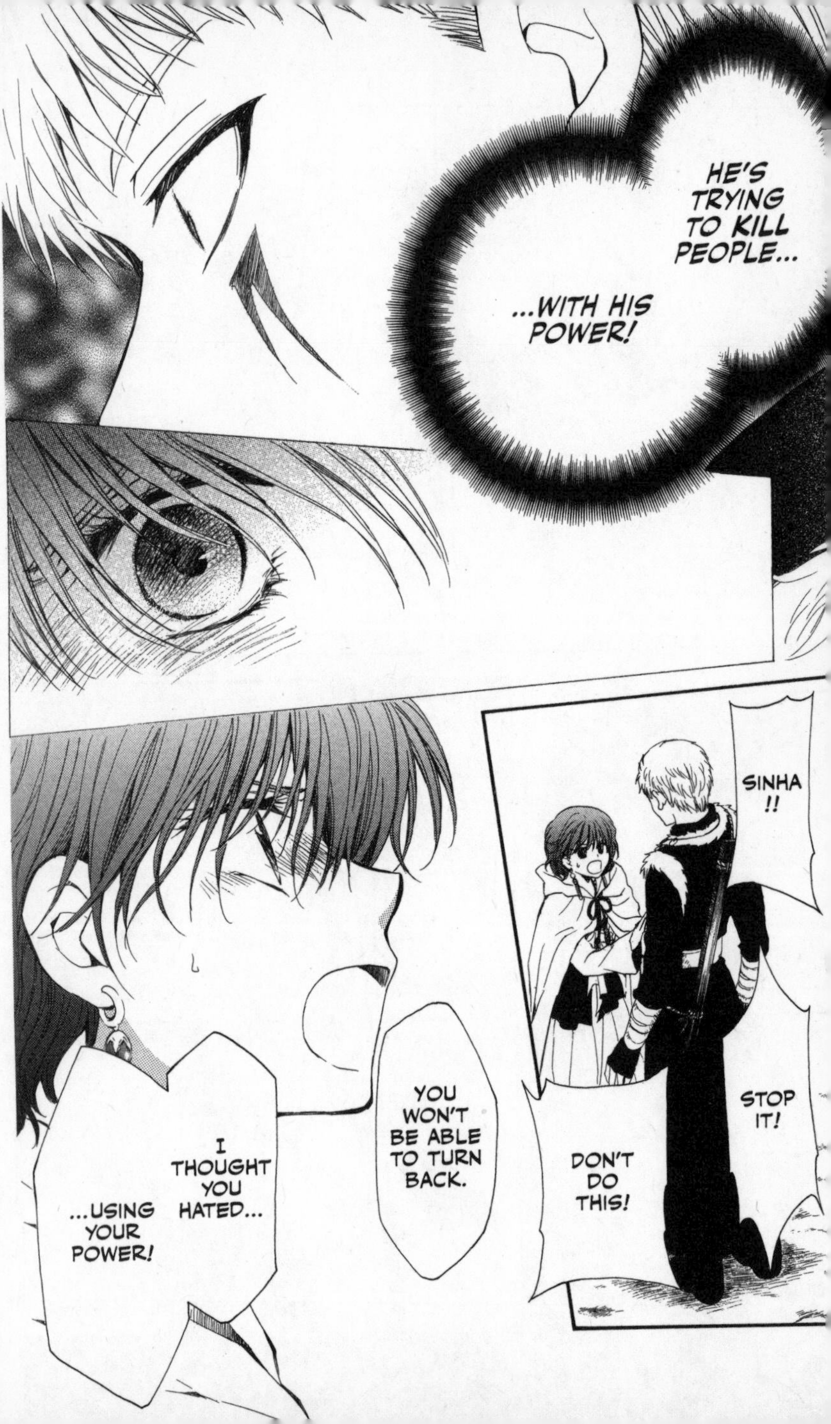
HE'S TRYING TO KILL PEOPLE...
...WITH HIS POWER!
SINHA !!
STOP IT!
DON'T DO THIS!
YOU WON'T BE ABLE TO TURN BACK.
I THOUGHT YOU HATED...
...USING YOUR POWER!

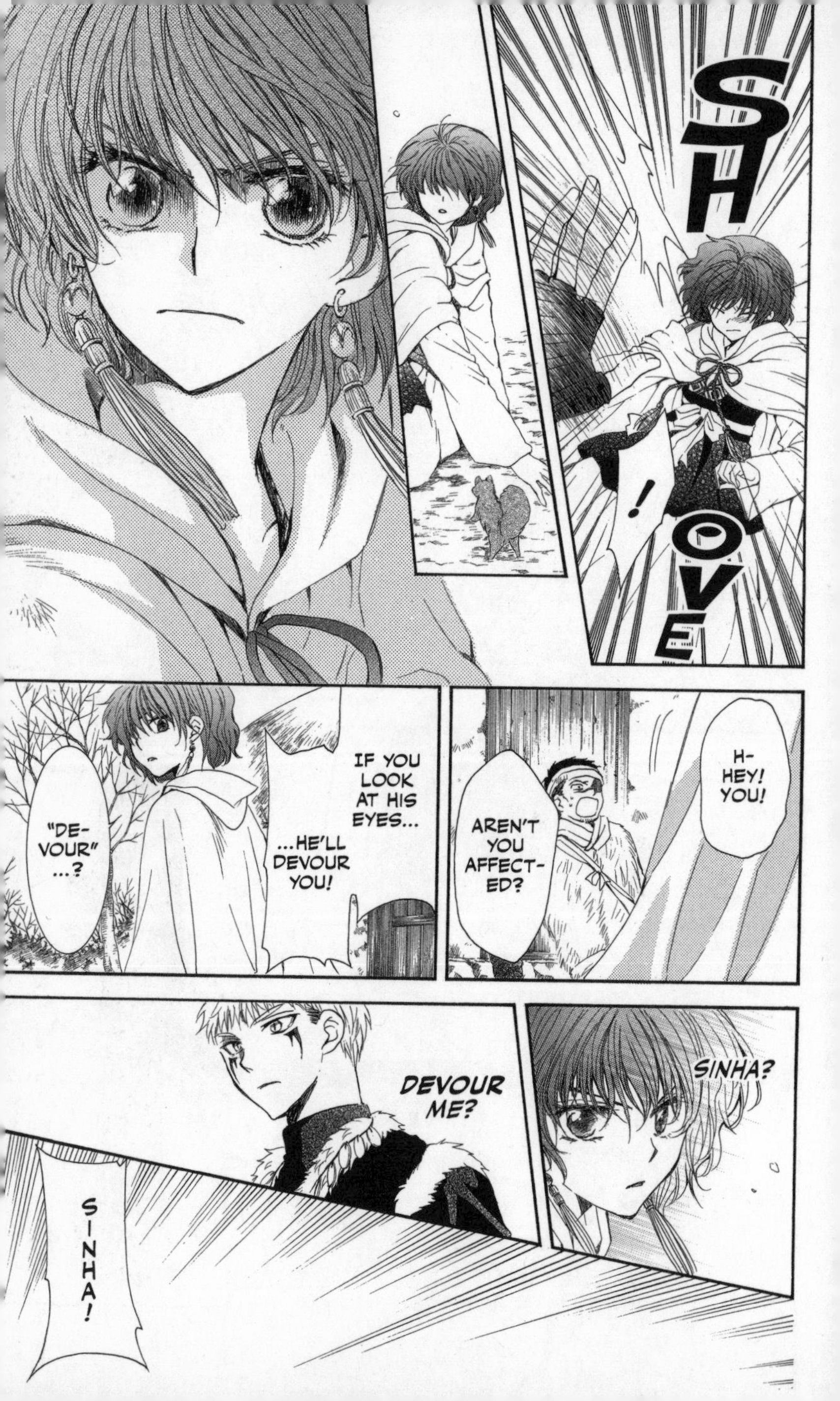
SHOVE
!
H-HEY! YOU!
AREN'T YOU AFFECTED?
IF YOU LOOK AT HIS EYES...
...HE'LL DEVOUR YOU!
"DE-VOUR"...?
SINHA?
DEVOUR ME?
SINHA!

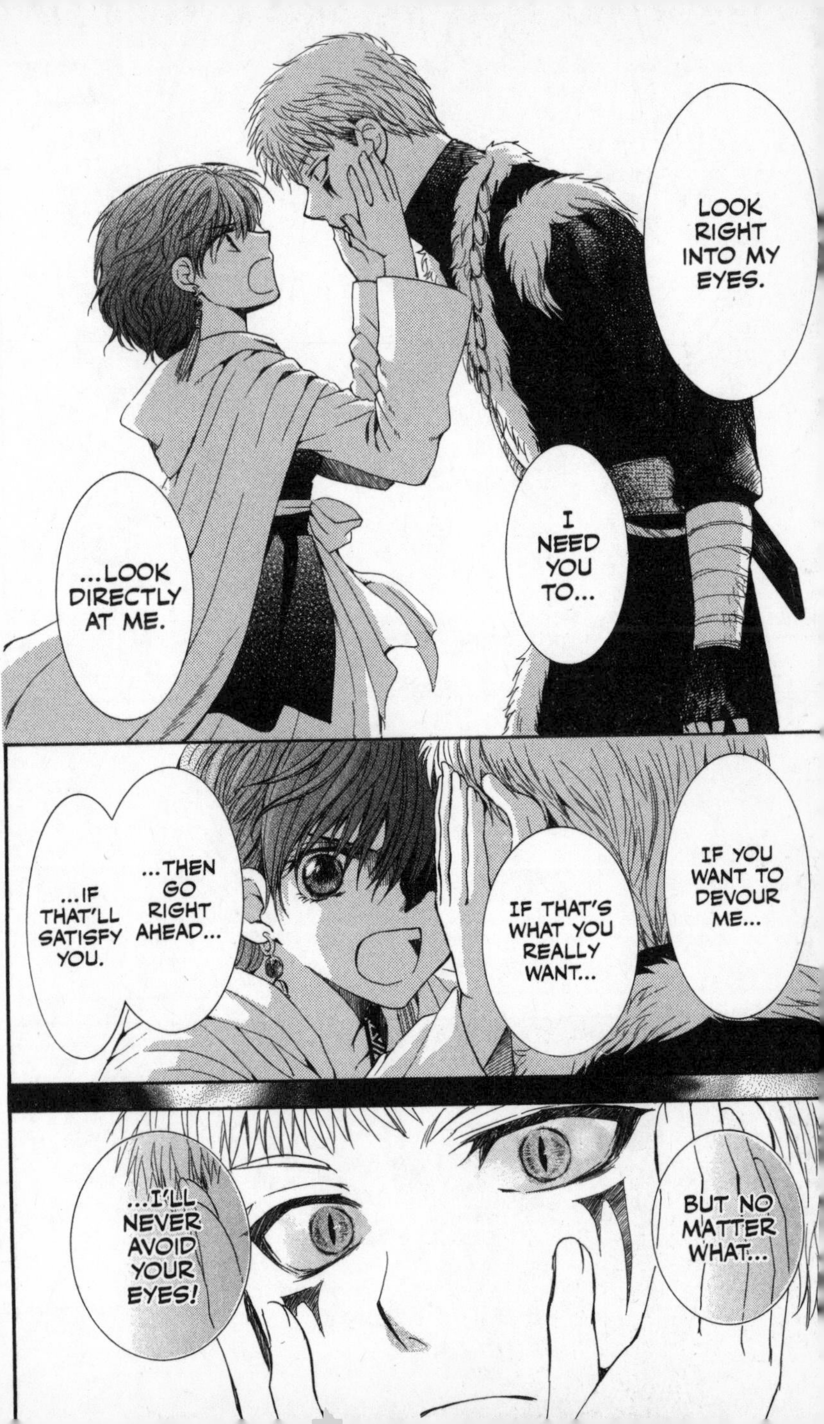
LOOK RIGHT INTO MY EYES.
I NEED YOU TO...
...LOOK DIRECTLY AT ME.
IF YOU WANT TO DEVOUR ME...
IF THAT'S WHAT YOU REALLY WANT...
...THEN GO RIGHT AHEAD...
...IF THAT'LL SATISFY YOU.
BUT NO MATTER WHAT...
...I'LL NEVER AVOID YOUR EYES!

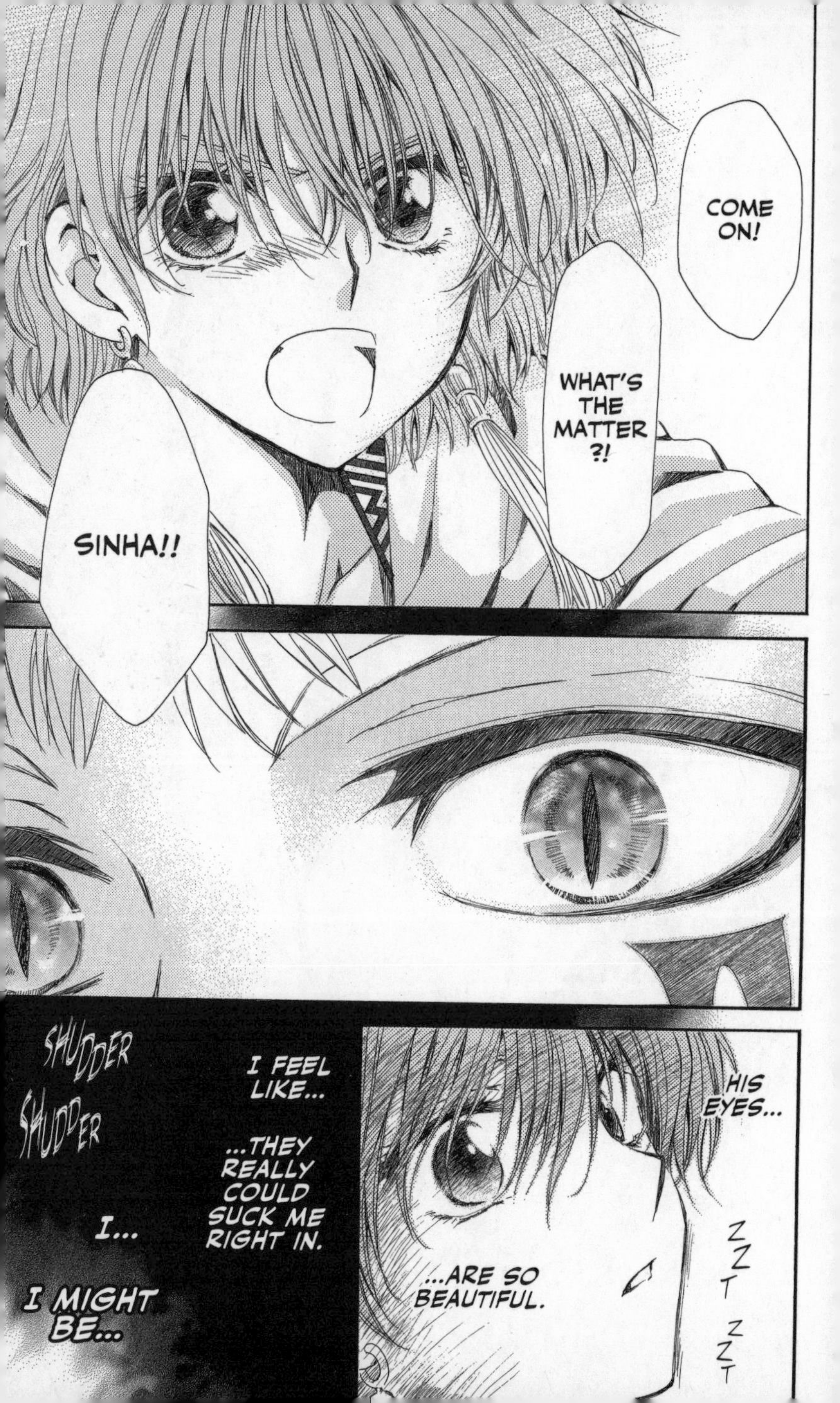
COME ON!
WHAT'S THE MATTER ?!
SINHA!!
HIS EYES...
...ARE SO BEAUTIFUL.
ZZT ZZT
I FEEL LIKE...
...THEY REALLY COULD SUCK ME RIGHT IN.
SHUDDER SHUDDER
I...
I MIGHT BE...

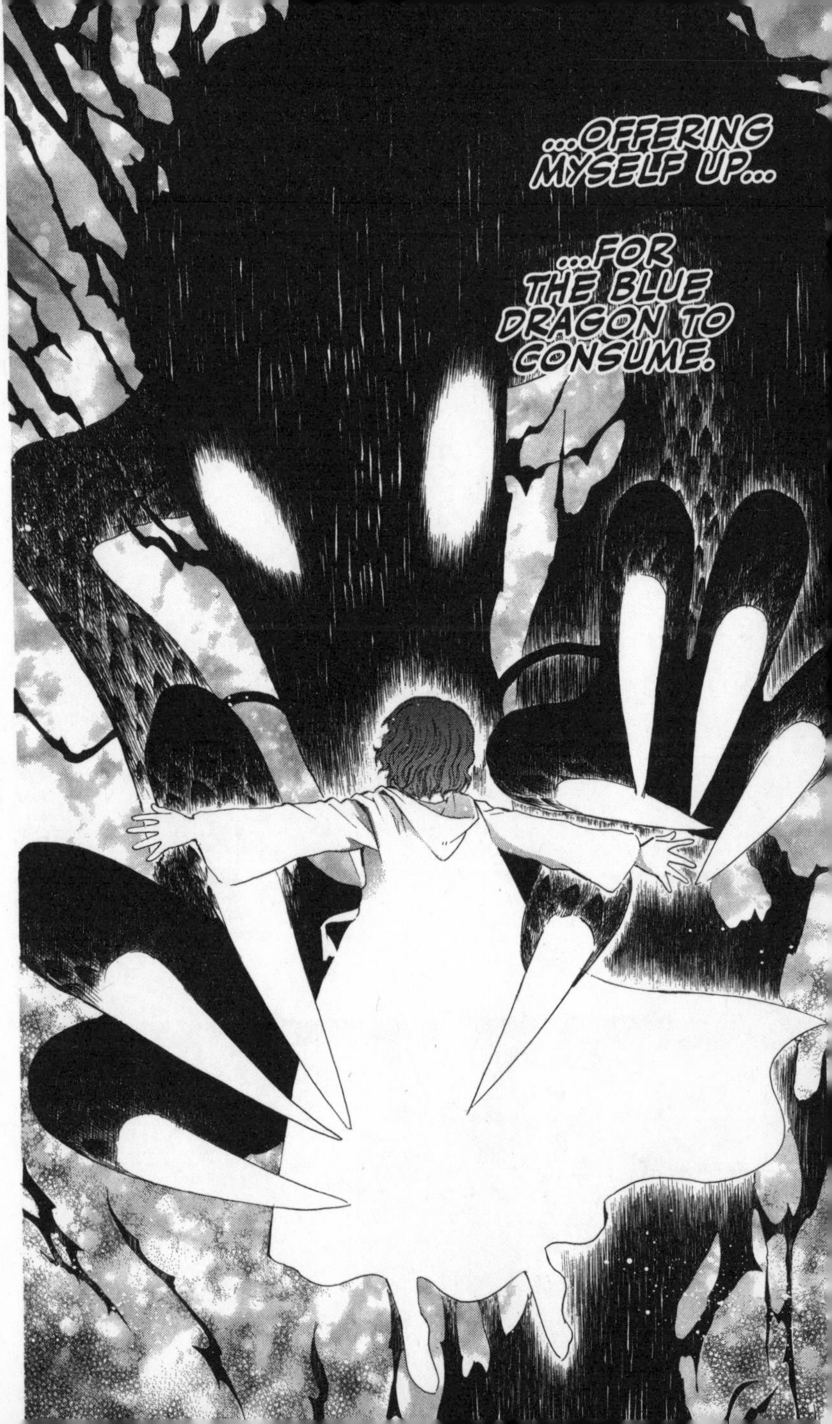
...OFFERING MYSELF UP...
...FOR THE BLUE DRAGON TO CONSUME.

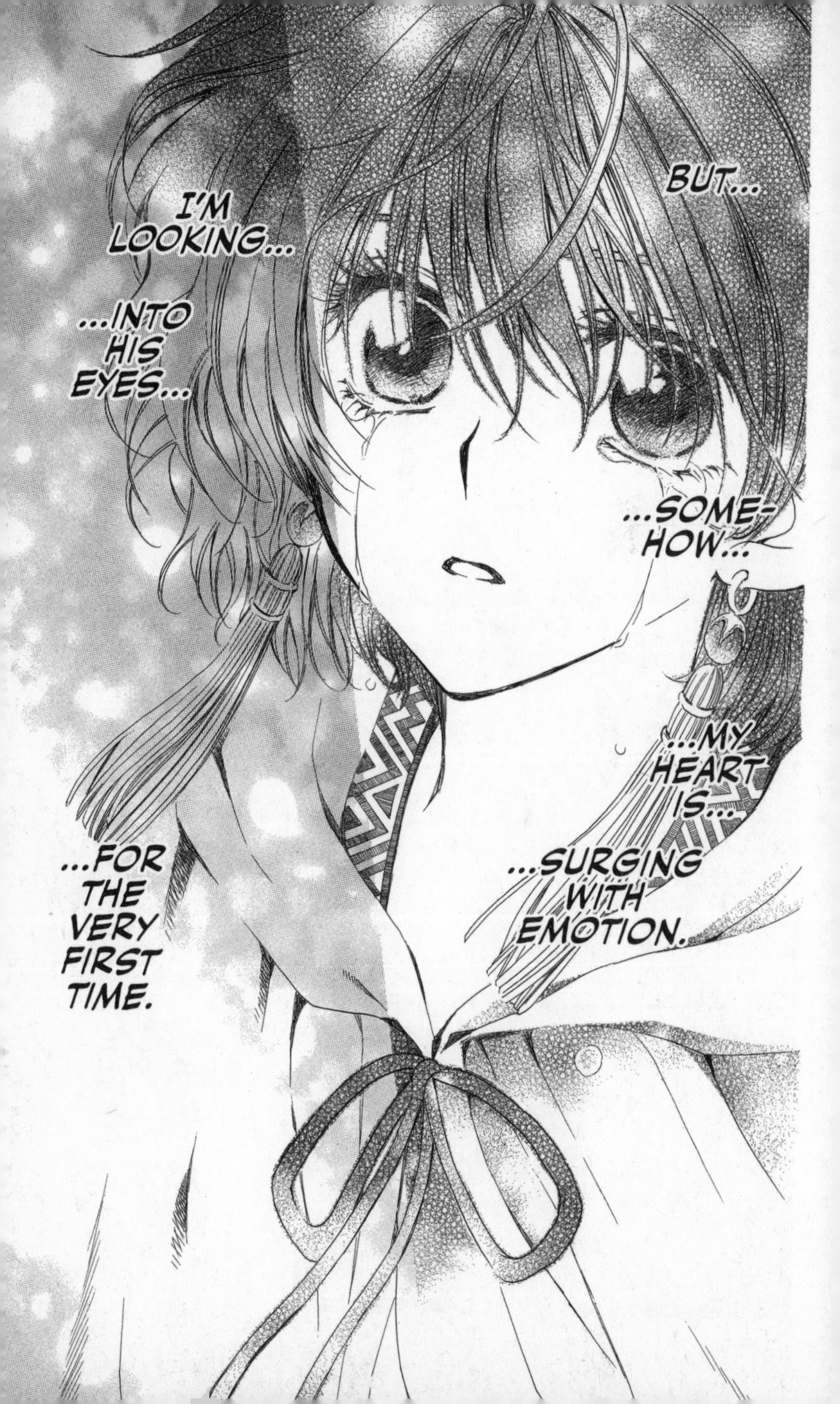
I'M LOOKING...
...INTO HIS EYES...
...FOR THE VERY FIRST TIME.
BUT...
...SOME-HOW...
...MY HEART IS...
...SURGING WITH EMOTION.

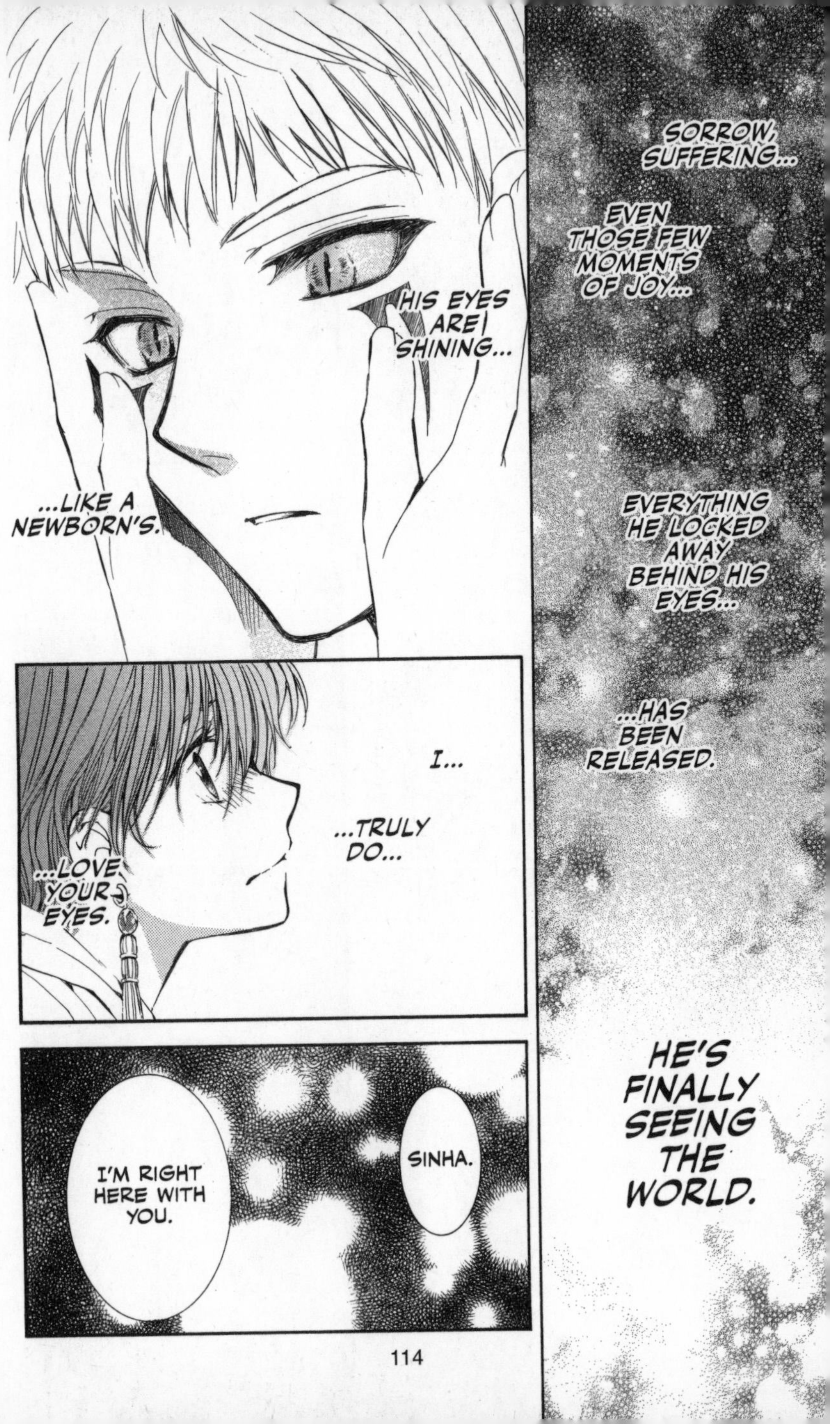
SORROW, SUFFERING...
EVEN THOSE FEW MOMENTS OF JOY...
EVERYTHING HE LOCKED AWAY BEHIND HIS EYES...
...HAS BEEN RELEASED.
HE'S FINALLY SEEING THE WORLD.
HIS EYES ARE SHINING...
...LIKE A NEWBORN'S.
I...
...TRULY DO...
...LOVE YOUR EYES.
SINHA.
I'M RIGHT HERE WITH YOU.

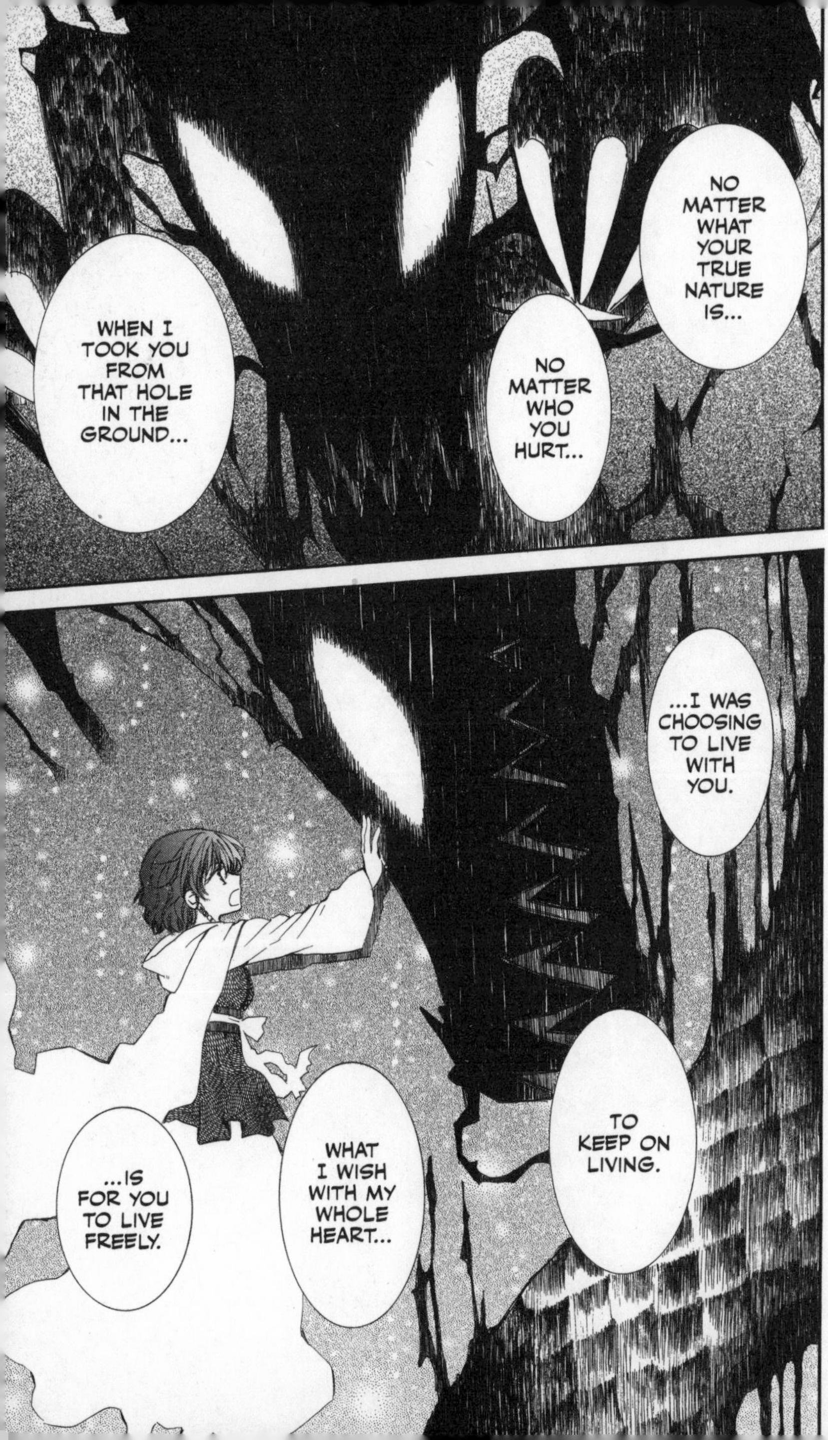
NO MATTER WHAT YOUR TRUE NATURE IS...
NO MATTER WHO YOU HURT...
WHEN I TOOK YOU FROM THAT HOLE IN THE GROUND...
...I WAS CHOOSING TO LIVE WITH YOU.
TO KEEP ON LIVING.
WHAT I WISH WITH MY WHOLE HEART...
...IS FOR YOU TO LIVE FREELY.

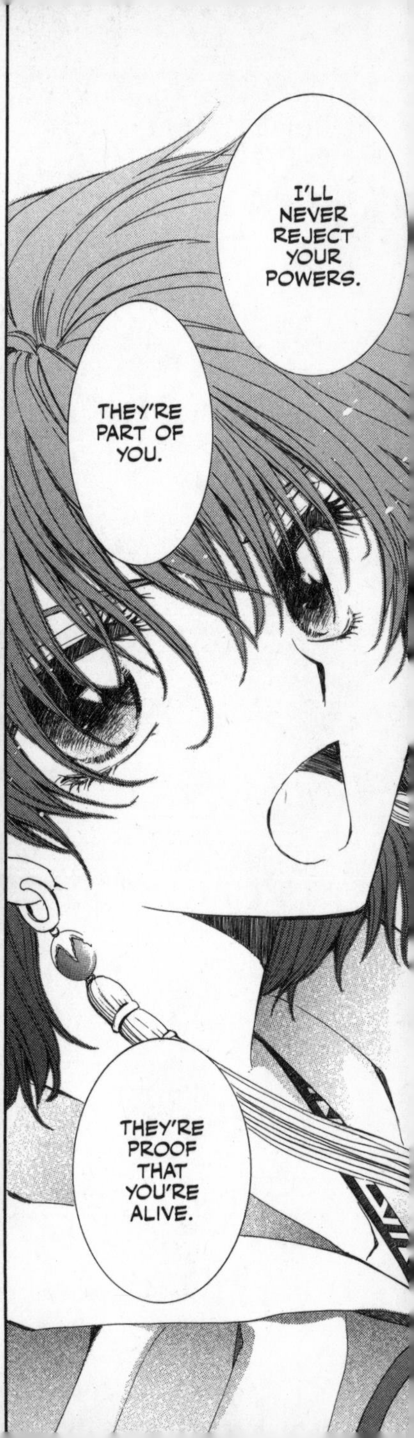
I'LL NEVER REJECT YOUR POWERS.
THEY'RE PART OF YOU.
THEY'RE PROOF THAT YOU'RE ALIVE.

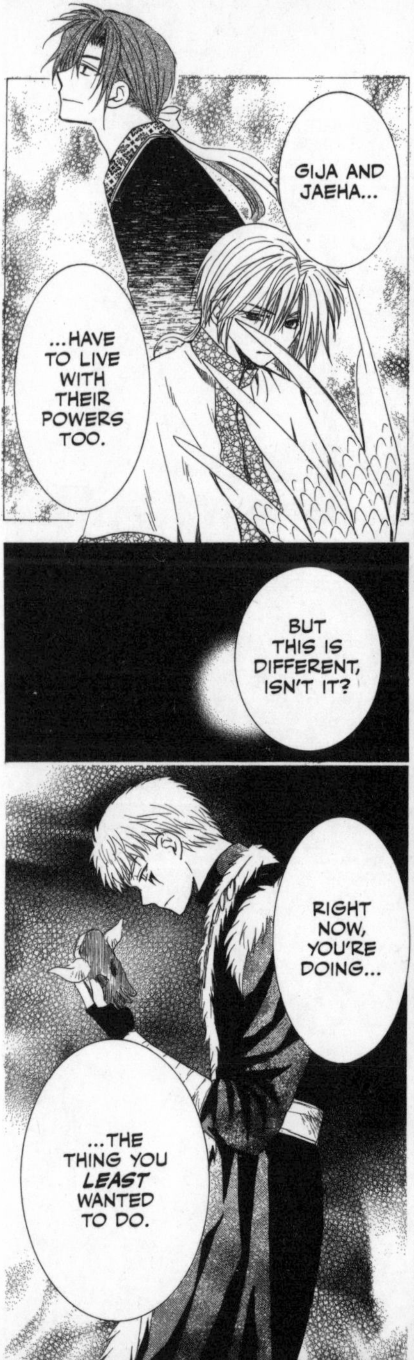
GIJA AND JAEHA...
...HAVE TO LIVE WITH THEIR POWERS TOO.
BUT THIS IS DIFFERENT, ISN'T IT?
RIGHT NOW, YOU'RE DOING...
...THE THING YOU ***LEAST*** WANTED TO DO.

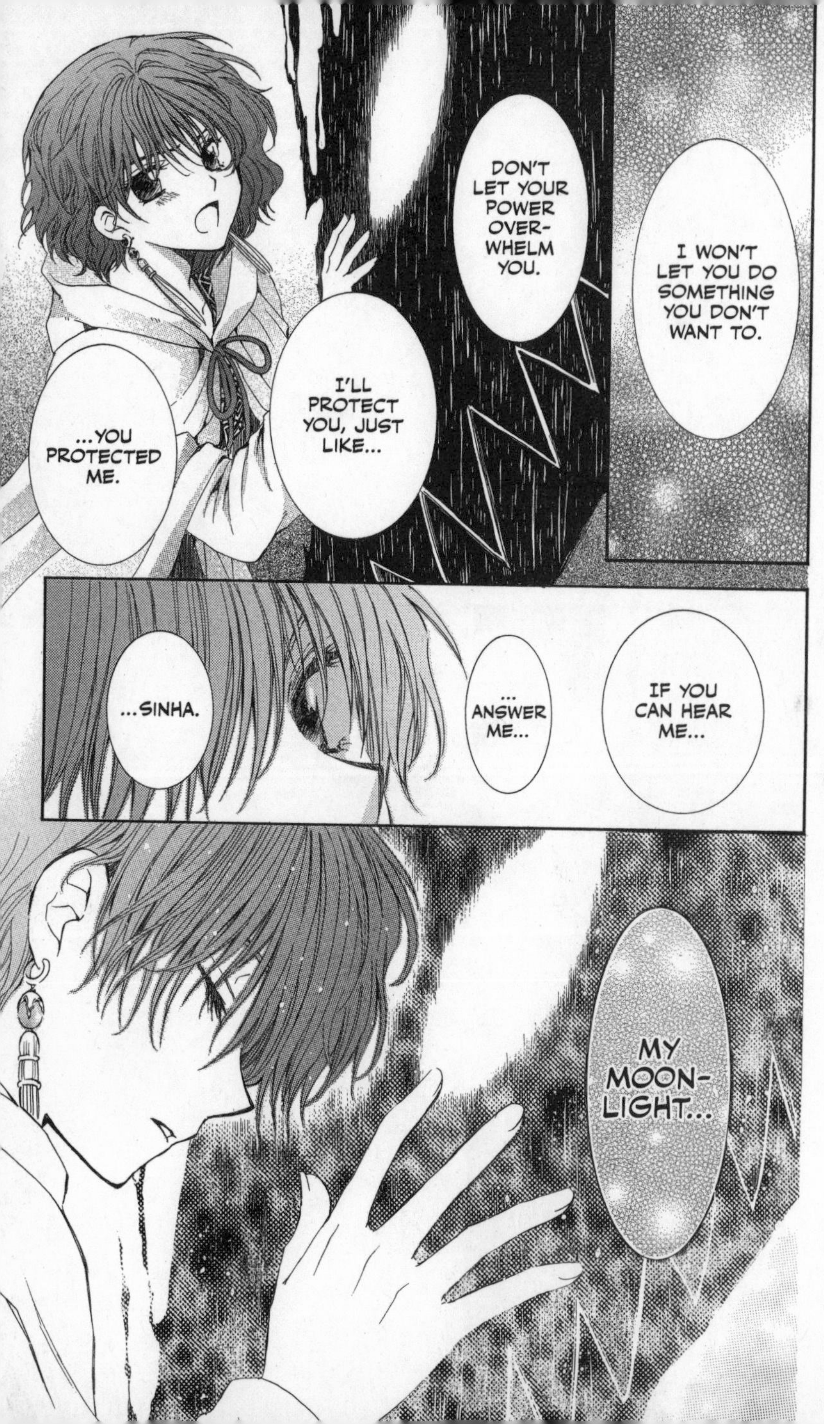
I WON'T LET YOU DO SOMETHING YOU DON'T WANT TO.
DON'T LET YOUR POWER OVER-WHELM YOU.
I'LL PROTECT YOU, JUST LIKE...
...YOU PROTECTED ME.
IF YOU CAN HEAR ME...
...ANSWER ME...
...SINHA.
MY MOON-LIGHT...

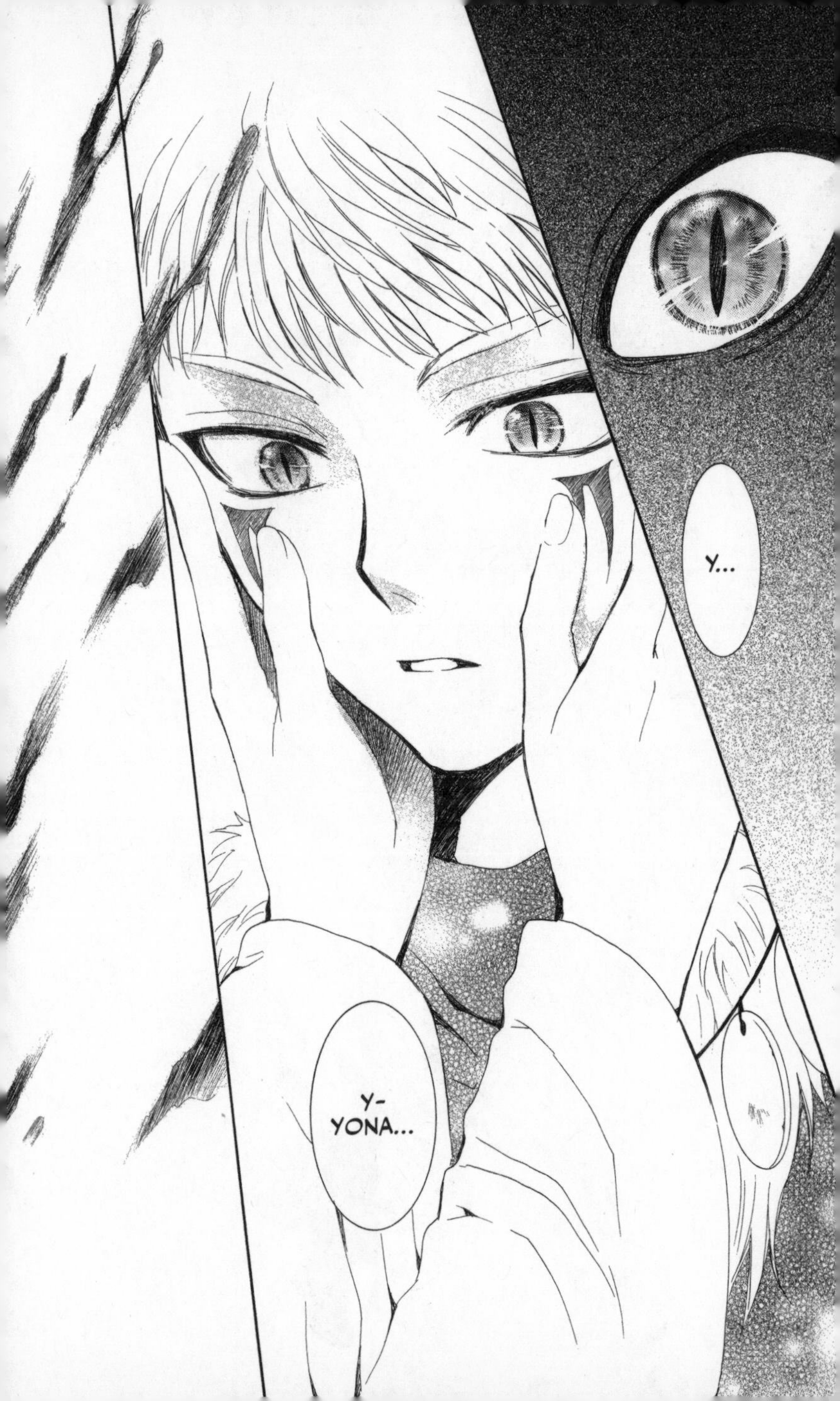
Y...
Y-
YONA...

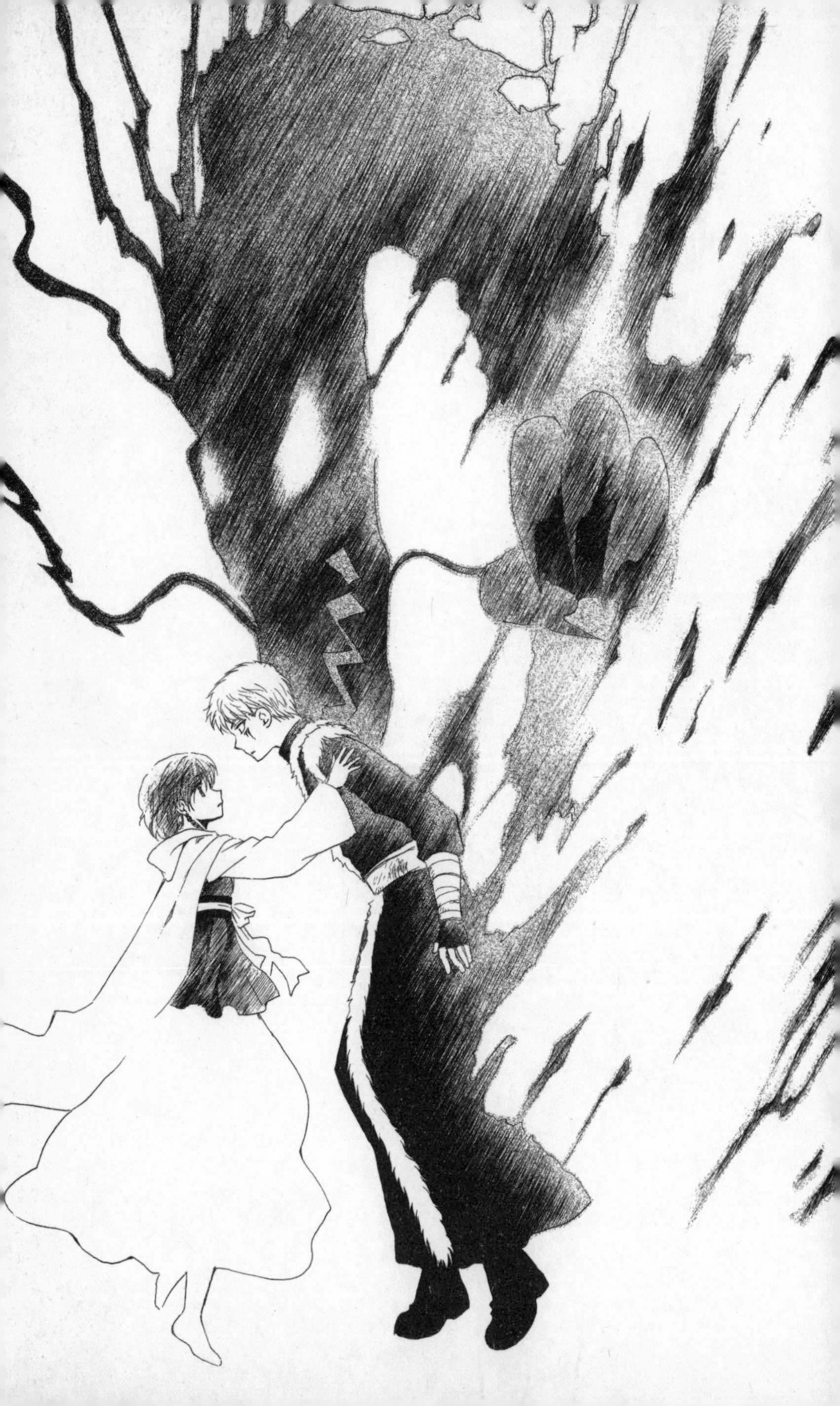

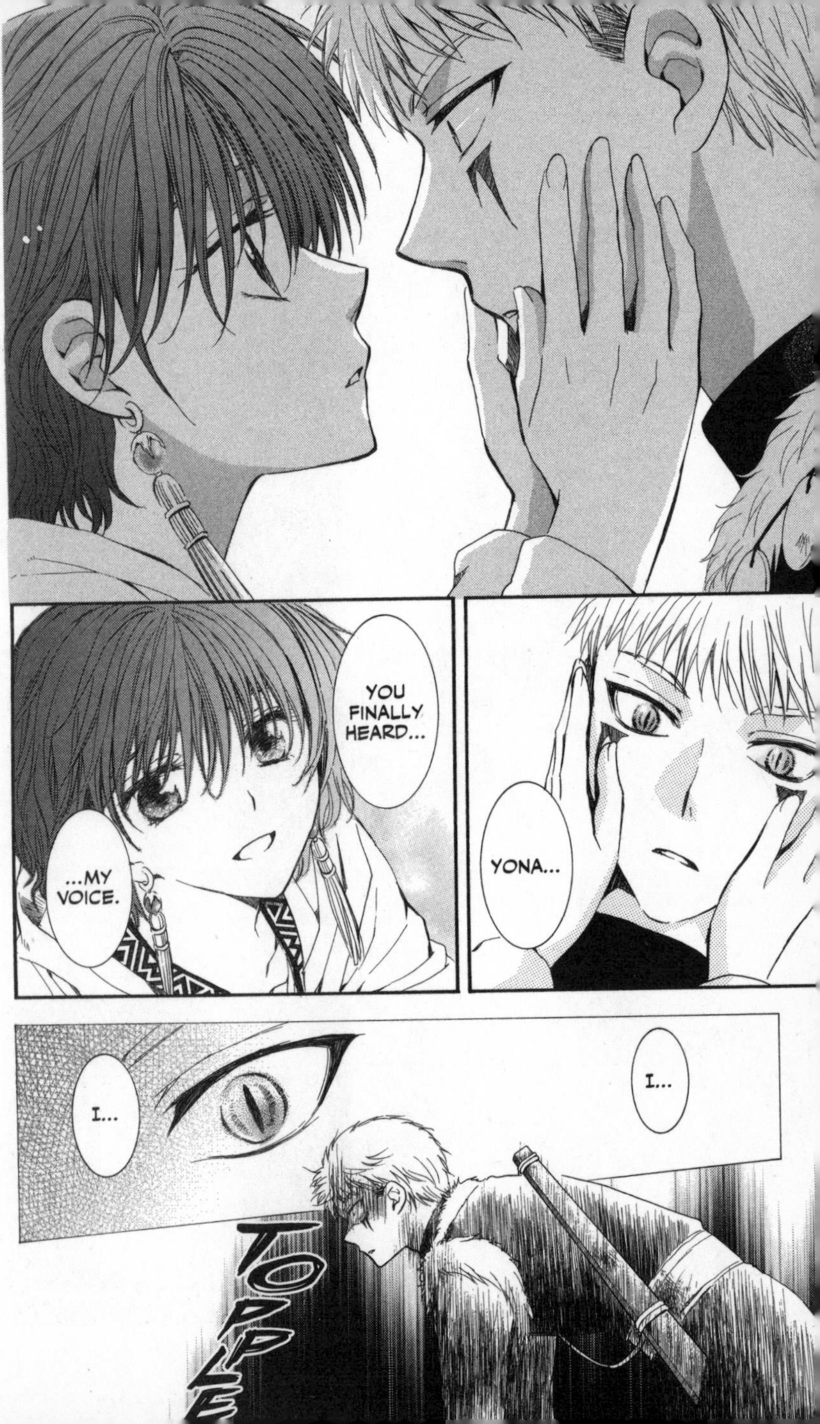
YONA...
YOU FINALLY HEARD...
...MY VOICE.
I...
I...
TOPPLE

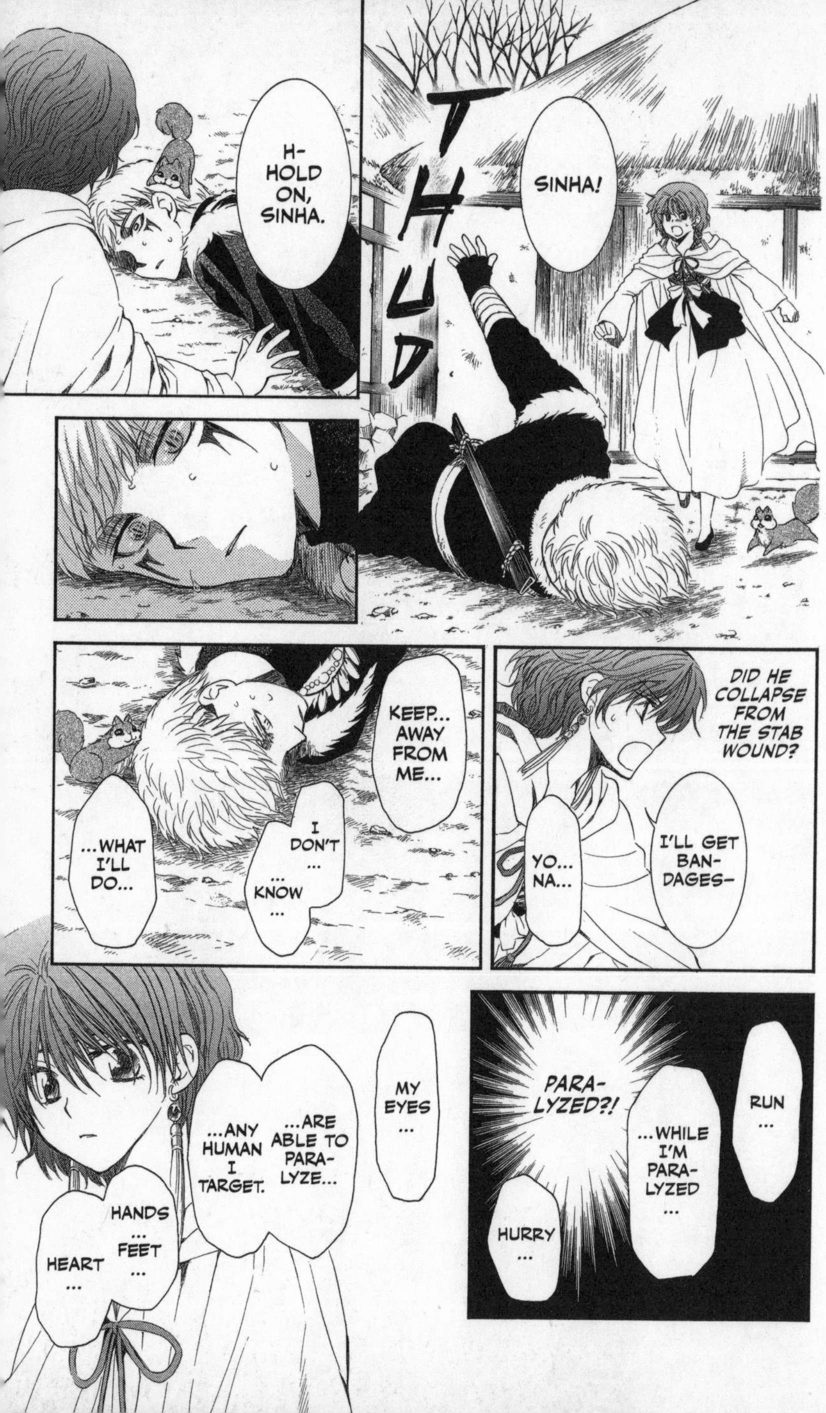
SINHA!
THUD
H- HOLD ON, SINHA.
DID HE COLLAPSE FROM THE STAB WOUND?
I'LL GET BAN-DAGES—
YO... NA...
KEEP... AWAY FROM ME...
I DON'T ... ... KNOW ...
...WHAT I'LL DO...
RUN ...
...WHILE I'M PARA-LYZED ...
PARA-LYZED?!
HURRY ...
MY EYES ...
...ARE ABLE TO PARA-LYZE...
...ANY HUMAN I TARGET.
HANDS ... FEET ...
HEART ...

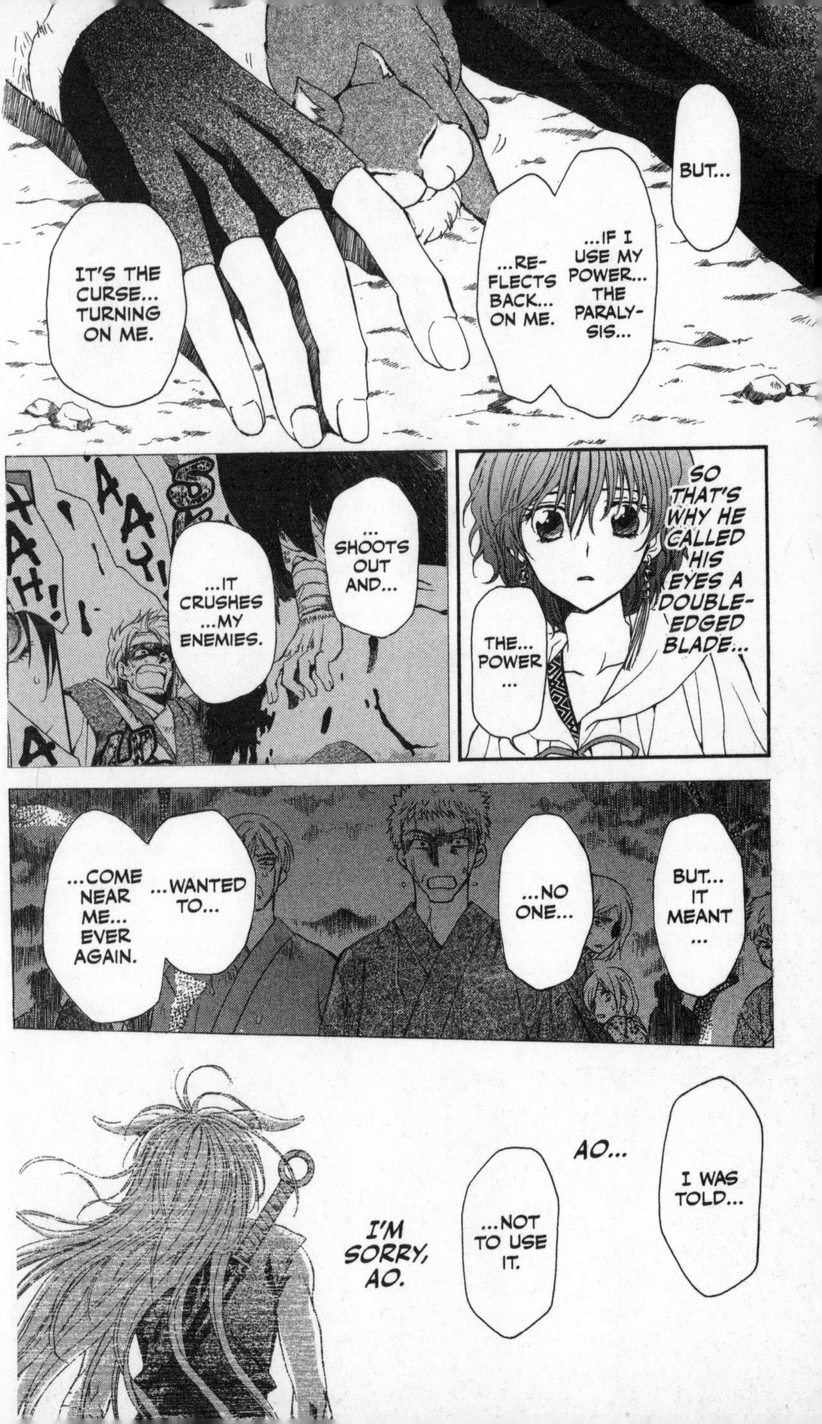
BUT...
...IF I USE MY POWER... THE PARALYSIS...
...RE-FLECTS BACK... ON ME.
IT'S THE CURSE... TURNING ON ME.
SO THAT'S WHY HE CALLED HIS EYES A DOUBLE-EDGED BLADE...
THE... POWER ...
... SHOOTS OUT AND...
...IT CRUSHES ...MY ENEMIES.
BUT... IT MEANT ...
...NO ONE...
...WANTED TO...
...COME NEAR ME... EVER AGAIN.
I WAS TOLD...
AO...
...NOT TO USE IT.
I'M SORRY, AO.

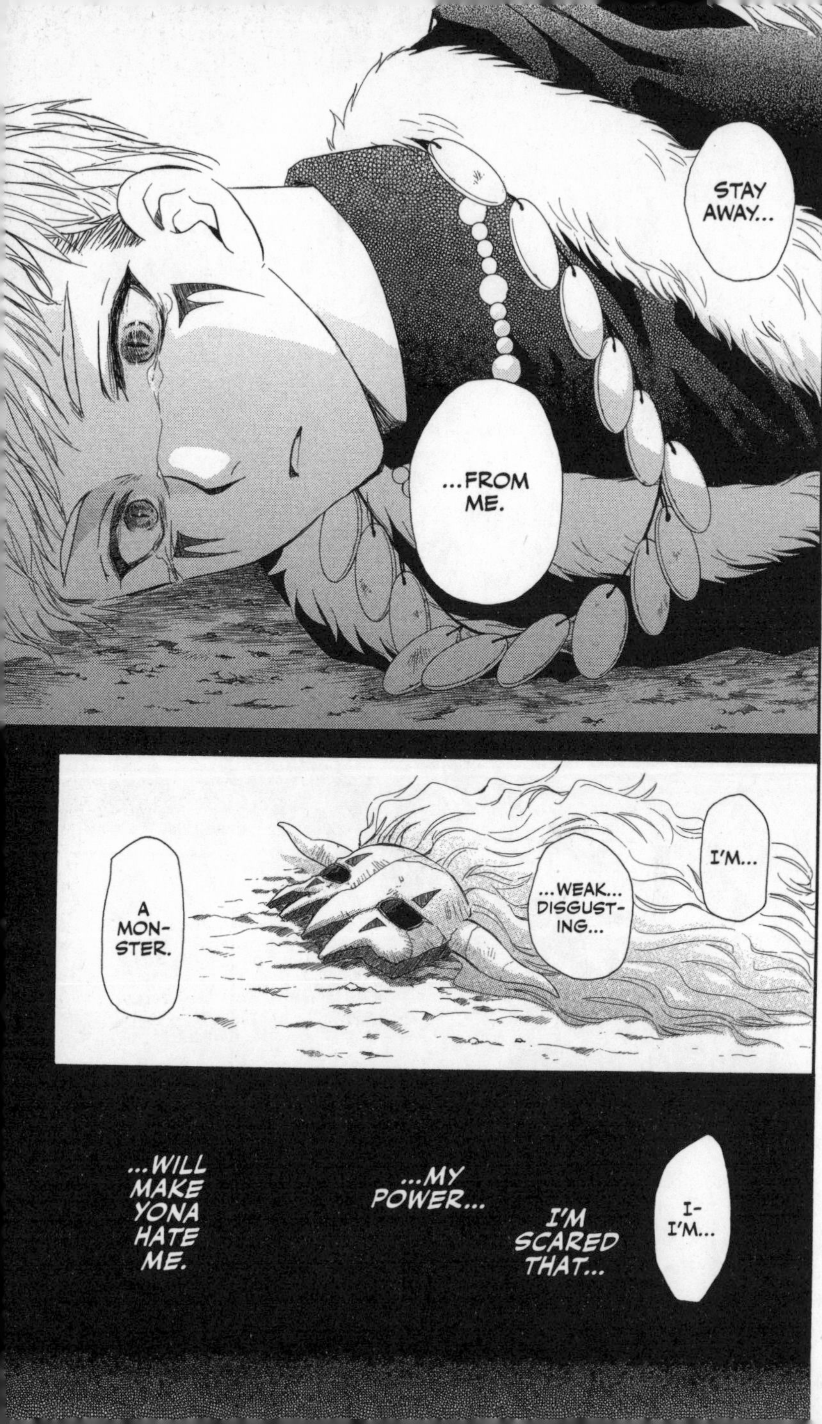
STAY AWAY...
...FROM ME.
I'M...
...WEAK... DISGUST-ING...
A MON-STER.
I- I'M...
I'M SCARED THAT...
...MY POWER...
...WILL MAKE YONA HATE ME.

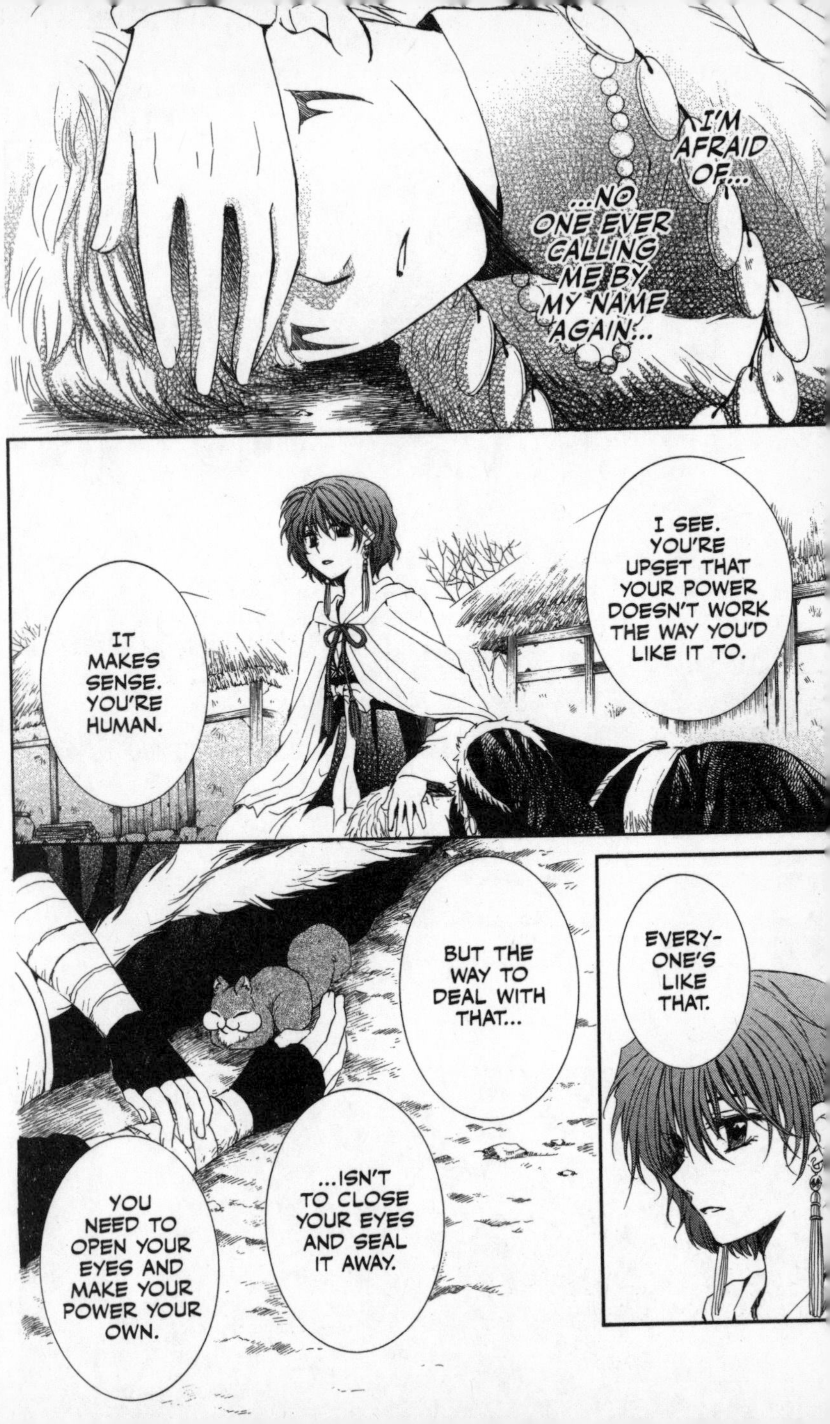
I'M AFRAID OF...
...NO ONE EVER CALLING ME BY MY NAME AGAIN...
I SEE. YOU'RE UPSET THAT YOUR POWER DOESN'T WORK THE WAY YOU'D LIKE IT TO.
IT MAKES SENSE. YOU'RE HUMAN.
EVERY-ONE'S LIKE THAT.
BUT THE WAY TO DEAL WITH THAT...
...ISN'T TO CLOSE YOUR EYES AND SEAL IT AWAY.
YOU NEED TO OPEN YOUR EYES AND MAKE YOUR POWER YOUR OWN.

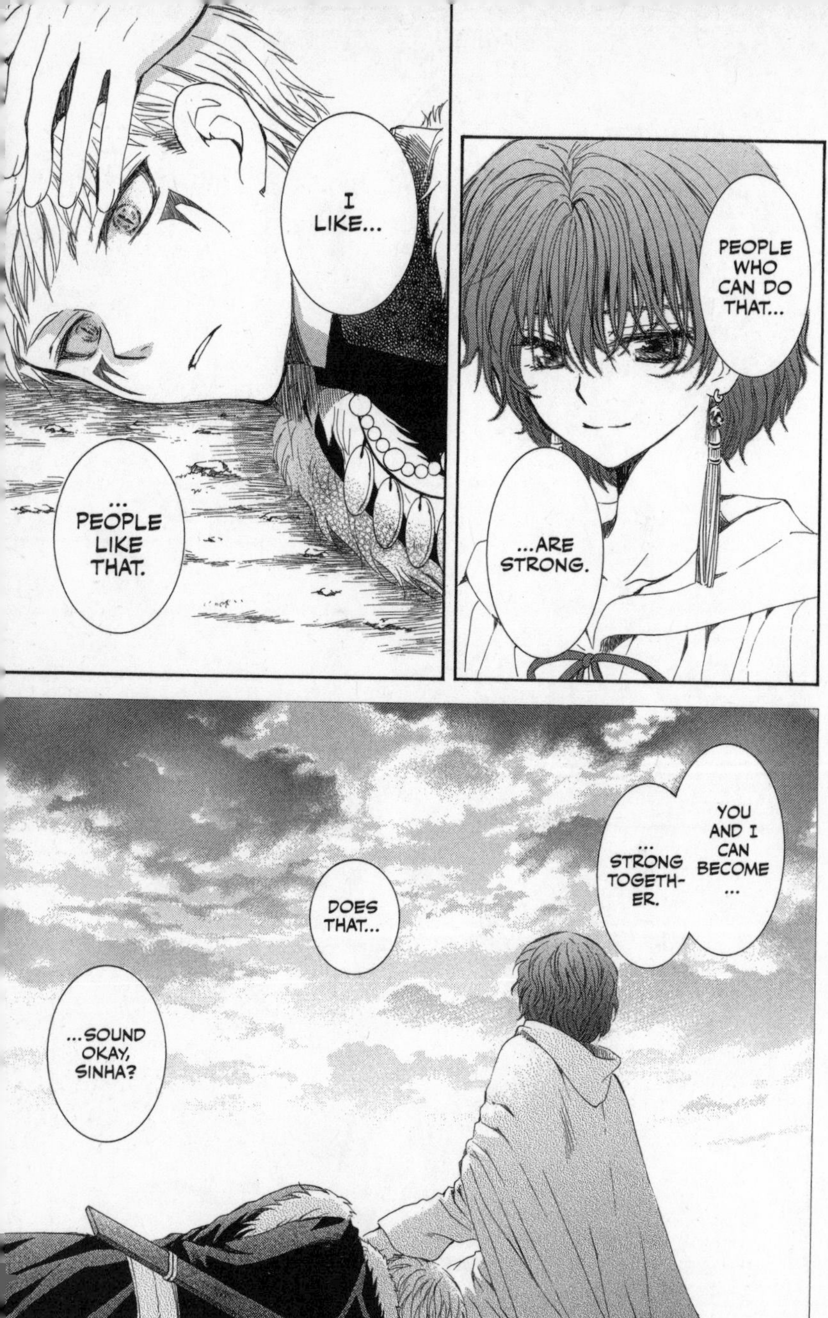
PEOPLE WHO CAN DO THAT...
...ARE STRONG.
I LIKE...
...PEOPLE LIKE THAT.
YOU AND I CAN BECOME...
...STRONG TOGETHER.
DOES THAT...
...SOUND OKAY, SINHA?

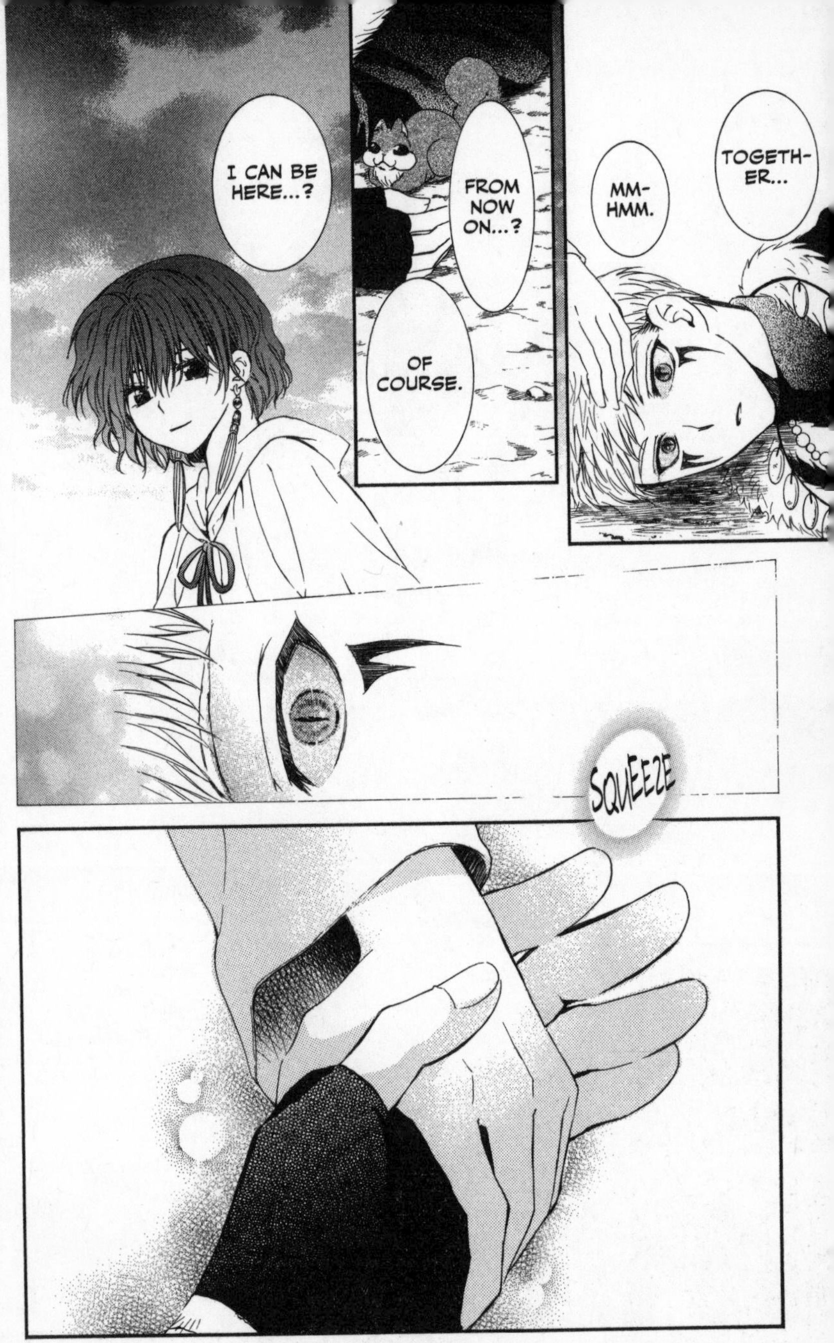
TOGETH-ER...
MM-HMM.
FROM NOW ON...?
OF COURSE.
I CAN BE HERE...?
SQUEEZE

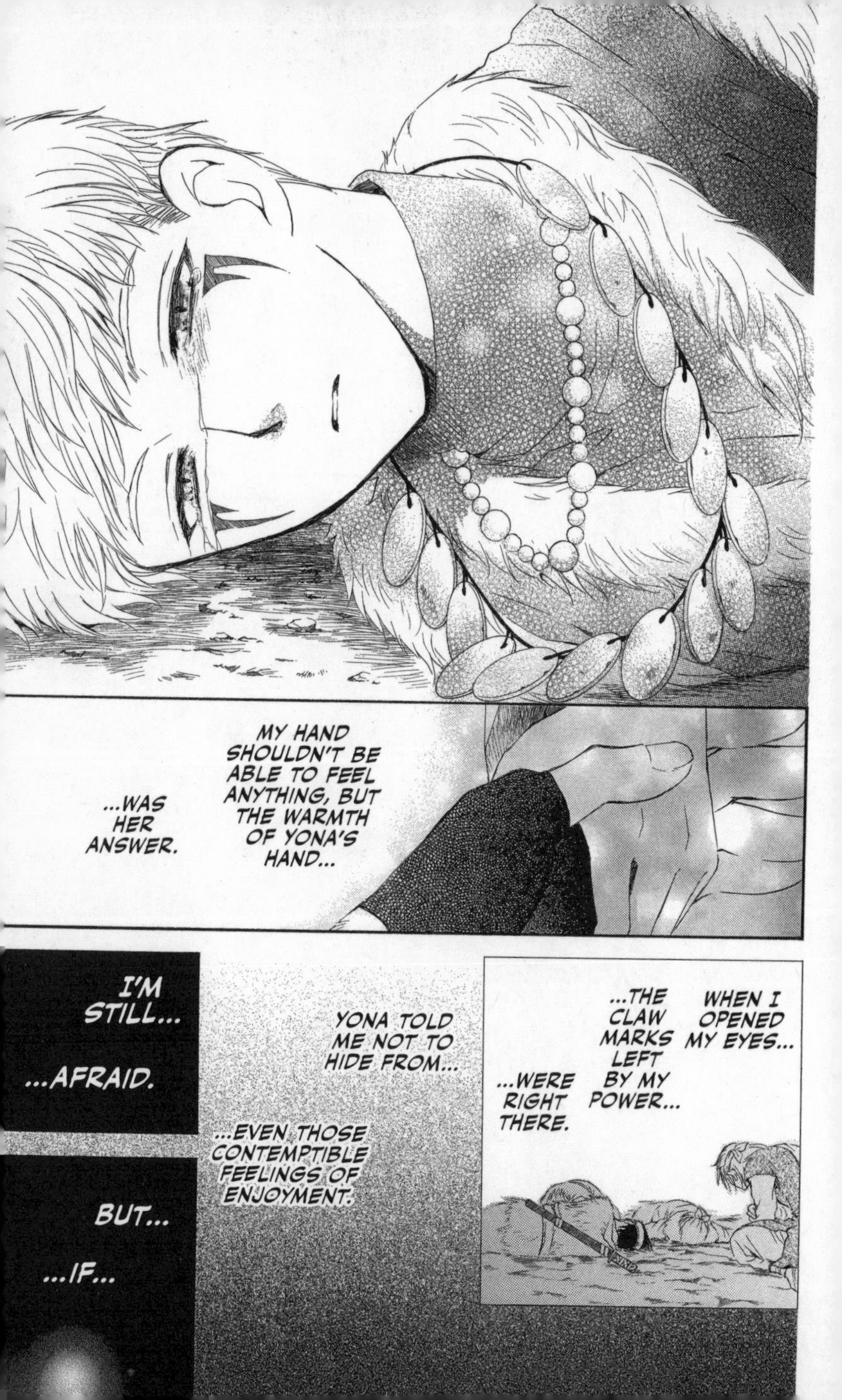

MY HAND SHOULDN'T BE ABLE TO FEEL ANYTHING, BUT THE WARMTH OF YONA'S HAND...
...WAS HER ANSWER.
WHEN I OPENED MY EYES...
...THE CLAW MARKS LEFT BY MY POWER...
...WERE RIGHT THERE.
YONA TOLD ME NOT TO HIDE FROM...
...EVEN THOSE CONTEMPTIBLE FEELINGS OF ENJOYMENT.
I'M STILL...
...AFRAID.
BUT...
...IF...

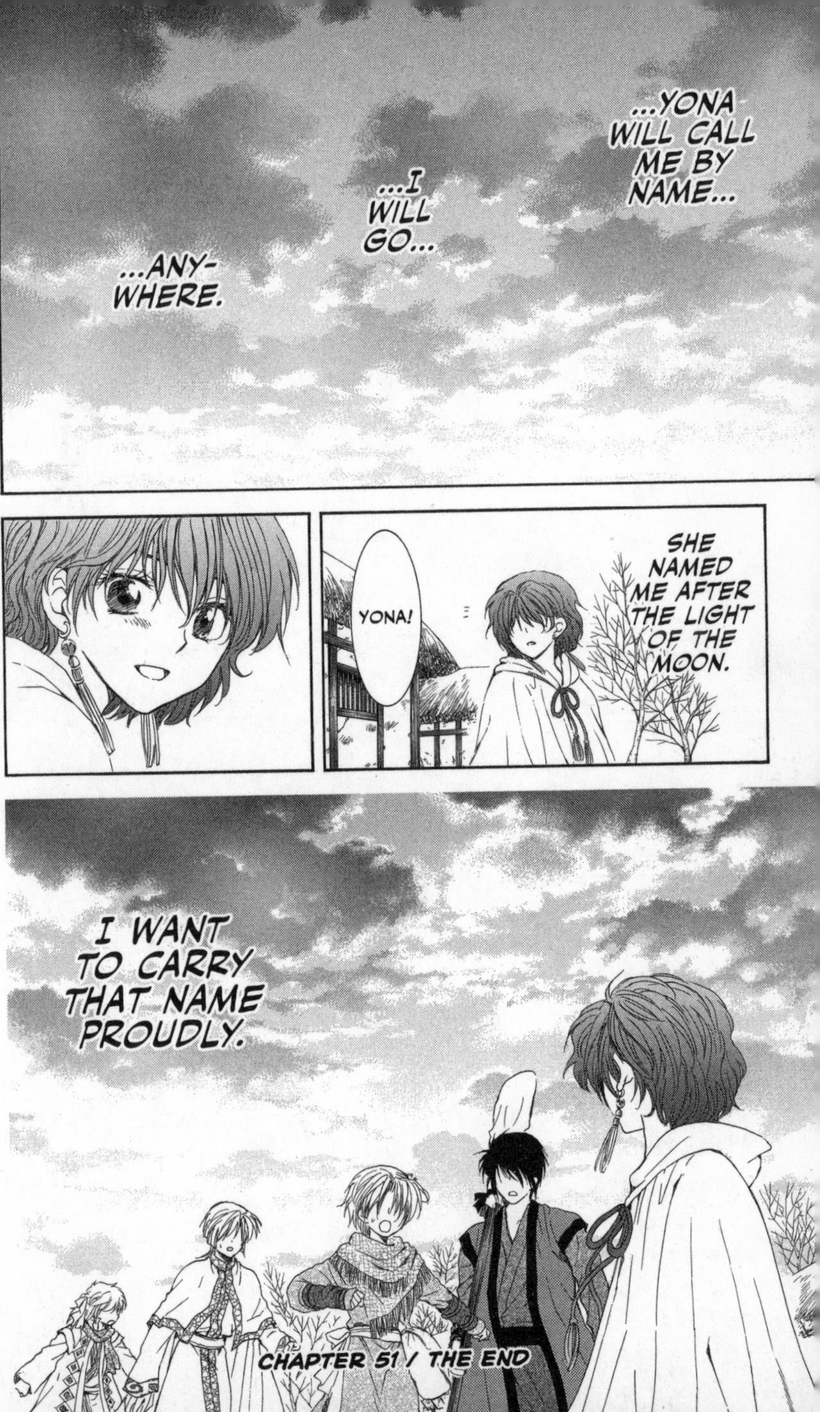
...YONA WILL CALL ME BY NAME...
...I WILL GO...
...ANY-WHERE.
SHE NAMED ME AFTER THE LIGHT OF THE MOON.
YONA!
I WANT TO CARRY THAT NAME PROUDLY.
CHAPTER 51 / THE END

Chapter 52: An Arrow Piercing a Stone

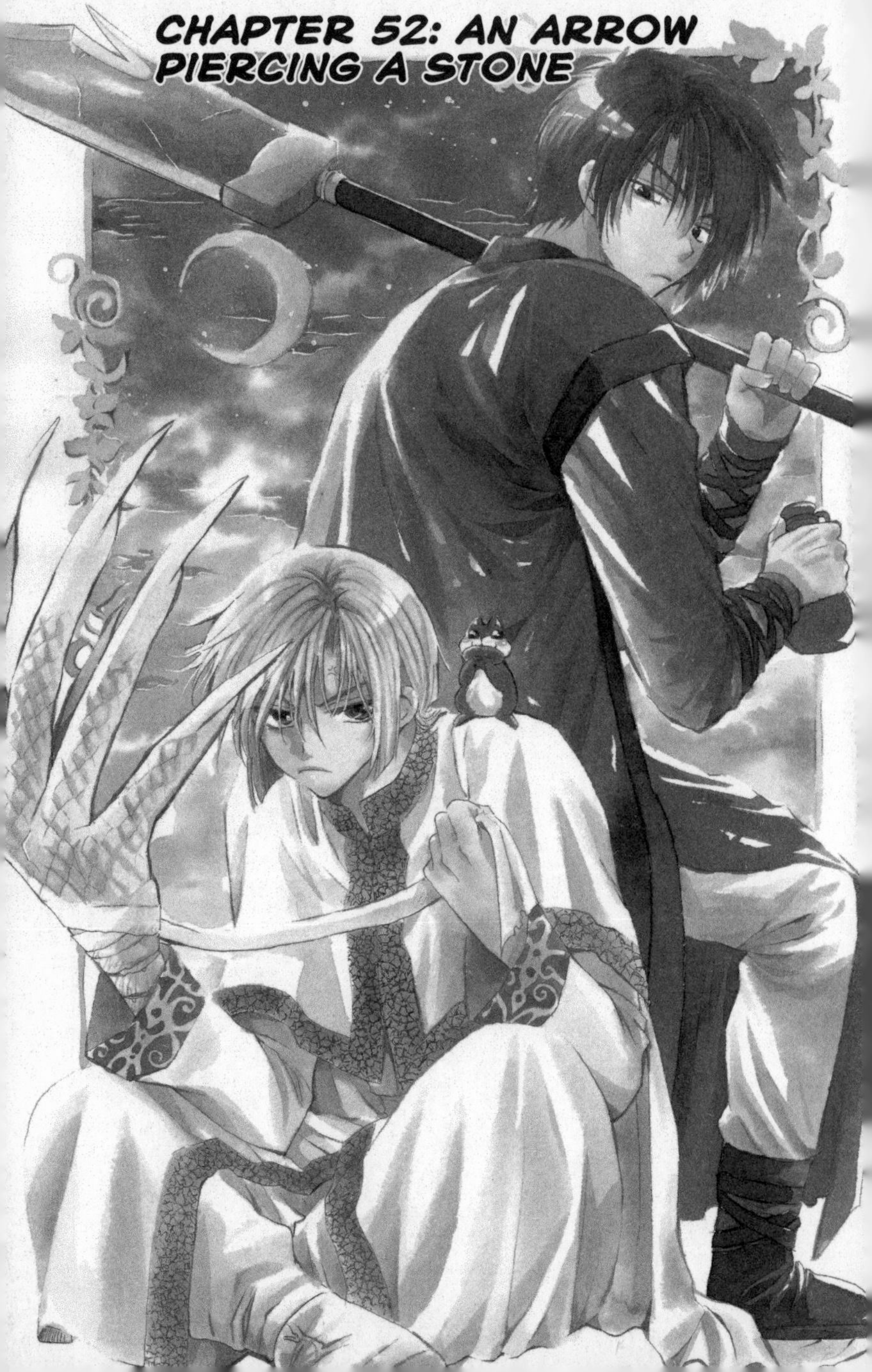

Gija Treats Sinha's Injuries

Wants to wash Sinha's bloody clothes, but water is a scarce, valuable resource in this village
Jaeha, could you take me to a river?
You act like it's easy.
Strolling through the sky
HOP
You're heavy...
It's cold, so the fabric's not drying very well.
It's all frayed too...
You snagged it with your claw, didn't you?
Sinha, wear these clothes for now.
Sinha...
He lent them to me...
Next time you have laundry, let me handle it.
Fixing Sinha's clothes
Gija has several identical outfits.

I have a blog where I post things about my day and my work. If you're interested, please check it out!
I don't update it very often, though...

Blog name: Mizuho Kusanagi's NG Life

URL: http://yaplog.jp/sanaginonaka/

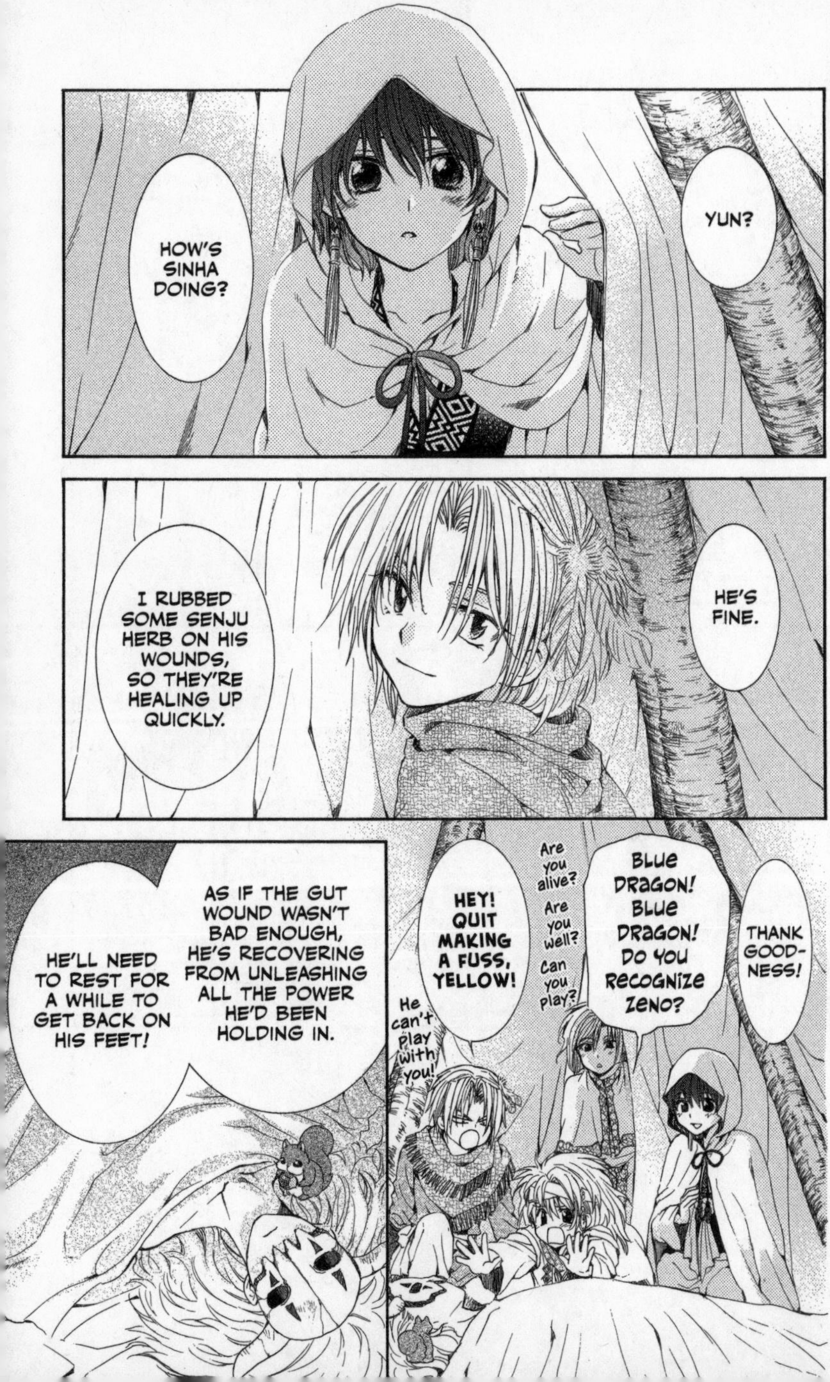
YUN?
HOW'S SINHA DOING?
HE'S FINE.
I RUBBED SOME SENJU HERB ON HIS WOUNDS, SO THEY'RE HEALING UP QUICKLY.
THANK GOODNESS!
Blue Dragon! Blue Dragon! Do you recognize Zeno?
Are you alive? Are you well? Can you play?
HEY! QUIT MAKING A FUSS, YELLOW!
He can't play with you!
AS IF THE GUT WOUND WASN'T BAD ENOUGH, HE'S RECOVERING FROM UNLEASHING ALL THE POWER HE'D BEEN HOLDING IN.
HE'LL NEED TO REST FOR A WHILE TO GET BACK ON HIS FEET!

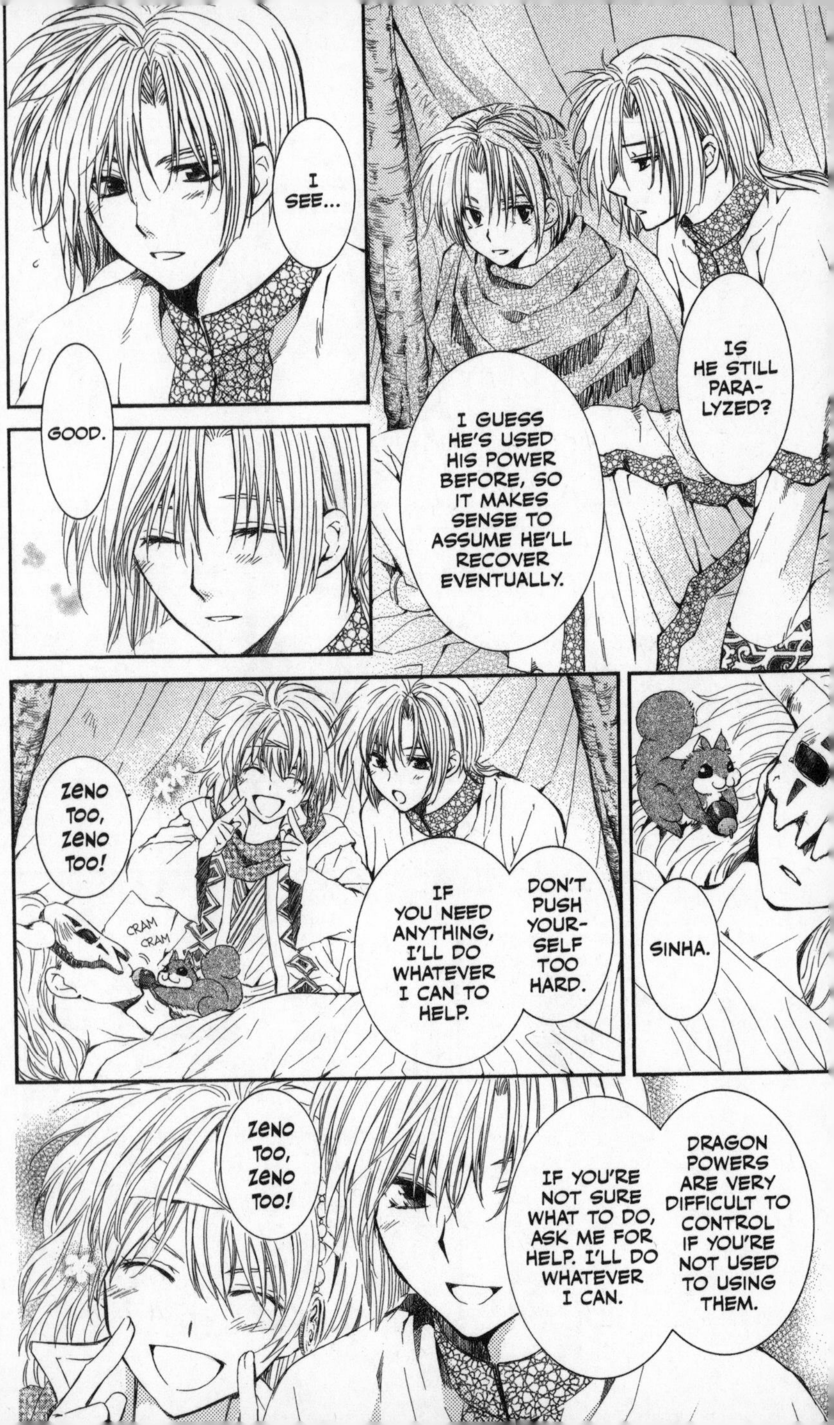
IS HE STILL PARA-LYZED?
I GUESS HE'S USED HIS POWER BEFORE, SO IT MAKES SENSE TO ASSUME HE'LL RECOVER EVENTUALLY.
I SEE...
GOOD.
SINHA.
DON'T PUSH YOUR-SELF TOO HARD.
IF YOU NEED ANYTHING, I'LL DO WHATEVER I CAN TO HELP.
CRAM CRAM
ZENO TOO, ZENO TOO!
DRAGON POWERS ARE VERY DIFFICULT TO CONTROL IF YOU'RE NOT USED TO USING THEM.
IF YOU'RE NOT SURE WHAT TO DO, ASK ME FOR HELP. I'LL DO WHATEVER I CAN.
ZENO TOO, ZENO TOO!

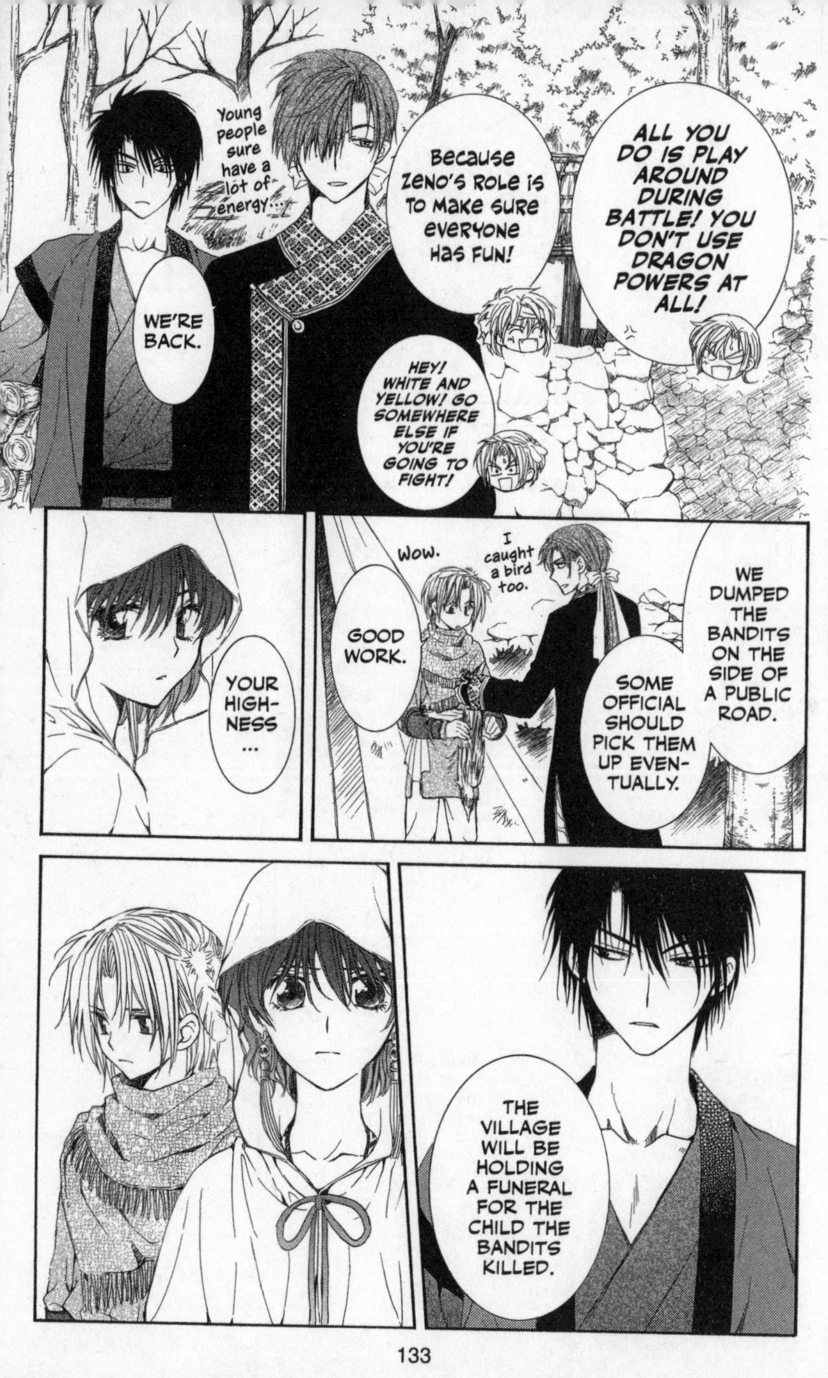
ALL YOU DO IS PLAY AROUND DURING BATTLE! YOU DON'T USE DRAGON POWERS AT ALL!
Because Zeno's role is to make sure everyone has fun!
Young people sure have a lot of energy...
HEY! WHITE AND YELLOW! GO SOMEWHERE ELSE IF YOU'RE GOING TO FIGHT!
WE'RE BACK.
WE DUMPED THE BANDITS ON THE SIDE OF A PUBLIC ROAD.
SOME OFFICIAL SHOULD PICK THEM UP EVENTUALLY.
I caught a bird too.
Wow.
GOOD WORK.
YOUR HIGHNESS...
THE VILLAGE WILL BE HOLDING A FUNERAL FOR THE CHILD THE BANDITS KILLED.

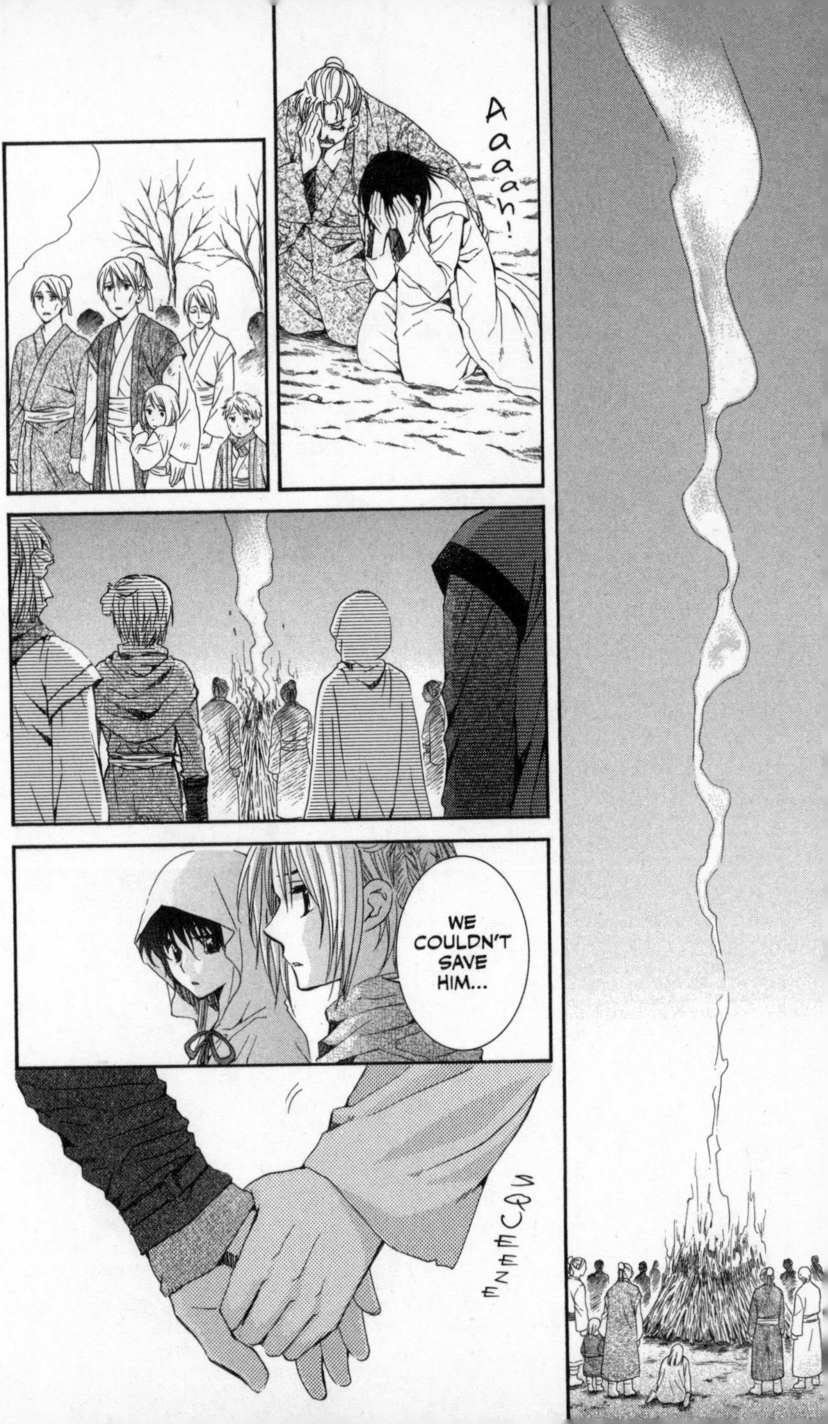

Aaaah!
WE COULDN'T SAVE HIM...
SQUEEZE

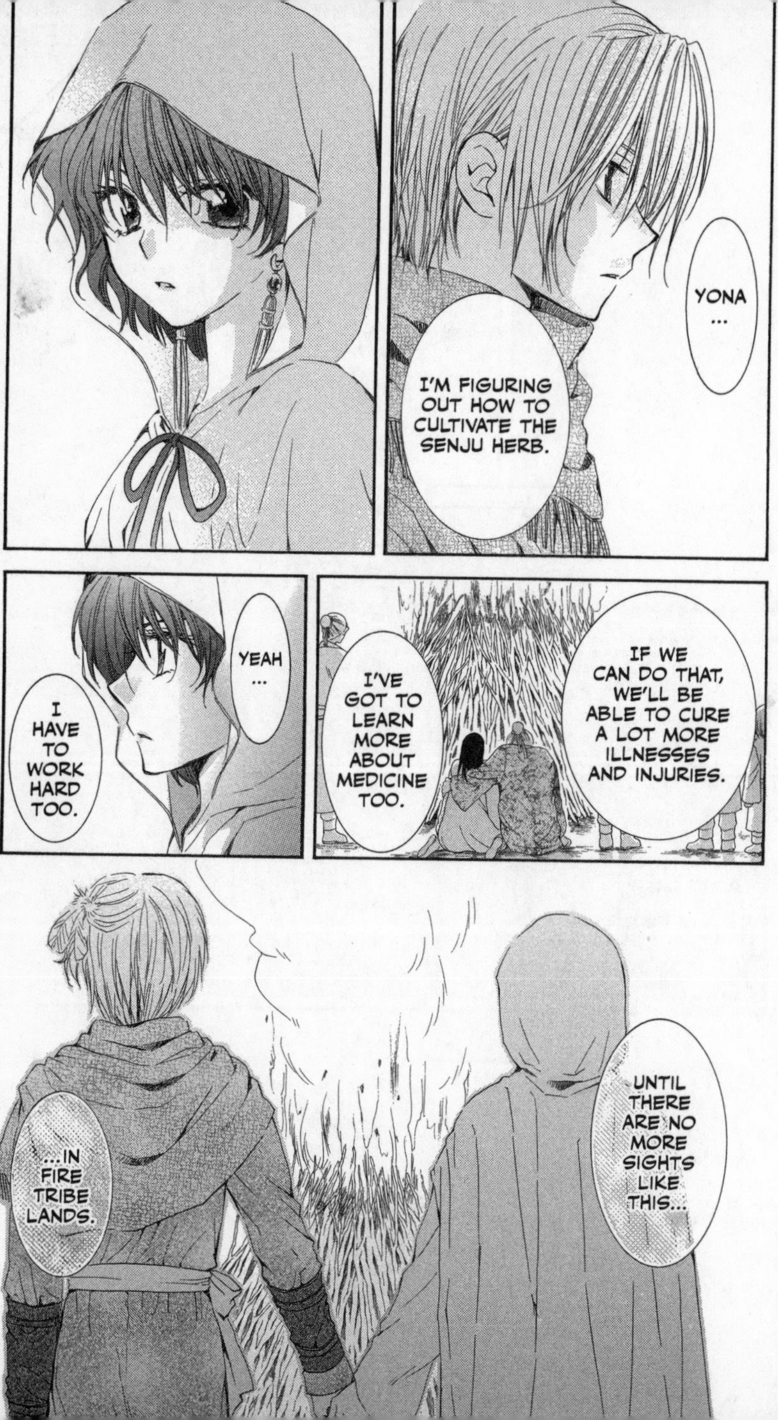
YONA ...
I'M FIGURING OUT HOW TO CULTIVATE THE SENJU HERB.
IF WE CAN DO THAT, WE'LL BE ABLE TO CURE A LOT MORE ILLNESSES AND INJURIES.
I'VE GOT TO LEARN MORE ABOUT MEDICINE TOO.
YEAH ...
I HAVE TO WORK HARD TOO.
UNTIL THERE ARE NO MORE SIGHTS LIKE THIS...
...IN FIRE TRIBE LANDS.

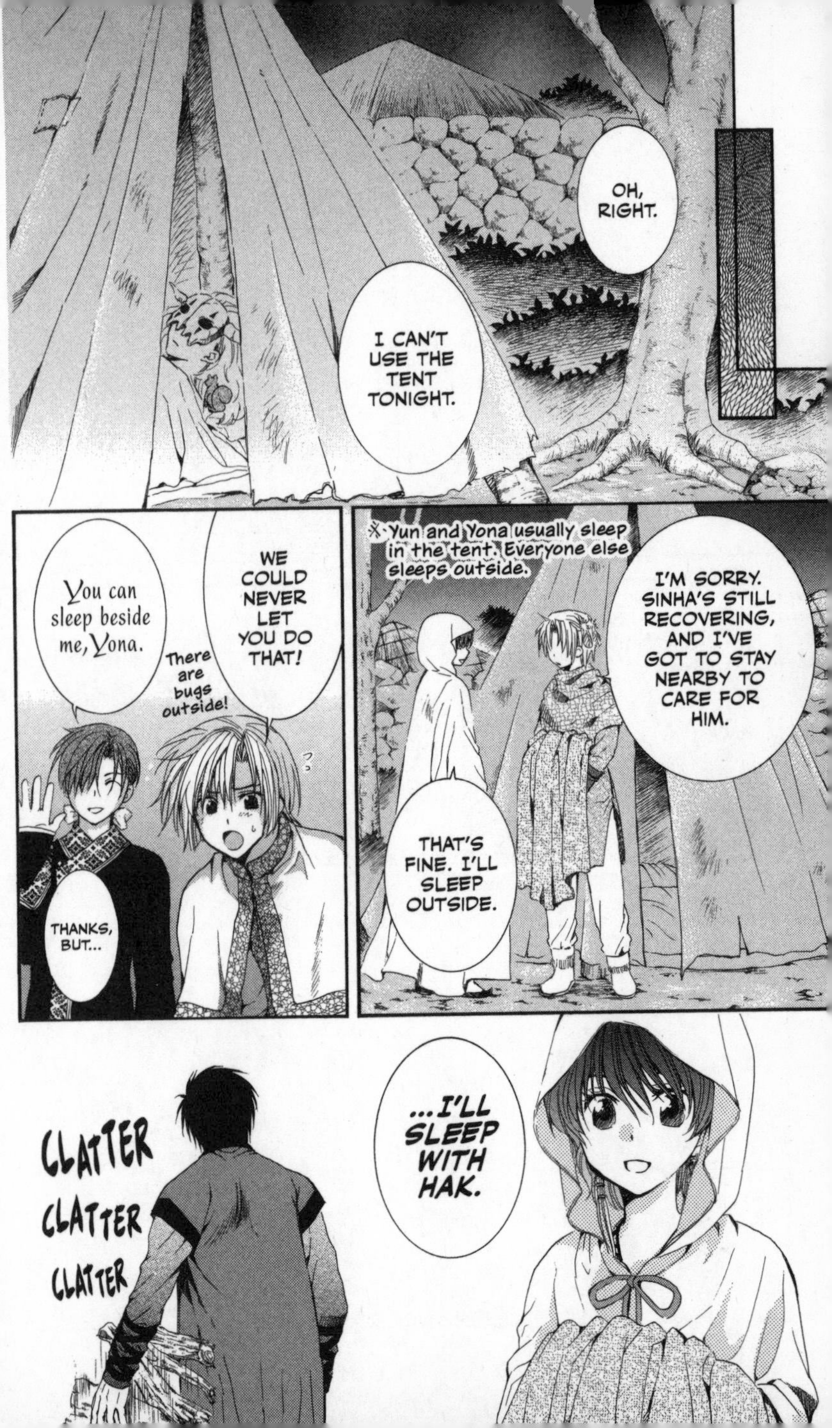
OH, RIGHT.
I CAN'T USE THE TENT TONIGHT.
※Yun and Yona usually sleep in the tent. Everyone else sleeps outside.
I'M SORRY. SINHA'S STILL RECOVERING, AND I'VE GOT TO STAY NEARBY TO CARE FOR HIM.
THAT'S FINE. I'LL SLEEP OUTSIDE.
WE COULD NEVER LET YOU DO THAT!
There are bugs outside!
You can sleep beside me, Yona.
THANKS, BUT...
...I'LL SLEEP WITH HAK.
CLATTER
CLATTER
CLATTER

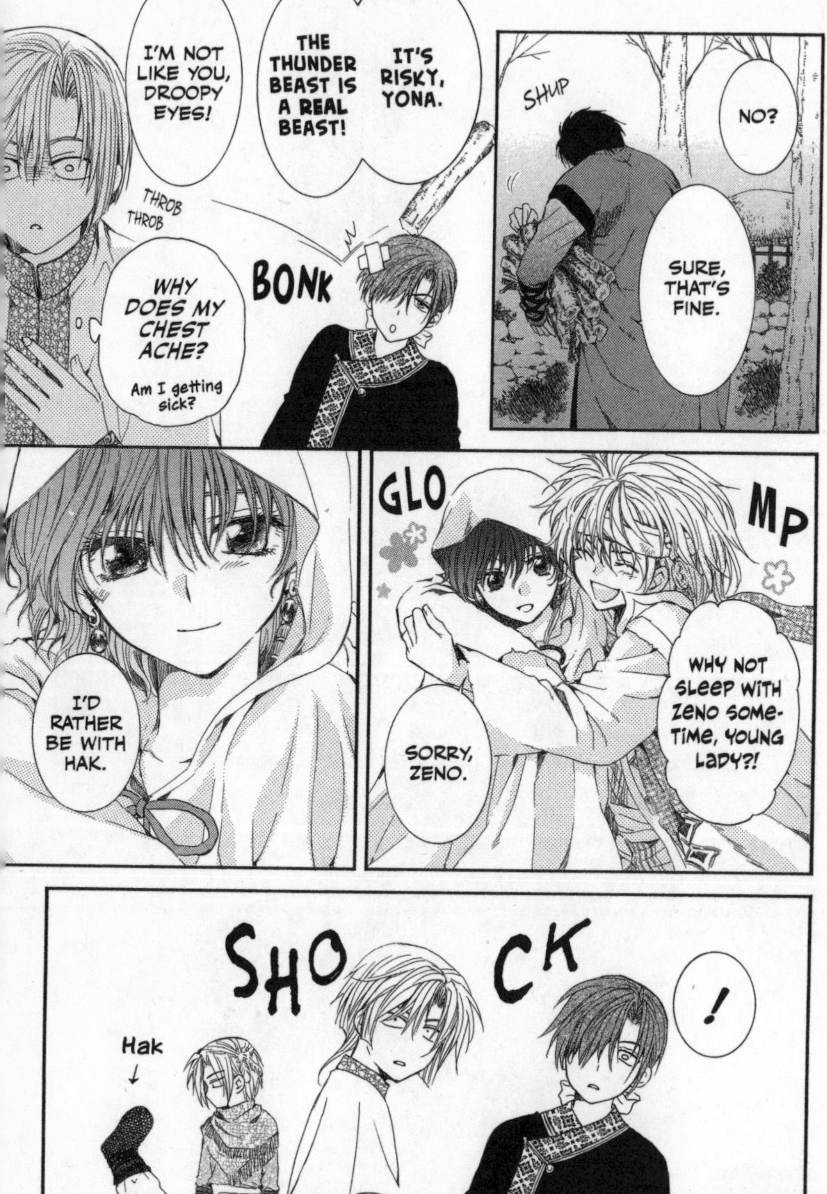
SHUP
NO?
SURE, THAT'S FINE.
IT'S RISKY, YONA.
THE THUNDER BEAST IS A REAL BEAST!
I'M NOT LIKE YOU, DROOPY EYES!
BONK
THROB THROB
WHY DOES MY CHEST ACHE?
Am I getting sick?
GLO
MP
WHY NOT SLEEP WITH ZENO SOME-TIME, YOUNG LADY?!
SORRY, ZENO.
I'D RATHER BE WITH HAK.
SHO
CK
!
Hak ↓

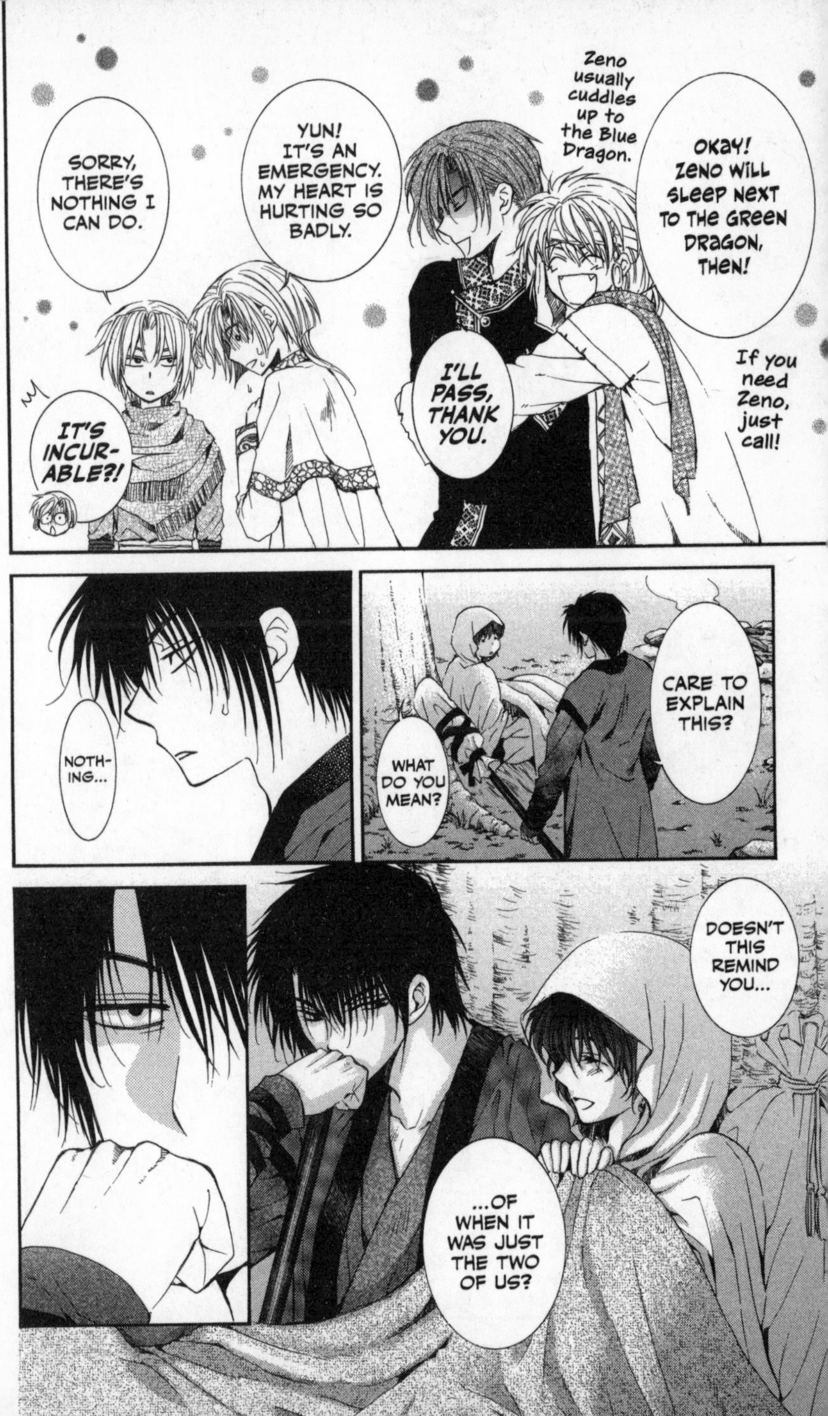
Zeno usually cuddles up to the Blue Dragon.
OKAY! ZENO WILL SLEEP NEXT TO THE GREEN DRAGON, THEN!
If you need Zeno, just call!
I'LL PASS, THANK YOU.
YUN! IT'S AN EMERGENCY. MY HEART IS HURTING SO BADLY.
SORRY, THERE'S NOTHING I CAN DO.
IT'S INCURABLE?!
CARE TO EXPLAIN THIS?
WHAT DO YOU MEAN?
NOTH-ING...
DOESN'T THIS REMIND YOU...
...OF WHEN IT WAS JUST THE TWO OF US?

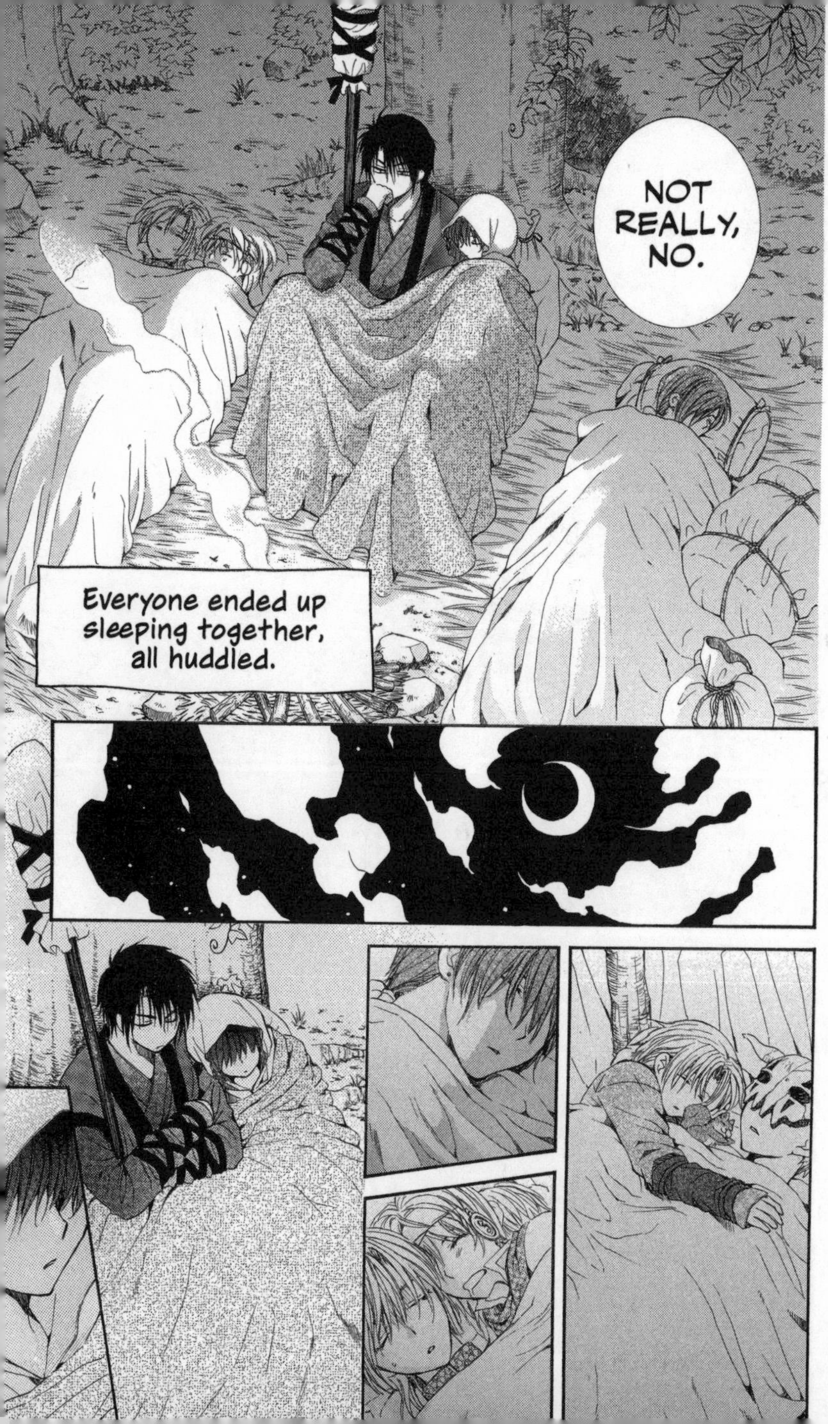
NOT REALLY, NO.
Everyone ended up sleeping together, all huddled.

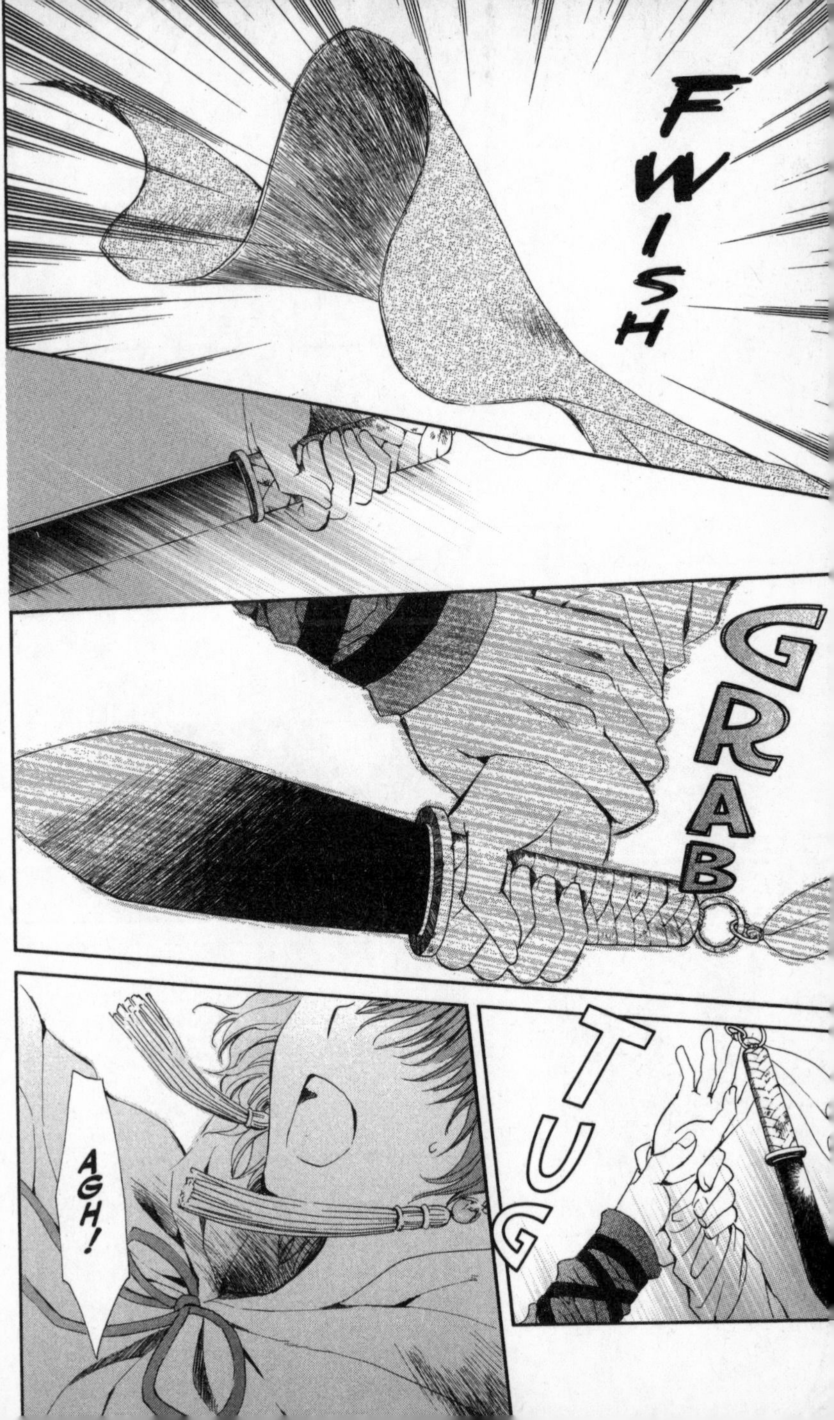
FWISH
GRAB
TUG
AGH!

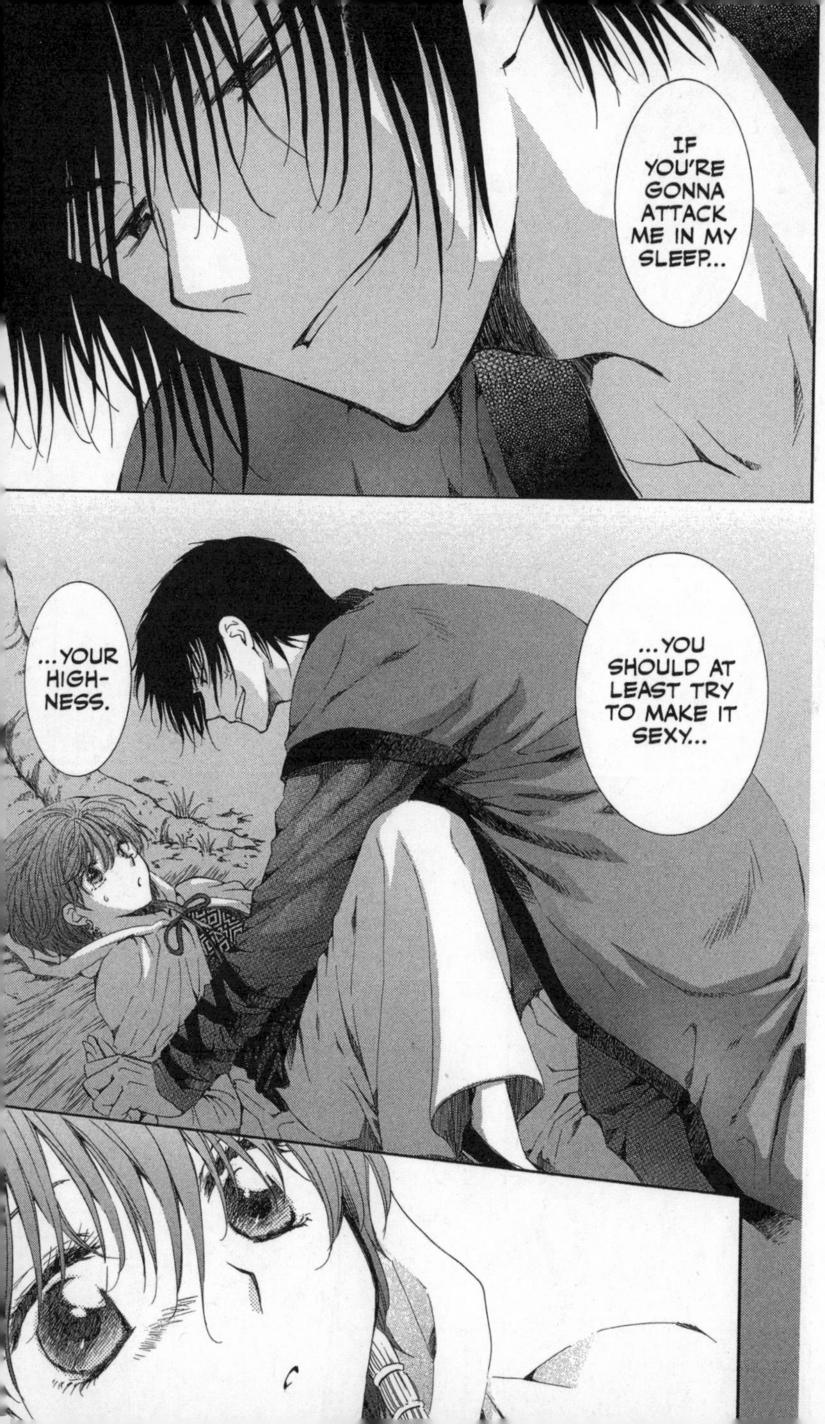
IF YOU'RE GONNA ATTACK ME IN MY SLEEP...
...YOU SHOULD AT LEAST TRY TO MAKE IT SEXY...
...YOUR HIGH-NESS.

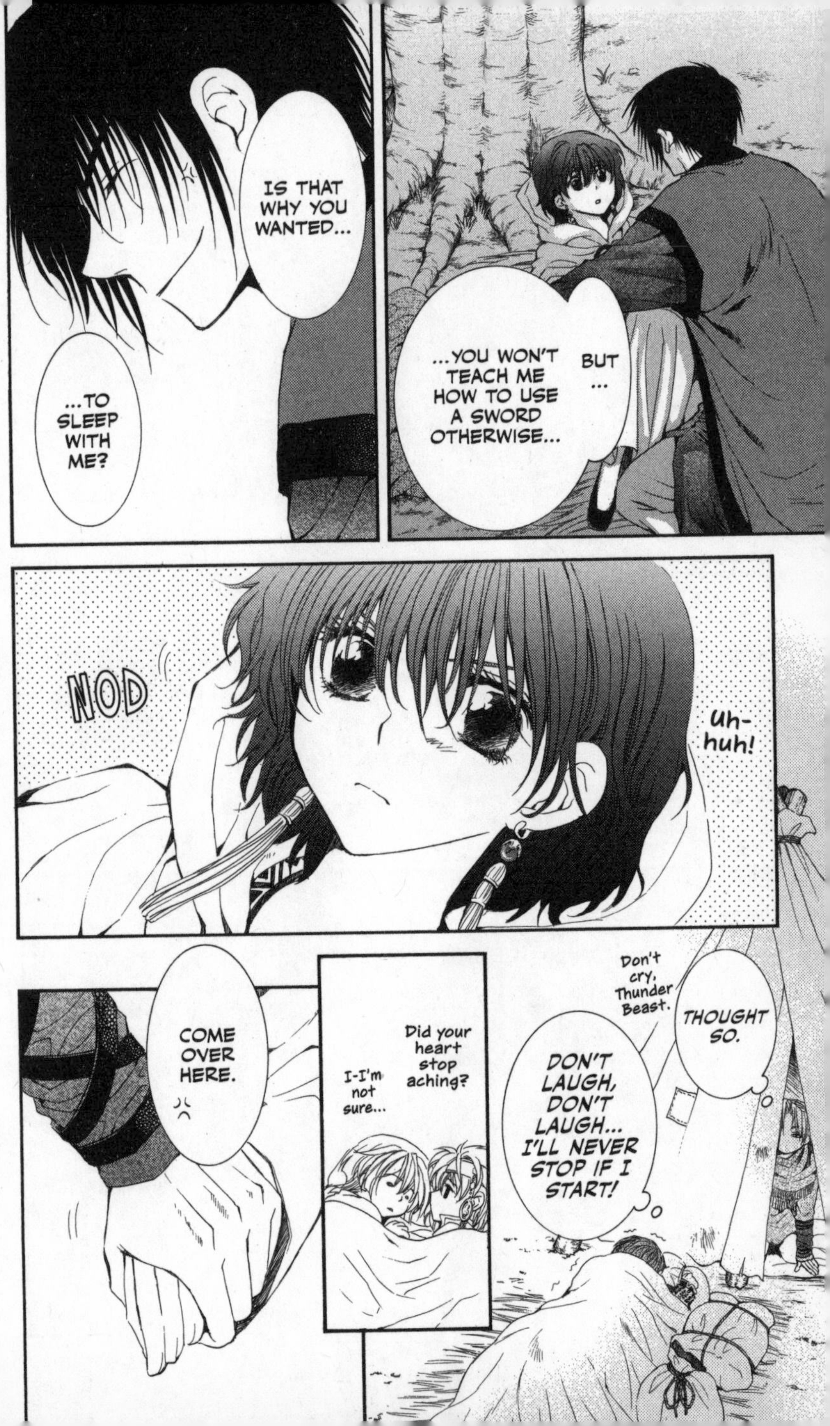
BUT...
...YOU WON'T TEACH ME HOW TO USE A SWORD OTHERWISE...
IS THAT WHY YOU WANTED...
...TO SLEEP WITH ME?
Uh-huh!
NOD
THOUGHT SO.
Don't cry, Thunder Beast.
DON'T LAUGH, DON'T LAUGH... I'LL NEVER STOP IF I START!
Did your heart stop aching?
I-I'm not sure...
COME OVER HERE.

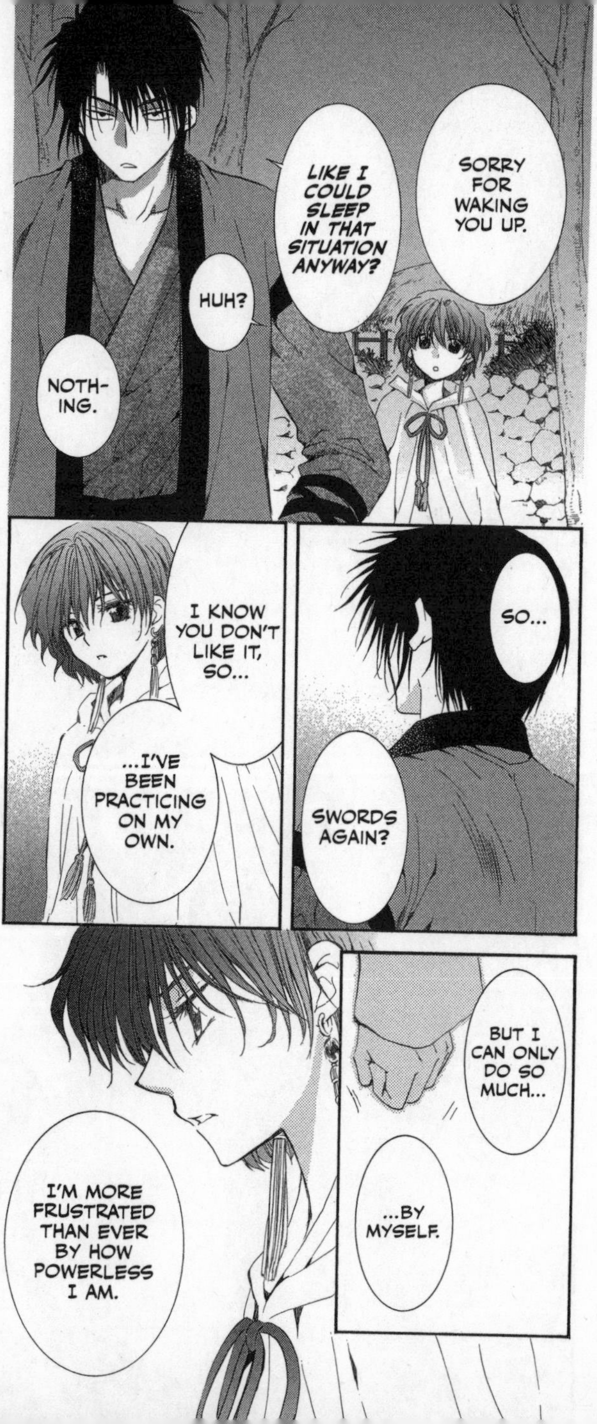
SORRY FOR WAKING YOU UP.
LIKE I COULD SLEEP IN THAT SITUATION ANYWAY?
HUH?
NOTHING.
SO...
SWORDS AGAIN?
I KNOW YOU DON'T LIKE IT, SO...
...I'VE BEEN PRACTICING ON MY OWN.
BUT I CAN ONLY DO SO MUCH...
...BY MYSELF.
I'M MORE FRUSTRATED THAN EVER BY HOW POWERLESS I AM.

Will there be new developments in this chapter?

One of my readers commented that Gija feels hurt that Yona wanted to sleep with Hak, but he thinks nothing of the fact that she usually sleeps with Yun. He totally thinks of Yun as a girl. (LOL!)

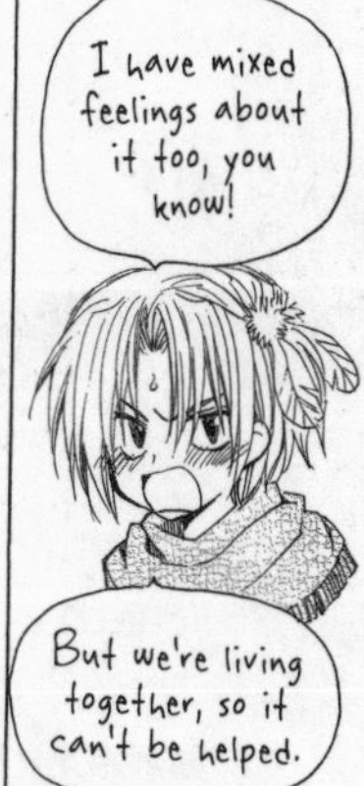
I have mixed feelings about it too, you know!
But we're living together, so it can't be helped.

Yun is a sensitive 15-year-old boy. Gija forgets that. Yona forgets it too.

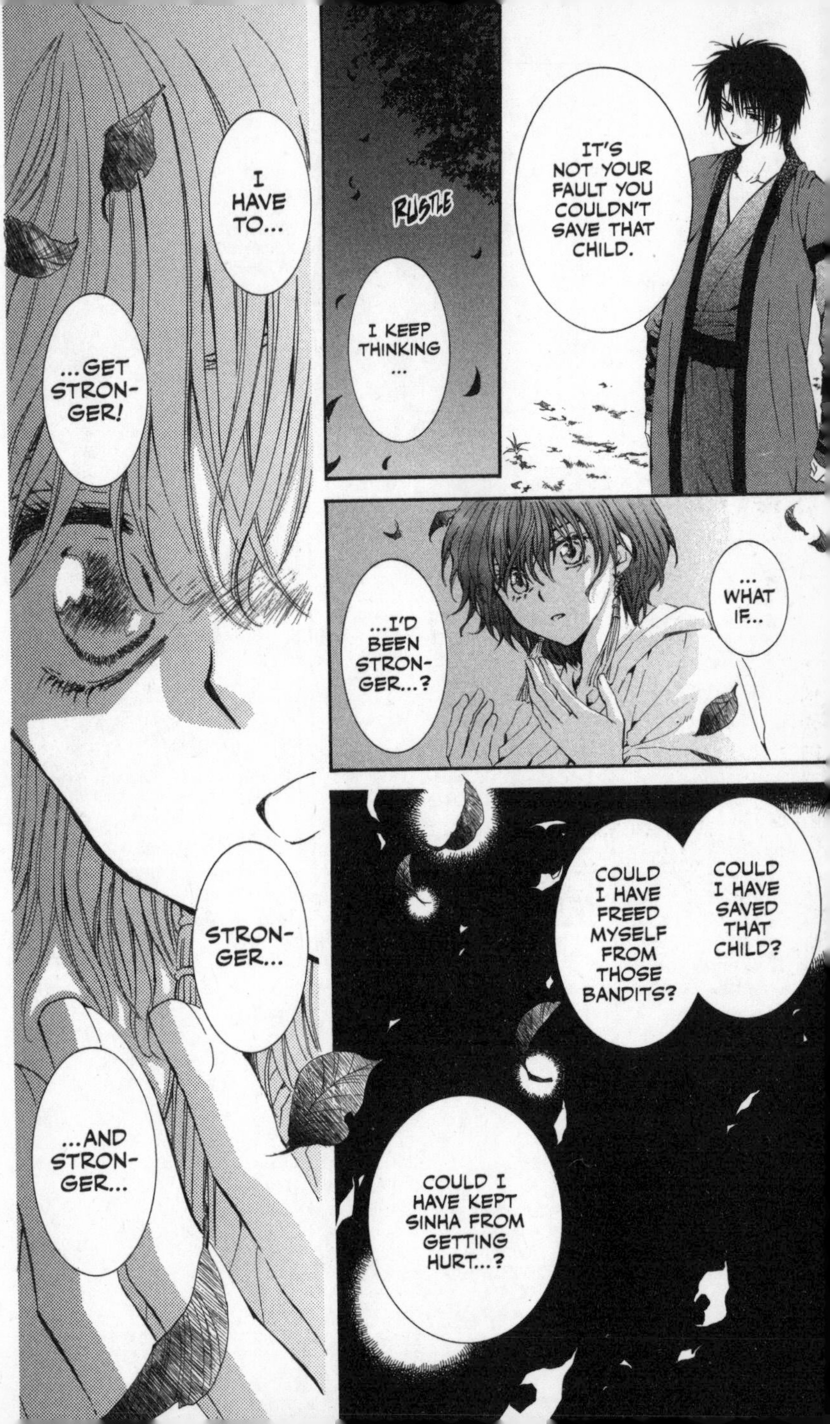

IT'S NOT YOUR FAULT YOU COULDN'T SAVE THAT CHILD.
RUSTLE
I KEEP THINKING ...
... WHAT IF...
...I'D BEEN STRON-GER...?
COULD I HAVE SAVED THAT CHILD?
COULD I HAVE FREED MYSELF FROM THOSE BANDITS?
COULD I HAVE KEPT SINHA FROM GETTING HURT...?
I HAVE TO...
...GET STRON-GER!
STRON-GER...
...AND STRON-GER...

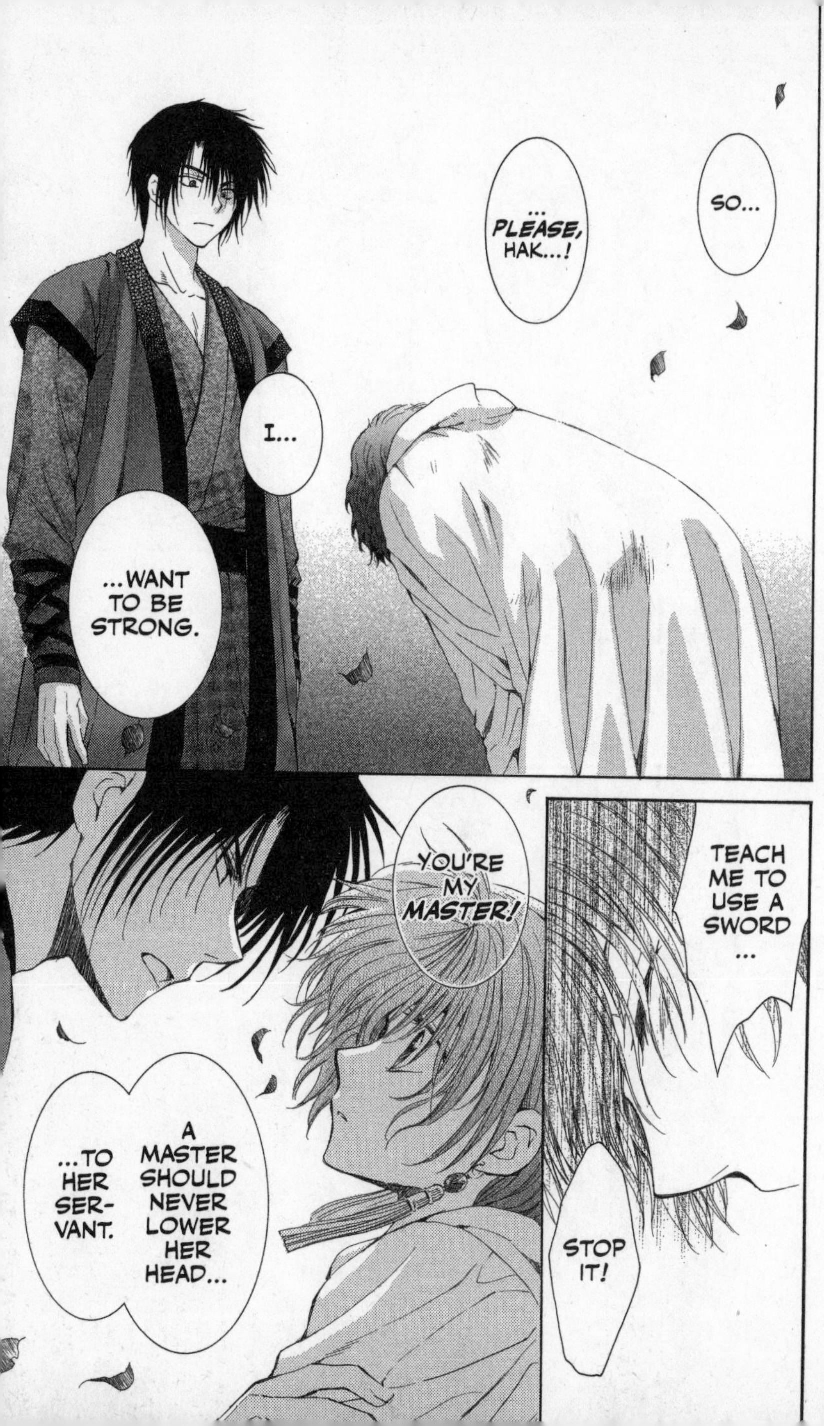
SO...
...PLEASE, HAK...!
I...
...WANT TO BE STRONG.
TEACH ME TO USE A SWORD...
STOP IT!
YOU'RE MY MASTER!
A MASTER SHOULD NEVER LOWER HER HEAD...
...TO HER SERVANT.

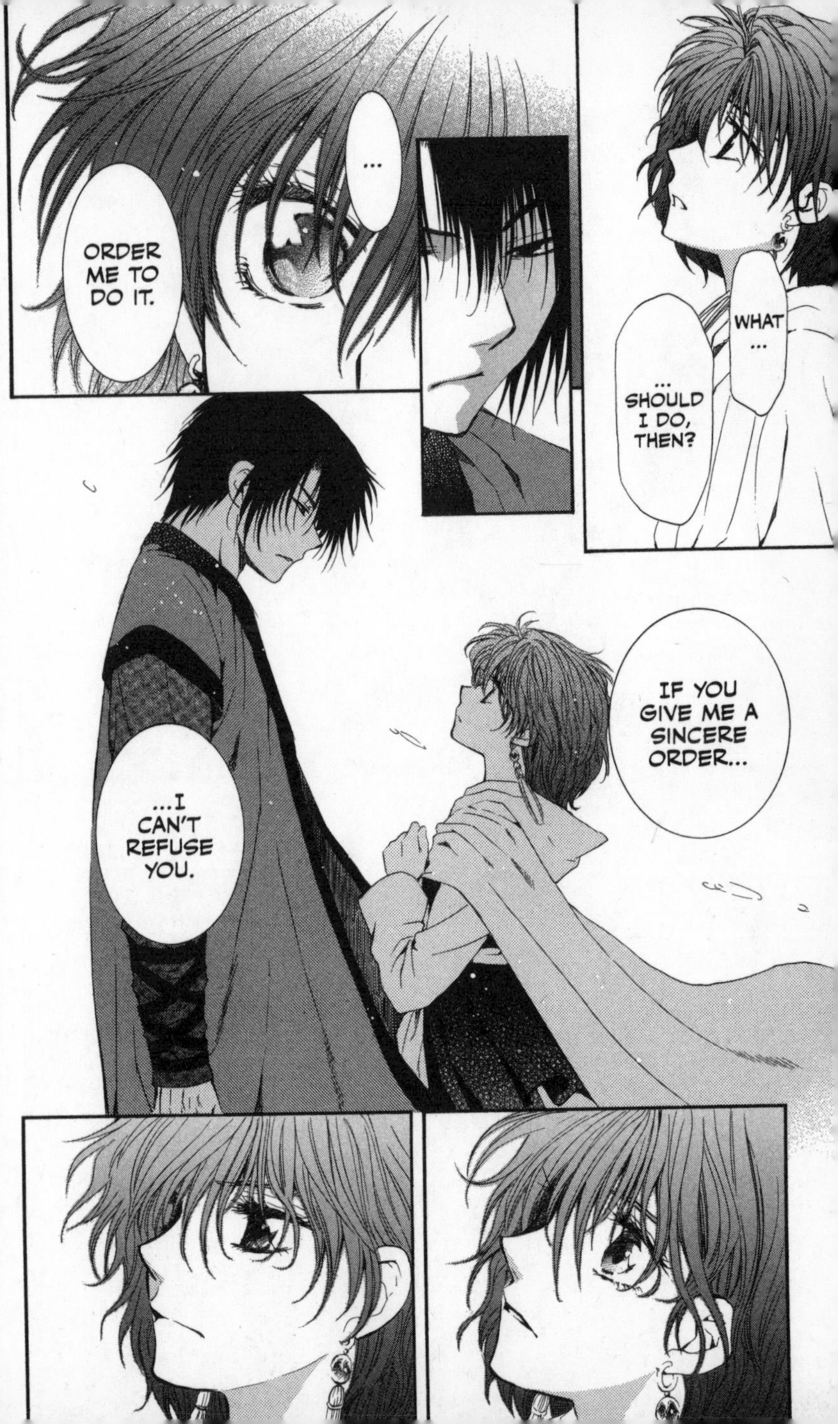
WHAT ...
... SHOULD I DO, THEN?
...
ORDER ME TO DO IT.
IF YOU GIVE ME A SINCERE ORDER...
...I CAN'T REFUSE YOU.

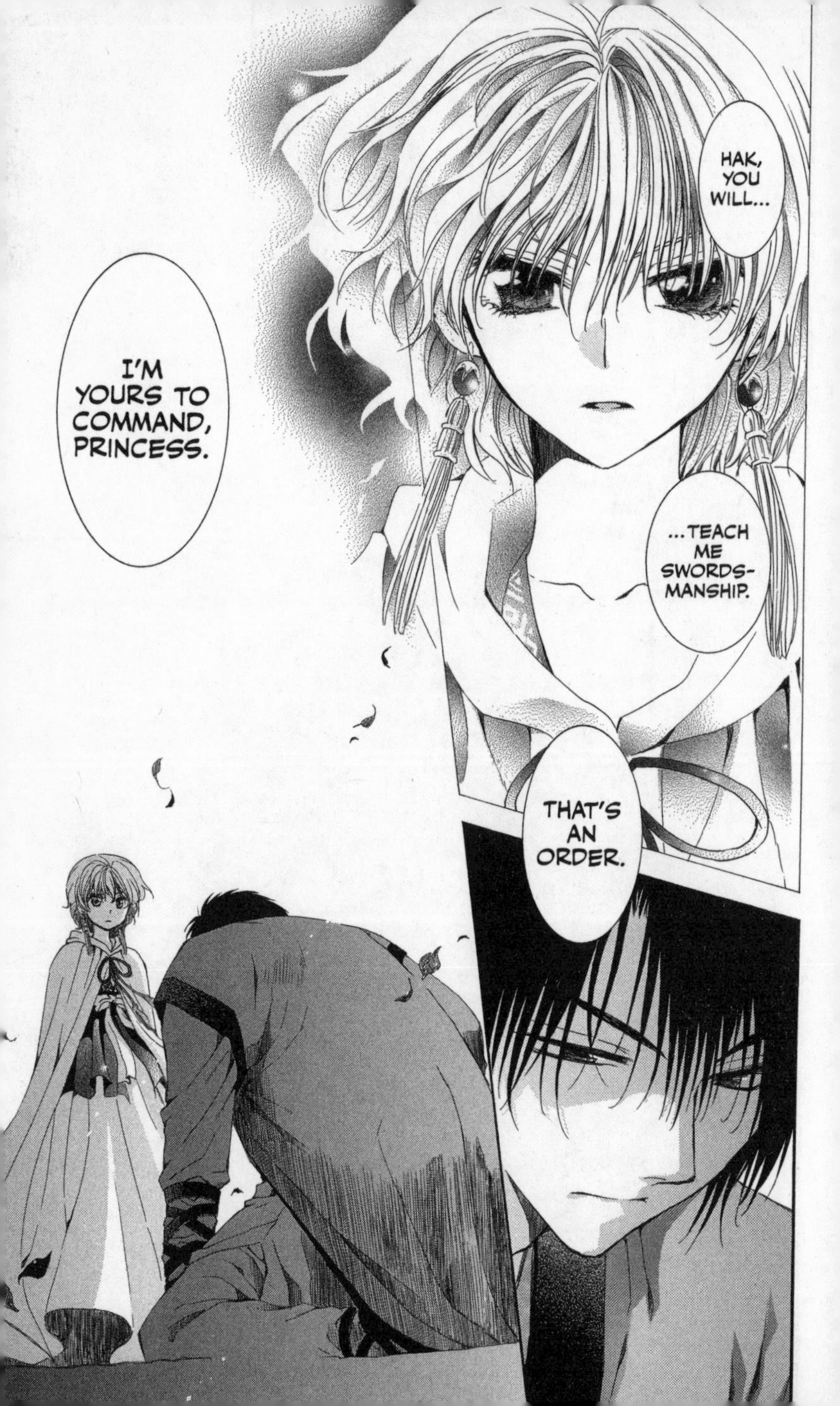
HAK, YOU WILL...
...TEACH ME SWORDS-MANSHIP.
THAT'S AN ORDER.
I'M YOURS TO COMMAND, PRINCESS.

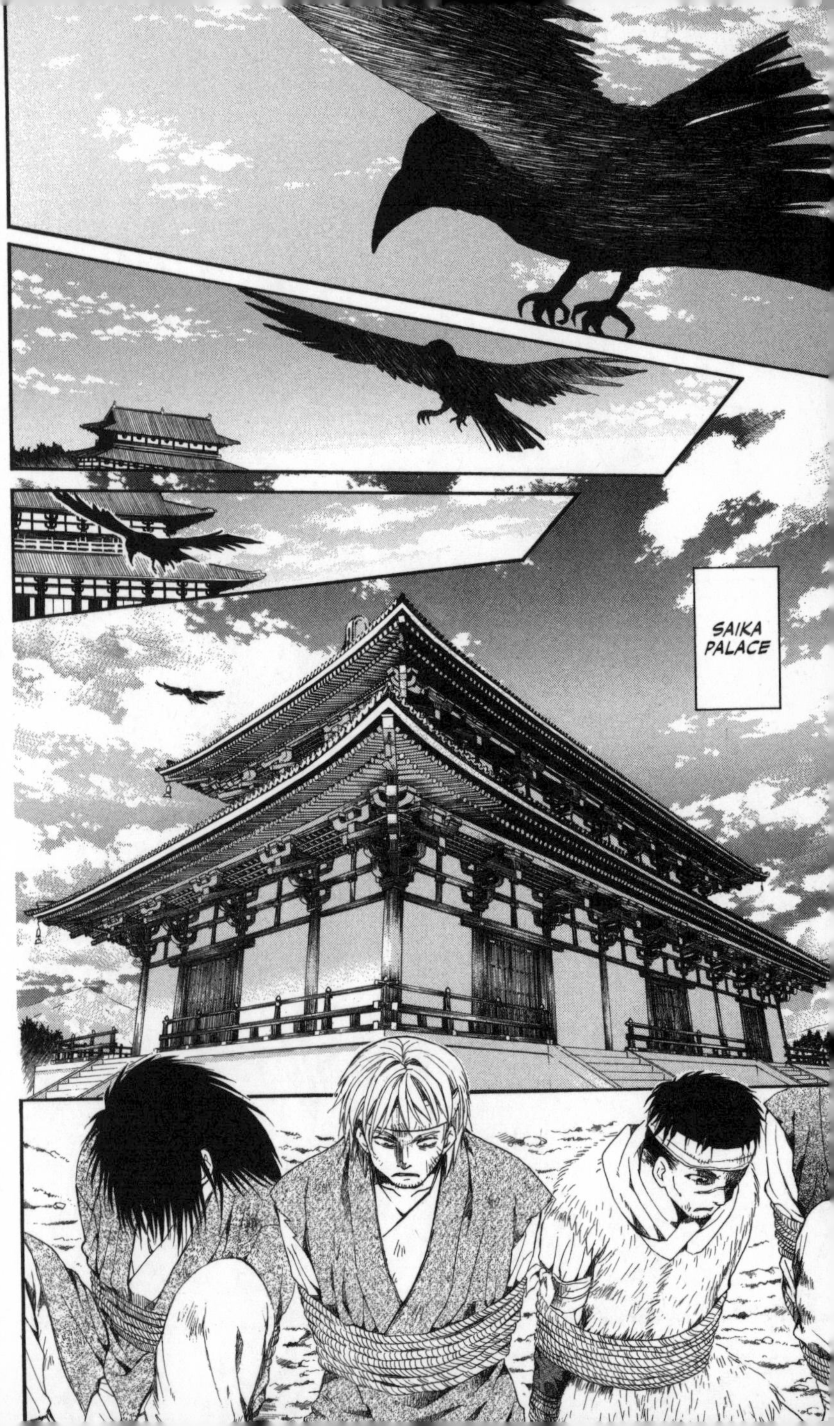
SAIKA PALACE

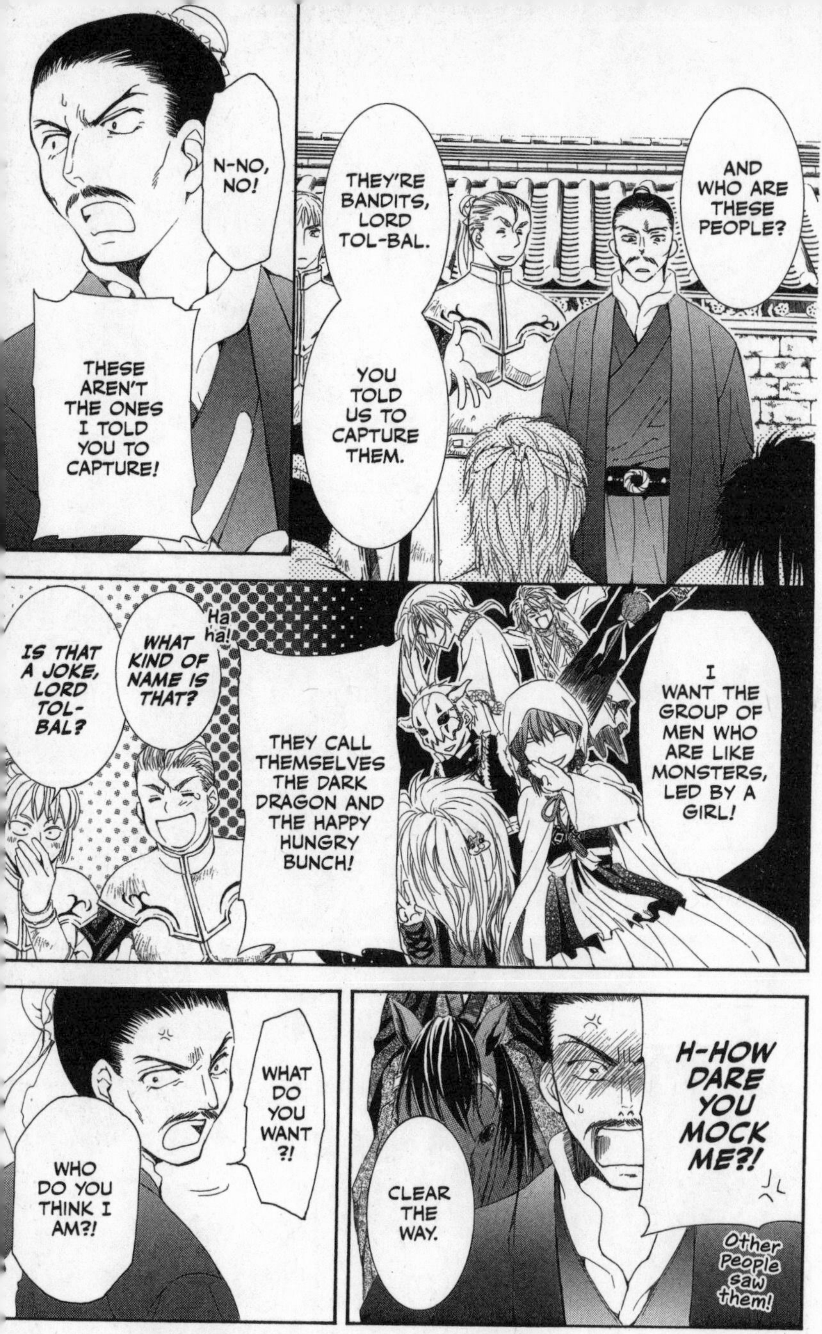
AND WHO ARE THESE PEOPLE?
THEY'RE BANDITS, LORD TOL-BAL.
YOU TOLD US TO CAPTURE THEM.
N-NO, NO!
THESE AREN'T THE ONES I TOLD YOU TO CAPTURE!
I WANT THE GROUP OF MEN WHO ARE LIKE MONSTERS, LED BY A GIRL!
THEY CALL THEMSELVES THE DARK DRAGON AND THE HAPPY HUNGRY BUNCH!
Ha ha!
WHAT KIND OF NAME IS THAT?
IS THAT A JOKE, LORD TOL-BAL?
H-HOW DARE YOU MOCK ME?!
Other People saw them!
CLEAR THE WAY.
WHAT DO YOU WANT?!
WHO DO YOU THINK I AM?!

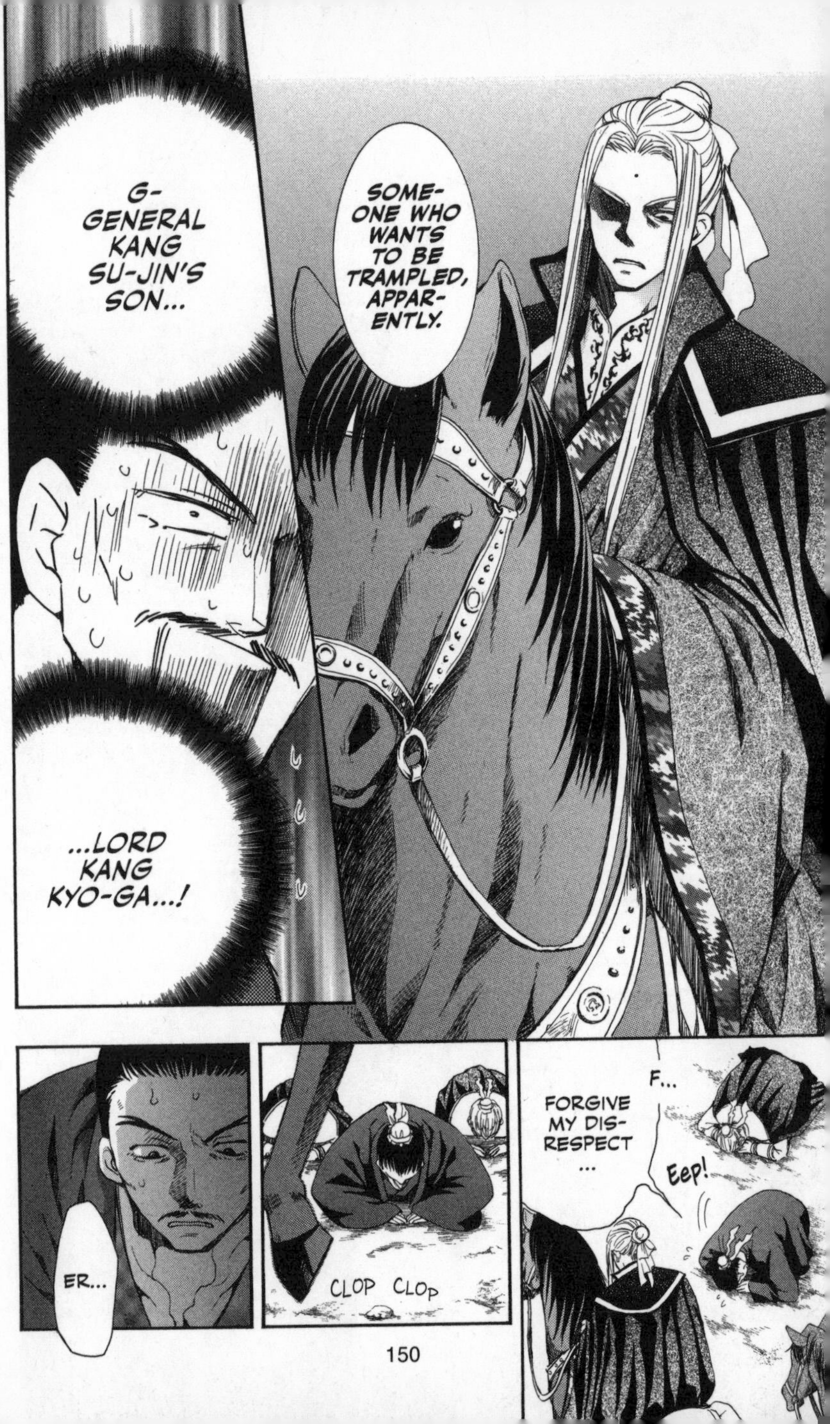
SOME-ONE WHO WANTS TO BE TRAMPLED, APPAR-ENTLY.
G-GENERAL KANG SU-JIN'S SON...
...LORD KANG KYO-GA...!
F...
FORGIVE MY DIS-RESPECT ...
Eep!
CLOP CLOP
ER...

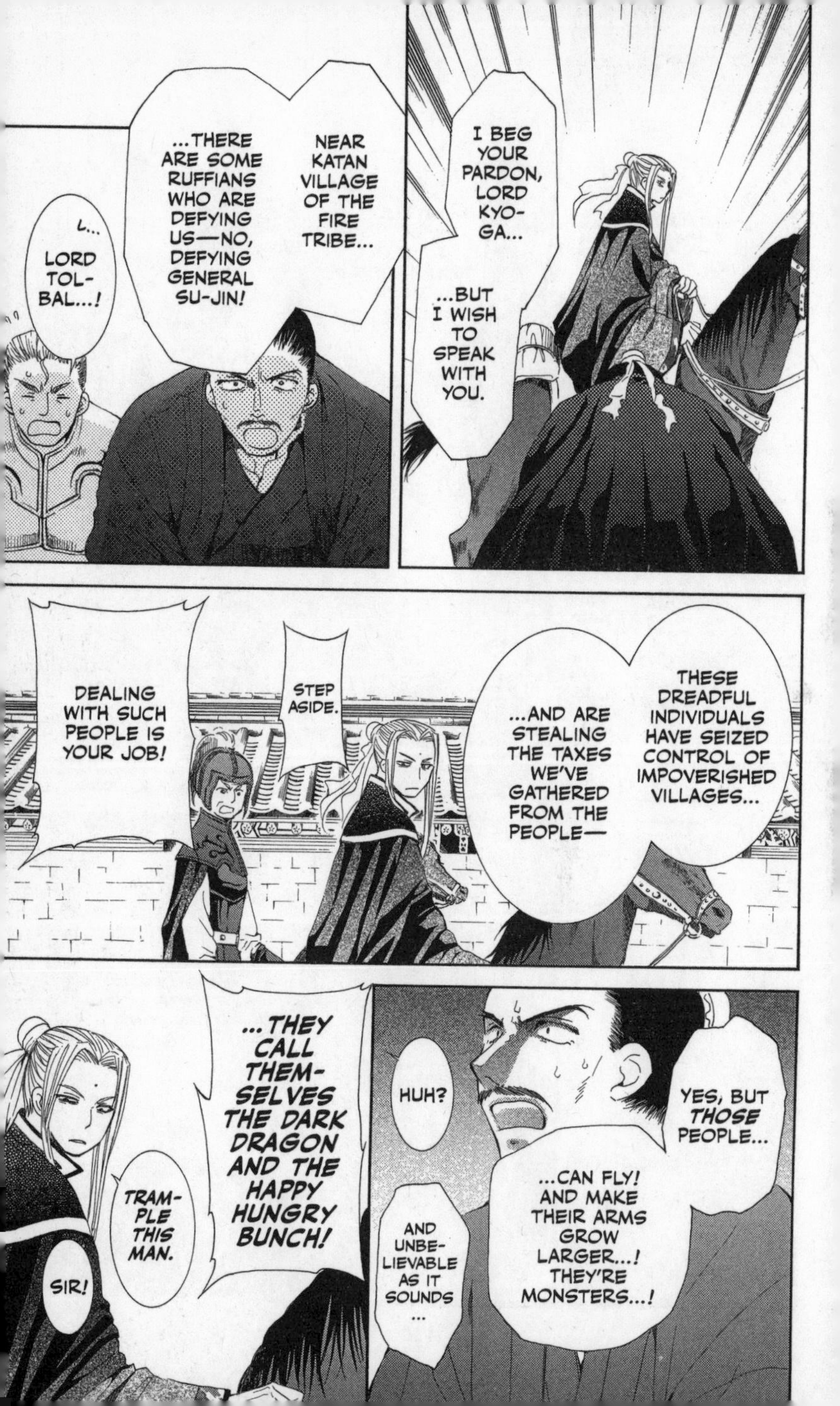
I BEG YOUR PARDON, LORD KYO-GA...
...BUT I WISH TO SPEAK WITH YOU.
NEAR KATAN VILLAGE OF THE FIRE TRIBE...
...THERE ARE SOME RUFFIANS WHO ARE DEFYING US—NO, DEFYING GENERAL SU-JIN!
L... LORD TOL-BAL...!
THESE DREADFUL INDIVIDUALS HAVE SEIZED CONTROL OF IMPOVERISHED VILLAGES...
...AND ARE STEALING THE TAXES WE'VE GATHERED FROM THE PEOPLE—
STEP ASIDE.
DEALING WITH SUCH PEOPLE IS YOUR JOB!
YES, BUT *THOSE* PEOPLE...
HUH?
...CAN FLY! AND MAKE THEIR ARMS GROW LARGER...! THEY'RE MONSTERS...!
AND UNBE-LIEVABLE AS IT SOUNDS...
...THEY CALL THEM-SELVES THE DARK DRAGON AND THE HAPPY HUNGRY BUNCH!
TRAM-PLE THIS MAN.
SIR!

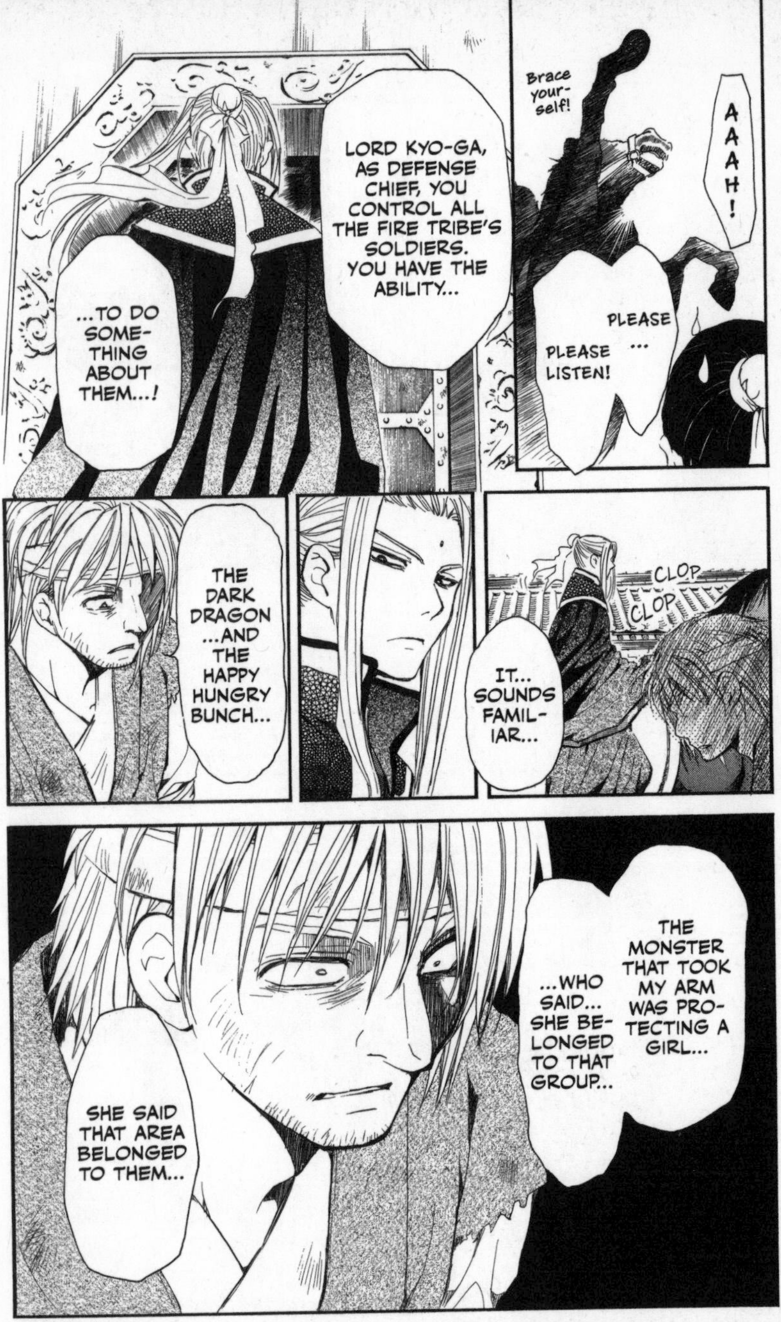
AAAH!
Brace yourself!
PLEASE... PLEASE LISTEN!
LORD KYO-GA, AS DEFENSE CHIEF, YOU CONTROL ALL THE FIRE TRIBE'S SOLDIERS. YOU HAVE THE ABILITY...
...TO DO SOMETHING ABOUT THEM...!
CLOP
CLOP
IT... SOUNDS FAMILIAR...
THE DARK DRAGON ...AND THE HAPPY HUNGRY BUNCH...
THE MONSTER THAT TOOK MY ARM WAS PROTECTING A GIRL...
...WHO SAID... SHE BELONGED TO THAT GROUP...
SHE SAID THAT AREA BELONGED TO THEM...

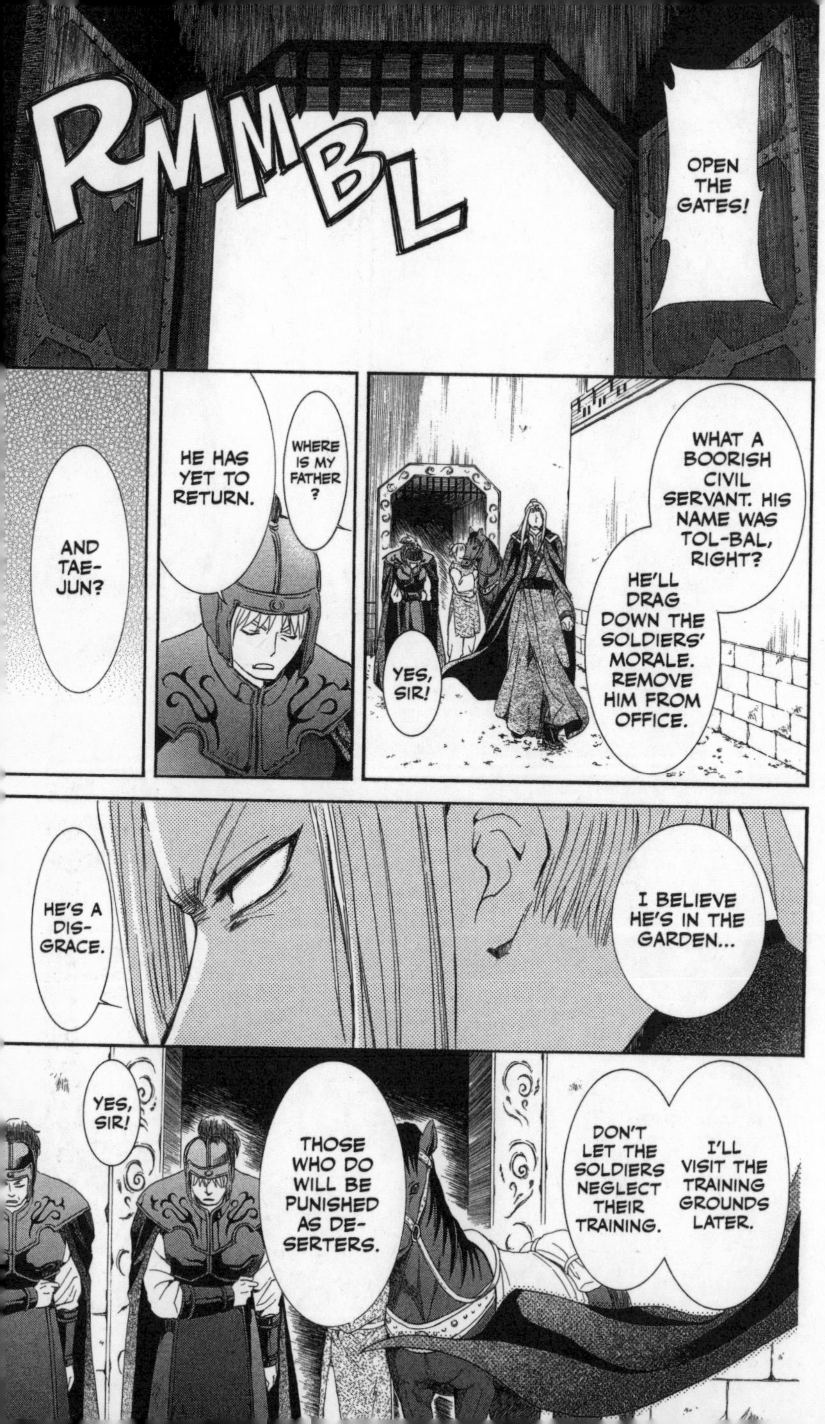
OPEN THE GATES!
RMMBL
WHAT A BOORISH CIVIL SERVANT. HIS NAME WAS TOL-BAL, RIGHT?
HE'LL DRAG DOWN THE SOLDIERS' MORALE. REMOVE HIM FROM OFFICE.
YES, SIR!
WHERE IS MY FATHER?
HE HAS YET TO RETURN.
AND TAE-JUN?
I BELIEVE HE'S IN THE GARDEN...
HE'S A DISGRACE.
I'LL VISIT THE TRAINING GROUNDS LATER.
DON'T LET THE SOLDIERS NEGLECT THEIR TRAINING.
THOSE WHO DO WILL BE PUNISHED AS DESERTERS.
YES, SIR!

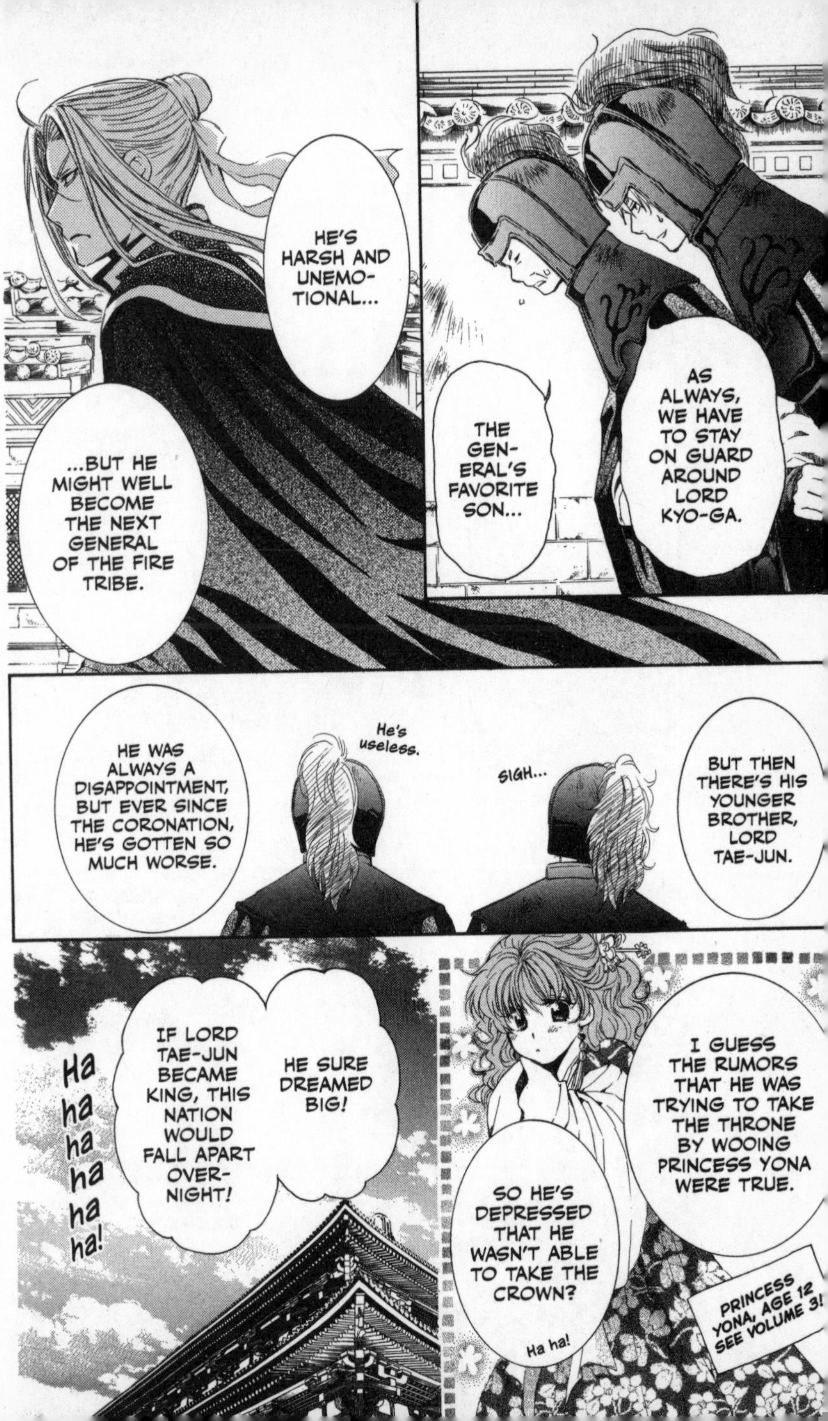
AS ALWAYS, WE HAVE TO STAY ON GUARD AROUND LORD KYO-GA.
THE GENERAL'S FAVORITE SON...
HE'S HARSH AND UNEMOTIONAL...
...BUT HE MIGHT WELL BECOME THE NEXT GENERAL OF THE FIRE TRIBE.
BUT THEN THERE'S HIS YOUNGER BROTHER, LORD TAE-JUN.
SIGH...
He's useless.
HE WAS ALWAYS A DISAPPOINTMENT, BUT EVER SINCE THE CORONATION, HE'S GOTTEN SO MUCH WORSE.
I GUESS THE RUMORS THAT HE WAS TRYING TO TAKE THE THRONE BY WOOING PRINCESS YONA WERE TRUE.
SO HE'S DEPRESSED THAT HE WASN'T ABLE TO TAKE THE CROWN?
Ha ha!
PRINCESS YONA, AGE 12 SEE VOLUME 3!
HE SURE DREAMED BIG!
IF LORD TAE-JUN BECAME KING, THIS NATION WOULD FALL APART OVERNIGHT!
Ha ha ha ha ha ha!

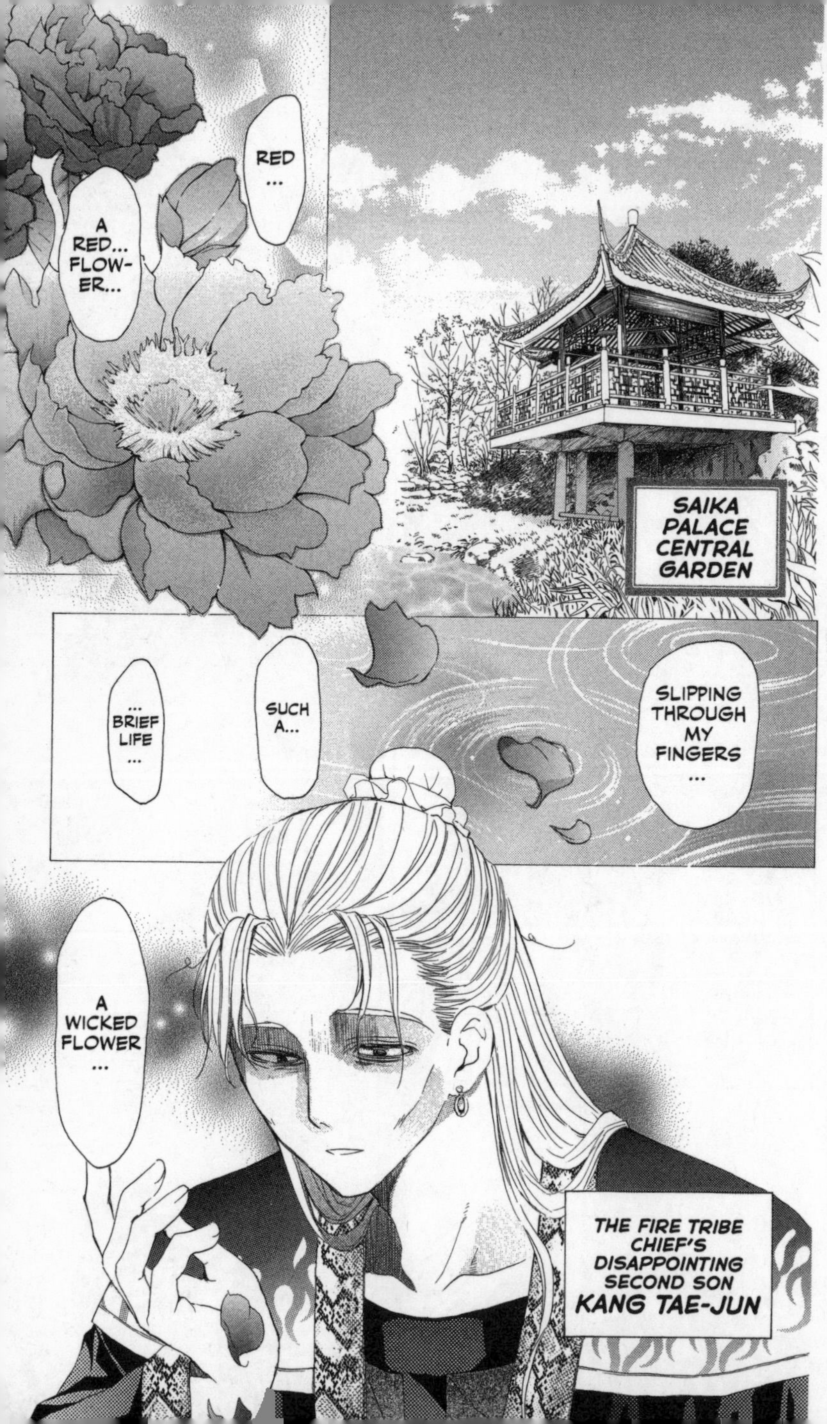
SAIKA PALACE CENTRAL GARDEN
RED ...
A RED... FLOWER-ER...
SLIPPING THROUGH MY FINGERS ...
SUCH A...
... BRIEF LIFE ...
A WICKED FLOWER ...
THE FIRE TRIBE CHIEF'S DISAPPOINTING SECOND SON KANG TAE-JUN

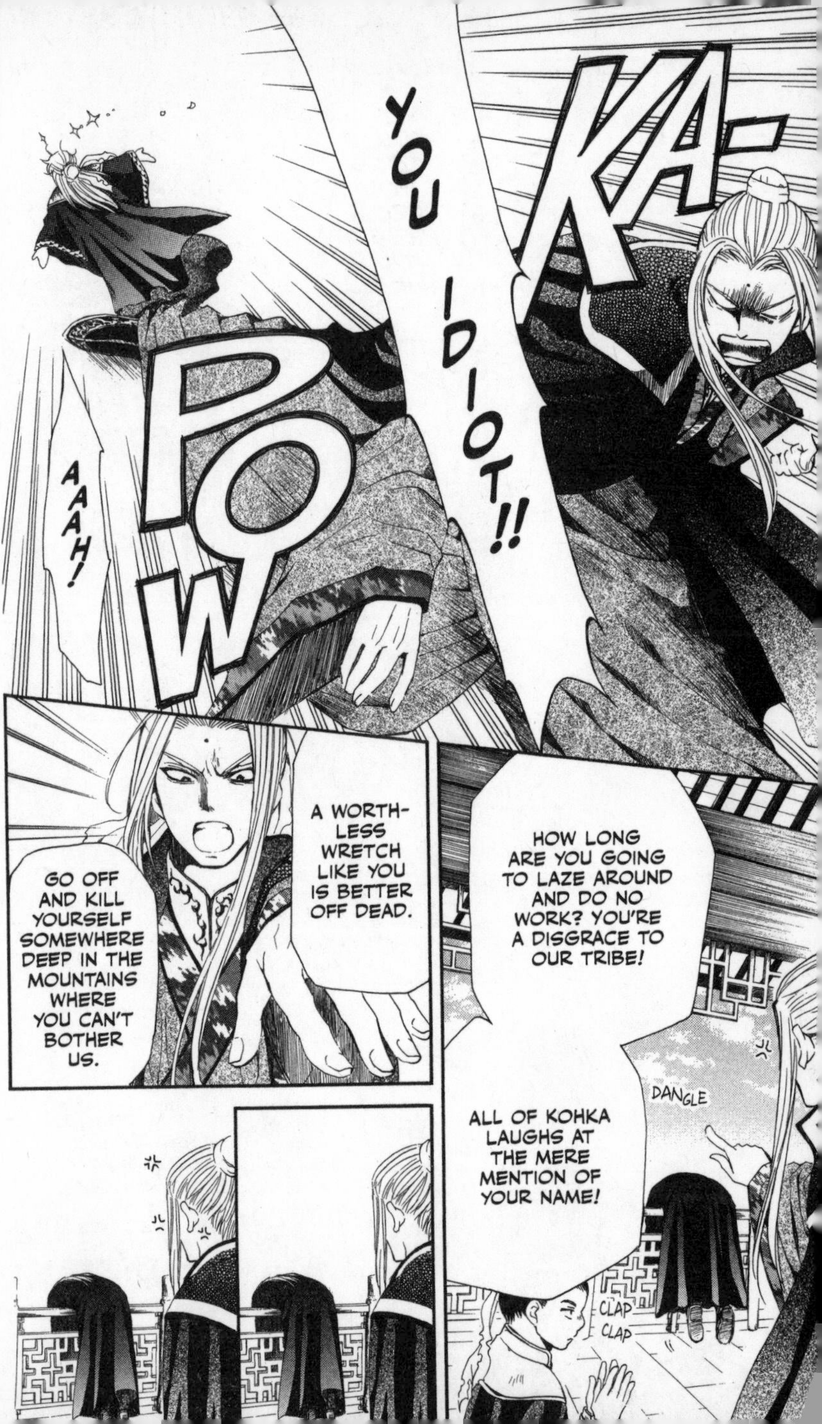
KA-
POW
YOU IDIOT!!
AAAH!
HOW LONG ARE YOU GOING TO LAZE AROUND AND DO NO WORK? YOU'RE A DISGRACE TO OUR TRIBE!
DANGLE
ALL OF KOHKA LAUGHS AT THE MERE MENTION OF YOUR NAME!
CLAP CLAP
A WORTHLESS WRETCH LIKE YOU IS BETTER OFF DEAD.
GO OFF AND KILL YOURSELF SOMEWHERE DEEP IN THE MOUNTAINS WHERE YOU CAN'T BOTHER US.

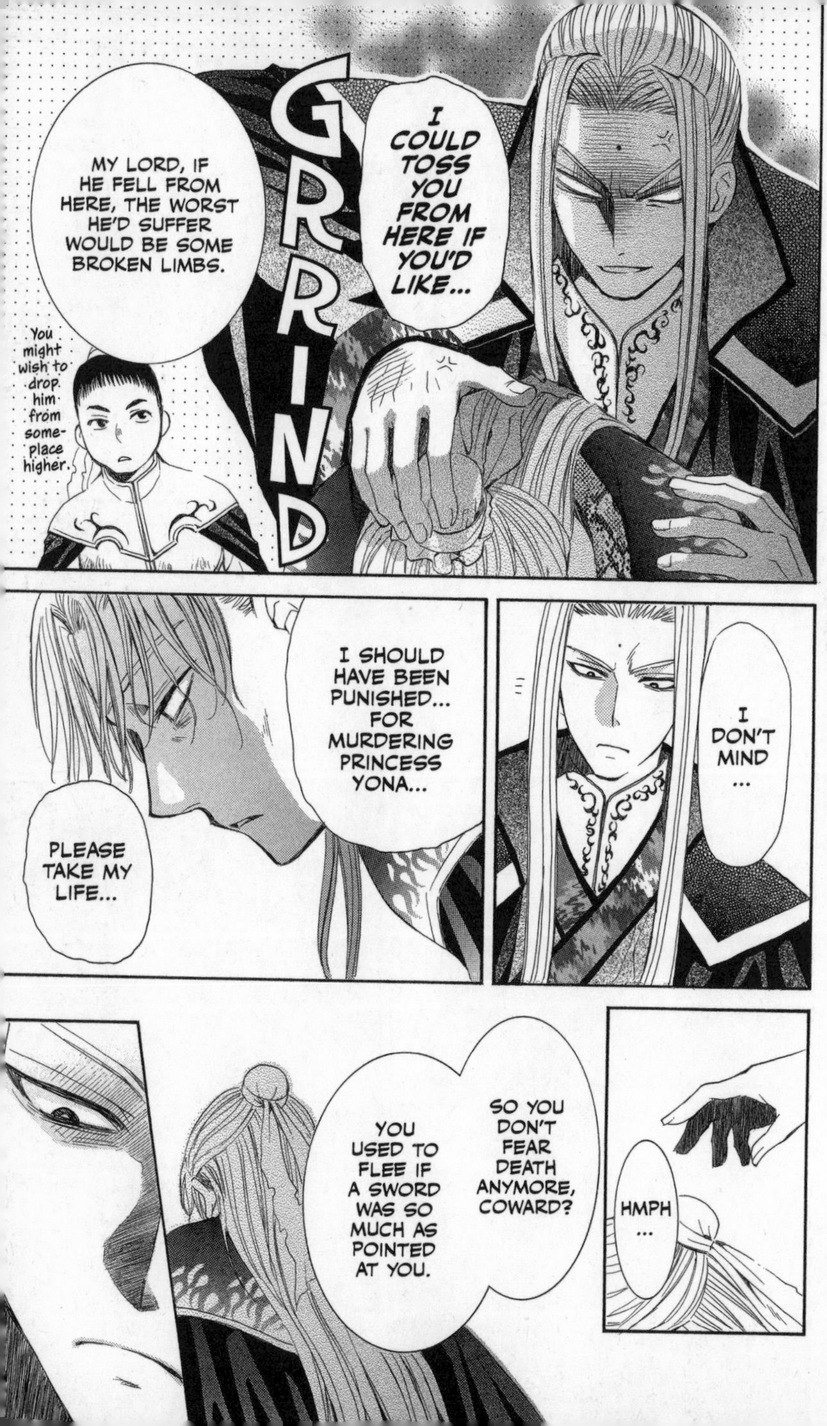
I COULD TOSS YOU FROM HERE IF YOU'D LIKE...
GRRIND
MY LORD, IF HE FELL FROM HERE, THE WORST HE'D SUFFER WOULD BE SOME BROKEN LIMBS.
You might wish to drop him from some-place higher.
I DON'T MIND ...
I SHOULD HAVE BEEN PUNISHED... FOR MURDERING PRINCESS YONA...
PLEASE TAKE MY LIFE...
HMPH ...
SO YOU DON'T FEAR DEATH ANYMORE, COWARD?
YOU USED TO FLEE IF A SWORD WAS SO MUCH AS POINTED AT YOU.

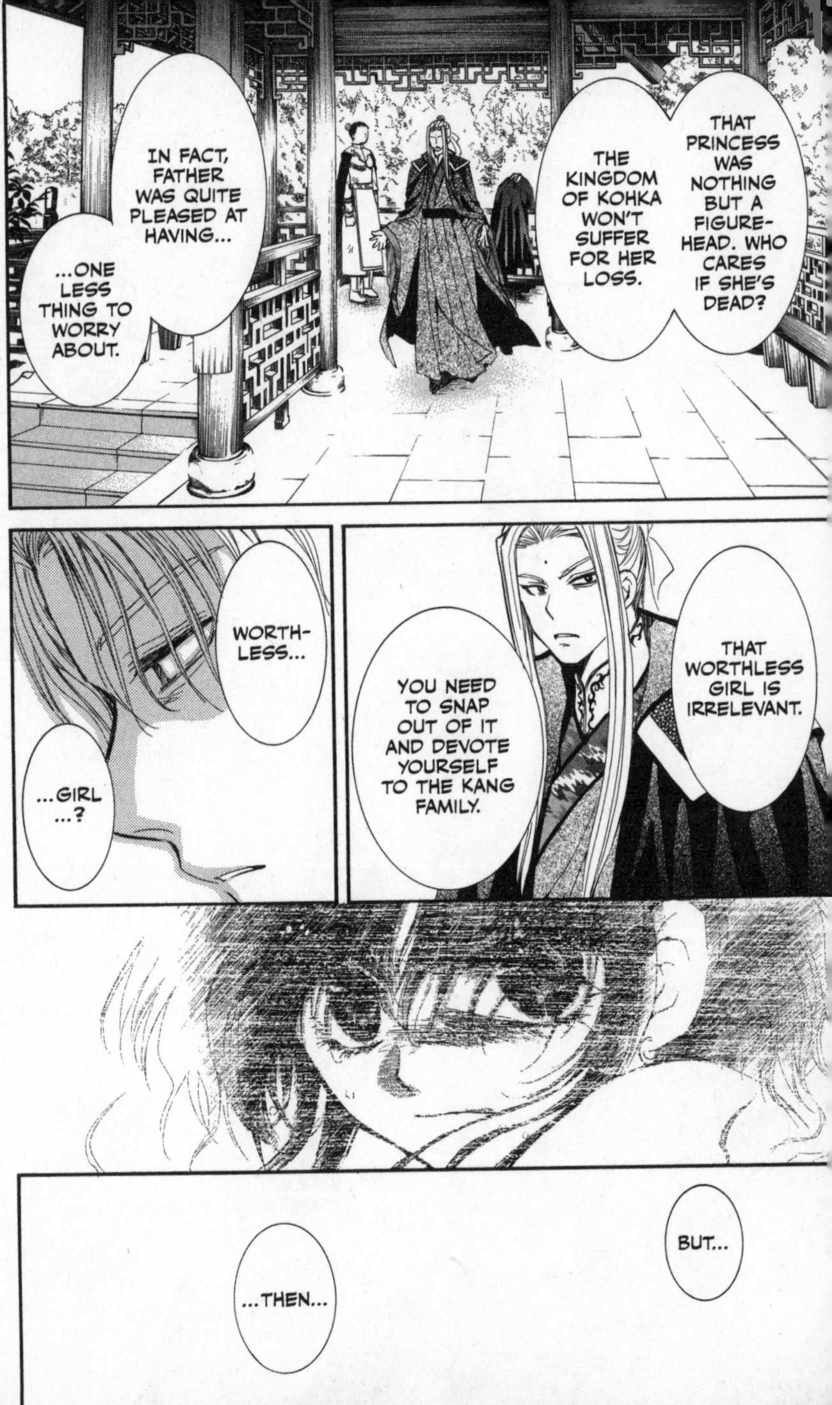
THAT PRINCESS WAS NOTHING BUT A FIGURE-HEAD. WHO CARES IF SHE'S DEAD?
THE KINGDOM OF KOHKA WON'T SUFFER FOR HER LOSS.
IN FACT, FATHER WAS QUITE PLEASED AT HAVING...
...ONE LESS THING TO WORRY ABOUT.
THAT WORTHLESS GIRL IS IRRELEVANT.
YOU NEED TO SNAP OUT OF IT AND DEVOTE YOURSELF TO THE KANG FAMILY.
WORTH-LESS...
...GIRL ...?
BUT...
...THEN...

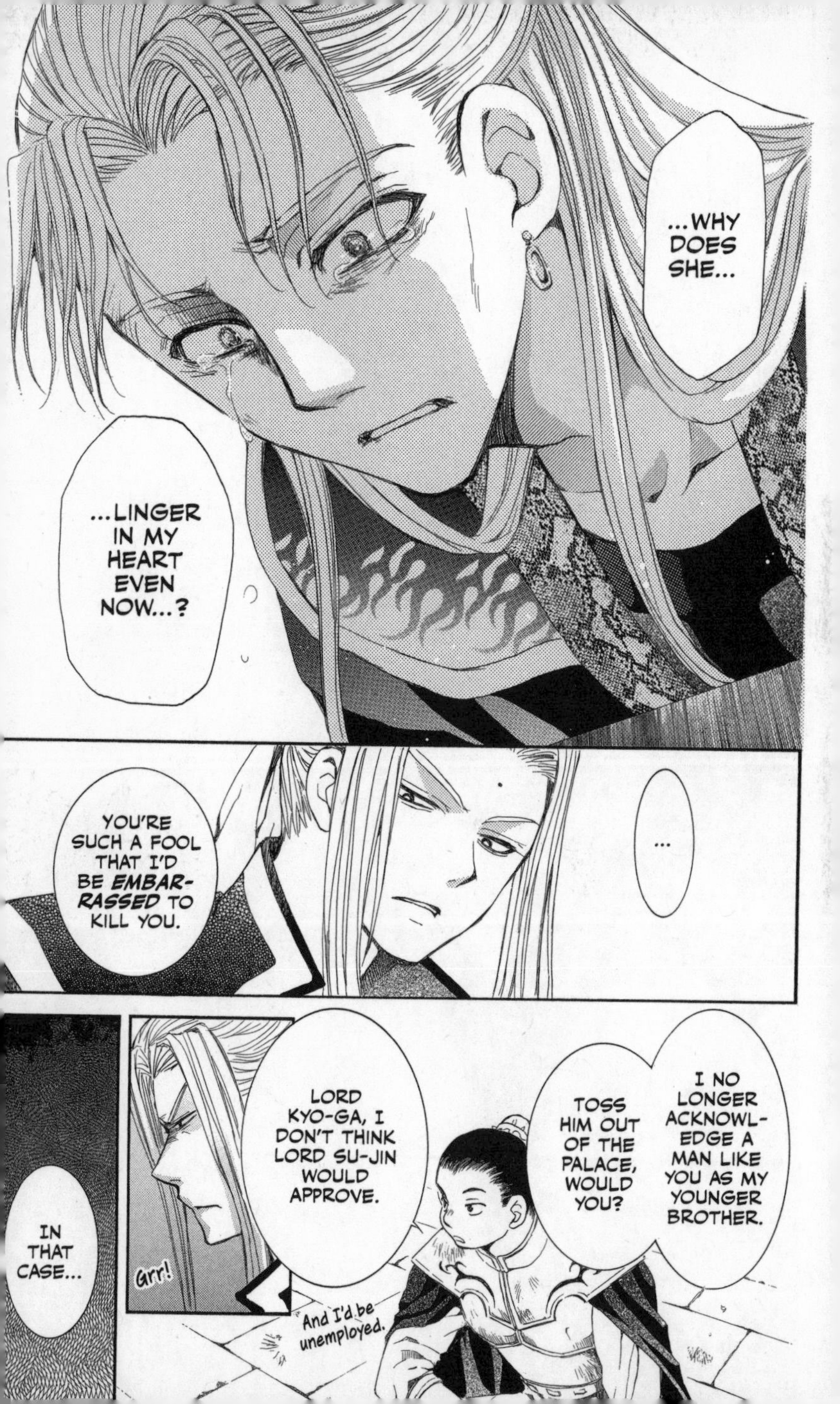
...WHY DOES SHE...
...LINGER IN MY HEART EVEN NOW...?
...
YOU'RE SUCH A FOOL THAT I'D BE *EMBARRASSED* TO KILL YOU.
I NO LONGER ACKNOWLEDGE A MAN LIKE YOU AS MY YOUNGER BROTHER.
TOSS HIM OUT OF THE PALACE, WOULD YOU?
LORD KYO-GA, I DON'T THINK LORD SU-JIN WOULD APPROVE.
And I'd be unemployed.
Grr!
IN THAT CASE...

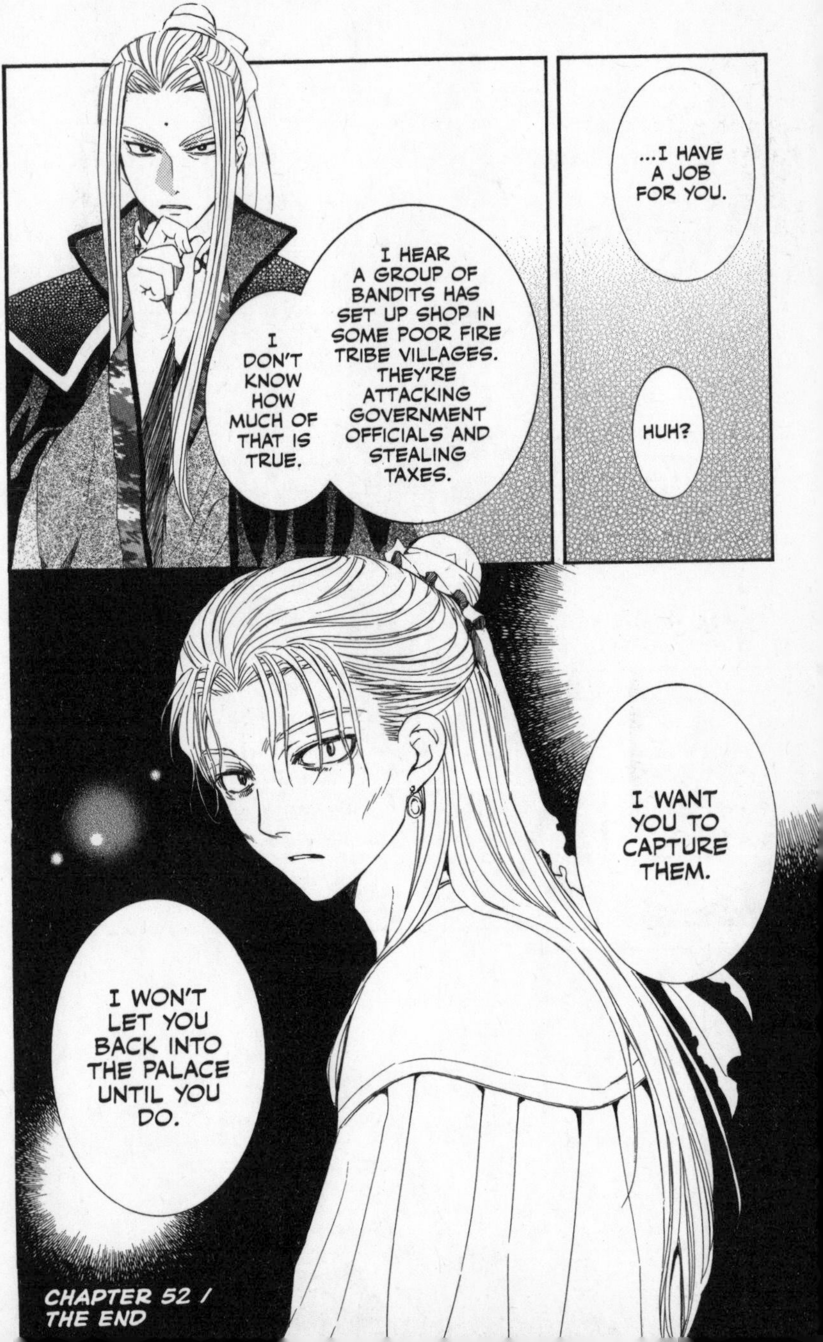
...I HAVE A JOB FOR YOU.
HUH?
I HEAR A GROUP OF BANDITS HAS SET UP SHOP IN SOME POOR FIRE TRIBE VILLAGES. THEY'RE ATTACKING GOVERNMENT OFFICIALS AND STEALING TAXES.
I DON'T KNOW HOW MUCH OF THAT IS TRUE.
I WANT YOU TO CAPTURE THEM.
I WON'T LET YOU BACK INTO THE PALACE UNTIL YOU DO.
CHAPTER 52 / THE END

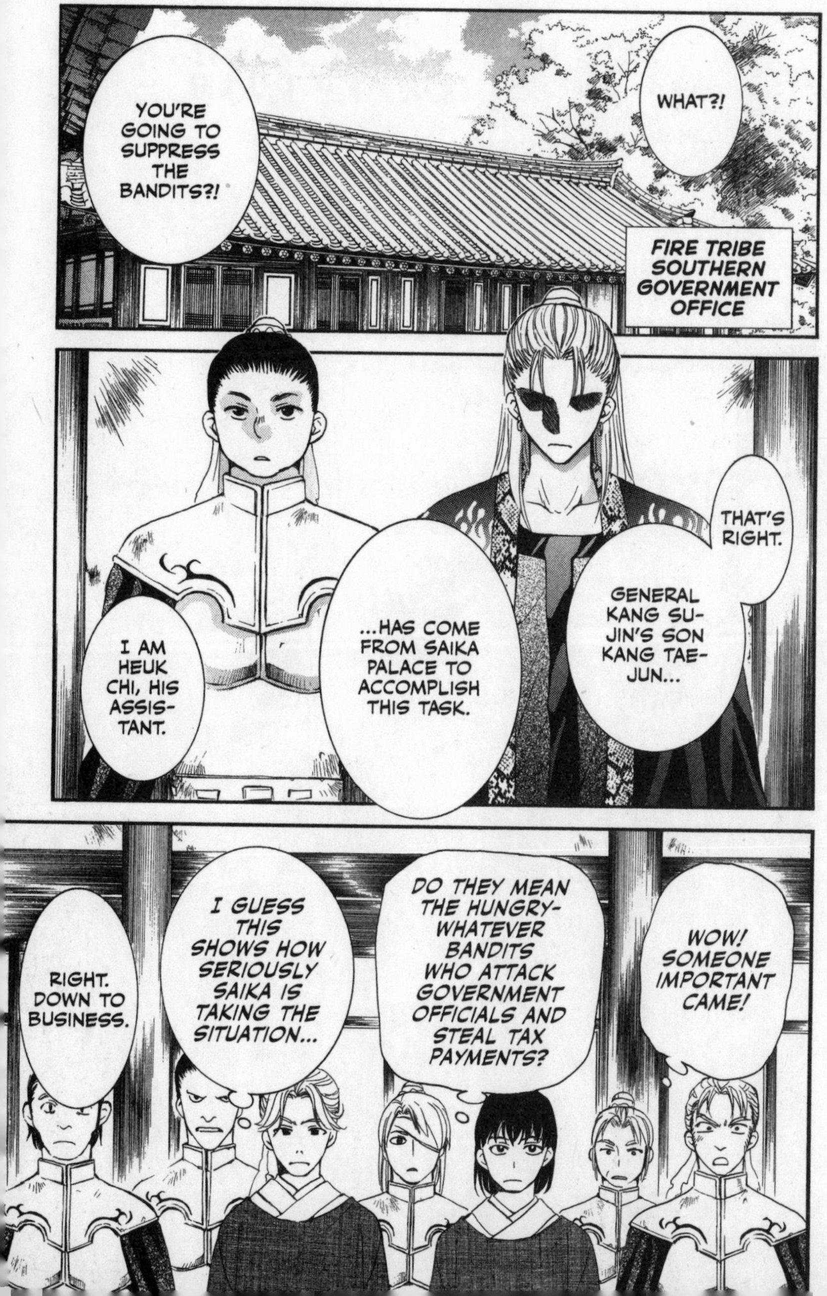
WHAT?!
YOU'RE GOING TO SUPPRESS THE BANDITS?!
FIRE TRIBE SOUTHERN GOVERNMENT OFFICE
THAT'S RIGHT.
GENERAL KANG SU-JIN'S SON KANG TAE-JUN...
...HAS COME FROM SAIKA PALACE TO ACCOMPLISH THIS TASK.
I AM HEUK CHI, HIS ASSISTANT.
WOW! SOMEONE IMPORTANT CAME!
DO THEY MEAN THE HUNGRY-WHATEVER BANDITS WHO ATTACK GOVERNMENT OFFICIALS AND STEAL TAX PAYMENTS?
I GUESS THIS SHOWS HOW SERIOUSLY SAIKA IS TAKING THE SITUATION...
RIGHT. DOWN TO BUSINESS.

CHAPTER 53: LORD TAE-JUN'S DEATH WISH

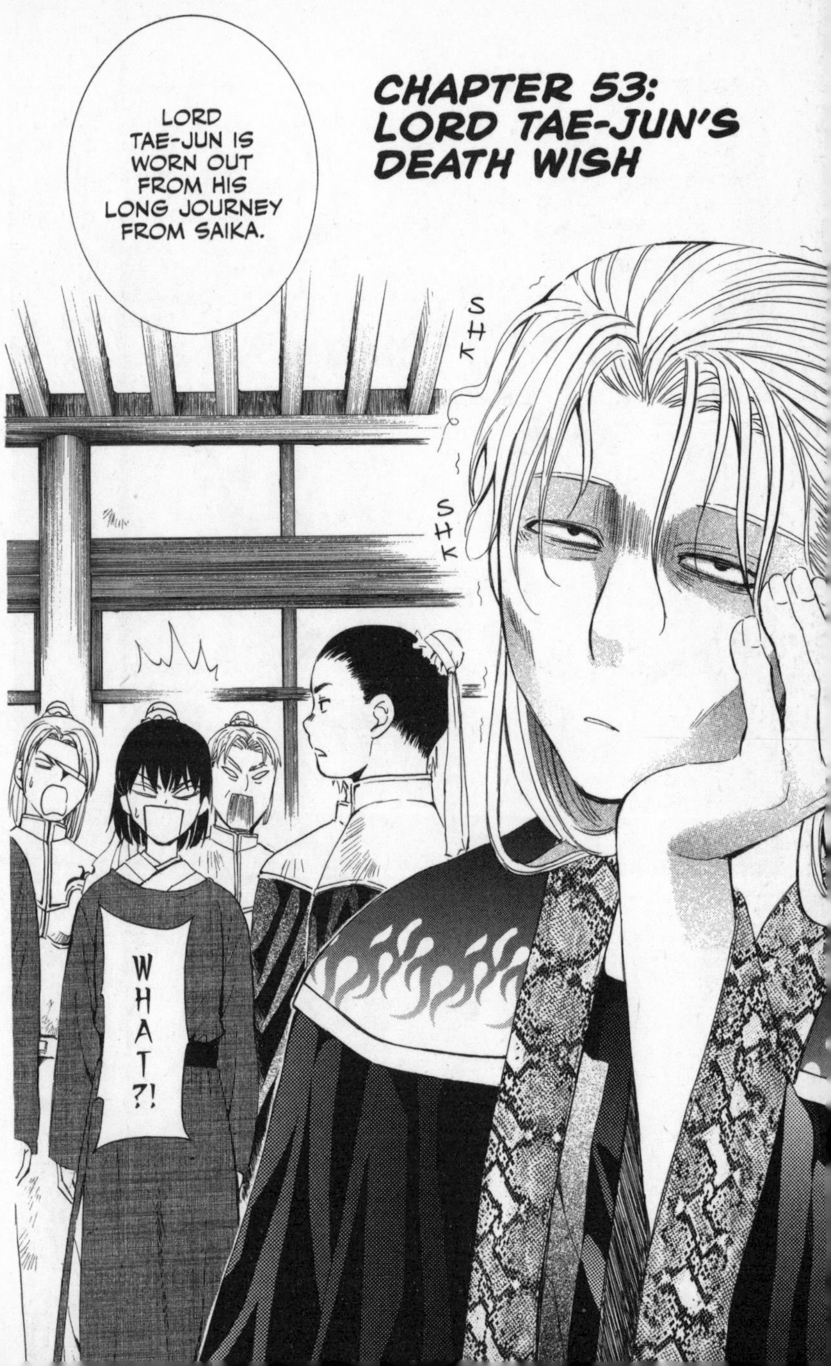
LORD TAE-JUN IS WORN OUT FROM HIS LONG JOURNEY FROM SAIKA.
SHK
SHK
WHAT?!

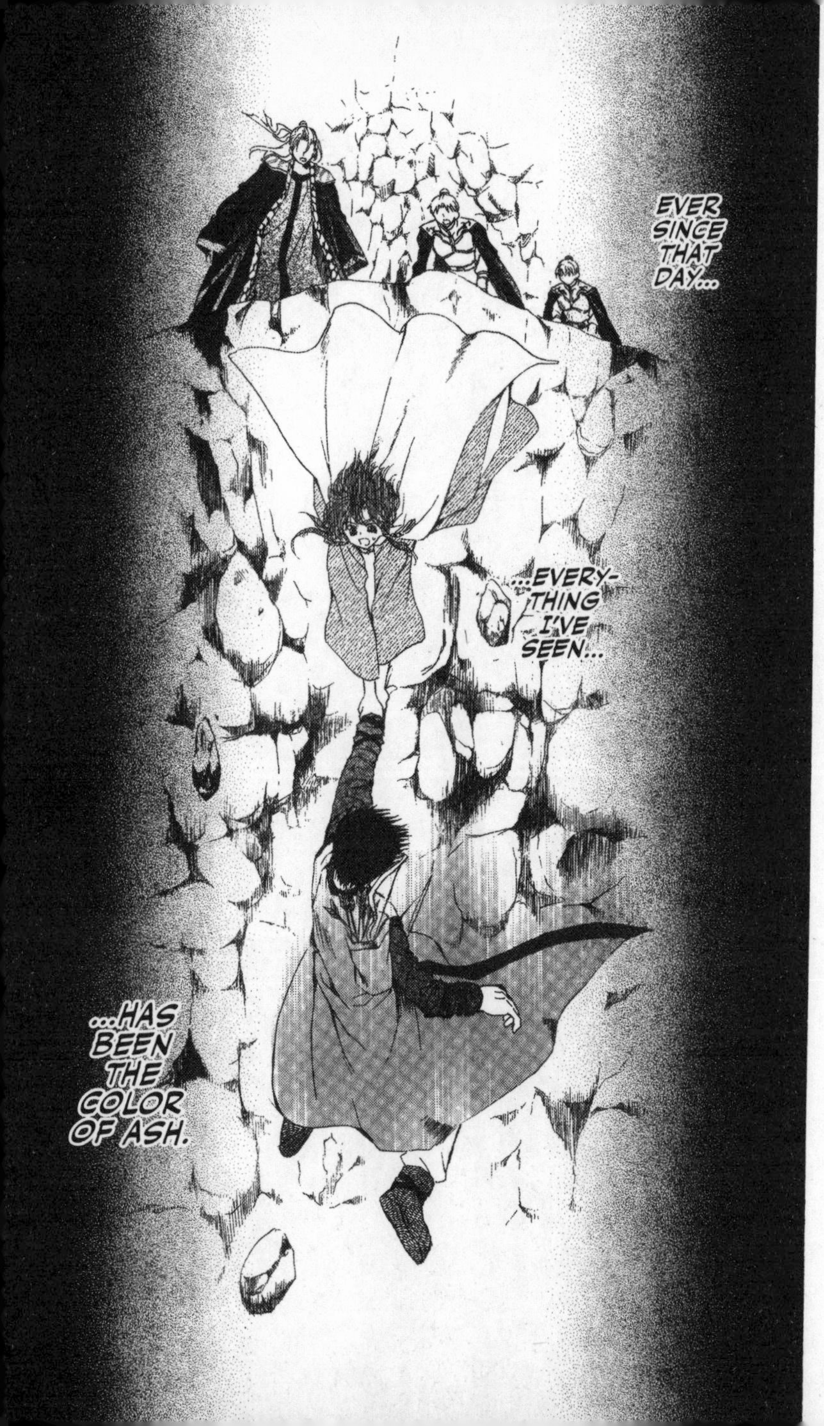
EVER SINCE THAT DAY...
...EVERYTHING I'VE SEEN...
...HAS BEEN THE COLOR OF ASH.

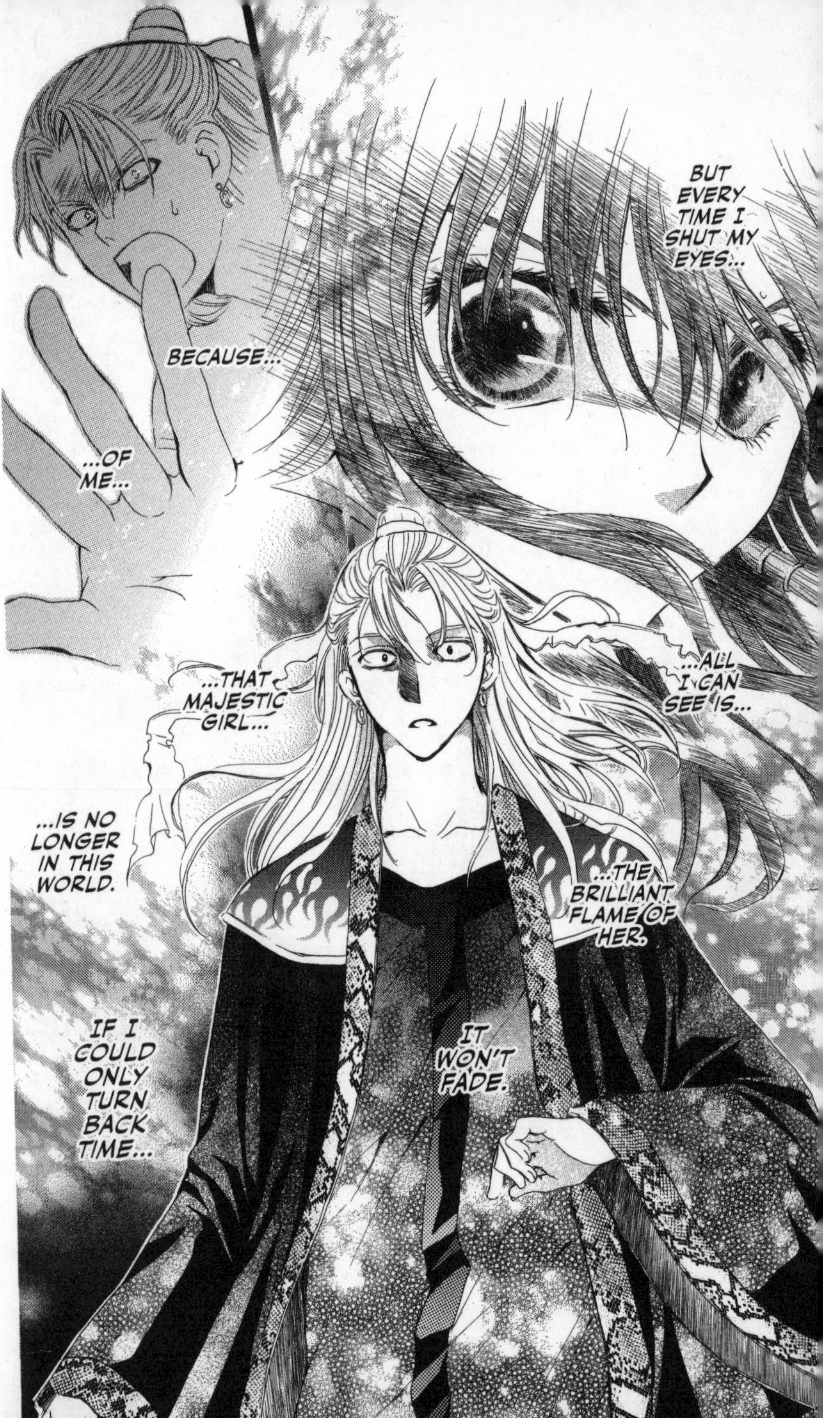
BUT EVERY TIME I SHUT MY EYES...
...ALL I CAN SEE IS...
...THE BRILLIANT FLAME OF HER.
IT WON'T FADE.
BECAUSE...
...OF ME...
...THAT MAJESTIC GIRL...
...IS NO LONGER IN THIS WORLD.
IF I COULD ONLY TURN BACK TIME...

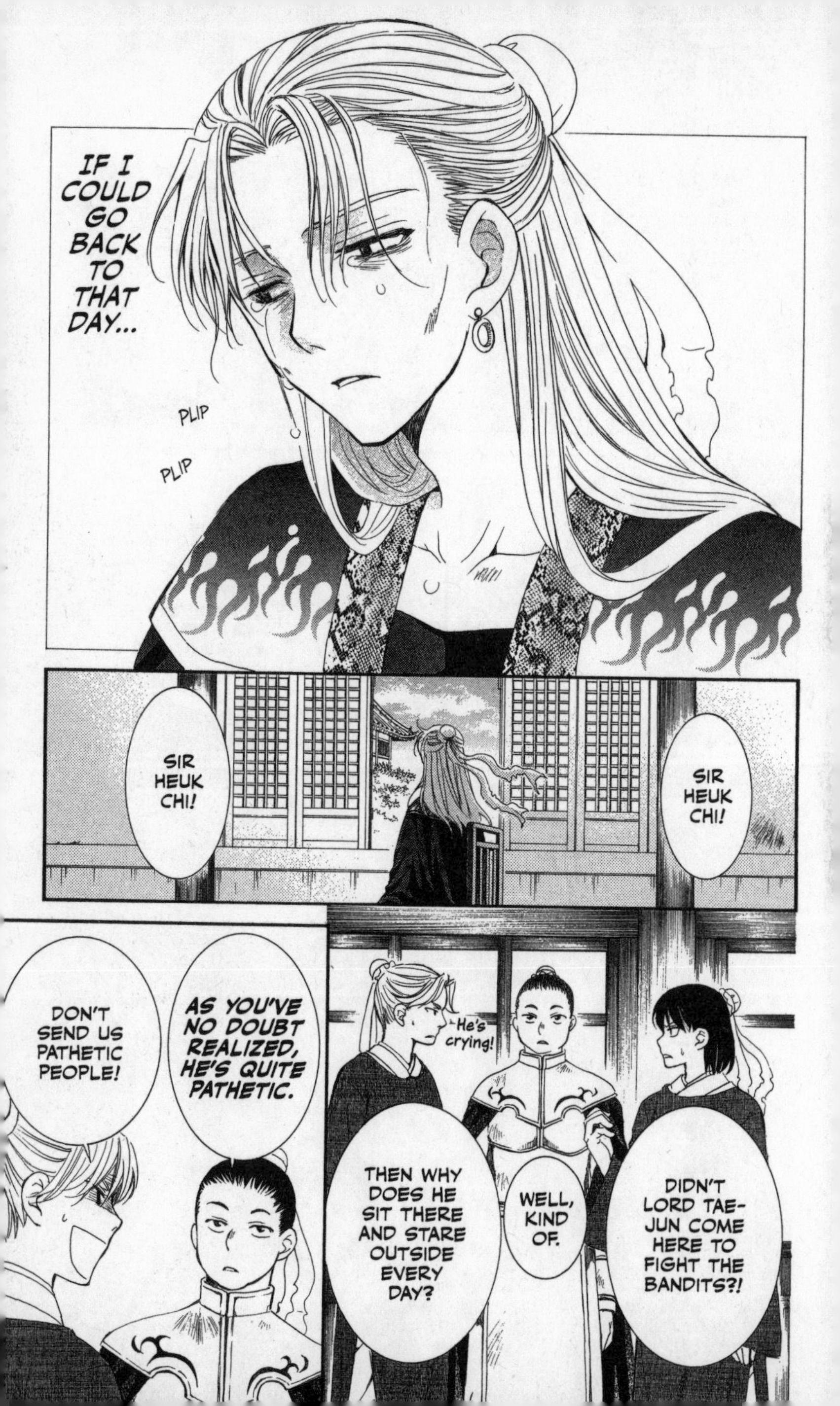
IF I COULD GO BACK TO THAT DAY...
PLIP
PLIP
SIR HEUK CHI!
SIR HEUK CHI!
He's crying!
DIDN'T LORD TAE-JUN COME HERE TO FIGHT THE BANDITS?!
WELL, KIND OF.
THEN WHY DOES HE SIT THERE AND STARE OUTSIDE EVERY DAY?
AS YOU'VE NO DOUBT REALIZED, HE'S QUITE PATHETIC.
DON'T SEND US PATHETIC PEOPLE!

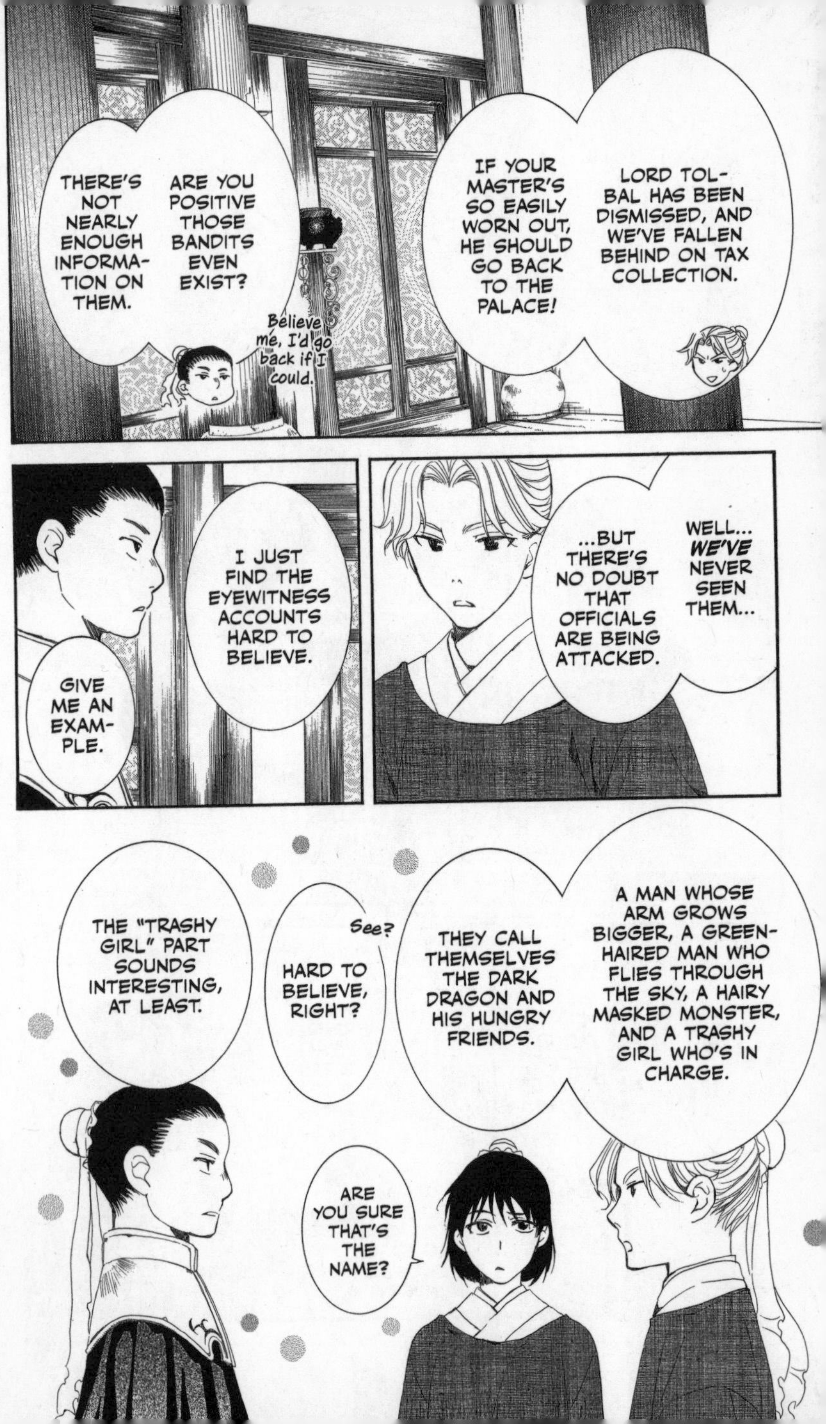
LORD TOL-BAL HAS BEEN DISMISSED, AND WE'VE FALLEN BEHIND ON TAX COLLECTION.
IF YOUR MASTER'S SO EASILY WORN OUT, HE SHOULD GO BACK TO THE PALACE!
Believe me, I'd go back if I could.
ARE YOU POSITIVE THOSE BANDITS EVEN EXIST?
THERE'S NOT NEARLY ENOUGH INFORMATION ON THEM.
WELL... *WE'VE* NEVER SEEN THEM...
...BUT THERE'S NO DOUBT THAT OFFICIALS ARE BEING ATTACKED.
I JUST FIND THE EYEWITNESS ACCOUNTS HARD TO BELIEVE.
GIVE ME AN EXAMPLE.
A MAN WHOSE ARM GROWS BIGGER, A GREEN-HAIRED MAN WHO FLIES THROUGH THE SKY, A HAIRY MASKED MONSTER, AND A TRASHY GIRL WHO'S IN CHARGE.
THEY CALL THEMSELVES THE DARK DRAGON AND HIS HUNGRY FRIENDS.
See?
HARD TO BELIEVE, RIGHT?
THE "TRASHY GIRL" PART SOUNDS INTERESTING, AT LEAST.
ARE YOU SURE THAT'S THE NAME?

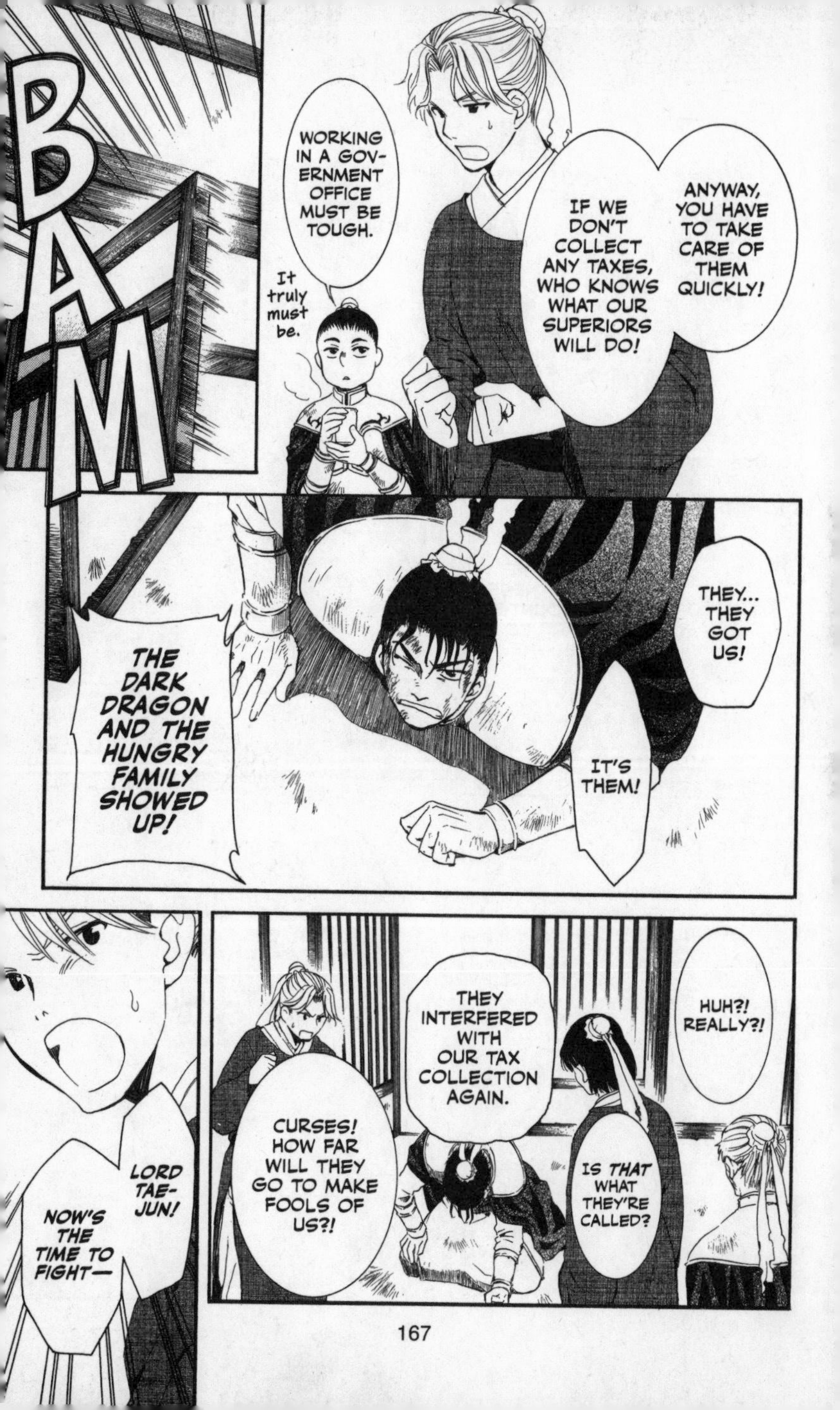
ANYWAY, YOU HAVE TO TAKE CARE OF THEM QUICKLY!
IF WE DON'T COLLECT ANY TAXES, WHO KNOWS WHAT OUR SUPERIORS WILL DO!
WORKING IN A GOVERNMENT OFFICE MUST BE TOUGH.
It truly must be.
BAM
THEY... THEY GOT US!
IT'S THEM!
THE DARK DRAGON AND THE HUNGRY FAMILY SHOWED UP!
HUH?! REALLY?!
IS *THAT* WHAT THEY'RE CALLED?
THEY INTERFERED WITH OUR TAX COLLECTION AGAIN.
CURSES! HOW FAR WILL THEY GO TO MAKE FOOLS OF US?!
LORD TAE-JUN!
NOW'S THE TIME TO FIGHT—

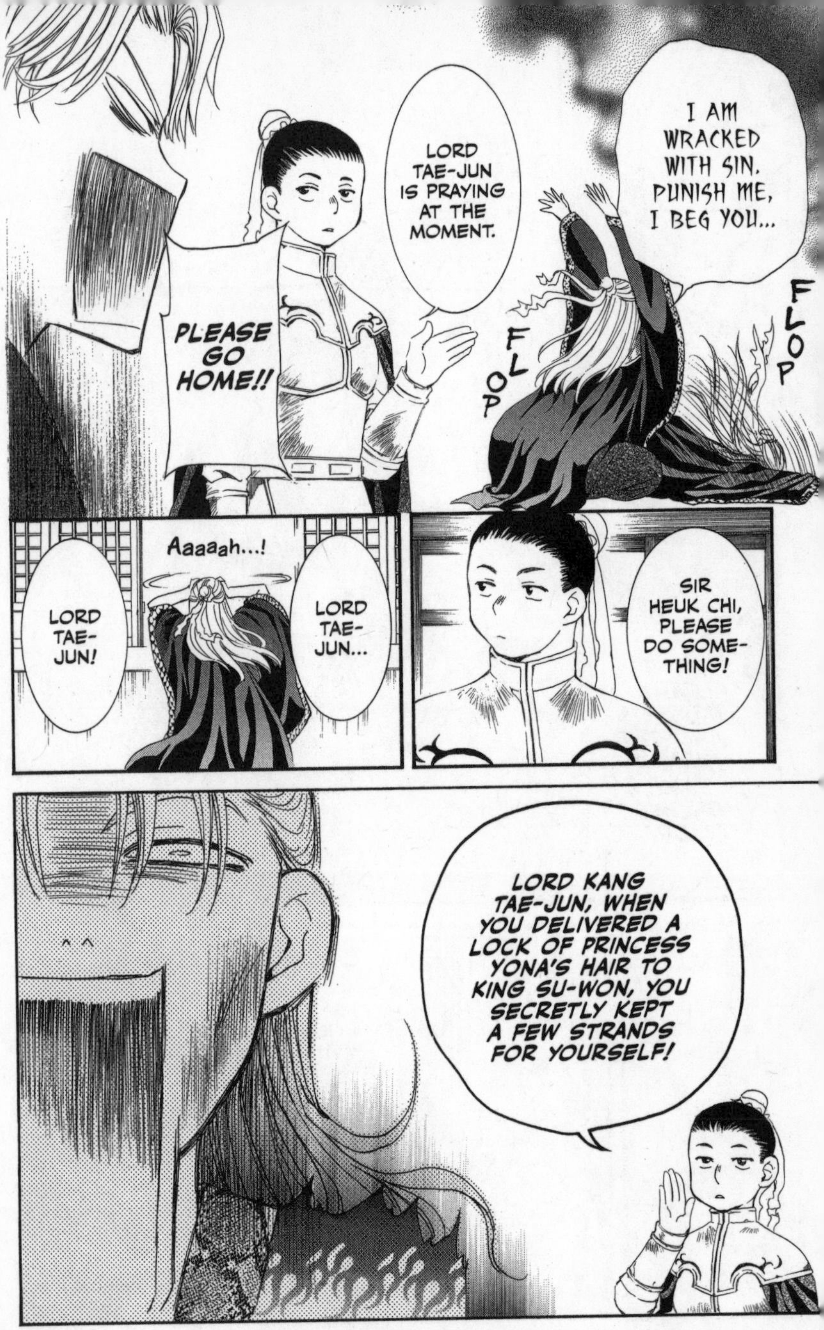
I AM WRACKED WITH SIN. PUNISH ME, I BEG YOU...
FLOP
FLOP
LORD TAE-JUN IS PRAYING AT THE MOMENT.
PLEASE GO HOME!!
SIR HEUK CHI, PLEASE DO SOME-THING!
LORD TAE-JUN...
Aaaaah...!
LORD TAE-JUN!
LORD KANG TAE-JUN, WHEN YOU DELIVERED A LOCK OF PRINCESS YONA'S HAIR TO KING SU-WON, YOU SECRETLY KEPT A FEW STRANDS FOR YOURSELF!

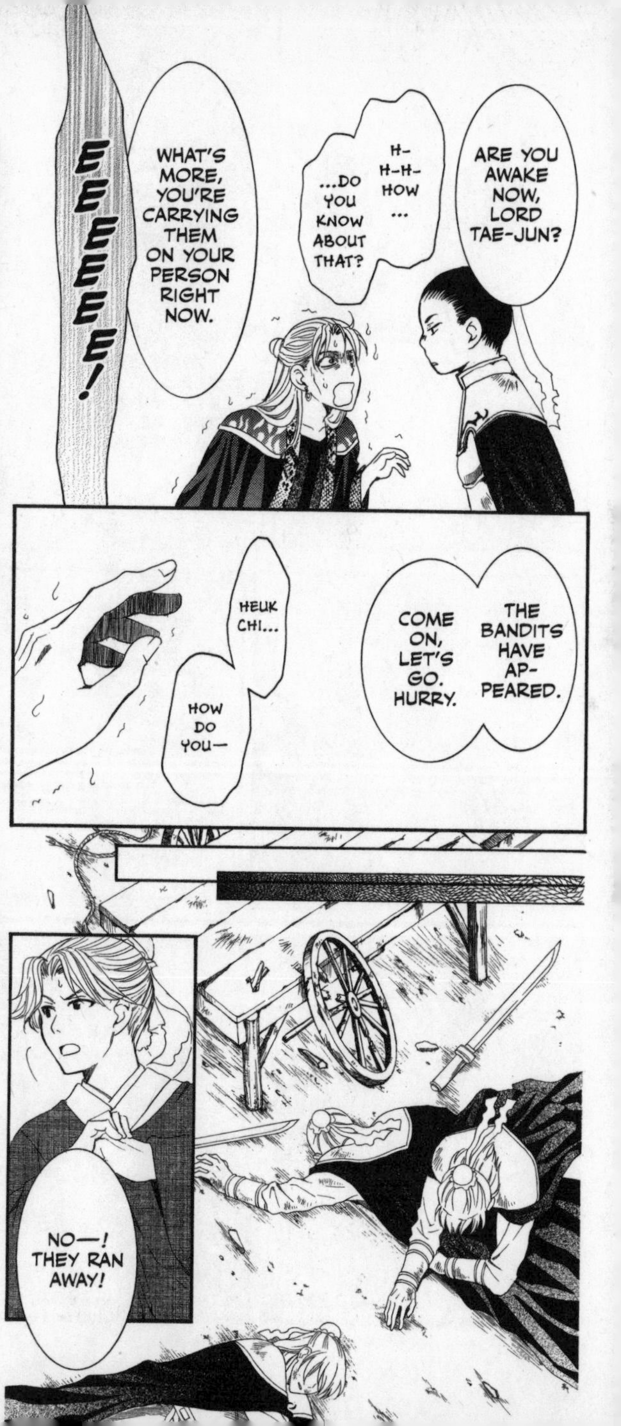
ARE YOU AWAKE NOW, LORD TAE-JUN?
H-H-H-HOW ...
...DO YOU KNOW ABOUT THAT?
WHAT'S MORE, YOU'RE CARRYING THEM ON YOUR PERSON RIGHT NOW.
EEEEEE!
THE BANDITS HAVE AP-PEARED.
COME ON, LET'S GO. HURRY.
HEUK CHI...
HOW DO YOU—
NO—! THEY RAN AWAY!

Pu-kyu in Chapter 52

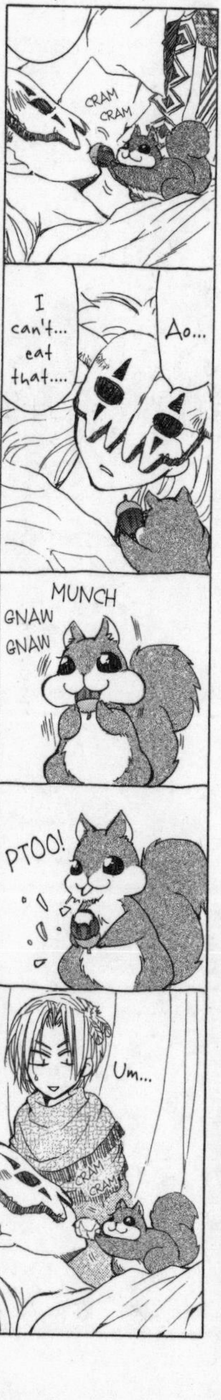
CRAM CRAM
Ao...
I can't... eat that....
MUNCH
GNAW GNAW
PTOO!
Um...
CRAM CRAM

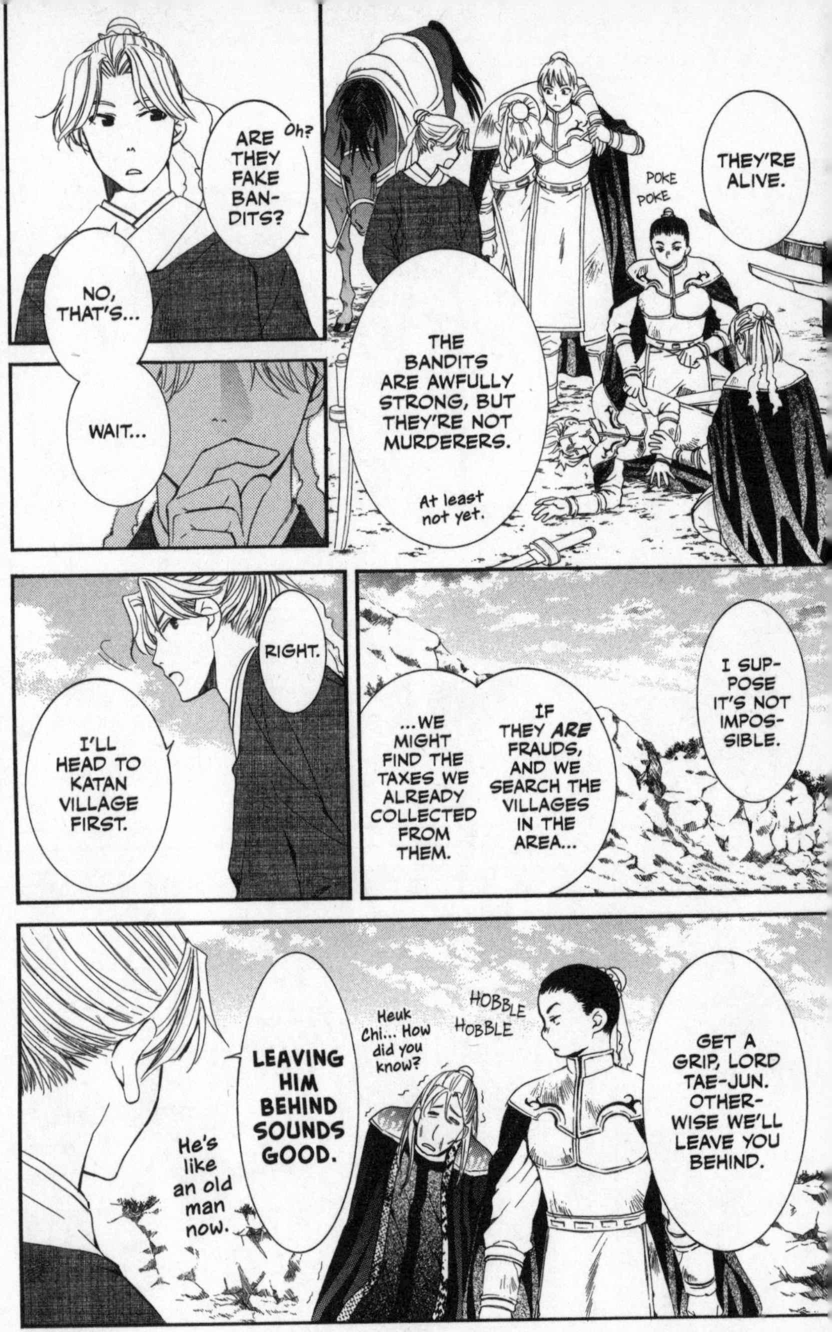
THEY'RE ALIVE.
POKE POKE
THE BANDITS ARE AWFULLY STRONG, BUT THEY'RE NOT MURDERERS.
At least not yet.
Oh?
ARE THEY FAKE BAN-DITS?
NO, THAT'S...
WAIT...
I SUP-POSE IT'S NOT IMPOS-SIBLE.
IF THEY ARE FRAUDS, AND WE SEARCH THE VILLAGES IN THE AREA...
...WE MIGHT FIND THE TAXES WE ALREADY COLLECTED FROM THEM.
RIGHT.
I'LL HEAD TO KATAN VILLAGE FIRST.
GET A GRIP, LORD TAE-JUN. OTHER-WISE WE'LL LEAVE YOU BEHIND.
HOBBLE HOBBLE
Heuk Chi... How did you know?
LEAVING HIM BEHIND SOUNDS GOOD.
He's like an old man now.

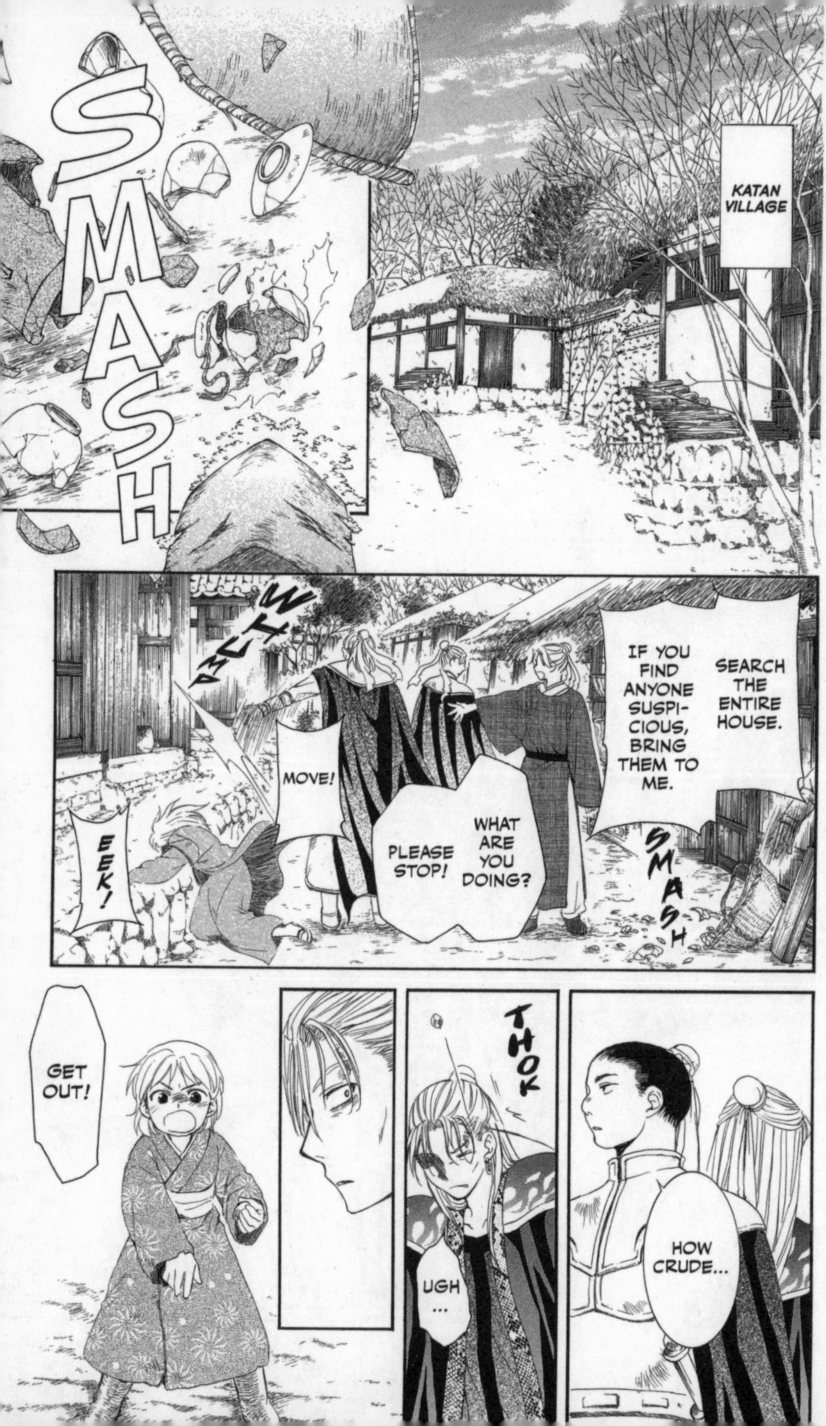
KATAN VILLAGE
SMASH
SEARCH THE ENTIRE HOUSE.
IF YOU FIND ANYONE SUSPICIOUS, BRING THEM TO ME.
SMASH
WHAT ARE YOU DOING?
PLEASE STOP!
MOVE!
WHUMP
EEK!
HOW CRUDE...
THOK
UGH ...
GET OUT!

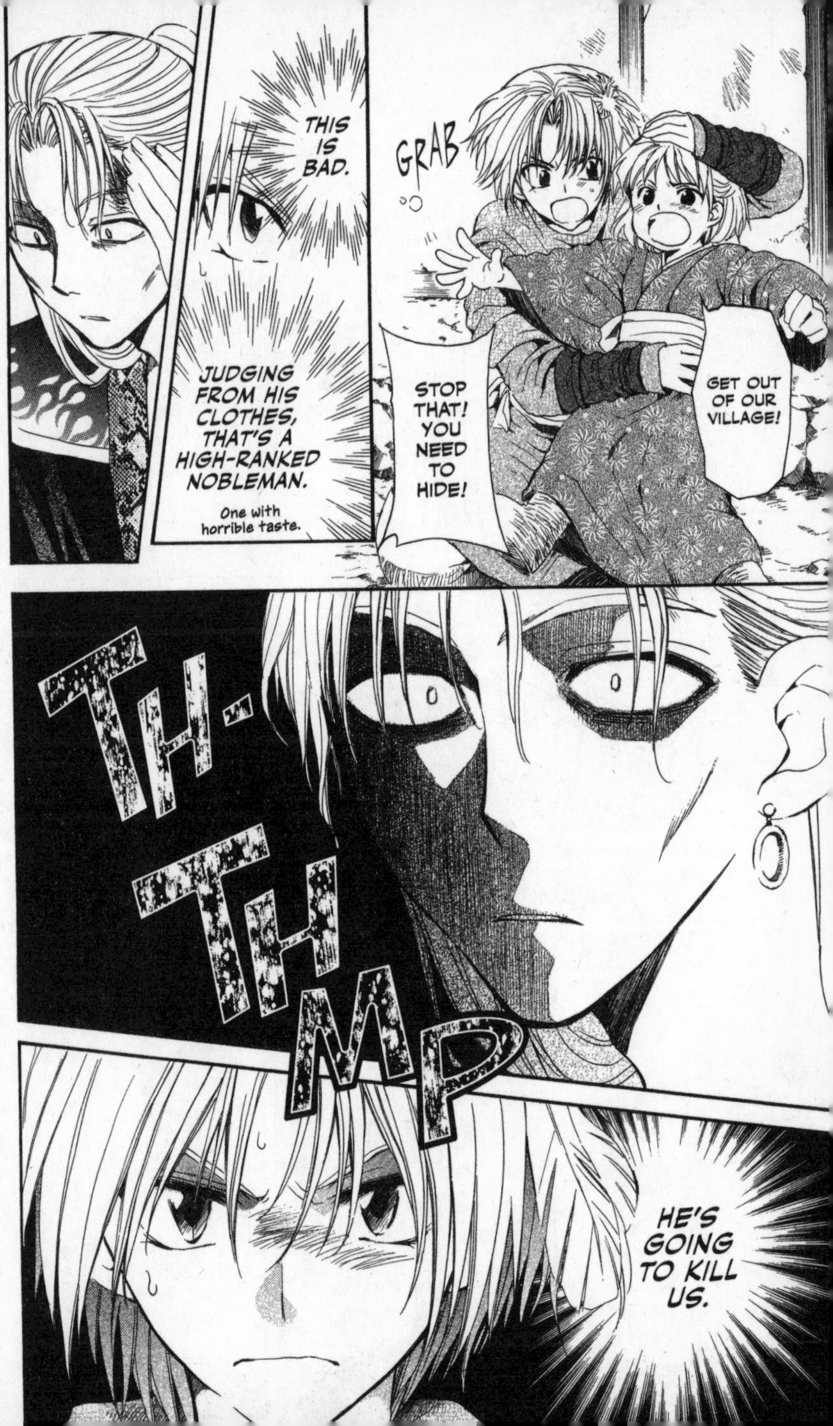

GRAB
GET OUT OF OUR VILLAGE!
STOP THAT! YOU NEED TO HIDE!
THIS IS BAD.
JUDGING FROM HIS CLOTHES, THAT'S A HIGH-RANKED NOBLEMAN.
One with horrible taste.
TH-TH-THMP
HE'S GOING TO KILL US.

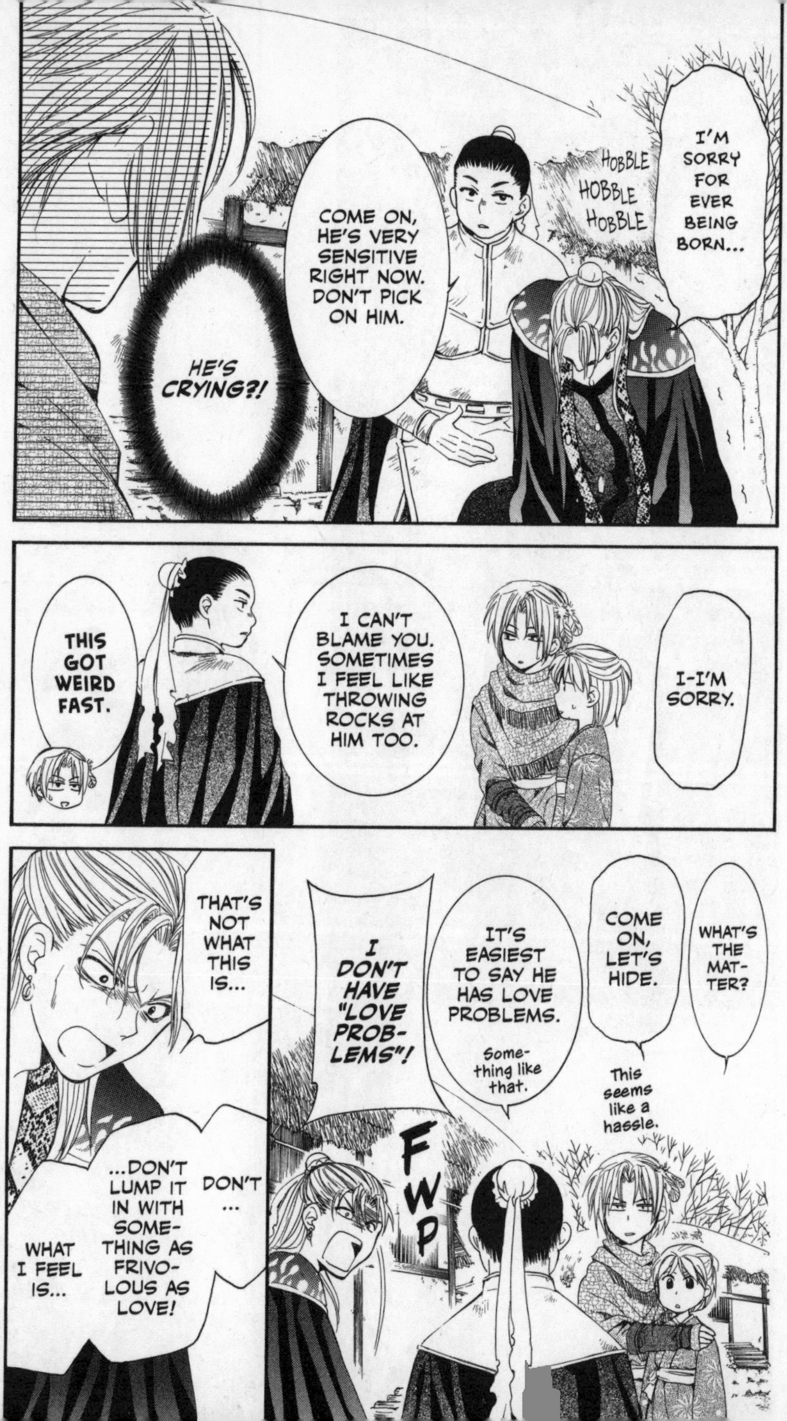
I'M SORRY FOR EVER BEING BORN...
HOBBLE HOBBLE HOBBLE
COME ON, HE'S VERY SENSITIVE RIGHT NOW. DON'T PICK ON HIM.
HE'S CRYING?!
I-I'M SORRY.
I CAN'T BLAME YOU. SOMETIMES I FEEL LIKE THROWING ROCKS AT HIM TOO.
THIS GOT WEIRD FAST.
WHAT'S THE MAT-TER?
COME ON, LET'S HIDE.
This seems like a hassle.
IT'S EASIEST TO SAY HE HAS LOVE PROBLEMS.
Some-thing like that.
I DON'T HAVE "LOVE PROB-LEMS"!
FWP
THAT'S NOT WHAT THIS IS...
DON'T...
...DON'T LUMP IT IN WITH SOME-THING AS FRIVO-LOUS AS LOVE!
WHAT I FEEL IS...

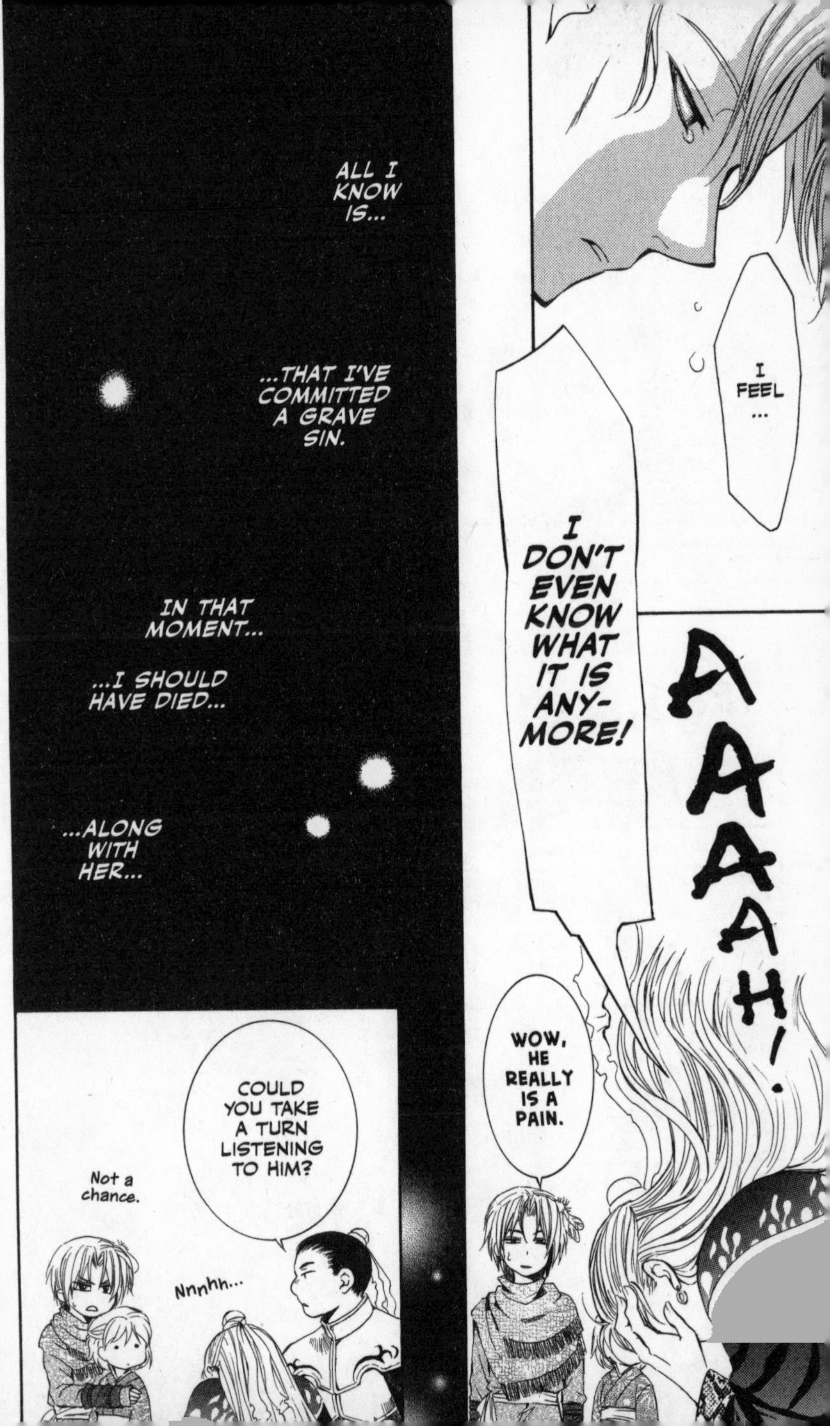
I FEEL...
I DON'T EVEN KNOW WHAT IT IS ANYMORE!
AAAAH!
WOW, HE REALLY IS A PAIN.
ALL I KNOW IS...
...THAT I'VE COMMITTED A GRAVE SIN.
IN THAT MOMENT...
...I SHOULD HAVE DIED...
...ALONG WITH HER...
COULD YOU TAKE A TURN LISTENING TO HIM?
Nnnhh...
Not a chance.

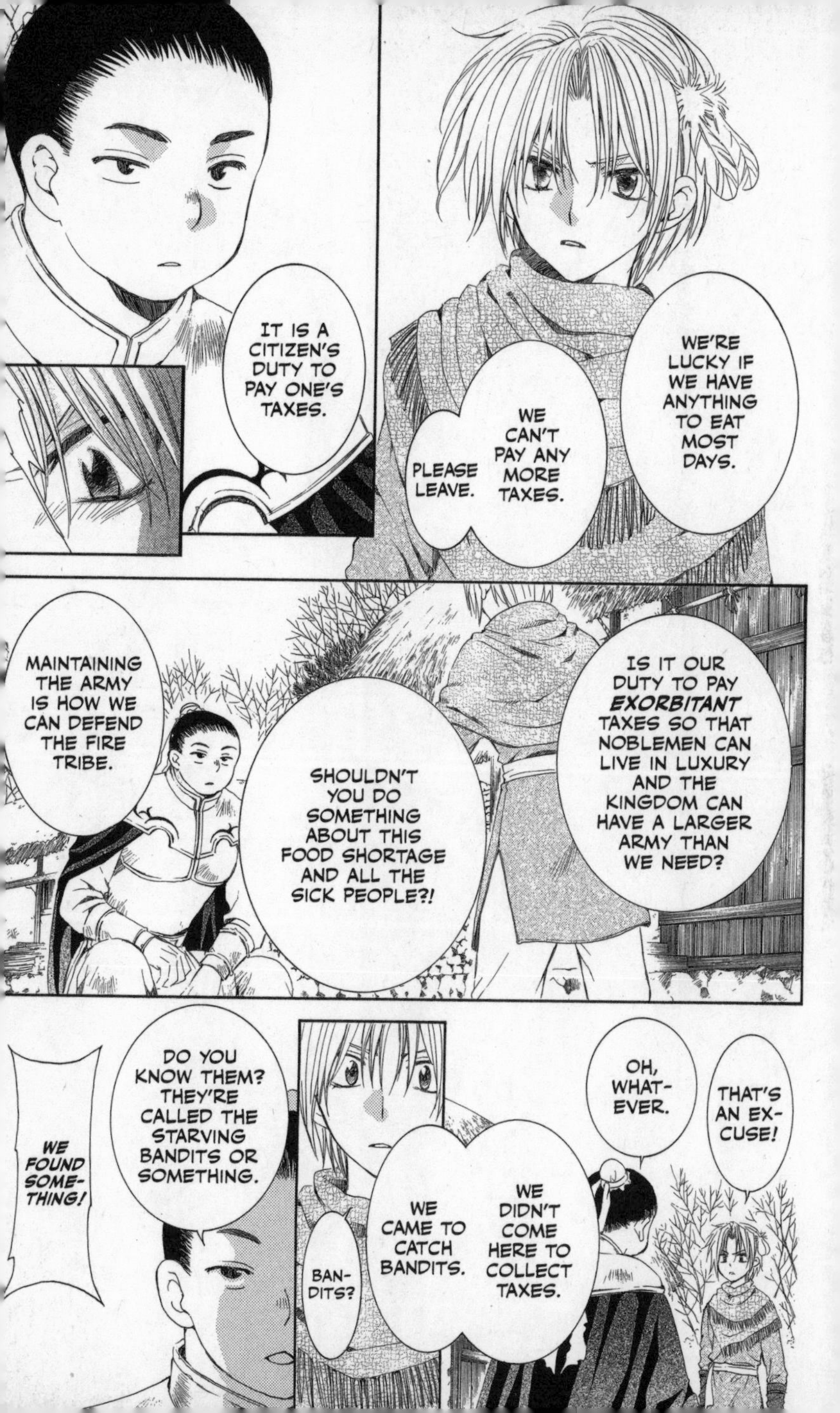
WE'RE LUCKY IF WE HAVE ANYTHING TO EAT MOST DAYS.
WE CAN'T PAY ANY MORE TAXES.
PLEASE LEAVE.
IT IS A CITIZEN'S DUTY TO PAY ONE'S TAXES.
IS IT OUR DUTY TO PAY ***EXORBITANT*** TAXES SO THAT NOBLEMEN CAN LIVE IN LUXURY AND THE KINGDOM CAN HAVE A LARGER ARMY THAN WE NEED?
SHOULDN'T YOU DO SOMETHING ABOUT THIS FOOD SHORTAGE AND ALL THE SICK PEOPLE?!
MAINTAINING THE ARMY IS HOW WE CAN DEFEND THE FIRE TRIBE.
THAT'S AN EX-CUSE!
OH, WHAT-EVER.
WE DIDN'T COME HERE TO COLLECT TAXES.
WE CAME TO CATCH BANDITS.
BAN-DITS?
DO YOU KNOW THEM? THEY'RE CALLED THE STARVING BANDITS OR SOMETHING.
WE FOUND SOME-THING!

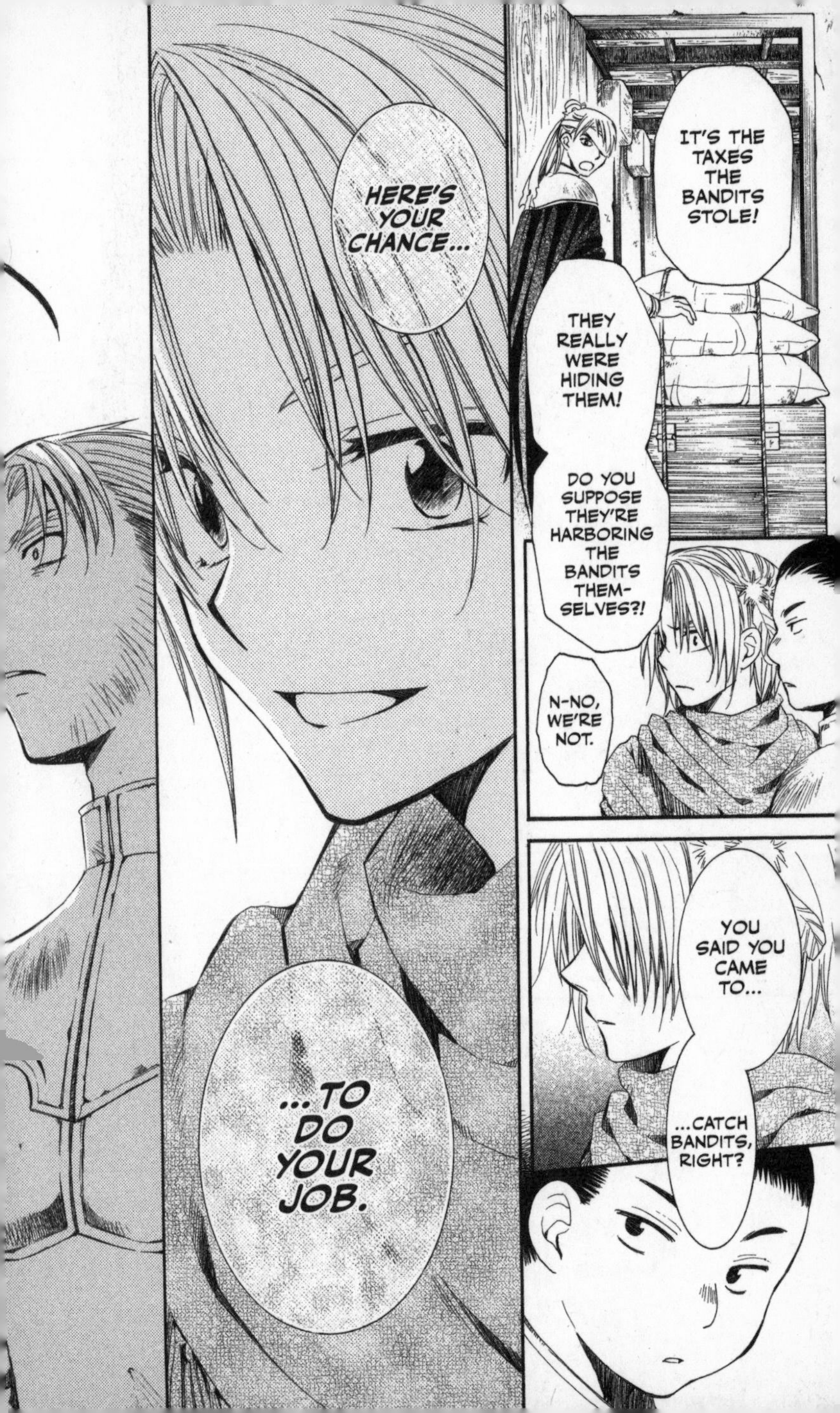
IT'S THE TAXES THE BANDITS STOLE!
THEY REALLY WERE HIDING THEM!
DO YOU SUPPOSE THEY'RE HARBORING THE BANDITS THEM-SELVES?!
N-NO, WE'RE NOT.
YOU SAID YOU CAME TO...
...CATCH BANDITS, RIGHT?
HERE'S YOUR CHANCE...
...TO DO YOUR JOB.

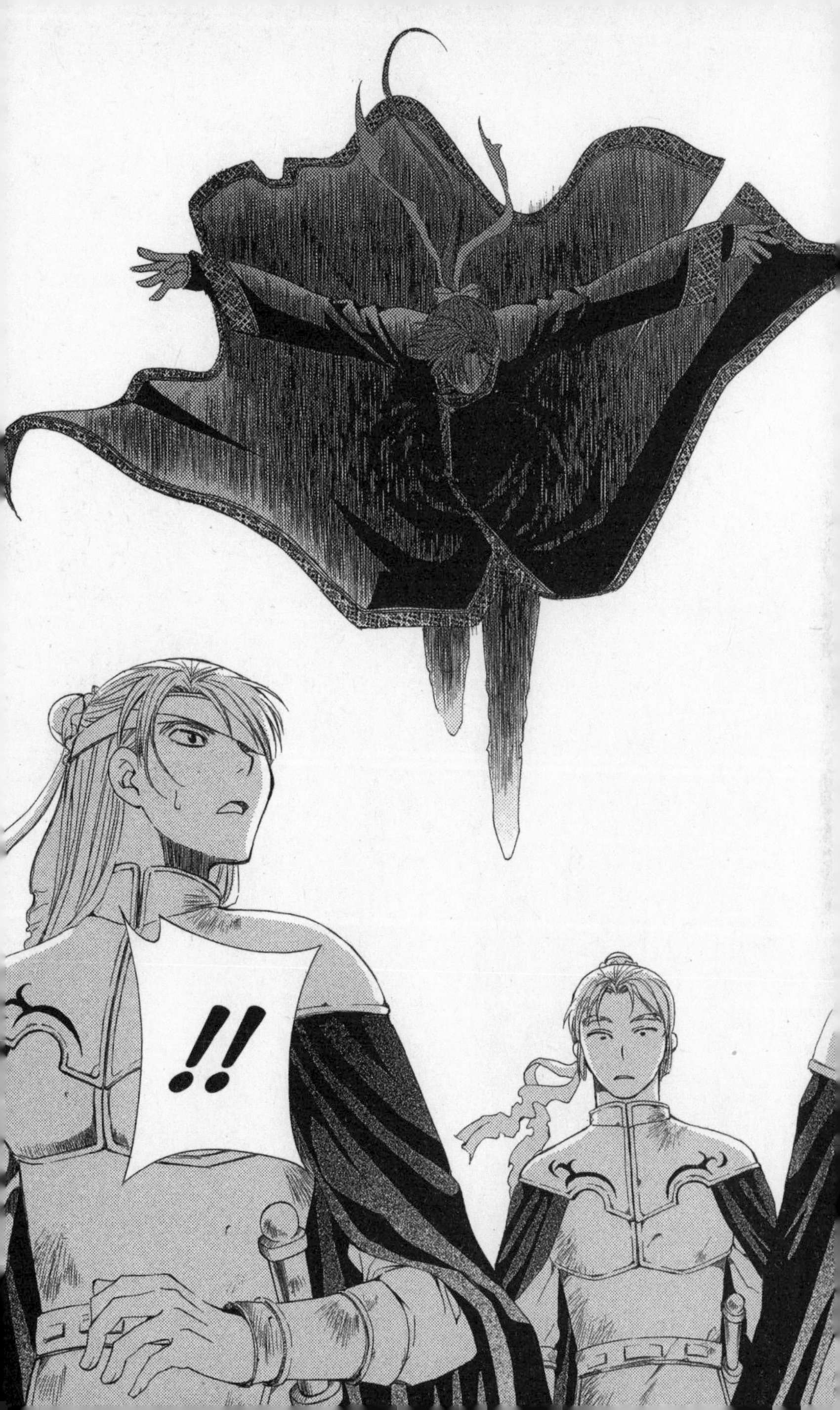
!!

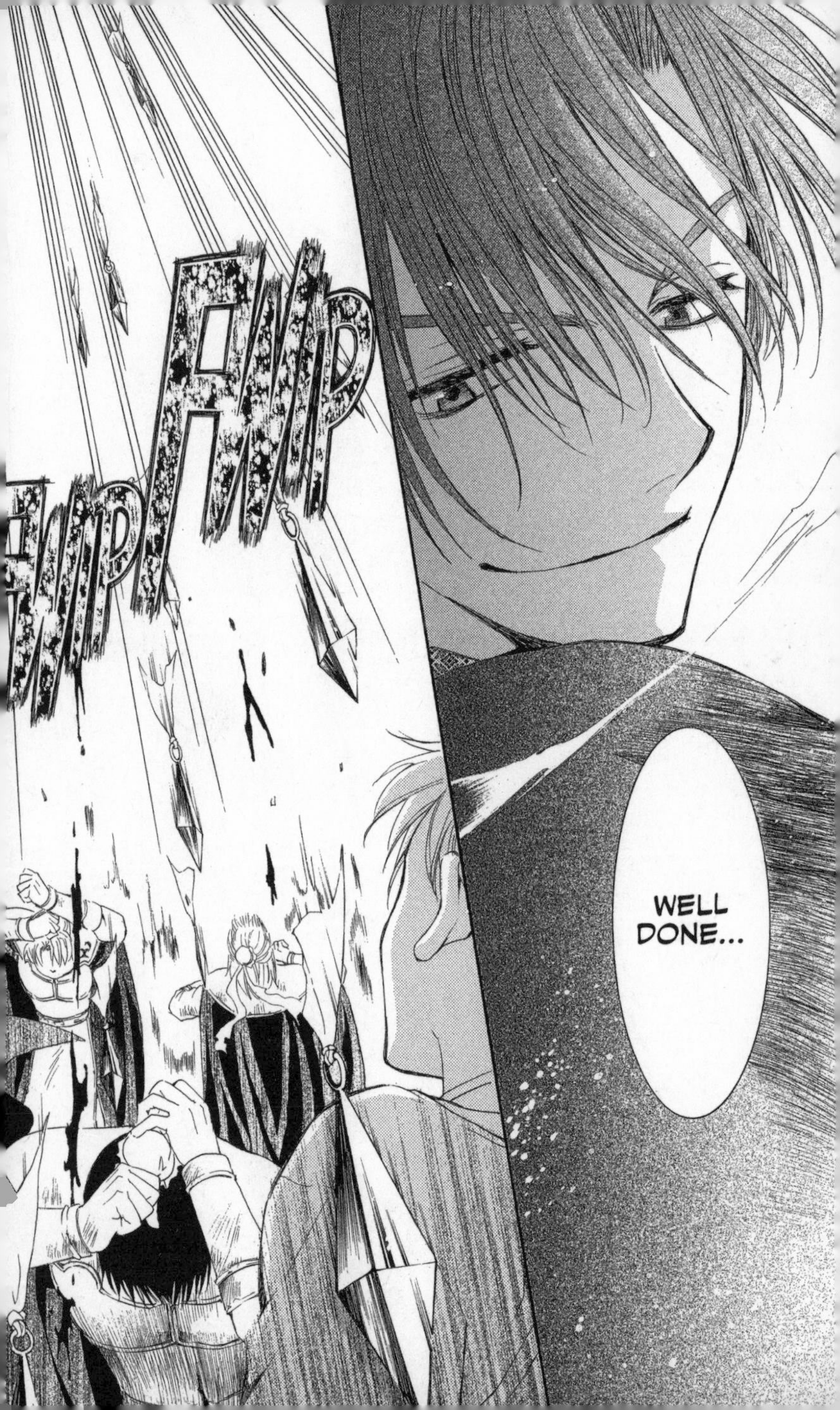
WELL DONE...
FWIP
FWIP

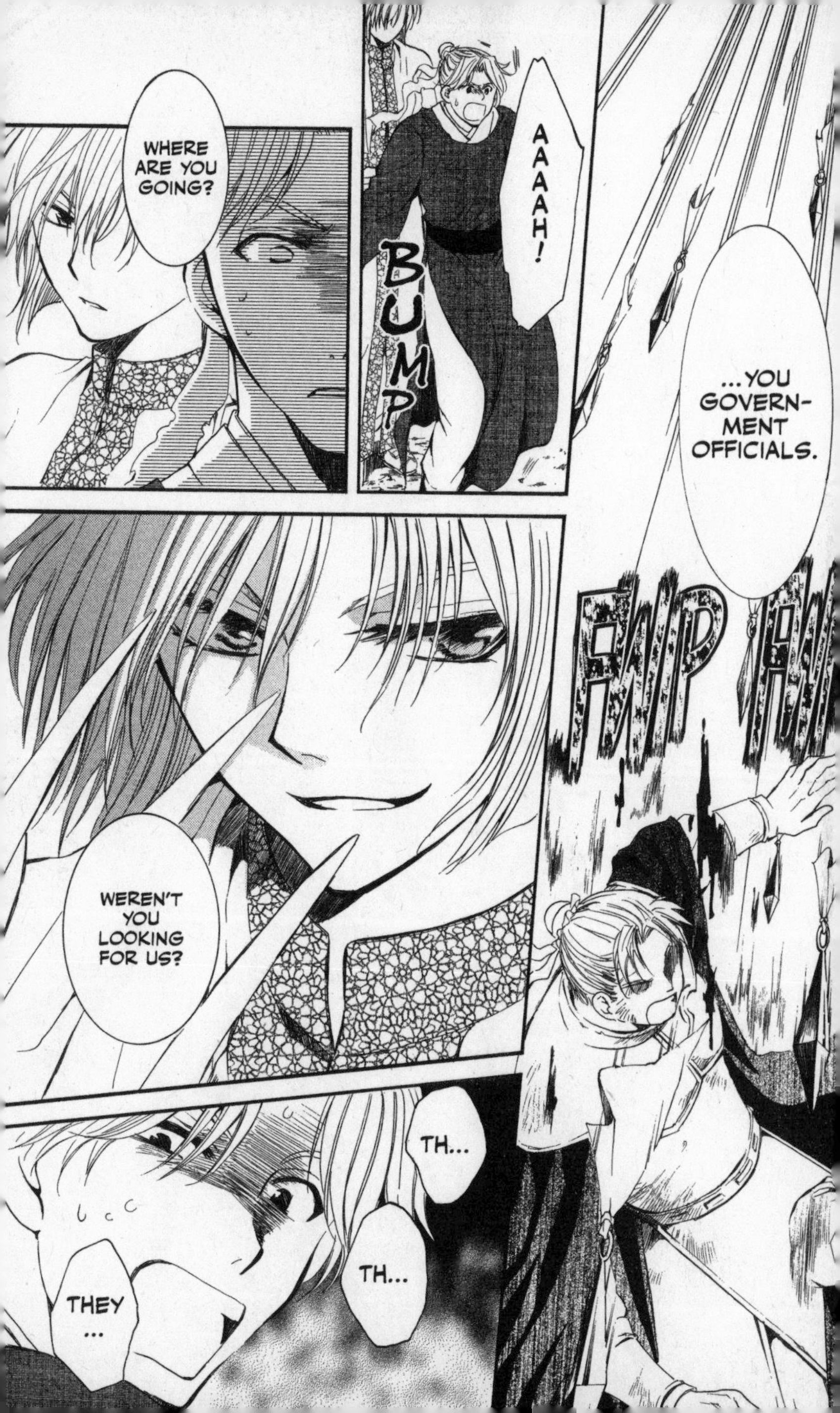
...YOU GOVERNMENT OFFICIALS.
FWIP FWIP
AAAAH!
BUMP
WHERE ARE YOU GOING?
WEREN'T YOU LOOKING FOR US?
TH...
TH...
THEY ...

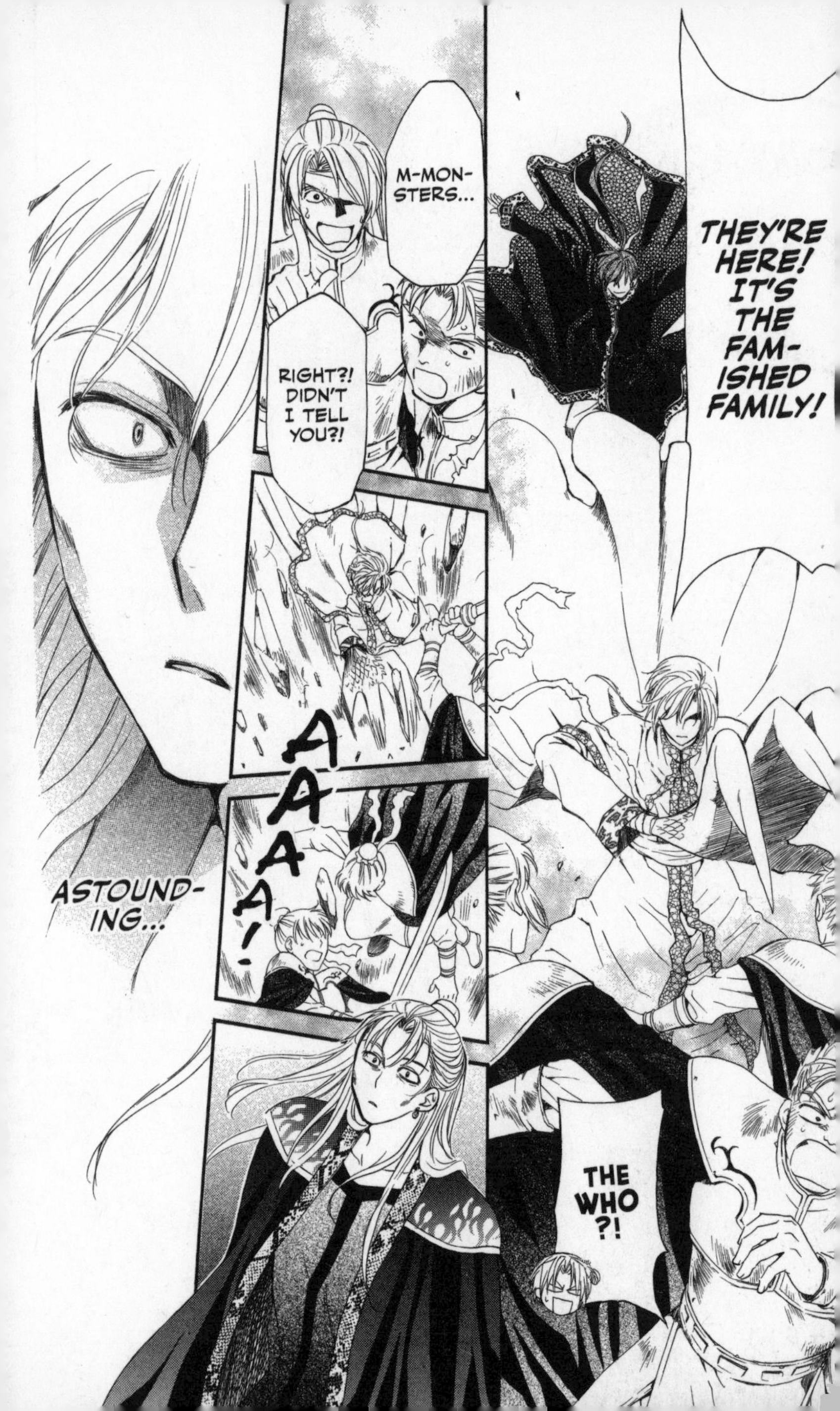
THEY'RE HERE! IT'S THE FAM-ISHED FAMILY!
THE WHO?!
M-MON-STERS...
RIGHT?! DIDN'T I TELL YOU?!
AAAAA!
ASTOUND-ING...

THE GOD OF DEATH...
THE GOD OF DEATH HAS APPEARED...!
HE'S FINALLY COME...
...TO TAKE MY LIFE...

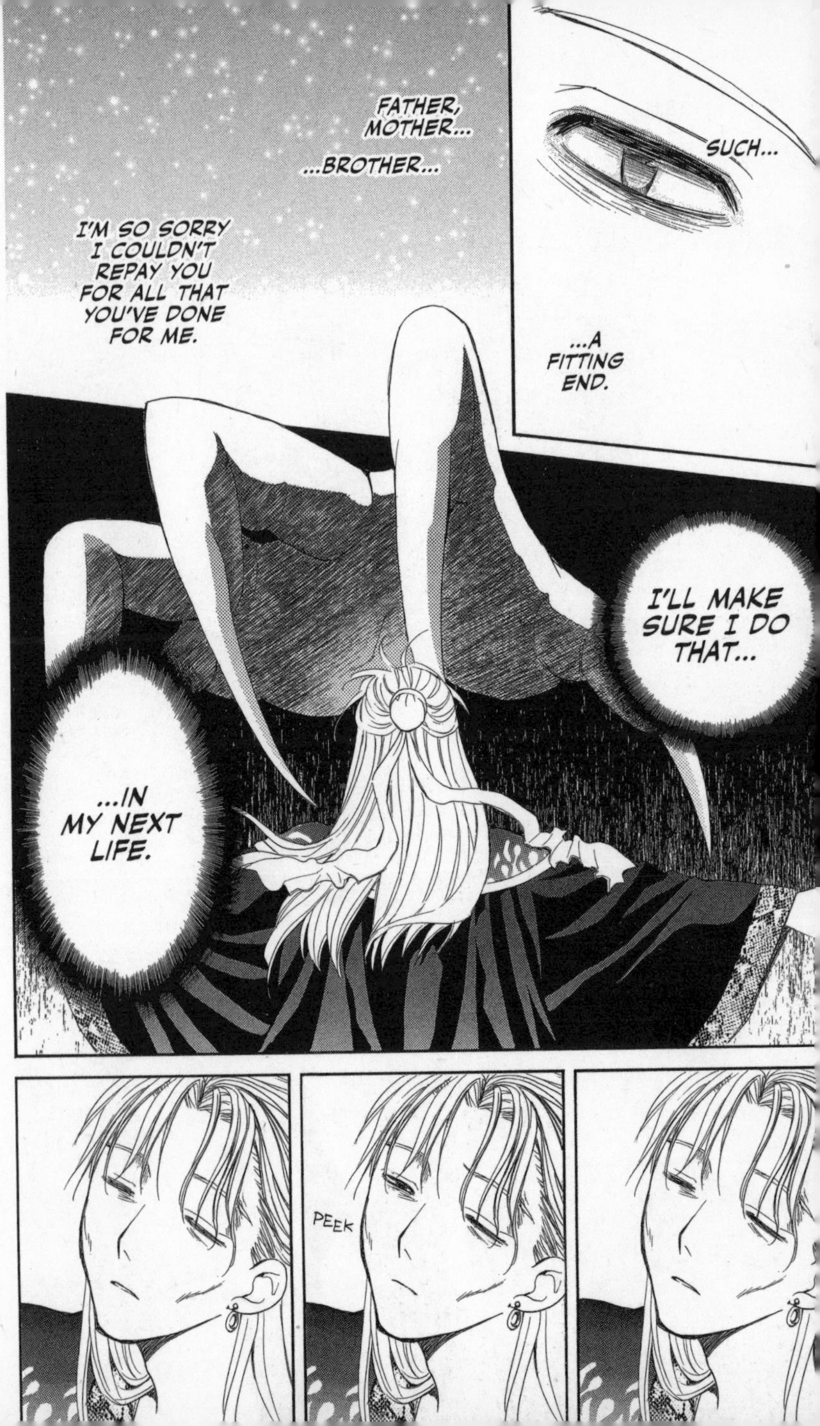
SUCH...
...A FITTING END.
FATHER, MOTHER...
...BROTHER...
I'M SO SORRY I COULDN'T REPAY YOU FOR ALL THAT YOU'VE DONE FOR ME.
I'LL MAKE SURE I DO THAT...
...IN MY NEXT LIFE.
PEEK

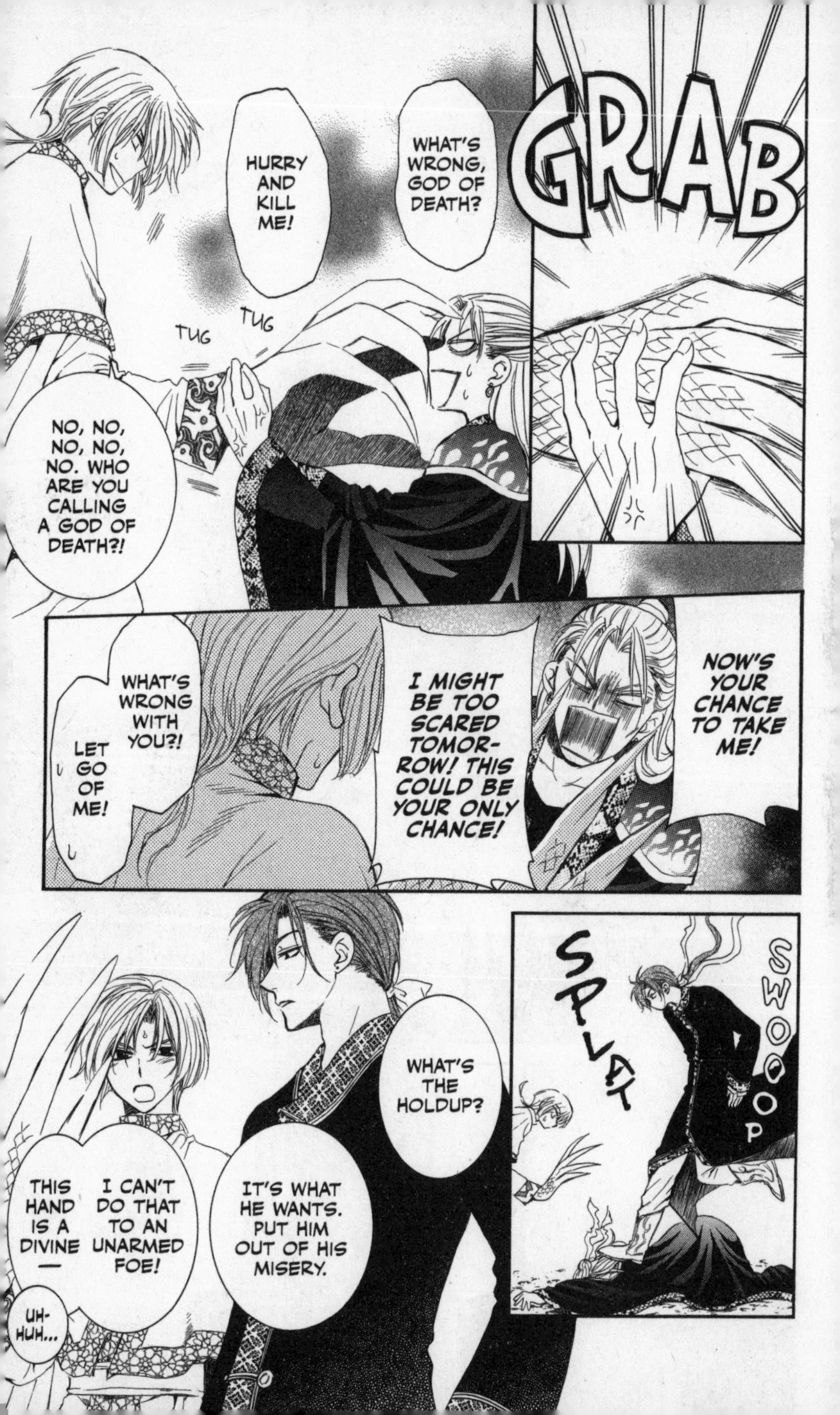
GRAB
WHAT'S WRONG, GOD OF DEATH?
HURRY AND KILL ME!
TUG
TUG
NO, NO, NO, NO, NO. WHO ARE YOU CALLING A GOD OF DEATH?!
NOW'S YOUR CHANCE TO TAKE ME!
I MIGHT BE TOO SCARED TOMORROW! THIS COULD BE YOUR ONLY CHANCE!
WHAT'S WRONG WITH YOU?!
LET GO OF ME!
SWOOOP
SPLAT
WHAT'S THE HOLDUP?
IT'S WHAT HE WANTS. PUT HIM OUT OF HIS MISERY.
I CAN'T DO THAT TO AN UNARMED FOE!
THIS HAND IS A DIVINE—
UH-HUH...

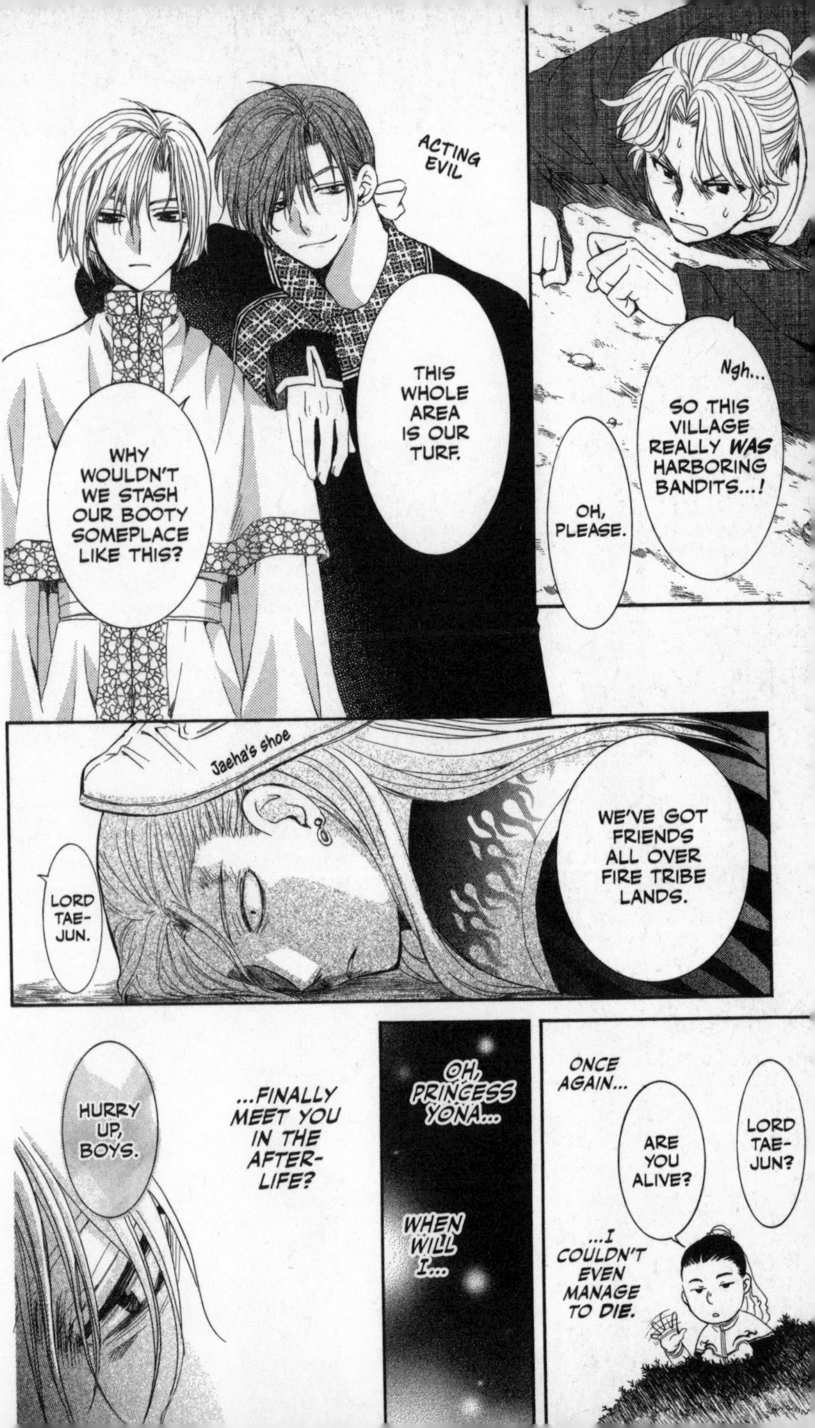

Ngh...
SO THIS VILLAGE REALLY *WAS* HARBORING BANDITS...!
OH, PLEASE.
ACTING EVIL
THIS WHOLE AREA IS OUR TURF.
WHY WOULDN'T WE STASH OUR BOOTY SOMEPLACE LIKE THIS?
WE'VE GOT FRIENDS ALL OVER FIRE TRIBE LANDS.
Jaeha's shoe
LORD TAE-JUN.
LORD TAE-JUN?
ONCE AGAIN...
ARE YOU ALIVE?
...I COULDN'T EVEN MANAGE TO *DIE*.
OH, PRINCESS YONA...
WHEN WILL I...
...FINALLY MEET YOU IN THE AFTER-LIFE?
HURRY UP, BOYS.

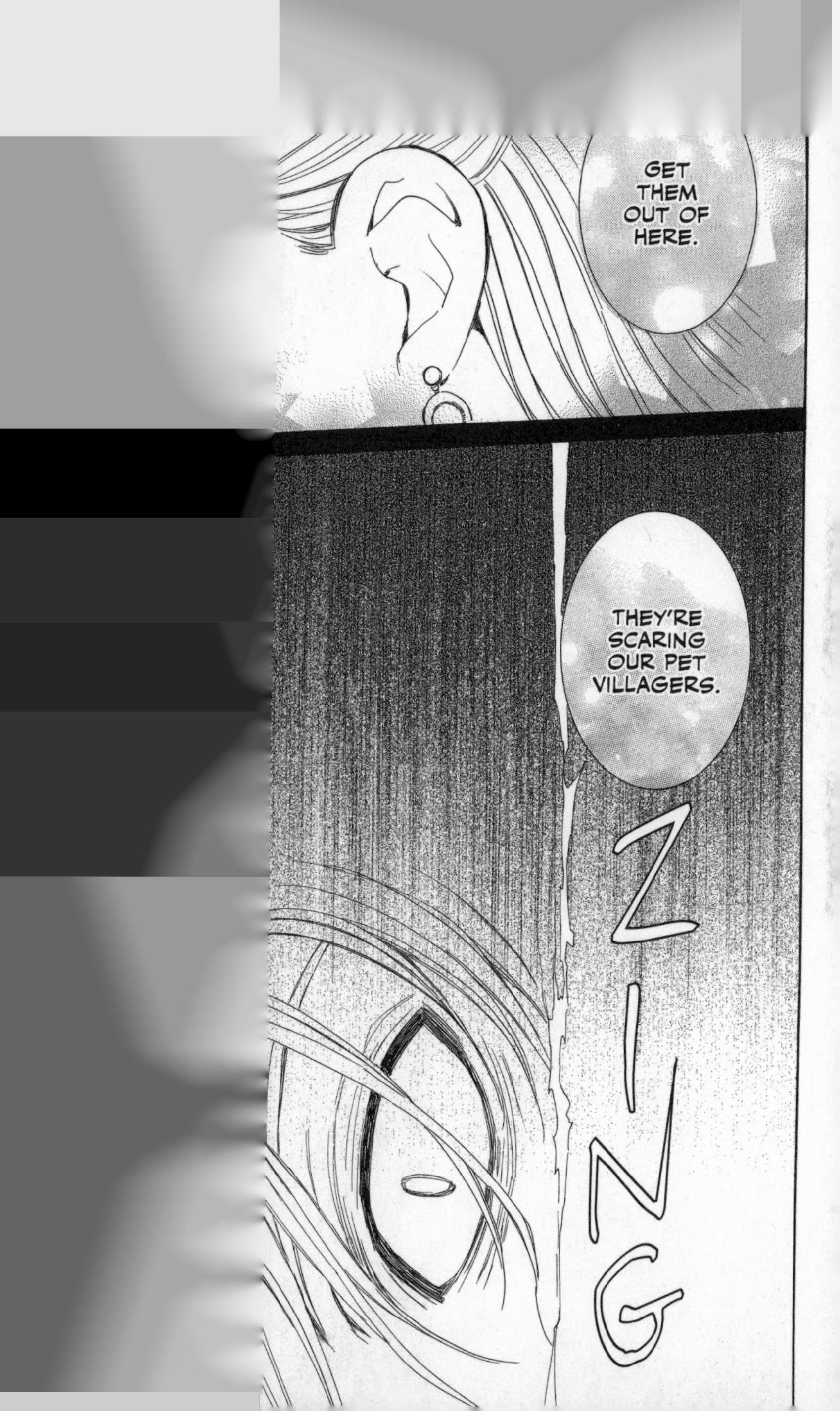
GET THEM OUT OF HERE.
THEY'RE SCARING OUR PET VILLAGERS.
ZING

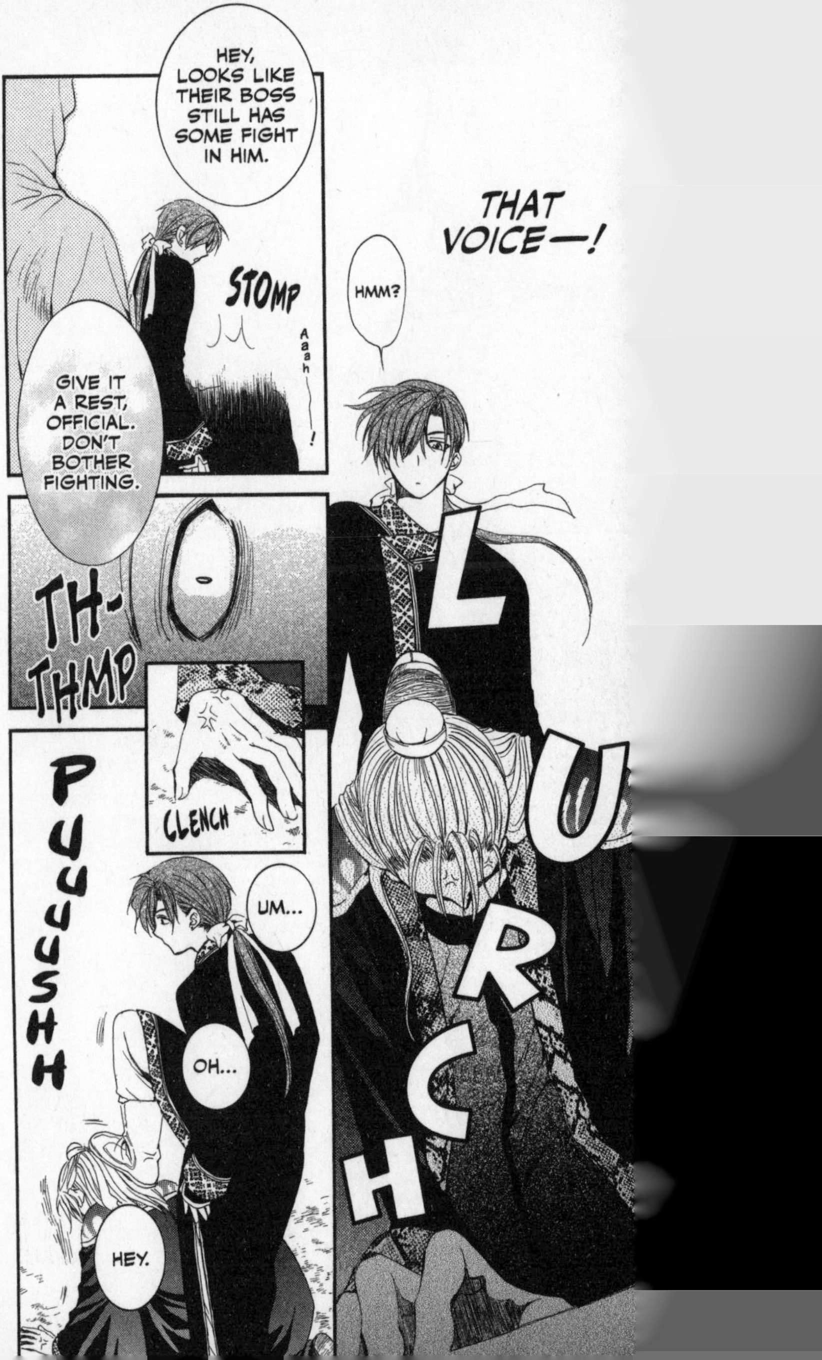
THAT VOICE—!
HMM?
LURCH
HEY, LOOKS LIKE THEIR BOSS STILL HAS SOME FIGHT IN HIM.
STOMP
Aaah—!
GIVE IT A REST, OFFICIAL. DON'T BOTHER FIGHTING.
TH-THMP
CLENCH
UM...
OH...
PUUUUSHH
HEY.

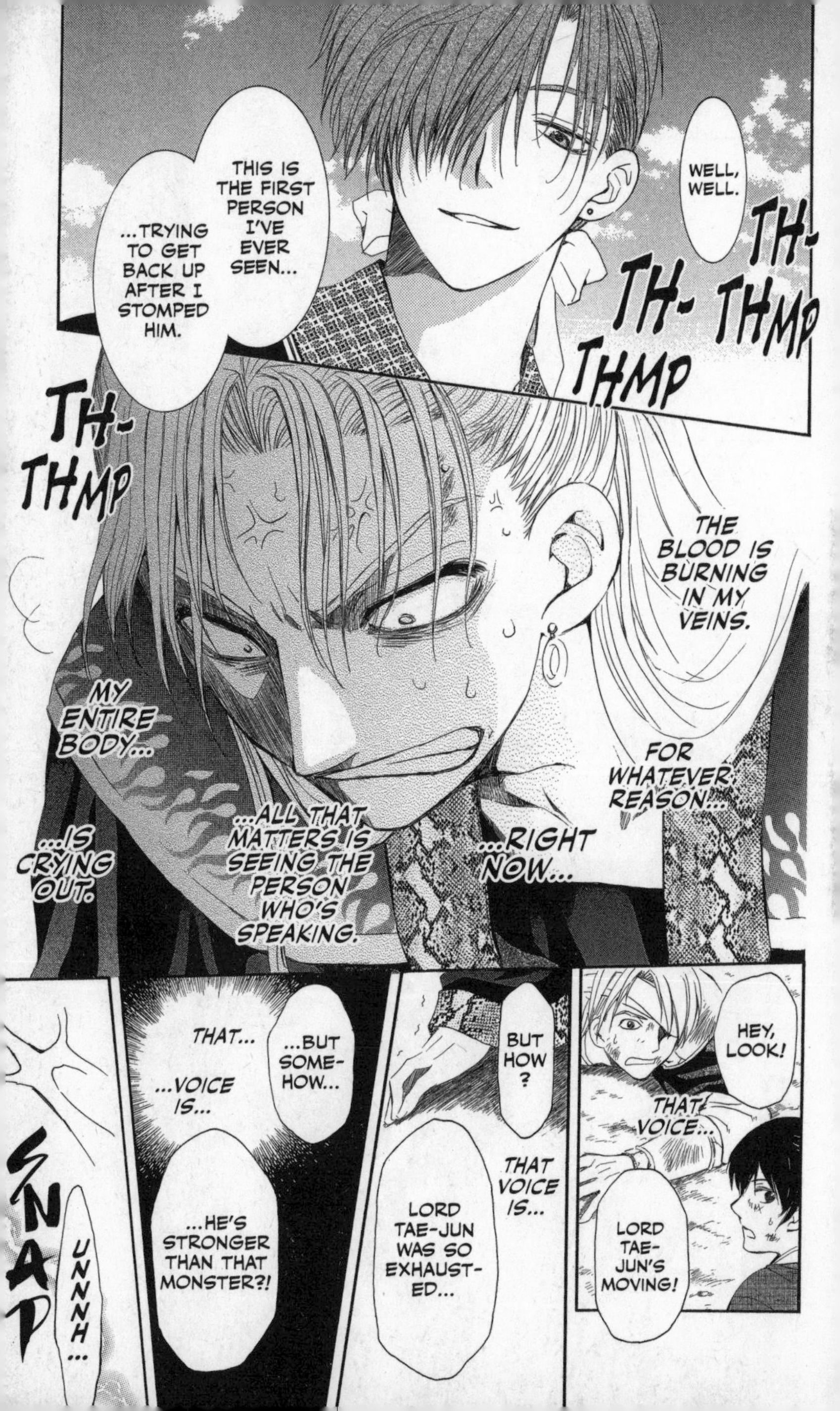
WELL, WELL.
THIS IS THE FIRST PERSON I'VE EVER SEEN...
...TRYING TO GET BACK UP AFTER I STOMPED HIM.
TH-THMP
TH-THMP
TH-THMP
THE BLOOD IS BURNING IN MY VEINS.
MY ENTIRE BODY...
...IS CRYING OUT.
FOR WHATEVER REASON...
...RIGHT NOW...
...ALL THAT MATTERS IS SEEING THE PERSON WHO'S SPEAKING.
HEY, LOOK!
THAT VOICE...
LORD TAE-JUN'S MOVING!
BUT HOW?
THAT VOICE IS...
LORD TAE-JUN WAS SO EXHAUSTED...
...BUT SOMEHOW...
THAT...
...VOICE IS...
...HE'S STRONGER THAN THAT MONSTER?!
UNNNH...
SNAP

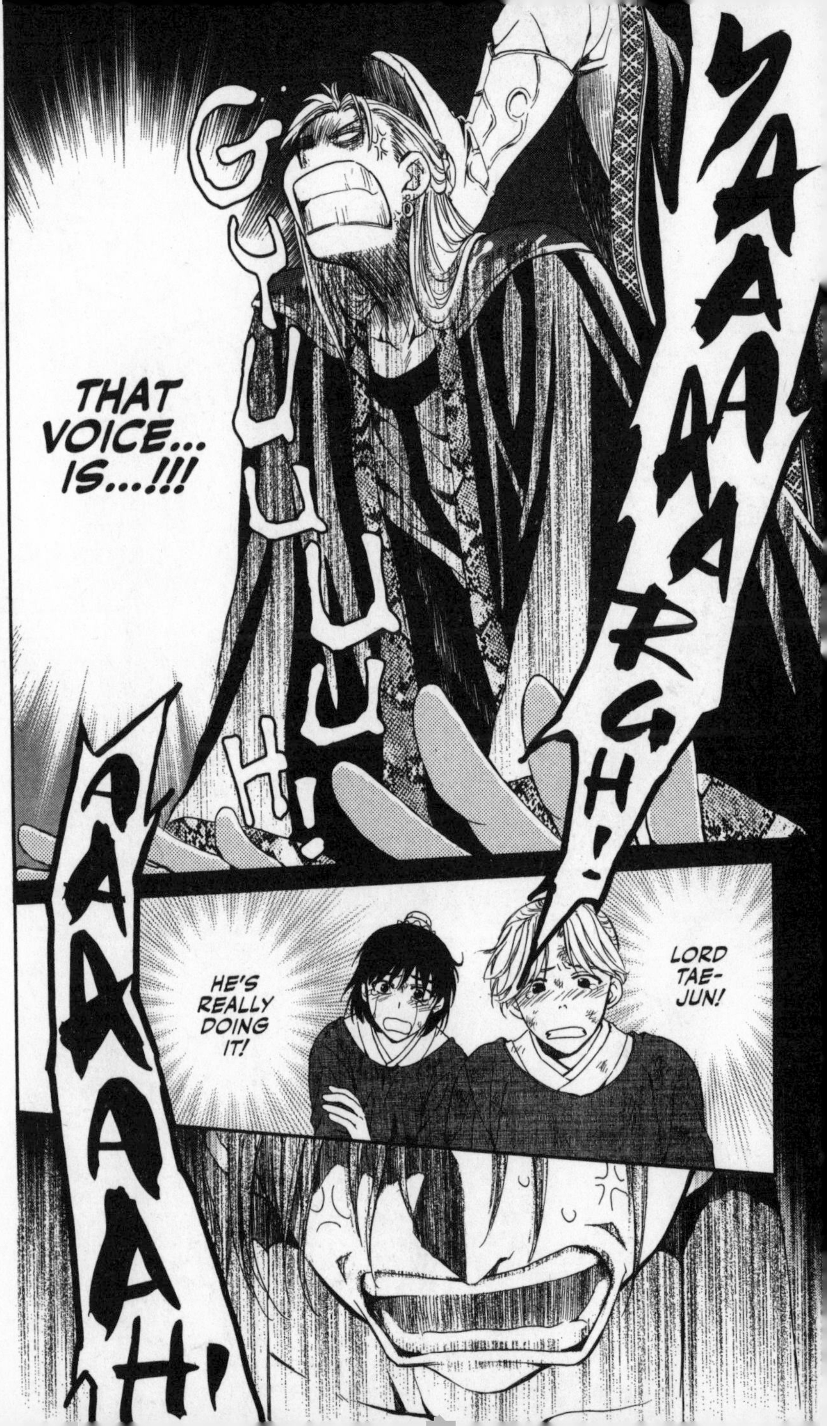

YAAAAARGH!
GUUUH!
THAT VOICE... IS...!!!
LORD TAE-JUN!
HE'S REALLY DOING IT!
AAAAAAH!

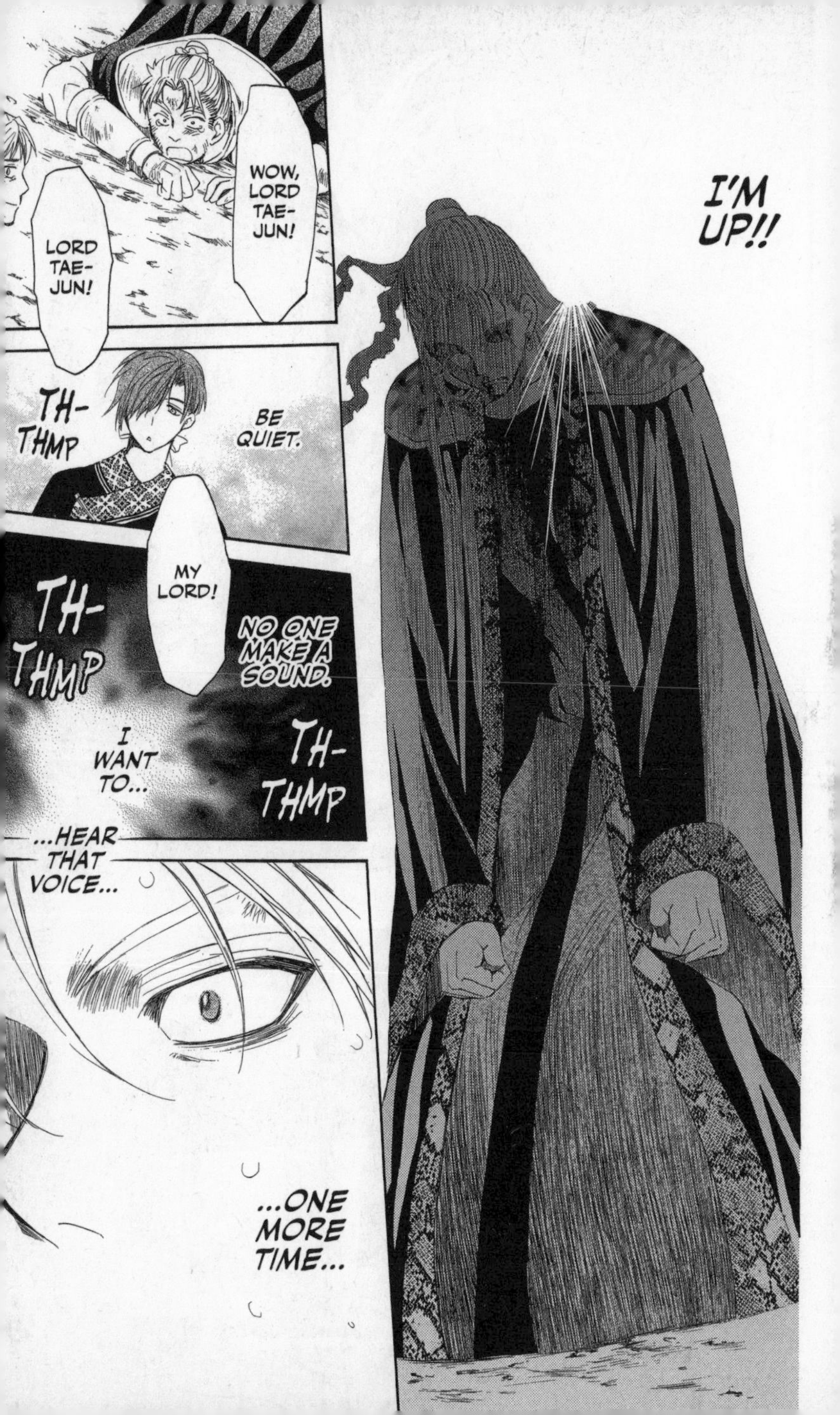
I'M UP!!
WOW, LORD TAE-JUN!
LORD TAE-JUN!
BE QUIET.
TH-THMP
MY LORD!
NO ONE MAKE A SOUND.
TH-THMP
TH-THMP
I WANT TO...
...HEAR THAT VOICE...
...ONE MORE TIME...

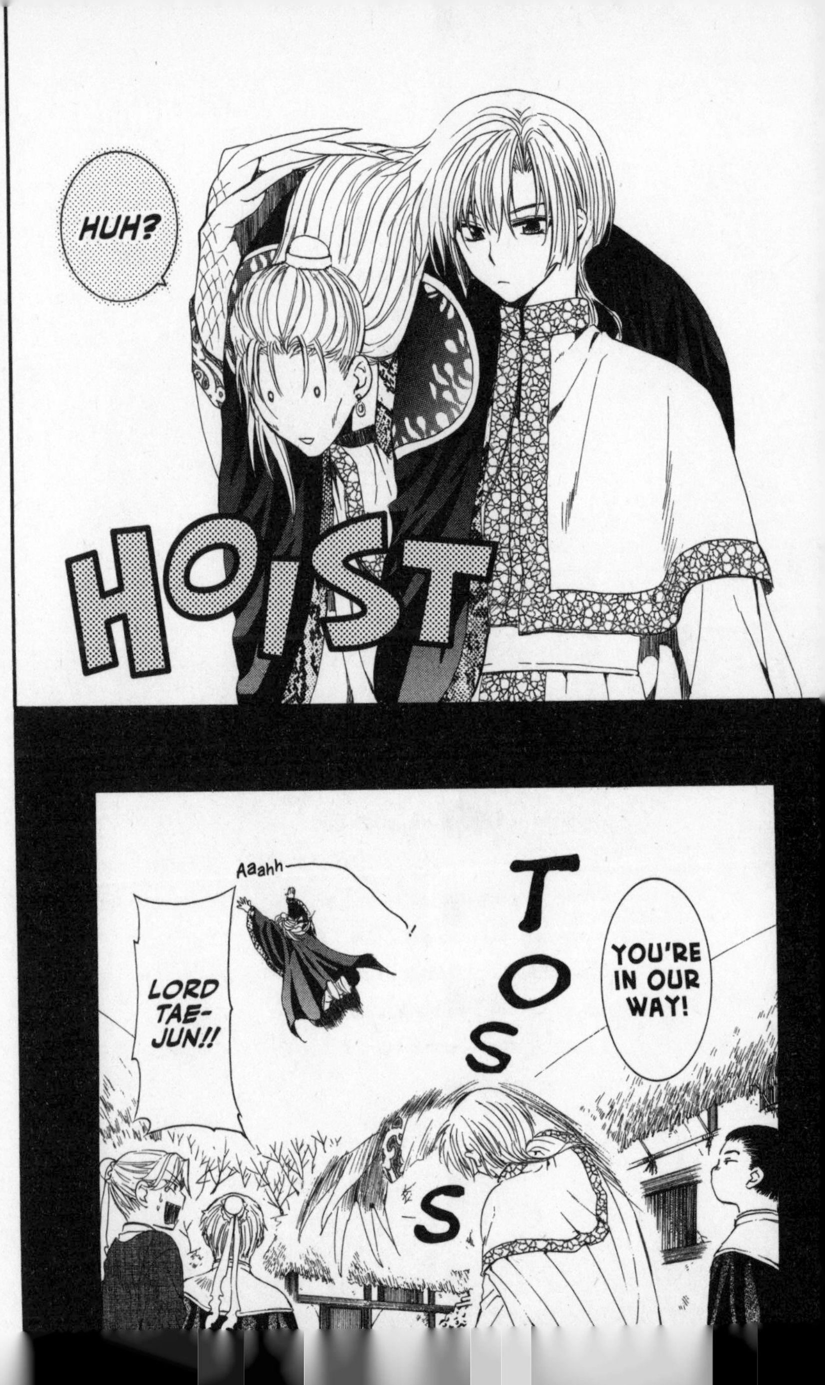
HUH?
HOIST
TOSS
YOU'RE IN OUR WAY!
Aaahh
LORD TAE-JUN!!

Born on February 3 in Kumamoto Prefecture in Japan, Mizuho Kusanagi began her professional manga career with *Yoiko no Kokoroe* (The Rules of a Good Child) in 2003. Her other works include *NG Life*, which was serialized in *Hana to Yume* and *The Hana to Yume* magazines and published by Hakusensha in Japan. *Yona of the Dawn* was adapted into an anime in 2014.

YONA OF THE DAWN
VOL.9
Shojo Beat Edition

STORY AND ART BY
MIZUHO KUSANAGI

English Adaptation/Ysabet Reinhardt MacFarlane
Translation/JN Productions
Touch-Up Art & Lettering/Lys Blakeslee
Design/Yukiko Whitley
Editor/Amy Yu

Akatsuki no Yona by Mizuho Kusanagi
© Mizuho Kusanagi 2012
All rights reserved.
First published in Japan in 2012 by HAKUSENSHA, Inc., Tokyo.
English language translation rights arranged with
HAKUSENSHA, Inc., Tokyo.

Printed in the U.S.A.

Published by VIZ Media, LLC
P.O. Box 77010
San Francisco, CA 94107

10 9 8 7 6 5 4 3 2 1
First printing, December 2017

www.viz.com   www.shojobeat.com

PARENTAL ADVISORY
YONA OF THE DAWN is rated T for Teen and is
recommended for ages 13 and up. This volume
contains violence and suggestive themes.
ratings.viz.com